# Success in Accounting and Costing

**Success Studybooks**

# Success in

# ACCOUNTING AND COSTING

Geoffrey Whitehead, B.Sc.(Econ.)
and
Arthur Upson, F.C.M.A., A.C.I.S., M.B.I.M.

**John Murray**

© Geoffrey Whitehead and Arthur Upson 1982

First published 1982
by John Murray (Publishers) Ltd
50 Albemarle Street, London W1X 4BD

Filmset by Latimer Trend & Company Ltd, Plymouth
Printed in Hong Kong by
Wing King Tong Ltd

British Library Cataloguing in Publication Data

Whitehead, Geoffrey
Success in accounting and costing.
1. Cost accounting
I. Title II. Upson, Arthur
657'.42      HF5686.C8

ISBN 0–7195–3835–1

# Foreword

Modern accounting may appear to be a matter of electronic wizardry but a computer can only be as good as the data and programs with which it is supplied. It follows that we need a growing body of accountants who understand industry and commerce in accountancy terms and can turn this knowledge into useful programs, supplied with accurate, up-to-date data.

*Success in Accounting and Costing*, together with its companion volume, *Problems and Projects*, has been designed to carry students beyond the levels covered by *Success in Principles of Accounting* to more advanced levels, giving particular attention to costing and the syllabuses of the Business Education Council's National awards, second year studies: Accounting II and Quantitative and Accounting Methods.

The books also offer an excellent introduction to management accounting, and will be of benefit to any student whose course covers the study of costing, including those working for BEC Higher National awards, the Royal Society of Arts (Cost Accounting II and III), London Chamber of Commerce ('Costing' Intermediate and Higher), degree courses in business studies, the Diploma of Management Studies and the intermediate examinations of professional bodies such as the Institute of Cost and Management Accountants, Association of Certified Accountants, Institute of Chartered Accountants, Institute of Public Finance and Accountancy and the Chartered Institute of Secretaries (Management Accounting). The books are also appropriate to TEC courses which relate to costing aspects of industry, and to courses in catering and hotel management.

*Success in Accounting and Costing* and its companion, *Problems and Projects*, cover a wide span of subject-matter and provide students with a demanding programme of work. *Problems and Projects* contains answers (many of them fully displayed) to all the questions in the core book, plus extra problems and projects. Lecturers and students will therefore need to be selective and concentrate on those sections which relate directly to the syllabuses they follow.

Ideally the two books should be studied together if students are to obtain maximum benefit. However, the core book *can* be studied alone by the more advanced student, for fast assimilation and revision, and *Problems and Projects* can also be used independently by teachers and lecturers for classwork, or by students working on their own.

Important features of the course are the detailed Unit on the Companies Act 1981 and the explanation of the proposals for Inflation Accounting in Statement of Standard Accounting Practice No. 16 (SSAP 16). All balance sheets in the book have been presented in the new formats required by Schedule 1 of the Companies Act 1981.

G. W. and A. U.

# Acknowledgments

We would like to express our sincere thanks to the many people who have helped us in writing this book. In particular we are grateful to those who read and criticized the text at various stages and made valuable suggestions: Lionel Millmore, Brighton Technical College, David Cox, Worcester Technical College, Alan Wood, formerly Watford College and Bill Jarvis, Birmingham Polytechnic. For editorial care and meticulous work we are grateful to those who contributed at different stages: Judith Samson, Helen Wright, Jean and Keith Macqueen, Anne Webster of John Murray, and Irene Slade, editor of the Success Studybooks series.

An especial thanks goes to our long-suffering wives for their patience and forbearance during the preparation of this book.

G. W. and A. U.

The kind assistance of the following organizations is also acknowledged: The Institute of Cost and Management Accountants, for graphs, diagrams and examination questions; George Vyner Limited for the Simplex weekly page (Fig. 3.1); Bass Limited (Fig. 18.5). The formats for the Profit and Loss Account and balance sheet from the Companies Act 1981 are reproduced by permission of the Controller of Her Majesty's Stationery Office.

# Contents

# Unit One

# Introduction

## 1.1 Principles of Accounting

The first level of accounting studies is usually described as Principles of
Accounting. Another book in the Success Studybooks series, *Success in
Principles of Accounting*, covers this area of work and includes Book-keeping
to the Trial Balance and Book-keeping to Final Accounts levels. In the United
Kingdom examination system, all elementary accounting syllabuses for the
General Certificate of Education O level, the Certificate of Secondary
Education and Stage I syllabuses of the Royal Society of Arts and similar
bodies are met by *Success in Principles of Accounting* and its accompanying
*Answer Book* where the answer to every question from the main text is fully
displayed in examination answer form.

## 1.2 Accounting and Costing

A study of accounting beyond the level of *Success in Principles of Accounting*
requires mastery of another branch of knowledge: costing (or management
accounting). For many years costing has been regarded as a separate subject
within accounting studies, if only because it is such an extensive topic. More
recently some examination boards have attempted to break down the barriers
between the various sections of accountancy subjects and have brought costing
studies into their general syllabuses. This attitude has much to recommend it.
In particular, both the second-year syllabuses of the Business Education
Council's National Courses, Accounting II and Quantitative and Accounting
Methods, contain large sections on costing. Accordingly we have included
Units on costing in *Success in Accounting and Costing* and we hope they will
serve as a useful introduction to the subject.

The BEC syllabus, Quantitative and Accounting Methods, has a statistical
element which this book does not attempt to cover. The companion volume,
*Success in Statistics* by Fred Caswell, deals with all the required statistics.

## 1.3 Problems and Projects

Accompanying this Studybook is a companion volume, *Success in Accounting
and Costing: Problems and Projects*, which gives answers to the exercises in
this volume. In addition it includes more questions for practice together with
their answers. The majority of the answers to numerical questions are fully
displayed in the form in which the authors would recommend you to present
your examination answers. For ease of reference the exercises in *Problems and
Projects* correspond to, and continue, the exercises in the Studybook.

## 1.4   How to Study

Although it is possible to embark on *Success in Accounting and Costing* without any previous knowledge of accounting, you would be well advised to study the principles of accounting first, since, particularly in accounting, every stage of the work is based upon principles laid down at an earlier stage. If you have already completed a course in principles of accounting, you should revise these studies before proceeding.

If you are preparing for an examination, you should obtain a syllabus or a set of course guidelines from the relevant examining body. This will tell you the topics which form the subject-matter of your course. As you master each topic, you should work the exercises in each Unit and a really conscientious student should also attempt the corresponding exercises in *Problems and Projects*. The displayed answers in that book will enable you to check your own work.

It is sometimes possible to obtain sets of past examination papers from an examining body. It is highly desirable that you work through several examination papers. First of all, take as much time as you need but then, as the examination approaches, train yourself to attempt a paper in the strict time limit allowed. At the end of that time evaluate your own likely score and assess your prospects of success. Then go through the paper again and refer to this Studybook to check on those parts of the paper you were unable to answer.

# Unit Two

# The Basic Concepts of Accounting

## 2.1 Accounting and the Mixed Economy

In 1842 George Eliot wrote in *Silas Marner* of 'the days when the spinning-wheels hummed busily in the cottages'. There was then no real need for advanced accounting techniques. Production and manufacturing were largely a domestic affair, and the profits of a man's industry gradually accumulated around him. The time to strike a balance sheet was when he was gathered to his Maker, and the things he could not take with him were shared among his heirs. Uniformity of procedure was not important, or at least not to the general public, and the entire affairs of Government could be financed from Customs and Excise duties on a small range of commodities.

In the modern mixed economy things are rather different. Out of a Gross National Product in 1979 of £163 649m the British Government spent £84 906m; £8 829m was required just to pay the interest on the National Debt. In 1869, when Gladstone was Prime Minister, the entire United Kingdom budget was only £67m so that, today, the interest on the National Debt alone is over 130 times Gladstone's total expenditure. If these enormous sums are to be collected from the public, it is essential to ensure some uniform system of calculation which is recognized as being 'just' between all parties in the community. The 'rewards to factors' paid out in one period as rent, wages, interest and profit must be calculated and accounted for in some uniform way so that public sector funds can be secured to run the social services and finance those non-profitable activities which the private sector is unwilling to undertake.

It is this need to secure equity in taxation that has been the major drive behind the establishment of agreed accounting concepts, though some of them are much older. The 'prudence' concept is an ancient one which says that the owner of a business should never regard a profit as actually made until it is realized. Thus if stocks you happen to hold rise in value and can be sold at a higher price than that for which you purchased them, it is not a profit until you actually sell them and realize the profit. Before you sell, the market price may fall again and the rise in value would have been delusory.

Beside the need to preserve equity in taxation, the whole system of accounting is a control system at a variety of levels. The basic accounting concepts are part of this control system, which operates both internally for the better management of the firm itself and externally to ensure uniformity between firms and to prevent a variety of abuses.

## 2.2   The Control Features Inherent in Accounting Systems

Accounting seeks to control the activities of an organization at several different levels. We may designate these levels as follows:

(i) **Internally** — to ensure an accurate record of receipts, payments, movements of stock, purchases, sales, use of assets and consumable stocks and to control misappropriations, theft and the dishonesty of employees.

(ii) **Comparatively** — to give managerial control of cost centres, departments, plants, etc. in order to achieve maximum efficiency from area to area and from one period of time to another.

(iii) **Externally** — to ensure that records are kept in conformity with accepted standards of accounting practice, so that they will bear comparison with the accounts of other business units, and survive scrutiny by interested parties such as the auditors, the Inland Revenue Department, the shareholders and official bodies such as the Council of the Stock Exchange.

As to (i), internal accounting, the accountant must devise an adequate system of work, using such principles as the separation of responsibilities. Frequently people empowered to collect money are not empowered to disburse it; petty cash may only be paid out against approved vouchers; cheques must be signed by two approved persons, and so on.

As to (ii), comparative accounting, the accountant must devise an adequate system of cost records, and of overhead allocation and absorption. Regular reports may be called for; statistical controls devised, and a policy of *management by exceptions* will rigorously investigate any variance between expected and actual costs.

You will already be familiar with these ideas, including aspects of external accounting which are the bases of elementary accounting. In this book we are developing the elementary rules given in *Success in Principles of Accounting* into more advanced fields. Before doing so we shall go over the basic concepts implied in (iii) above.

## 2.3   The Fundamental Concepts of Accounting

These may be listed as:

(a) business entity;
(b) money as the stable unit of account;
(c) the objectivity concept;
(d) the going-concern concept;
(e) the accruals concept;
(f) the consistency concept;
(g) the prudence concept;
(h) the concepts of substance and materiality.

### (a) The Concept of Business Entity

Every business exists as a real, separate unit distinct from all other units, and even distinct from its owners. This is sometimes recognized by law. In the

United Kingdom, for example, a limited-liability company has a separate legal status independent of its shareholders; it is an incorporation, which means it has been given authority to act in a business capacity. Partnerships, sole traders and clubs are not corporations and do not have a separate legal status, but as far as accountancy is concerned they are still business entities. The accountant distinguishes between the business and its owner and includes an item of expense, if it is appropriate to the business, or excludes it, if it is a personal expense of the proprietor. This, then, is one aspect of control in accounting: we must constantly bear in mind the nature of the business unit of which we are keeping the records.

One development from the concept of business entity is the concept of stewardship. Those who are running the business are accountable to those who own the business for the proper management of its affairs and for the profits it produces. Where a sole trader is running the business himself it might seem strange to regard him as a steward. The concept becomes clearer if we think of one partner needing to account for his conduct of the business to his fellow partners; in the case of a limited company the directors must certainly account to the shareholders for their conduct of the company's affairs.

### (b) Money as the Stable Unit of Account

Money is a common denominator which is used to value all transactions, assets, etc. It enables a total monetary value to be set upon the business, and upon the net worth of the business to the owner or owners. The presumption is that money is stable in value, which of course is not true in times of inflation, when debts incurred in one period are repaid in a later period in currency units which have meanwhile depreciated. *Inflation accounting* (or *current cost accounting*) attempts to grapple with this problem (see Unit 20).

### (c) The Objectivity Concept

This concept holds that the accountant will choose values for any data he uses which are based on the facts so far as they can be ascertained, and are susceptible to verification by an outside observer. They are not the subjective hunches of people within the firm. Where a choice has to be made—for example, in selecting a particular method of calculating depreciation—the impact of such a subjective choice will be somewhat reduced if the method is consistently applied from year to year (see Unit 2.3(f)).

The remaining five fundamental concepts of accounting have achieved general recognition over the course of centuries, but are now enshrined in the Companies Act 1981, Schedule 1 (Sections 10–15). They have been adopted in the Act largely in the form in which they appear in SSAP 2 (Statement of Standard Accounting Practice No. 2). The Statements of Standard Accounting Practice are the results of the deliberations of an Accounting Standards Committee, which was set up in 1969 and now embodies representatives of all the major accounting bodies in the United Kingdom. The Committee exists to propose definitive standards of financial accounting and reporting for the joint approval of the Councils of the governing bodies of the six major professional accountancy bodies. This ensures a uniform approach to accounting by members of the six institutes.

The following Statements of Standard Accounting Practice have been issued to date:

SSAP 1    Accounting for the results of associated companies;
SSAP 2    Disclosure of accounting policies;
SSAP 3    Earnings per share;
SSAP 4    The accounting treatment of government grants;
SSAP 5    Accounting for VAT;
SSAP 6    Extraordinary items and prior year adjustments;
SSAP 7    (Provisional) Accounting for changes in the purchasing power of money (withdrawn January 1978);
SSAP 8    The treatment of taxation under the imputation system in the accounts of companies;
SSAP 9    Stocks and work-in-progress;
SSAP 10   Statements of source and application of funds;
SSAP 11   Accounting for deferred taxation (withdrawn October 1978);
SSAP 12   Accounting for depreciation;
SSAP 13   Accounting for research and development;
SSAP 14   Group accounts;
SSAP 15   Accounting for deferred taxation;
SSAP 16   Current cost accounting;
SSAP 17   Accounting for post balance sheet events;
SSAP 18   Accounting for contingencies.

The full text is available in the handbook *Accounting Standards* published by the Institute of Chartered Accountants in England and Wales, PO Box 433, London EC2 2BJ.

The same basic concepts are also laid down in IAS 1, the International Accounting Standard, *Disclosure of Accounting Policies*, which applies to international financial statements issued on or after January 1, 1975.

### (d) The Going-concern Concept

This concept holds that when an accountant prepares a set of final accounts for any organization he does so on the basis that it is a going concern which is likely to continue in existence for the conceivable future to the best of his knowledge. If it is not likely to do so, but is going to cease trading shortly, the value of the business assets might be quite different, and the accountant has to make an interested party (such as a potential buyer or investor) aware of the likely changes. Thus a transport lorry might be valued on the books of a going concern at a figure representing original cost less depreciation to date. If it were to be sold at the best price it might fetch much less than its present value on the books — or it might possibly fetch more. A quite different valuation of assets on the balance sheet might be made if the business is to cease to trade, and a *profit on realization* or *loss on realization* might need to be taken into account. In the absence of any such likelihood, the accounts are prepared on the understanding that the business will continue to operate.

## (e) The Accruals Concept

The accruals concept holds that where final accounts are drawn up for a particular trading period they will include all the profits and all the losses for that period. *Accruals* are debts which have collected and are due for payment. Thus, if a sale is made in November, as part of the trading period ending on December 31, it would be included in the sales figure for the period even if the actual payment is not received until January, which is in the next financial period. Similarly, the expenses of the business should include every item of expense for the period under review even if it is not to be paid until the next period. (This principle, which is the basis of *adjustments* in final accounts, is dealt with in *Success in Principles of Accounting*.)

## (f) The Consistency Concept

In advanced accounting the use of accounts as a means of comparing one period with another or one department with another is often more important than in elementary accounting where the chief preoccupation is that of finding out the actual profits. When accountancy is used as a tool of management to make decisions about things like the closure of plants, the expansion of depots or making investments in a particular firm, it is essential that the accounts should be prepared consistently. For example, a firm whose profitability is declining could be made to appear profitable if the asset *land and buildings* was revalued to a higher figure. The decline of profits on normal trading might be masked by the capital profit made by writing-up the value of the asset. It is therefore essential to have a sound set of rules on which the profession is agreed. This ensures that uniform and consistent behaviour is followed from year to year, from department to department, from plant to plant, and so on. Any change in treatment between one year and another on such matters as the method of depreciating assets, for example, would require a clear statement of the change and the reasons for it. It would then be usual to demonstrate the effects of the change by showing the impact of the calculations on the final accounts (a) under the old method and (b) under the new method. This would prevent any misunderstanding.

## (g) The Prudence Concept

This traditional concept, which is as old as accountancy itself, holds that a businessman should be prudent in all his book-keeping practices. He should never take a profit until it is actually realized, but always accept a loss when there is reasonable prospect of one being incurred. If we are prudent we value stocks at cost price or net realizable value, whichever is the lower. If stocks have risen in value we are not advised to value them at the higher figure—and thus take the profit on them before they have been sold. By contrast, where we suspect that a debt is bad we are advised to write the debt off as irrecoverable (accepting the loss even before we are sure it has occurred) and even where we cannot pinpoint any particular bad debtor we are entitled to make a *provision for bad debts* which will take account of past experience. If we know that in our particular trade 5 per cent of outstanding debts cannot be collected, on average, we should reduce our profits by this figure, that is, 5 per cent of the outstanding debts.

### (h) The Concepts of Substance and Materiality

The accounts should bring out the true substance of the firm's financial position, showing the facts fully and fairly for all to see. They should not mask or conceal essential elements. It used to be a common practice for loans to directors to be hidden among other loans to *bona fide* customers, or to be repaid on the last day of the financial year and borrowed back next morning in a 'bed and breakfast' arrangement. On the other hand, where the cost of an item is comparatively modest, it may not be considered material and is therefore included with others to save too complex a presentation. Thus a small payment for an asset not strictly describable as plant and machinery might be included in that description to save an extra line on the balance sheet.

By contrast, where an item is sufficiently large to represent an important part of the entire business (say $2\frac{1}{2}$ per cent of the expenses) or where it has changed significantly over the year and therefore represents a change in management policy or business style, an accountant would deem it material. The aim is to display separately any matter that is material, but to avoid a welter of detail.

Materiality is usually a matter for professional judgment, and a guideline statement has been issued to members by the Institute of Chartered Accountants in England and Wales. It is also a statutory requirement that accountants should exercise this judgment when preparing accounts to give a 'true and fair view' of the affairs of a company, under the Companies Acts 1948–1981. It therefore has both a professional and a statutory duty aspect for accountants.

## 2.4   Accounting Policies

Accounting policies are defined in SSAP 2 as the specific accounting bases selected by the management to be followed in the preparation of the published accounts. These are bases which are considered most appropriate in the firm's circumstances and those most likely to present fairly the firm's results for the accounting period and its financial position at the close of the trading period.

There are a number of recognized alternative bases for calculating profits and valuing assets, and it is expected that where accounts are published the accounting policies which have been followed will be disclosed in a note to the accounts. Thus, if depreciation is being calculated by a particular method (there are eight or ten possible methods) this will be explained. There are recognized alternative bases for, among others, the following:

(*a*)  depreciation of fixed assets;
(*b*)  writing down intangible assets such as goodwill, research and development expenditure, etc.;
(*c*)  amortization of leases, patents, etc.;
(*d*)  deferred taxation;
(*e*)  conversion of foreign currencies;

(f) repairs and renewals;
(g) property valuations;
(h) hire purchase and instalment transactions;
(i) stock and work-in-progress;
(j) leasing and rental transactions.

SSAP 2 lays down that any change in accounting policies or any departure from the four basic concepts should be explained by a clear statement giving the reasons. In the absence of any such statement it will be assumed that the basic concepts have been followed and that the firm's accounting policies are unchanged.

## 2.5 The Application of Accounting Concepts

You will already be familiar with many aspects of the application of accounting concepts, which form a background to elementary accounting and the preparation of final accounts. Here we shall review only some of these elementary points and extend others to cover a wider set of circumstances. The application of accounting concepts to different types of business entity is contained in later Units of this book, and the basic principles should be borne in mind at all times and in all accounting situations. Each section that follows is an illustration of an important aspect of the application of these general principles.

Each business entity has its own special considerations and its specialized accounting techniques. Generally, the simpler types of business are adequately treated by traditional accounting principles. More advanced businesses are governed by Parliamentary controls of one kind or another, so that accounting concepts are reinforced by statute law to a greater or lesser degree. The Partnership Act 1890, for example, is less restrictive than the Companies Acts 1948–1981, and the specialist Acts of Parliament for many of the public sector authorities include accounting provisions and review procedures which have to be complied with by these authorities.

Later Units of this book consider the accounting activities for each type of business and go beyond elementary treatment.

At this stage it is sufficient to look at the application of accounting concepts to two elements of accounting practice, *stock valuation* and *depreciation*.

### Stock Valuation
Statement of Standard Accounting Practice No. 9 is the definitive statement on stock valuation. The full text is available in the handbook *Accounting Standards* (see p. 6).

Stocks are of many types, including:

(a) goods or other assets purchased for resale, for example, tyres sold as spares;
(b) consumable stores like oil, petrol, and other items which are not part of the end-product;

(c) raw materials and components purchased for incorporation into products for sale, for example, pig iron, gear boxes;

(d) products and services in intermediate stages of completion, for example, work-in-progress and units awaiting incorporation into the finished product;

(e) finished goods.

The essential statement in SSAP 9 is:

*Stocks and work-in-progress normally need to be stated at cost, or, if lower, at net realizable value.*

Although at first sight this appears to be a clear definition, we soon find ourselves asking: what exactly was the cost of this item of stock? Was it the purchase price? Or should we add the transport charges for delivery, the warehousing costs while it was in stock, the equitable proportion of overheads incurred?

In accounting, the aim is to discover as accurately as possible the profit earned during any particular trading period, and at the same time to establish the value of the assets and their relationship to the owner(s) of the business at the closing date. This is not easy to do, because sometimes an acceptable system of valuing the assets from the profit-measuring point of view results in a distorted valuation of the asset on the balance sheet, and vice versa.

What value should be placed upon stock is always a debatable question to some extent, and if we consider work-in-progress as an example, it is clear that such valuation is not easy. Let us imagine a plant producing finished goods as a result of a continuous-belt system. Raw materials (valued at cost price), come in at one end and finished goods leave at the other. At closing time on the last day of the financial year, the work-in-progress (or partly-finished goods) consists of work in every stage of production from raw materials (on which work has hardly started) to goods which are almost finished and about to leave the plant. Not only has value been added to the extent of direct wages and other direct costs embodied in the work to date, but a fair share of the overhead costs must also be charged to each unit. If we average out the costs across all units passing through the factory, assuming that the flow is even, we can place a value on work-in-progress, but it is only an estimate.

Similar considerations apply to the stock of finished goods, except that these will all be valued at such a figure that the value includes the entire costs of manufacture, both direct and indirect (overheads). Since finished goods incur further costs in distribution, marketing and selling, it could be argued that even finished goods should be valued at a figure which takes into account the distance to the final retail outlet.

SSAP 9 defines cost as *the expense incurred in obtaining the stock and bringing it to its present location and condition.* Net realizable value is defined as *the actual or estimated selling price net of trade discounts and less all costs to completion (of partly-finished goods) and all selling and marketing expenses.*

Stock consisting of a collection of items bought at different prices, as, for example, in inflationary times, can be allocated for use in different ways, and different valuations for the remainder will be reached. In retail trade, for example, it is usual to use stock in rotation, using the oldest items first, before they start to deteriorate. In inflationary times, this means that the cheapest items are disposed of first, on a *first in, first out* (FIFO) basis. Where goods are not subject to deterioration and where trade is not competitive, so that the price charged to the consumer may not have much effect upon sales, it would be sensible to invoice the customer on the basis of the current cost of material, charging the cost of the most recent items purchased, plus profit. This is called LIFO or *last in, first out*. Sometimes, when prices are rising fast, it might be appropriate to charge the customer on the basis of the replacement price. This means guessing by how much prices will have risen when we come to replenish stock and charging this estimated figure for any unit of stock used. Another method is AVCO (weighted average cost). Using AVCO, new average prices are fixed each time that goods or purchases are taken into stock, and it is these AVCO prices which are charged to jobs, contracts, and so on. It does not follow that the method the accountant uses to price the stock will bear any relationship to the actual units of stock issued by the storekeeper. We will now consider the effect of stock valuation on the profit, and the balance sheet value of stock in hand, by three methods. These are:

> FIFO    (first in, first out)
> LIFO    (last in, first out)
> AVCO    (weighted average cost)

Suppose that the stock of 12 identical items was purchased as follows: 3 for £5 each, 8 for £6 each and 1 at £10. Suppose that 6 items are sold, at prices which rose over the period, to yield a total of £76. Under the three systems we have:

**Table 2.1    Valuation of closing stock calculated by the three methods**

|  | FIFO £ | LIFO £ | AVCO £ |
|---|---|---|---|
| Sales | 76 | 76 | 76 |
| Cost of sales | 33 | 40 | 36.48 |
|  | $(3 \times 5) + (3 \times 6)$ | $(1 \times 10) + (5 \times 6)$ | $(6 \times 6.08)$ |
| Profit | 43 | 36 | 39.52 |
| Value of stock at close | 40 | 33 | 36.48 |
|  | $(5 \times 6) + (1 \times 10)$ | $(3 \times 5) + (3 \times 6)$ | $(6 \times 6.08)$ |

From Table 2.1 we can see that the valuation of stock affects both the profit deemed to have been made in the period and the value of the stock at close which will appear on the balance sheet. We can comment on each as follows:

(i) **FIFO.** This gives the largest profit and the largest value of stock at the close of the year. If all this profit was withdrawn, the cash left would only be sufficient to buy 3.3 units at the current price of £10 per unit, to replace the 6 items sold.

(ii) **LIFO.** This gives the smallest profit and the smallest stock value at the end of the period. If all the profit was withdrawn, the cash available would be sufficient to purchase 4 units at the current price of £10 per unit. This is also not very satisfactory as 6 units have been used up in the period.

(iii) **AVCO.** This gives results which fall between the other two.

The conclusion is that both the profit for any period and the valuation to be placed upon the asset *stock* reflect the method of valuation chosen. For this reason it is essential to be consistent from year to year in the method adopted. If the method is varied, the financial result will vary too so any comparison made with previous years will be misleading: it will reflect the change in accounting method rather than the change in business activities.

A fuller description of the use of FIFO, LIFO and AVCO is given in Unit 10.

## 2.6   Accounting for Depreciation

Depreciation is the process of allocating charges for the use of assets in proportion to the service they have provided in the accounting period. The original cost of the asset is *capitalized*, which means that it is recorded in an asset account (a real account) as distinct from an expense account (a nominal account). This original cost is reduced each year by the amount of depreciation charged to the Profit and Loss Account. The balance sheet value of any asset is therefore that portion of its original cost which has not been treated as an expense and written off the profits in the years since the asset was acquired.

There are three important points about the whole process of asset use.

(i) We must first identify and record the cost of the asset. This may mean recording its purchase price, but it is more likely that it will also involve some capitalization of revenue expenses. Thus if a machine costs £5 000 ex works, plus £150 delivery charges, plus £750 labour costs of installation, the full cost of the asset is £5 900. The asset must be recorded at this figure, the Delivery Charges Account and Wages Account being reduced (credited) by the amount to be capitalized (£150 and £750 respectively).

(ii) The useful life of the asset often needs to be known in the calculations. This can only be an estimate, and regard should be taken of the accounting principles of prudence and objectivity. Where an asset use varies from time period to time period, it may be necessary to set up some monitoring system to determine the depreciation charge—for example, machine-hours run or mileage covered. This would replace the 'asset life' approach, which is appropriate to assets in constant use throughout their lifetime.

(iii) Most assets have a residual value or scrap value which can be recovered when they are finally disposed of. Thus, the net cost of the asset, depreciating over the lifetime, is the original cost less the residual value. The residual value can rarely be more than a guess, but as it is viewed conservatively—under the prudence rule—it is often only a small part of the original cost, and errors in the estimate are immaterial.

There are several methods of depreciation, and brief descriptions are given below. The essential thing is to choose a method that is *appropriate* and *rational* in the circumstances, and then apply it *consistently* over the years. The decline in value of the asset is not the only cost incurred as the years pass: there are also the maintenance and repair costs associated with its use. Since a new asset usually breaks down less frequently and needs replacement of parts less often than an ageing asset, maintenance and repair costs are low in the early years and tend to increase later on. Some methods of calculating depreciation such as the diminishing-balance method, write off more in the early years than in the later years. Consequently this method tends to achieve an even combination of depreciation and service costs over the lifetime of the asset.

The subject is covered for professional accountants in SSAP 12, *Accounting for Depreciation*, which explains the general principles.

There are three main methods of calculating depreciation.

### (a) The Straight-line Method

By this method, which is also known as the *fixed-instalment method*, the asset is regarded as giving steady service over the years, without any significant maintenance costs; the depreciation charge is therefore related to the lifetime of use. An inventory of office equipment such as filing cabinets and shelving might depreciate in this way. The formula is:

$$\text{Depreciation charge} = \frac{\text{Original cost } less \text{ Residual value}}{\text{Lifetime in years}}$$

Thus, for an asset costing £500, deemed to have a residual value of £50 and a life of ten years, the calculation would be

$$\text{Depreciation charge} = \frac{£500 - £50}{10} = £45 \text{ per annum}$$

Over the lifetime of the asset, the book value declines in a regular way to the residual value. In the above example, the value would reduce over the years in the following way: £500, £455, £410 and so on until it reached £95 and finally £50.

**Lease amortization.** The term depreciation is not really appropriate to the wastage of a lease as the years pass, and the term *amortization* (from the French word *mort* — dead) is used instead. While leases are usually amortized using the straight-line method, in most cases it is necessary to provide for *dilapidations*. This means that the premises must be repaired so that the tenant can return them to the landlord in good condition at the end of the period.

### (b) The Diminishing-balance Method

This method is also known as the *reducing* — or *declining* — *balance method*. In this instance the charge is a decreasing charge — to offset the increasing maintenance charges. A large amount is written off in the early years, but this percentage deduction is made on the diminishing balance of the asset. The disadvantage of this method is that an asset with a short life has to be excessively depreciated in the first year. So to clear an asset with a life of only three years we need a 90 per cent rate. For a £1 000 asset we would need to write off £900 in Year 1, £90 in Year 2 and £9 in Year 3. (This also illustrates the fact that this method does not eliminate an asset completely; a negligible amount has to be written off in the final year.) Clearly this is an unsatisfactory spread over a three-year lifetime. Using the example in (*a*) above, over five years, a depreciation rate of 36.9 per cent leads to the following reductions in value:

|              | Year 1 | Year 2 | Year 3 | Year 4 | Year 5 | Year 6 |
|--------------|--------|--------|--------|--------|--------|--------|
| At start     | £500   | £316   | £199   | £126   | £80    | £50    |
| Depreciation | £184   | £117   | £73    | £46    | £30    |        |

The formula for calculating the rate of depreciation is:

$$r = 100\left(1 - \sqrt[n]{\frac{RV}{P}}\right)$$

where *r* is the percentage rate of depreciation, *n* the number of years of the life-time, *RV* the residual value and *P* the principal (net cost of the asset).

A very rough estimate of a suitable rate is found by doubling the rate used in the straight-line method in (*a*) above. Thus, if an asset has a five-year life, when a 20 per cent charge would be appropriate for the straight-line method, a 40 per cent charge would be suitable for the diminishing-balance method. Naturally, such a rough estimate will not reduce the asset value exactly to the residual value, but it will be near enough for the accountant to regard the difference as immaterial. This rough estimate is sometimes called the *double-declining method*.

### (*c*)  The Sum of the Digits Method

This requires a diminishing amount to be written off. We write down the number of years to run—for example 5, 4, 3, 2 and 1 year—as the asset approaches the end of its life. The sum of these digits is 15. We then write off the same fraction of the *net* cost as the digit bears to the sum of the digits; that is, in the first year (with 5 years of life left) we write off $\frac{5}{15}$, in the next year $\frac{4}{15}$ and so on. Thus, in Year 1, $\frac{5}{15}$ of £450 (£500−£50 residue)=£150. In Year 2, $\frac{4}{15}$ of £450=£120, etc.

Using the same example as in (*a*) and (*b*) above we have:

|                | Year 1 | Year 2 | Year 3 | Year 4 | Year 5 | Year 6 |
|----------------|--------|--------|--------|--------|--------|--------|
| At start       | £500   | £350   | £230   | £140   | £80    | £50    |
| Depreciation   | $(\frac{5}{15})$ £150 | $(\frac{4}{15})$ £120 | $(\frac{3}{15})$ £90 | $(\frac{2}{15})$ £60 | $(\frac{1}{15})$ £30 |  |

The charge for depreciation reduces year by year, to compensate for the rise in maintenance charges.

There are several other methods of calculating depreciation, some of which are highly sophisticated. But on the whole, these methods are not widely used and we shall consider them only in brief.

(*d*) **The Annuity Method**

This method regards any purchase of an asset as a use of capital which, in other circumstances, would yield interest to the proprietor(s). A notional sum for interest is therefore added to the asset account each year and this total (asset *plus* interest) is written down by equal instalments. The business is thus charged for the use of the asset, an amount which includes the interest lost by rejecting other investment opportunities.

(*e*) **The Insurance Policy Method**

Here an insurance policy is taken out to provide enough funds to replace the asset at the end of its life. The advantage is that the lump sum payable on maturity of the policy is provided from outside the business, and is fixed in amount and not subject to losses as other investments sometimes are.

The book-keeping is rather involved and varies with the arrangements made by the accountant. He may decide to value the policy at the sum paid, plus an addition for interest at some notional rate, or he may value it at surrender value. Using the first method as an example, and imagining the asset to be a lease, the entries are:

(i) Premiums payable in advance, on Day 1 each year

> Dr. Lease Policy Account
> Cr. Bank Account

with the annual premium paid.

(ii) On Day 365

> Dr. Profit and Loss Account
> Cr. Lease Redemption Fund Account

with the annual amount charged for depreciation.

(iii) On Day 365 an entry must be made to take account of the notional rate of interest earned by the policy:

> Dr. Lease Policy Account
> Cr. Lease Redemption Fund Account

with the interest deemed to have been earned.

(iv) When the policy matures, the cash received is entered as follows:

> Dr. Bank Account
> Cr. Lease Policy Account

Any balance either way on the Lease Policy Account represents a difference between how much the policy actually earned and the notional interest we estimated it would earn. This balance would be cleared to the Lease Redemption Fund Account.

(v) The lease which has expired would then be cleared by the following entries:

> Dr. Lease Redemption Fund Account
> Cr. Lease Account

If there is an outstanding debit balance on the Lease Redemption Fund Account it would be written off against the Profit and Loss Account, while if it was a favourable balance it would be retained to start off the Lease Redemption Fund Account on the new lease.

In any given year, the balance sheet shows two assets, a Lease Account and a Lease Policy Account, and only one liability, the Lease Redemption Fund Account.

## (f) The Sinking Fund Method

In this method an asset remains on the books at its original cost. Each year an amount called the *sinking fund instalment* is debited to the Profit and Loss Account as the depreciation charge for the year, and credited to the Provision for Depreciation Account. At the same time a similar sum of money is invested in securities outside the business. This provides a sinking fund investment from which, when the time arrives, funds can be realized by selling the investments to purchase a replacement for the worn-out or obsolete asset. Any interest earned during the lifetime of the fund is reinvested to increase the fund. This method is less used than formerly because it requires funds to be invested outside the business, at a lower rate of interest than can be earned by most firms inside the business itself.

## (g) The Revaluation Method

This method is dealt with in *Success in Principles of Accounting*. It is used for assets which cannot be depreciated by normal methods because they change in value in an erratic way. Thus, herds and flocks, investments, trade marks and copyrights, loose tools, moulds and patterns may change from time to time in an irregular way. The method can be illustrated as follows:

|  | £ |
|---|---|
| Opening stock | 27 000 |
| Purchases during year | 62 000 |
|  | 89 000 |
| *Less* Closing stock | 43 000 |
| Charge for asset use in year | £46 000 |

The entry *purchases* includes not only the actual purchase, but also the capitalized costs of creating assets—for example, if the tool room makes moulds and jigs for permanent use in the business, the labour and overhead costs would be capitalized and charged to the Loose Tools Account.

Revaluation is also used in the case of premises and land where *appreciation* of the asset may have taken place. If buildings, for example, are not increased in value as the price of premises rises on the open market, their existence on the balance sheet at out-of-date prices constitutes a hidden reserve in the business and may lead to the purchase of the business by outsiders for the purpose of *asset-stripping.* This implies that the purchase of the business is made not with the intention of trading as a going concern but in order to sell its assets piecemeal and achieve the profits thus released. This practice closes down factories which are still viable, throws employees out of work, decreases the wealth-creating forces in the country and transfers to the asset-stripper the capital accumulated by the original investors.

By revaluing the premises at a realistic figure, the assets on the balance sheet rise to their correct value and the capital gain is taken into account. Being a capital gain, and not a revenue gain, the profit cannot be credited to the Profit and Loss Account, but instead is credited to the Capital Account (in the case of sole traders or partners) or to a Capital Reserve Account, such as the Premises Revaluation Account (in the case of a limited company). Capital profits of this type may not be distributed to the shareholders as dividend, but they do increase the ordinary shareholders' interest in the company.

## 2.7    The Impact of Depreciation on Profits

Clearly a charge made to a Profit and Loss Account for depreciation purposes affects the profits, reducing them by the amount of the charge, and reducing the asset value on the balance sheet. A number of points arise from these effects.

(*a*) The financial results will be affected by any change in depreciation, and therefore the chief aim of the accountant is to secure *consistency* between one period and another. Where the appraisal of financial results is achieved by comparing the current year with preceding years, any inconsistency about depreciation (different charges in successive years for the use of the same asset) is clearly undesirable. Where it has been necessary to change the basis used, mention of this must be made unequivocally in a *Note to the accounts*, and the reason for the change and its effects explained.

(*b*) While depreciation reduces the profit, and therefore reduces the distribution of profits to the proprietors, it does not, in fact, reduce the cash available in the system. The reduction in profit is balanced out by the reduction in asset values. This means that funds which are the result of the reduced distribution of profits exist somewhere in the system. These funds may be in the form of cash, but may easily be diverted into other uses such as increased wages or the purchase of unnecessary assets or stocks of consumables. It follows that the creation of sinking funds and other liquid reserves is highly desirable so that funds are earmarked for particular purposes – plant replacement and renewal, motor vehicle replacement, etc. The new assets are rarely the same as the existing ones because of technological change, and, in inflationary times rarely cost the same amount. The adequacy of the reserves created is, therefore, of great concern.

(*c*) It might be thought that depreciation should be set as high as possible, thus reducing the profits and the amount of tax payable. In fact, depreciation is not allowed as an expense for tax purposes: any deduction for depreciation on the accounts is added back again when the Inland Revenue Department assesses the business for tax purposes. Instead, there are *capital allowances* which are unrelated to the rate of depreciation, and reflect Government policy instead. Thus, at times of severe unemployment, capital allowances for new investment may be 100 per cent and the whole of the value of a new asset is deductible in the first year. This encourages firms to re-tool, for example, and thus provides work in the machine-tool industry. The depreciation process is not affected by the manipulations of the profit to satisfy the tax system. Therefore it would be wrong, at a time when capital allowances are 100 per cent, to write down the value of the asset on the books to zero just because the full capital allowance against tax had been claimed. The balance sheet could not possibly give a 'true and fair view' of the business assets if assets which were nearly new were not shown because of 100 per cent depreciation.

## 2.8   Exercises

1. What are Statements of Standard Accounting Practice? Why have the accountancy bodies felt it would be helpful to issue such statements?

2. 'Accountants should always be prudent.' Explain the concept of prudent behaviour in accounting, giving examples.

3. 'Stock should appear in the financial accounts at the lower of cost or net realizable value.' Explain why this Statement of Standard Accounting Practice is not as clear as it appears to be. What methods of valuing stock are in use and what is their impact upon the financial accounts?

4. A trader buys goods at £37 per unit and sells them at £64 per unit. At the end of the financial year he has 110 units in stock of which 25 were damaged by foam used to extinguish a fire. They are now valued at only £14 each. What value would you place on the stock?

5. A five-year lease is purchased for £7 000 on January 1, 19. . . Depreciation is made by equal instalments over the five-year period. Show the Lease Account for the five years.

6. A combine-harvester is purchased for £15 000 on January 1, 19. . . It is decided to use the double-declining method for calculating depreciation, the asset being deemed to have a life of eight years. Show the Asset Account for the first three years. (Calculations to be made to the nearest £1.)

*Note:* This and all other sets of exercises are contained, together with many additional ones, in *Problems and Projects*, the companion volume. The answers to all questions are given there, many of them fully displayed.

# Unit Three

# Applying Basic Concepts:
# 1. The Accounts of Small Traders and Incomplete Records

## 3.1 Introduction

Before the Inland Revenue demanded such a large share of the national income, many businessmen did not keep accounting records. The success of a business could be judged by the gradual accumulation of wealth, and the time to strike a balance sheet was at the death of the proprietor. Even today there is no compulsion for sole traders or partnerships to keep written records, although it is an offence to go bankrupt without proper accounts.

Any system that is less than a full double-entry system is potentially inadequate, but many small traders find a full double-entry system time-consuming and unnecessary. The *Simplex System* is one of the best which is available commercially and is widely used. It is described briefly in Unit 3.2.

Other systems, which record only half the double entry required for a transaction, are called *single-entry systems*, and anything more rudimentary is called *incomplete records*. Preparing accounts from incomplete records taxes the ingenuity of the accountant — and wastes a great deal of his time too. Successful preparation of such accounts in many cases depends on the perseverance of the accountant.

It is often said that tax evasion is rife among people concerned with small businesses because of the opportunities that exist for hiding the truth if records are incomplete. This would be the case if it were not for the long memory of the Inland Revenue Department and its ability to compare records across the length and breadth of the country. Accounts that appear to be fraudulent (because they show a lower profit than similar businesses in similar situations) are soon detected. The trader is called to give an explanation and failure to satisfy the tax inspector leads to an assessment well above the stated level of income. Any appeal must then be justified to the Inland Revenue Commissioners, who will usually require proof of the statements made.

Another occasion for action by the Inland Revenue against traders arises when a person who is not paying a fair share of tax is seen to achieve a steady growth of wealth, while those who are paying tax in full may find this difficult to achieve. The *increased-net-worth method* of finding profits (described in *Success in Principles of Accounting* and summarized here in Unit 3.3) is a fundamental technique for dealing with incomplete records.

The Inland Revenue, when reviewing the growth of a business, is interested in seeing how this growth has been achieved out of the declared profits in earlier years. There is a popular misconception that one only needs a clever accountant to escape paying tax. This is not true. An accountant may give his client valuable advice on many topics, but it is his professional duty to see that accounts are properly prepared, and this includes the correct calculation of tax due.

## 3.2 The Simplex System of Accounts

The Simplex System has two main features.

(i) Each page in the Simplex D Account Book (the D stands for Schedule D—the tax schedule for business profits) has room for a week's records, and these are quite separate from the records of all other weeks. Books do not need to be balanced off and balances brought down before the next week's records can begin.

(ii) The link between the week's records and the records for the rest of the year is achieved through a series of summaries, at the back of the book, which are really the nominal ledger accounts. The figures for sales (takings of the business) and expenditure (purchases of goods for resale, payments other than for stock and capital items) are entered in these summaries at the end of each week. By the end of the year these summaries provide grand totals of sales, purchases, wages, postage, and other expenses from which the Trading Account, Profit and Loss Account and balance sheet can easily be drawn up. Fig. 3.1 shows the weekly Simplex page.

## 3.3 The Increased-net-worth Method

This method of finding profits depends on the fact that a business can only grow—barring the introduction of extra capital or loans from outside the business—if it is making profits. Even then it must be profitable enough to support the owner in the manner to which he has become accustomed and still leave funds available to acquire extra fixed assets, extra stock and other working capital.

This explains why the balance sheet is such an important element in accounting, for it reveals the state of the business at any given moment, and when this is compared with a previous balance sheet the *increased net worth* can be discovered. In this type of calculation it is usual to call the balance sheet by its original name of a *Statement of Affairs*, since, with incomplete records, there are no accounts and therefore no balances to go on the balance sheet. The figures for the two Statements of Affairs are found from such records as are available and from astute questioning of the proprietor by the accountant.

The following example illustrates the increased-net-worth method.

### Example 3.1

M. Twain set up in business on July 1, 19.0, with capital of £3 000 in cash. During the first year he kept very few records of his transactions. On June 30, 19.1 the assets and liabilities of the business were:

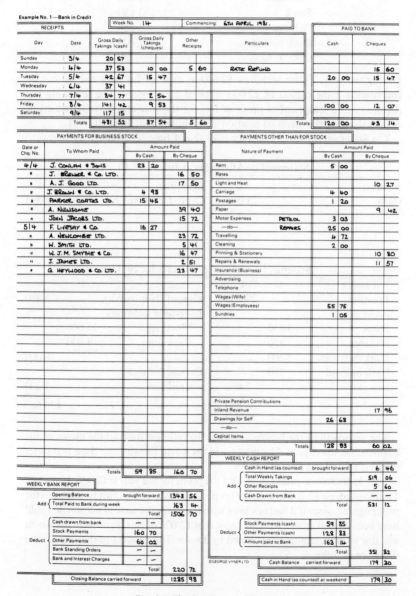

*Fig. 3.1 The Simplex weekly page*

|                             | £      |
|-----------------------------|--------|
| Freehold premises           | 27 000 |
| Mortgage on the premises    | 25 000 |
| Bank loan                   | 3 000  |
| Creditors                   | 1 200  |
| Stock                       | 3 850  |
| Debtors                     | 850    |
| Bank balance                | 2 600  |
| Cash in hand                | 380    |

During the year, Twain withdrew £2 800 in cash for his personal use but he contributed extra capital of £2 000 received as a legacy. The following are required: (a) a statement of profit or loss for the year and (b) a Statement of Affairs showing the financial position of the business at June 30, 19.1.

The Statement of Affairs on July 1, 19.0 and June 30, 19.1 are as follows:

Statement of Affairs (as at July 1, 19.0)

| Assets | £ | Liabilities | £ |
|--------|------|-------------|------|
| Cash | 3 000 | Capital (Net worth) | 3 000 |

Statement of Affairs (as at June 30, 19.1)

| Fixed assets | £ | £ | | £ | £ |
|--------------|------|--------|---------------------|--------|--------|
| Premises | | 27 000 | *Capital* (Net worth) | | 5 480 |
| *Current assets* | | | *Long-term liabilities* | | |
| Stock | 3 850 | | Mortgage | 25 000 | |
| Debtors | 850 | | Bank loan | 3 000 | |
| Bank balance | 2 600 | | | | 28 000 |
| Cash in hand | 380 | | *Current liabilities* | | |
| | | 7 680 | Creditors | | 1 200 |
| | | £34 680 | | | £34 680 |

The net worth of the business is what the business owes to the owner of the business, i.e. the capital. The increase in net worth shown from these two statements is £5 480 *less* £3 000=£2 480.

It looks therefore, prima facie, as if the profit for the year is £2 480. However, Twain withdrew £2 800 in cash for his personal use, which must be added to the profit figure—since if it had not been withdrawn the increase in net worth would have been £2 800 more. We also know that £2 000 of this increase in net worth was due to extra capital contributed by Twain. The answers to the exercise are therefore as follows:

(a) Statement of profit or loss for the year

|  | £ |
|---|---|
| Increase in net worth | 2 480 |
| *Add* Drawings | 2 800 |
|  | 5 280 |
| *Less* Extra capital contributed | 2 000 |
| Net profit | £3 280 |

(b) The Statement of Affairs as at June 30, 19.1 is given above.


## 3.4  Preparing Final Accounts from Incomplete Records

The information about a business provided by a calculation of the type shown in the above example is far from satisfactory. It would be much better to have a Trading and Profit and Loss Account and a balance sheet as at the last day of the financial year. Frequently sufficient evidence can be assembled to provide the figures required, and it is here that the ingenuity and patience of the accountant is needed.

Consider the figures required for a Trading Account. These are, as a minimum, the sales figure (and possibly sales returns), the purchases figure (and possibly purchases returns) and the opening and closing stocks.

The opening and closing stocks will have to be obtained if the Statement of Affairs is to be drawn up, so we can be sure that these figures will be made available, even if it means a physical stocktaking by the accountant himself.

The figure under 'Sales' in the Trading Account requires us to know the sales for the period, whether actually paid for or not. If a record of cash takings has been kept and debtors at the start and end of the year are known, the sales figure may be calculated as follows:

| Sales calculation | |
|---|---|
|  | £ |
| *Takings* | |
| Cash | 124 750 |
| Cheques | 38 250 |
|  | 163 000 |
| *Deduct* Debtors at start (We assume that they have all been paid in the period) | 5 850 |
|  | 157 150 |
| *Add* Debtors at close | 7 215 |
| Sales during year | £164 365 |

A simpler way to present the figures is in the form of a Total Debtors' Account.

### Total Debtors' Account

| 19.0 | | £ | 19.0 | | £ |
|---|---|---|---|---|---|
| Jan. 1 | Opening balances | 5 850 | | *Receipts* | |
| | Sales | ? | | Cash | 124 750 |
| | | | | Cheques | 38 250 |
| | | | Dec. 31 | Closing balances c/d | 7 215 |
| | | £170 215 | | | £170 215 |

| 19.1 | | £ |
|---|---|---|
| Jan. 1 | Opening balances b/d | 7 215 |

Therefore the missing figure, £164 365, is the sales for the year.

By the same argument, the purchases figure for the year is made up of the total payments to suppliers, less outstanding items at the start of the year (these will have been paid during the current year, but refer to the previous period), plus outstanding items at the end of the year. These will be paid in the next year, but must be included in the current year's purchases figure. Again, a Total Creditors' Account will reveal the missing figure, which in this case is £90 686.

### Total Creditors' Account

| 19.0 | | £ | 19.0 | | £ |
|---|---|---|---|---|---|
| | Sums paid to | | Jan. 1 | Balances b/d | 5 850 |
| | suppliers | 84 286 | | Purchases | ? |
| Dec. 31 | Closing balances | | | | |
| | c/d | 12 250 | | | |
| | | £96 536 | | | £96 536 |
| | | | 19.1 | | £ |
| | | | Jan. 1 | Balances b/d | 12 250 |

In examinations you will usually be provided with a set of information from which, using ingenuity, you can obtain the required figures. The example below illustrates the work involved.

**Example 3.2**

R. Cross is a plumber who does not keep proper books of account. From the information given below prepare a Trading and Profit and Loss Account for the year ended December 31, 19.0 and a Statement of Affairs at that date.

Statement of Affairs (as at January 1, 19.0)

| | £ | | £ |
|---|---|---|---|
| Motor vehicle | 2 300 | Capital | 5 150 |
| Tools and equipment | 1 600 | Creditors | 2 450 |
| Stock | 850 | Bank overdraft | 1 885 |
| Debtors | 4 540 | | |
| Rates in advance | 40 | | |
| Insurance prepaid | 120 | | |
| Cash in hand | 35 | | |
| | £9 485 | | £9 485 |

Cross's bank statements for the year show:

| | £ |
|---|---|
| Amounts received from customers (including opening cash in hand) | 8 452 |
| Amounts paid to suppliers | 3 485 |
| Purchase of tools and equipment | 585 |
| Repairs to motor vehicles | 230 |
| Petrol and oil | 685 |
| Rates and insurance paid | 430 |
| Proceeds of sale of family heirloom (extra capital) | 8 250 |

| Cash payments were analysed as follows: | £ |
|---|---|
| Rent | 1 040 |
| Wages | 2 560 |
| Office expenses | 156 |
| Printing and stationery | 140 |
| Sundries | 36 |

All these payments were made out of takings which had been received from customers, and were in addition to the sums actually banked. Cross also took £25 per week out of the business for his personal use, and gave £30 per week to his wife for housekeeping.

At December 31 he estimated as follows:

   (a) Stock was valued at £930.

   (b) Debtors outstanding were £3 150 and creditors unpaid totalled £645.

   (c) Rates in advance totalled £62 and insurance in advance £86.

   (d) Cash in hand (takings not yet banked) was £135.

   (e) Depreciation on the motor vehicle is to be taken at 20 per cent and on all tools and equipment at 25 per cent (to nearest £1).

We proceed as follows:

(i) The opening Statement of Affairs is essential for many of the calculations, and all the entries in it must either come into the accounts in some way or carry over into the final Statement of Affairs at the end of the year. (In the example we have been given this Statement, but in some cases it would be necessary to work it out.) It is important to ensure that every item in it is incorporated in either the Trading and Profit and Loss Account or in the final Statement of Affairs.

(ii) It is usually necessary to draw up a Cash Account and a Bank Account, and this is frequently done with the columns alongside one another in tabular form. In this example only a Bank Account is necessary. Every item in that Bank Account must affect the Trading and Profit and Loss Account in some way, or be carried through into the closing Statement of Affairs.

(iii) A Cash Account is not required in this case because all the cash used is actually part of the cash received from customers for services rendered. The opening cash balance is banked at the start of the year, and as it was received for work done in the previous year it reduces the amounts received by customers as far as the current year is concerned. The sums used as cash instead of being banked, increase the amounts received from customers.

(iv) A Total Debtors' Account reveals the sales figure, and a Total Creditors' Account reveals the purchases figure.

The accounts and balance sheet are set out in Fig. 3.2 (pp. 26–9).

### Bank Account

| 19.0 | | £ | 19.0 | | £ |
|---|---|---|---|---|---|
| | Received from | | | Overdraft (at start) | 1 885 |
| | customers | 8 452 | | Amounts paid to | |
| | Extra capital | | | suppliers | 3 485 |
| | contributed | 8 250 | | Tools and equipment | 585 |
| | | | | Repairs to motor | |
| | | | | vehicle | 230 |
| | | | | Petrol and oil | 685 |
| | | | | Rates and insurance | |
| | | | | paid | 430 |
| | | | | Balance c/d | 9 402 |
| | | £16 702 | | | £16 702 |
| 19.1 | | £ | | | |
| Jan. 1 | Balance b/d | 9 402 | | | |

### Total Debtors' Account

| 19.0 | | £ | 19.0 | | £ |
|---|---|---|---|---|---|
| Jan. 1 | Opening balances | 4 540 | | Amounts banked | 8 417 |
| | Sales | 13 954 | | Amounts received but not banked | |
| | | | | Rent | 1 040 |
| | | | | Wages | 2 560 |
| | | | | Office expenses | 156 |
| | | | | Printing and stationery | 140 |
| | | | | Sundries | 36 |
| | | | | Drawings (£55 per week) | 2 860 |
| | | | | Cash in hand | 135 |
| | | | | Balances at close c/d | 3 150 |
| | | £18 494 | | | £18 494 |

| 19.1 | | £ |
|---|---|---|
| Jan. 1 | Balances b/d | 3 150 |

### Total Creditors' Account

| 19.0 | | £ | 19.0 | | £ |
|---|---|---|---|---|---|
| | Cash paid to suppliers | 3 485 | Jan. 1 | Opening balances | 2 450 |
| | Balances at close c/d | 645 | | Purchases | 1 680 |
| | | £4 130 | | | £4 130 |

| | | | 19.1 | | £ |
|---|---|---|---|---|---|
| | | | Jan. 1 | Opening balances b/d | 645 |

(*continued overleaf*)

## Trading and Profit and Loss Account (for year ending December 31, 19.0)

| 19.0 | | £ | 19.0 | | £ |
|---|---|---|---|---|---|
| | Opening stock | 850 | | Sales | 13 954 |
| | Purchases | 1 680 | | | |
| | | 2 530 | | | |
| | Less Closing stock | 930 | | | |
| | | 1 600 | | | |
| | Gross profit c/d | 12 354 | | | |
| | | £13 954 | | | £13 954 |
| | | | | | |
| | Repairs to motor | | | | |
| | vehicle | 230 | | Gross profit b/d | 12 354 |
| | Petrol and oil | 685 | | | |
| | Rates and | | | | |
| | insurance | 430 | | | |
| | Add Balances | | | | |
| | at start | 160 | | | |
| | | 590 | | | |
| | Less Balances | | | | |
| | at end | 148 | | | |
| | | 442 | | | |
| | Rent | 1 040 | | | |
| | Wages | 2 560 | | | |
| | Office expenses | 156 | | | |
| | Printing and | | | | |
| | stationery | 140 | | | |
| | Sundries | 36 | | | |
| | Depreciation: | | | | |
| | Motor | | | | |
| | vehicle | 460 | | | |
| | Tools, etc. | 546 | | | |
| | | 1 006 | | | |
| | | 6 295 | | | |
| | Net profit | 6 059 | | | |
| | | £12 354 | | | £12 354 |

Balance sheet (as at December 31, 19.0)

| Fixed assets | £ | Capital | | £ |
|---|---|---|---|---|
| Motor vehicle (£2 300 | | At start | | 5 150 |
| less depreciation) | 1 840 | Add new capital | | 8 250 |
| | | | | 13 400 |
| Tools (£2 185 | | Add Profits | 6 059 | |
| less depreciation) | 1 639 | Less Drawings | 2 860 | 3 199 |
| | 3 479 | | | 16 599 |
| Current assets | | Current liabilities | | |
| Stock | 930 | Creditors | | 645 |
| Debtors | 3 150 | | | |
| Bank balance | 9 402 | | | |
| Cash in hand | 135 | | | |
| Rates in advance | 62 | | | |
| Insurance in | | | | |
| advance | 86 | | | |
| | 13 765 | | | |
| | £17 244 | | | £17 244 |

Fig. 3.2 Accounts and balance sheet for Example 3.2

## 3.5   Exercises

1.   What is meant by 'incomplete records'? What problems do incomplete records present to the accountant?

2.   R. Jones is a builder who does not keep proper records. He set up in business on January 1, 19. . with a capital of £5 800 in cash. His records of cash transactions are as follows: motor vehicle expenses £525; wages £2 760; sundry expenses £340. All this cash, except for £50 of his original capital which was not banked on January 1, is money he received from customers in cash for work done. In addition, he has also taken out £45 every week from his cash takings, for domestic purposes.

His bank records show the following situation: original capital banked £5 750; received from customers and banked £11 850; rent £1 400; rates £390; telephone £475; paid to suppliers £3 250; prize received from competition and used as extra capital £500; motor vehicle purchased £680; loose tools purchased £1 240; hire of tools £485.

On December 31, 19. . he owes suppliers £380 for materials, and is owed £1 950 by customers for work done. He has £235 cash in hand (this again is cash received for work done). The motor vehicle and the loose tools are to be depreciated by 25 per cent on cost. Closing stock is valued at £680.

Prepare the Trading and Profit and Loss Account and a Statement of Affairs for the year just ended.

## Unit Four

# Applying Basic Concepts: 2. Partnership Accounts

## 4.1 Recapitulation of Partnership Accounts

In *Success in Principles of Accounting* there is a full description of the elementary rules of accounting for partnerships. The chief points are:

(*a*) A partnership comes into existence when the partners agree to work together to provide some good or service. The agreement may be oral or written but it is best to have a formal agreement (the *deed of partnership*) drawn up so that all parties are clear about the terms of the partnership. The lawyer who draws up such an agreement usually suggests matters which should be covered in the document, notably the capital contributions of the partners, arrangements for any loans to the firm over and above the capital contributed and the division of the profit at the end of each financial year.

(*b*) Once the partnership has started, any point which causes difficulty, on which the parties have failed to specify exact terms, will be settled by reference to the Partnership Act of 1890 (in the United Kingdom).

(*c*) Where partners have not entered into any agreement, express or implied, about the division of profits at the end of the year, this Partnership Act rules as follows:

    (i) profits and losses are to be shared equally;
    (ii) no interest is to be allowed on capital;
    (iii) no interest is to be charged on drawings;
    (iv) no partner is allowed a salary;
    (v) loans to the business by a partner are entitled to interest at 5 per cent.

It is usual for the division of the profits to take place in an Appropriation Section of the Profit and Loss Account. The net profit appears on the credit side of the Appropriation Account, together with any interest on drawings charged to a partner. This total profit is then shared among the partners in the agreed way. Salaries to partners (if any) and interest on loans and interest on capital are debited to the Appropriation Account and credited to the partners' Current Accounts, before the residue of the profit is divided in the agreed way and credited to their Current Accounts.

Example 4.1 and the exercises in Unit 4.2 illustrate the basic principles of partnership accounting.

### Example 4.1

Allen and Brown are in partnership sharing profits and losses in the ratio 2:1. Their accounts are made up for the year ending December 31, 19.0. They have a clause in their partnership agreement which says that interest on capital will be payable at 12 per cent per annum, but that interest at the same rate will also be payable on drawings made during the year. This interest also applies to the balances on the partners' Current Accounts at the start of the year.

From the following information prepare the Profit and Loss Appropriation Account of the partnership and the other personal accounts of Allen and Brown as they would appear in their private ledger.

| Jan. 1, 19.0 | Current Account balance |
|---|---|
| Allen | £400 Cr. |
| Brown | £350 Dr. |

Drawings during year: Allen £1 500 per quarter drawn on the last day of March, June, September and December.
Brown £1 200 per quarter drawn on the same dates.
Capital on Jan. 1: Allen £30 000, Brown £25 000
Salary: Brown £4 000
The net profit made during the year was £24 508. Other assets and liabilities are (a) fixed assets £62 000, (b) current assets £9 600, (c) current liabilities £2 842.

The various accounts are shown in Fig. 4.1 (pp. 31–3)

### Appropriation Account (for year ending December 31, 19.0)

| 19.0 | | | £ | 19.0 | | | £ |
|---|---|---|---|---|---|---|---|
| Dec. 31 | Salary (Brown) | | 4 000 | Dec. 31 | Net profit b/d | | 24 508 |
| | Interest on capital | | | | Interest on Current | | |
| | Allen | 3 600 | | | A/c Brown | | 42 |
| | Brown | 3 000 | | | Interest on drawings | | |
| | | | 6 600 | | Allen | 270 | |
| | Interest on Current | | | | Brown | 216 | |
| | A/c Allen | 48 | | | | | 486 |
| | Share of residue | | | | | | |
| | Allen | 9 592 | | | | | |
| | Brown | 4 796 | 14 388 | | | | |
| | | | £25 036 | | | | £25 036 |

### Capital Account (Allen)

| | | | | 19.0 | | £ |
|---|---|---|---|---|---|---|
| | | | | Jan. 1 | Balance b/d | 30 000 |

### Capital Account (Brown)

| | | | | 19.0 | | £ |
|---|---|---|---|---|---|---|
| | | | | Jan. 1 | Balance b/d | 25 000 |

(*continued overleaf*)

### Current Account (Allen)

| 19.0 | | £ | 19.0 | | | £ |
|------|------|------|------|------|------|------|
| Dec. 31 | Drawings transferred | 6 270 | Jan. 1 | Balance b/d | | 400 |
| 31 | Balance c/d | 7 370 | Dec. 31 | Interest on Current A/c | | 48 |
| | | | 31 | Interest on capital | | 3 600 |
| | | | 31 | Share of residue ($\frac{2}{3}$) | | 9 592 |
| | | £13 640 | | | | £13 640 |

| 19.1 | | £ |
|------|------|------|
| Jan. 1 | Balance b/d | 7 370 |

### Current Account (Brown)

| 19.0 | | £ | 19.0 | | £ |
|------|------|------|------|------|------|
| Jan. 1 | Balance b/d | 350 | Dec. 31 | Salary | 4 000 |
| Dec. 31 | Interest on Current A/c | 42 | 31 | Interest on capital | 3 000 |
| 31 | Drawings transferred | 5 016 | 31 | Share of residue ($\frac{1}{3}$) | 4 796 |
| 31 | Balance c/d | 6 388 | | | |
| | | £11 796 | | | £11 796 |

| 19.1 | | £ |
|------|------|------|
| Jan. 1 | Balance b/d | 6 388 |

### Drawings Account (Allen)

| 19.0 | | Interest £ | £ | 19.0 | | £ |
|------|------|------|------|------|------|------|
| Mar. 31 | Bank | 135 | 1 500 | Dec. 31 | Transfer to Current A/c | 6 270 |
| June 30 | Bank | 90 | 1 500 | | | |
| Sept. 30 | Bank | 45 | 1 500 | | | |
| Dec. 31 | Bank | — | 1 500 | | | |
| 31 | Interest total | | 270 | | | |
| | | | £6 270 | | | £6 270 |

### Drawings Account (Brown)

| 19.0 | | Interest £ | £ | 19.0 | | £ |
|------|------|------|------|------|------|------|
| Mar. 31 | Bank | 108 | 1 200 | Dec. 31 | Transfer to Current A/c | 5 016 |
| June 30 | Bank | 72 | 1 200 | | | |
| Sept. 30 | Bank | 36 | 1 200 | | | |
| Dec. 31 | Bank | — | 1 200 | | | |
| 31 | Interest total | | 216 | | | |
| | | | £5 016 | | | £5 016 |

Balance sheet (as at December 31, 19.0)

| | £ | | | £ |
|---|---|---|---|---|
| Fixed assets | 62 000 | Capital | Allen | 30 000 |
| | | | Brown | 25 000 |
| | | | | 55 000 |
| Current assets | 9 600 | Current Accounts | £ | |
| | | Allen | 7 370 | |
| | | Brown | 6 388 | |
| | | | | 13 758 |
| | | Current liabilities | | 2 842 |
| | £71 600 | | | £71 600 |

*Fig. 4.1 Simple partnership accounts*

## 4.2  Adjusting Relationships between Partners

Partnership agreements are essentially a recognition of the qualities and abilities of the partners. One may have more knowledge or experience; another may be physically stronger, and so on. The agreement arrived at reflects the bargaining strength of the parties at a particular time. This agreement may, therefore, need adjusting occasionally as the situation changes. Younger partners gain experience as the years pass, older ones may take less responsibility and adopt a more advisory role. Partners may retire, or die, and new partners may be admitted. In these circumstances, there has to be some adjustment of the original arrangements. The adjustment involves the goodwill of the partnership.

### Goodwill and Partnerships

Business goodwill only appears on the books of the business of a sole trader if he has actually purchased the business at some earlier date and paid a sum for the goodwill as part of the purchase price. In such circumstances the asset *goodwill* is an *intangible asset*, and it is usual to write off such an asset over the first few years of the sole trader's business. With partnerships it is quite common to have a Goodwill Account appearing on the books, and it usually indicates that at some past date a rearrangement of the agreement between the partners has been put into effect. However, there are some disadvantages in having such an account on the books, because if the business should be sold it is unlikely that the goodwill at the time of the sale would be the same as the book valuation chosen earlier. Thus, if goodwill appears on the books at £5 000 but it is proposed to charge the purchaser £15 000, he will probably object. For this reason it is desirable, if the partners prefer, to effect the rearrangement without creating a Goodwill Account.

Goodwill has been defined as 'the probability that the old customer will resort to the old place' (*per* Lord Eldon, 1810). The implication is that a business which has done a certain volume of business in the past will continue to do the same business (and make the same profit) in the future. However, it is often much more than this. It may be the measure of a lifetime's work, the value of which is now to be transferred to a stranger. The consideration payable for such lifetime's work is debatable, but cannot be greater than the amount which the highest bidder will offer for it.

The valuation of goodwill is not easy and is always a matter of bargaining. Whatever value is placed upon it by the vendor, it does not follow that he can persuade the purchaser to pay it. Common valuations are:

   (i) $x$ years' purchase of the net profits;

  (ii) $x$ years' purchase of the super-profits.

*Super-profits* is a term used to distinguish between the net profit earned by the business and the true profit element in the net profit. Much of the reward earned by a trader is really only compensation for his labour, and interest on his capital invested in the business. By working and investing his capital in the business, he has lost opportunities for working and investing elsewhere. A dentist earning £12 000 per annum net profit whose salary as an employee would be £6 000 elsewhere and whose capital of £30 000 could earn 8 per cent elsewhere (£2 400), is really only making £3 600 true profit.

Goodwill is valued under the following circumstances:

(*a*) when a partnership is purchasing an existing business and actually purchasing the goodwill. This is the same situation as with a sole trader: the Goodwill Account is an intangible asset and is written off over the first few years of the new business.

(*b*) when there is a change in the profit-sharing ratios of the existing partners;

(*c*) when a new partner is admitted. The new partner is charged a premium for goodwill, since he is purchasing a right to a share in the future profits.

(*d*) when a partner retires;

(*e*) when a partner dies.

Leaving (*a*) aside as an elementary case, the other four examples involve negotiation between the various parties to arrive at a valuation to be placed upon all or part of the goodwill.

In addition to the difficulties in valuing the goodwill, there are also different ways of treating the book-keeping. These vary with circumstances and are referred to in the examples which follow.

Finally, we should note that when the profit-sharing ratios between partners have to be adjusted because of some change in the situation with respect to each other, a valuation is placed upon the goodwill of the business which is shared, using the old method of sharing profits that existed prior to the arrangement. This results either in the payment of money between them or in the allocation of an appropriate sum to their various Capital Accounts. The business then proceeds as before, with the subsequent profits being shared in the new way, until a further rearrangement becomes necessary.

Consider the following example of a rearrangement between partners:

**Example 4.2**

A, B and C who have been sharing profits $\frac{1}{2}$, $\frac{1}{3}$ and $\frac{1}{6}$ decide to rearrange their affairs as at January 1, 19. . . A has developed other interests and will take a less important role and only $\frac{1}{4}$ of the profits. The balance will be shared equally between B and C. Capital is as follows: A £12 000; B £8 000; C £4 000. The partners agree to value the goodwill at £12 000.

There are two methods of dealing with such rearrangements. One is by opening up a Goodwill Account and crediting each of the partners at the date of the rearrangement with an appropriate share of this goodwill. This method recognizes the existence of goodwill as an asset of the business. The two balance sheets, before and after the rearrangement, are shown in Fig. 4.2. The goodwill has been shared $\frac{1}{2}$, $\frac{1}{3}$ and $\frac{1}{6}$, to give increases in their Capital Accounts of A £6 000, B £4 000 and C £2 000. The other assets are shown as a net figure (i.e. any liabilities other than the capital have been deducted from the assets to show a net assets figure).

Balance sheet (as at January 1. 19. .)

|  | Before | After |  | Before | After |
|---|---|---|---|---|---|
|  | £ | £ |  | £ | £ |
| Goodwill | — | 12 000 | Capital A | 12 000 | 18 000 |
| Other assets (net) | 24 000 | 24 000 | B | 8 000 | 12 000 |
|  |  |  | C | 4 000 | 6 000 |
|  | £24 000 | 36 000 |  | £24 000 | 36 000 |

*Fig. 4.2 Rearrangements between partners — Goodwill Account opened*

In view of the disadvantages of already having a Goodwill Account on the books, it is often preferable to make the same rearrangement without opening such an account. The principle here is that if a partner is likely in future to have a more favourable share in the goodwill than in the past, he must pay for that privilege, whereas a partner who moves to a less favourable position is entitled to compensation for that loss. In considering the three partners' positions, we see that A is moving to a less favourable situation (only $\frac{1}{4}$ share in future compared with $\frac{1}{2}$ at present), B is improving his position slightly (from $\frac{1}{3}$ to $\frac{3}{8}$), and C is improving his position considerably (from $\frac{1}{6}$ to $\frac{3}{8}$).

Comparing the shares in a Goodwill Account of £12 000 under the old and new systems, we have:

|  |  | Old system £ |  | New system £ | Change in entitlement | Remedial action |
|---|---|---|---|---|---|---|
| A | $\frac{1}{2}$ | 6 000 | $\frac{1}{4}$ | 3 000 | £3 000 less | Credit A's Capital A/c £3 000 |
| B | $\frac{1}{3}$ | 4 000 | $\frac{3}{8}$ | 4 500 | £500 gain | Debit B's Capital A/c £500 |
| C | $\frac{1}{6}$ | 2 000 | $\frac{3}{8}$ | 4 500 | £2 500 gain | Debit C's Capital A/c £2 500 |

The resulting balance sheet before and after now appears as in Fig. 4.3.

Balance sheet (as at January 1, 19. .)

| | Before | After | | | Before | After |
|---|---|---|---|---|---|---|
| | £ | £ | | | £ | £ |
| Assets (net) | 24 000 | 24 000 | Capital A | | 12 000 | 15 000 |
| | | | B | | 8 000 | 7 500 |
| | | | C | | 4 000 | 1 500 |
| | £24 000 | 24 000 | | | £24 000 | 24 000 |

*Fig. 4.3 Rearrangements between partners—Goodwill Account not opened*

Note that the only difference between Fig. 4.2 and Fig. 4.3 is that in Fig. 4.3 the asset Goodwill is in the form of a *hidden reserve*. Imagine the business was sold on January 2 to a purchaser who paid the agreed price of £12 000 for the goodwill. In the case of Fig. 4.2, the purchase price of £36 000 would reimburse the partners for the sums invested over the years as capital. In the case of Fig. 4.3, they would be repaid their capital sums, and in addition they would have £12 000 to share for goodwill. In the proportions $\frac{1}{4}, \frac{3}{8}, \frac{3}{8}$ this would give A £3 000 extra, B £4 500 extra and C £4 500 extra. In each case this would raise their total remuneration to the same values as shown in Fig. 4.2.

## 4.3   Admission of a New Partner

When a new partner is admitted, three possible situations arise:

(*a*) The new partner takes over the share of a retiring or deceased partner. In this case there is no change in the existing shares and the new entrant merely replaces the retiring or deceased partner.

In any other circumstances the partners must in future give up a share of the profits to the new entrant. They can do this in two ways:

(*b*) Without disturbing the ratios in which they share profits at present— which means they give up the same proportions of their shares of the profit. Imagine two partners, X and Y, sharing $\frac{2}{3}$ and $\frac{1}{3}$, who agree to admit a new partner, Z, who is to have $\frac{1}{5}$ of the profits in future. One partner (X) must give up $\frac{2}{3}$ of $\frac{1}{5} = \frac{2}{15}$ and the other (Y) must surrender $\frac{1}{3}$ of $\frac{1}{5} = \frac{1}{15}$. This leaves them receiving profits as follows:

$$X \text{ receives } \tfrac{2}{3} \text{ less } \tfrac{2}{15} = \tfrac{8}{15}$$
$$Y \text{ receives } \tfrac{1}{3} \text{ less } \tfrac{1}{15} = \tfrac{4}{15}$$
$$Z \text{ receives } \tfrac{3}{15} = \tfrac{1}{5}$$

X's and Y's shares are still in the ratio of 2:1 as before. Book-keeping entries would be required to take account of Z's purchase of part of the goodwill.

(*c*) If the new entrant's arrival calls for a reallocation of the profits which disturbs the existing ratios between the original partners, this must be taken into account. For example, if X, Y and Z are to share profits $\frac{2}{5}$, $\frac{2}{5}$ and $\frac{1}{5}$ in future, the former 2:1 ratio between X and Y has been disturbed. This calls for an adjustment not only because Z has taken over part of the goodwill, but also because the relative shares of the goodwill held by X and Y have changed.

Examples 4.3 and 4.4 show the book-keeping involved under (b) and Example 4.5 shows that under (c).

**No change in the original partners' ratio of profits** (see (b) above).

**Example 4.3**

On January 1, A and B, who are in partnership, sharing profits $\frac{2}{3}$ and $\frac{1}{3}$, agree to admit C on payment of £1 500 for a $\frac{1}{4}$ share of the profits. As well as the £1 500 premium on entry, C will contribute £1 000 capital. The ratio in which A and B share profits will not be disturbed. Make the appropriate entries. (*Note:* Since C's future share is to be $\frac{1}{4}$ of the profits, A must give up $\frac{2}{3}$ of $\frac{1}{4}$ and B must surrender $\frac{1}{3}$ of $\frac{1}{4}$.)

This means that A gives up $\frac{2}{3} \times \frac{1}{4} = \frac{1}{6}$, and in future takes only $\frac{2}{3} - \frac{1}{6} = \frac{1}{2}$ of the profits. B gives up $\frac{1}{3} \times \frac{1}{4} = \frac{1}{12}$ and in future only takes $\frac{1}{3} - \frac{1}{12} = \frac{1}{4}$. The future division will therefore be $\frac{1}{2}$, $\frac{1}{4}$ and $\frac{1}{4}$ for C. A is still taking twice as large a share as B and no rearrangement of shares between them has taken place.

Three methods for dealing with the book-keeping are available:

**Method I.** The £1 500 is paid privately by C to the old partners who share it in the ratio $\frac{2}{3} : \frac{1}{3}$, i.e. £1 000 to A; £500 to B. No book-keeping for this is required as the premium never becomes partnership property. The only book-keeping is the entry of £1 000 new capital from C which is debited in the Bank Account and credited in C's Capital Account.

**Method II.** The £1 500 is paid into the business Bank Account by C and credited to the Capital Accounts of A and B in the ratio $\frac{2}{3} : \frac{1}{3}$. This is then withdrawn at once in cash, in full, with debit entries for withdrawal of capital in the Capital Accounts of A and B. There is at least some record on the books of the partnership of C's purchase of a quarter share of the future profits.

C's contribution of £1 000 capital is entered as in Method I.

**Method III.** The £1 500 is paid into the business Bank Account by C (debiting the Bank Account) with corresponding credits for £1 000 and £500 in A's and B's Capital Accounts. The funds are left in the business and represent extra capital contributed by the *existing* partners (although the actual source of the funds was C). The entries for C's £1 000 capital are the same as in Method I.

The three methods are illustrated in Fig. 4.4 (pp. 37–8).

**Method I:** *No record of premium on entry*

| Bank Account | | CB1 |
|---|---|---|
| 19.. | £ | |
| Jan. 1   Capital | J1   1 000 | |

| Capital Account (C) | | L3 |
|---|---|---|
| | 19.. | £ |
| | Jan. 1   Bank | J1   1 000 |

(*continued overleaf*)

**Method II:** *Premium recorded, but then withdrawn by original partners*

|  | Bank Account |  |  |  | CB1 |
|---|---|---|---|---|---|
| 19.. |  | £ | 19.. |  | £ |
| Jan. 1 | Capital (C)      J1 | 1 000 | Jan. 1 | Capital withdrawn A | 1 000 |
| 1 | Premium on entry J1 | 1 500 | 1 | Capital withdrawn B | 500 |

|  | Capital Account (A) |  |  |  | L1 |
|---|---|---|---|---|---|
| 19.. |  | £ | 19.. |  | £ |
| Jan. 1 | Bank | 1 000 | Jan. 1 | Balance (say) b/d | 8 000 |
|  |  |  | 1 | Share of premium  J1 | 1 000 |

|  | Capital Account (B) |  |  |  | L2 |
|---|---|---|---|---|---|
| 19.. |  | £ | 19.. |  | £ |
| Jan. 1 | Bank | 500 | Jan. 1 | Balance (say) b/d | 4 000 |
|  |  |  | 1 | Share of premium  J1 | 500 |

|  | Capital Account (C) |  |  |  | L3 |
|---|---|---|---|---|---|
|  |  |  | 19.. |  | £ |
|  |  |  | Jan. 1 | Bank | J1 | 1 000 |

**Method III:** *Premium recorded and left in the business*

|  | Bank Account |  | CB1 |
|---|---|---|---|
| 19.. |  | £ |  |
| Jan. 1 | Capital (C)      J1 | 1 000 |  |
| 1 | Premium on entry J1 | 1 500 |  |

|  | Capital Account (A) |  |  |  | L1 |
|---|---|---|---|---|---|
|  |  |  | 19.. |  | £ |
|  |  |  | Jan. 1 | Balance (say) b/d | 8 000 |
|  |  |  | 1 | Share of premium  J1 | 1 000 |

|  | Capital Account (B) |  |  |  | L2 |
|---|---|---|---|---|---|
|  |  |  | 19.. |  | £ |
|  |  |  | Jan. 1 | Balance (say) b/d | 4 000 |
|  |  |  | 1 | Share of premium  J1 | 500 |

|  | Capital Account (C) |  |  |  | L3 |
|---|---|---|---|---|---|
|  |  |  | 19.. |  | £ |
|  |  |  | Jan. 1 | Bank | J1 | 1 000 |

*Fig. 4.4 Admission of a new partner*

**Example 4.4**

A and B are in partnership sharing profits $\frac{2}{3}$ and $\frac{1}{3}$. On January 1, 19. . they agree to admit C with a capital of £1 000. C will take $\frac{1}{4}$ of the profits; the present ratio in which A and B share profits is not to be disturbed. C is unable to bring in any premium on entry and goodwill is valued at £6 000. Show the journal entries (*a*) where goodwill is to be recorded, (*b*) where goodwill is not to appear as a permanent asset on the books of the partnership.

It frequently happens that a new partner does not have enough funds to pay a premium on entry. In this case it is usual to recognize the past work of the existing partners by opening a Goodwill Account for the full value of the goodwill. This intangible asset would be balanced by credit entries in the Capital Accounts of the existing partners who thus share the asset in the original way: $\frac{2}{3}$ and $\frac{1}{3}$ in this example.

The journal entry for this is shown in Fig. 4.5, together with the journal entry for C's capital contribution.

| 19. . | | | | £ | £ |
|---|---|---|---|---|---|
| Jan. 1 | Goodwill Account | Dr. | L7 | 6 000 | |
| | Capital Account A | | L1 | | 4 000 |
| | Capital Account B | | L2 | | 2 000 |
| | Being goodwill entries on admission of new partner, C | | | | |
| Jan. 1 | Bank Account | Dr. | CB5 | 1 000 | |
| | Capital Account C | | L3 | | 1 000 |
| | Being capital contribution of the new partner | | | | |

*Fig. 4.5 Admission of a new partner who cannot afford a premium on entry*

We have already seen (in Unit 4.2) that there are good reasons for not having a Goodwill Account as a permanent feature of the accounts, and it can be readily removed as soon as the new partnership has begun. The Goodwill Account is simply written off against the partners' Capital Accounts, the loss being shared in the new agreed way. Since C is to have $\frac{1}{4}$ of the profits the calculations will be the same as those given earlier (see Example 4.3) and the new shares will be $\frac{1}{2}$, $\frac{1}{4}$ and $\frac{1}{4}$ (leaving the ratios between A and B undisturbed). The goodwill of £6 000 will thus be lost as follows: £3 000 by A and £1 500 each by B and C. The result is that A's Capital Account has effectively risen by £1 000, B's by £500 and C's has fallen by £1 500—which actually makes C's Capital Account overdrawn by £500.

Although it appears that the new partner has already lost his original capital contribution, this is in fact not so. The partnership has simply agreed to remove the Goodwill Account from the books, leaving it as a hidden reserve which may be realized at any time. Should a situation arise when the goodwill again needs to be valued, the Capital Accounts of the partners will at once be credited with the correct shares of the new valuation, and C's Capital Account will be restored with an appropriate sum which recognizes the new value of goodwill at the new point in time.

The journal entry for the elimination of the Goodwill Account is shown in Fig. 4.6.

| 19.. | | | | £ | £ |
|---|---|---|---|---|---|
| Jan. 1 | Capital Account A | Dr. | L1 | 3 000 | |
| | Capital Account B | Dr. | L2 | 1 500 | |
| | Capital Account C | Dr. | L3 | 1 500 | |
| | Goodwill Account | | L7 | | 6 000 |
| | Being writing off of goodwill at | | | | |
| | this date in the new agreed ratio | | | | |

*Fig. 4.6 Eliminating Goodwill Account from the books*

As an alternative short-cut method, the partners' Capital Accounts may be adjusted without any entries in the Goodwill Account. The calculation is made as follows:

| | Share of ownership of the goodwill | | Change in ownership | Remedial action necessary |
|---|---|---|---|---|
| | Before | After | | |
| A | £4 000 | £3 000 | Loss of £1 000 | Credit Capital A/c £1 000 |
| B | £2 000 | £1 500 | Loss of £500 | Credit Capital A/c £500 |
| C | — | £1 500 | Gain of £1 500 | Debit Capital A/c £1 500 |

Note that the remedial action compensates the losers for their losses and charges C for his gain. The journal entry would be as shown in Fig. 4.7.

| 19.. | | | | £ | £ |
|---|---|---|---|---|---|
| Jan. 1 | Capital Account C | Dr. | L3 | 1 500 | |
| | Capital Account A | | L1 | | 1 000 |
| | Capital Account B | | L2 | | 500 |
| | Being adjustment of | | | | |
| | Capital Accounts on | | | | |
| | admission of new | | | | |
| | partner, C | | | | |

*Fig. 4.7 Admitting a partner who cannot afford a premium — no Goodwill Account to be opened*

**Entrance of a new partner disturbs the previous arrangement** (see Unit 4.3(c)).

The general principle has already been stated. Where a partner moves to an improved position in the sharing out of future profits, he must pay for that improvement. Where a partner moves to a less satisfactory situation he is entitled to compensation for his agreement to take a smaller share in the future. Example 4.5 illustrates the book-keeping involved.

**Example 4.5**

X, Y and Z have capitals of £4 000, £4 000 and £2 000 respectively, and share profits in the ratio 2:2:1. They decide to admit W who will bring in £1 000 capital and £1 000 as a premium on entry. In future, profits will be shared in the ratio 4:3:2:1 (i.e. 10 shares in all) with W taking one share.

Assuming that the £1 000 premium is for the purchase of $\frac{1}{10}$ of the future profits, the total goodwill is valued at £10 000. The ownership of the goodwill is now as follows:

| | Share of ownership of goodwill | | Change in ownership | Remedial action necessary |
|---|---|---|---|---|
| | Before £ | After £ | | |
| X | 4 000 | 4 000 | None | None |
| Y | 4 000 | 3 000 | Loss of £1 000 | Credit Capital A/c £1 000 |
| Z | 2 000 | 2 000 | None | None |
| W | — | 1 000 | Gain of £1 000 | Debit Capital A/c £1 000 |

The journal entries will be as shown in Fig. 4.8, with the new partner's effective capital on entry being £1 000.

| 19.. | | | £ | £ |
|---|---|---|---|---|
| Jan. 1 | Bank A/c | Dr. | 2 000 | |
| | Capital A/c W | | | 2 000 |
| | Being capital £1 000 and premium on entry £1 000 (goodwill purchased) | | | |
| Jan. 1 | Capital A/c W | Dr. | 1 000 | |
| | Capital A/c Y | | | 1 000 |
| | Being entry to adjust for W's purchase of $\frac{1}{10}$ of the goodwill value from Y (share reduced from $\frac{2}{5}$ to $\frac{3}{10}$) | | | |

*Fig. 4.8 Admitting a partner whose entry disturbs the previous arrangements*

## 4.4 Exercises

1. Rogers and Moore conduct a merchanting business in partnership on the following terms:

(a) Interest is to be allowed on partners' Capital Accounts, and on Current Account balances at the start of the year, at 10 per cent per annum. No interest will be charged on drawings.

(*b*)  Rogers is to be credited with a partnership salary of £2 000 per annum.

(*c*)  The balance of profit in any year is to be shared by the partners in the ratio 1:2.

After preparing their Trading and Profit and Loss Account for the year ended March 31, 19. ., but before making any provision for interest on capital or for Rogers's partnership salary, the following balances remained on the books:

|  | £ | £ |
|---|---|---|
| *Capital Accounts:* | Dr. | Cr. |
| Rogers (as on April 1, previous year) | | 10 000 |
| Moore (as on April 1, previous year) | | 20 000 |
| *Current Accounts:* | | |
| Rogers | | 250 |
| Moore | | 500 |
| *Drawings Accounts:* | | |
| Rogers | 2 400 | |
| Moore | 3 800 | |
| Profit and Loss Account (net profit for year) | | 9 252 |
| Stock at March 31, 19. . | 13 650 | |
| Premises | 12 000 | |
| Plant and machinery, at cost | 8 650 | |
| Plant and machinery, depreciation | | 4 325 |
| Fixtures and fittings, at cost | 2 000 | |
| Fixtures and fittings, depreciation | | 1 500 |
| Trade debtors and creditors | 3 700 | 750 |
| Loan from B. Brightside | | 2 000 |
| Rent due at March 31, 19. . | | 280 |
| Insurance unexpired at March 31, 19. . | 140 | |
| Cash at bank, Current Account | 2 517 | |
| | £48 857 | £48 857 |

Prepare the Appropriation Section of the firm's Profit and Loss Account and the partners' Current Accounts for the year ended March 31, 19. ., together with the balance sheet as on that date. (Calculations to be made to the nearest £1.)

## Unit Five
# Applying Basic Concepts:
# 3. Manufacturing Accounts

## 5.1 Introduction

Manufacturing is the process by which natural resources from mines, forests, fields and seas are turned into consumer goods. In accounting these resources are classed under the general heading of *materials*, which have to be worked on by people during the manufacturing process. The human resources come under the general heading of *labour*. Some labour works directly on the product and is called *direct labour* while workers who are employed in other ways such as supervisory or factory administration, and only contribute indirectly, are called *indirect labour*, and form part of what is known as *overhead expenses*. Other overhead expenses are 'non-human' in character, such as rent, rates and telephone bills.

The advanced countries of the world are largely engaged in manufacturing, which forms the basis of much of their prosperity, creating a flood of consumer goods. The whole area of manufacturing forms a special branch of accountancy called *cost accountancy*, closely interrelated with *management accounting* (see Unit 8.1). Much of this book is concerned with cost accounting, and this introductory Unit shows how manufacturing is dealt with in Final Accounts, but the full processes of cost accounting are dealt with in Units 8–17.

## 5.2 The Basic Elements of Manufacturing Accounts

It is usual to prepare Manufacturing Accounts in two parts—the *prime cost section* and the *cost of manufactured goods section*. Stocks also present special problems in Manufacturing Accounts.

**The prime cost section.** Prime means first, and *prime costs* are those which are incurred as soon as the manufacturing process starts. We must have raw materials and labour to work on them; and usually some source of power is required for the various processes. All these basic requirements which are incorporated *directly* into the product are called *direct costs*. These costs also vary with the final output—for example, to make double the number of tables takes twice as much wood, and this gives rise to a third term, *variable costs*. These three terms are interchangeable.

The prime cost section of the Manufacturing Account lists all these costs and totals them to give the prime costs of the enterprise.

**The cost of manufactured goods section.** The prime costs thus obtained are then carried down into the second section of the Manufacturing Account, the cost of manufactured goods section. *Overheads* are then added to these prime costs to give the total costs of manufacture. Such items as factory rent, rates, salaries of supervision and managerial staff, are *overhead expenses*. They are also called *indirect costs* or *fixed costs* to distinguish them from the direct costs and variable costs mentioned above. A manager's salary, for example, does not vary with output; he can supervise the production of 8 000 items just as easily as he can 800.

**Stocks in manufacturing.** In *Success in Principles of Accounting* we saw how to prepare a Trading Account, and we met stocks, both opening stocks and closing stocks. These were, of course, stocks of finished goods which were being bought and sold — but in the main activity of manufacturing businesses we do not buy finished goods, only the raw materials to make into finished goods. At the end of the financial year, when we do the stocktaking, there are three kinds of stock to count. First there is the *stock of raw materials*, then there is the *stock of work-in-progress*, sometimes called the *stock of partly-finished goods*, and finally, there is the *stock of finished goods*.

The second group is the most difficult to value. For example, between the start and the finish of the production line a furniture manufacturer would have many partly-finished units, ranging from sawn planks which have barely started the production process, to nearly-finished articles, needing merely labelling and packaging. Clearly, it will require some calculation to find the value of this work-in-progress. The accountant has to decide what value to place upon it and whether to include overhead charges as well as prime costs in the calculations. It is probably most common to value the work-in-progress at factory cost, that is to say, at prime cost (raw materials, labour and other variable costs) plus overheads (a proportion of total overhead costs being added). If this procedure is adopted, the work-in-progress appears in the second part of the Manufacturing Account, that is, in the cost of manufactured goods section. It is therefore usual to have three stock figures in Manufacturing Accounts exercises, to reflect what happens in real life.

## 5.3    The Final Accounts of a Manufacturer

A manufacturer's Final Accounts include the following sections of work which must be prepared:

(*a*) a Manufacturing Account in two parts — a prime cost section and a cost of manufactured goods section;

(*b*) a Trading Account;

(*c*) a Profit and Loss Account;

(*d*) an Appropriation Account if the firm is a partnership or a limited company;

(*e*) a balance sheet.

This is a fairly lengthy series of activities and for textbook and examination purposes it is usually only necessary to produce the Manufacturing Account and Trading Account.

Fig. 5.1 shows a manufacturer's accounts prepared in this way. Work through them carefully and make sure that you understand the preparation of each part.

**Example 5.1**

A. Prefabricator is a manufacturer. Prepare his Manufacturing Account and Trading Account for the year ending December 31, 19. . from the figures given below and carry the gross profit to the Profit and Loss Account.

|  |  | £ |
|---|---|---:|
| Stocks at January 1, 19. . | | |
| | Raw materials | 2 100 |
| | Work-in-progress | 3 500 |
| | Finished goods | 7 250 |
| Purchase of raw materials | | 31 250 |
| Sales | | 84 275 |
| Returns in | | 405 |
| Factory | | |
| | Wages (variable) | 12 250 |
| | Power (variable) | 815 |
| | Salaries (overhead) | 8 500 |
| | Rent and rates (overhead) | 750 |
| Stocks at December 31, 19. . | | |
| | Raw materials | 7 250 |
| | Work-in-progress | 4 550 |
| | Finished goods | 8 500 |
| Factory | | |
| | Lighting (overhead) | 800 |
| | Repairs (overhead) | 1 200 |
| | Depreciation (overhead) | 1 275 |
| Warehouse | | |
| | Wages | 8 625 |
| | Rates | 1 100 |

The accounts are set out as in Fig. 5.1 (pp. 45–6).

Manufacturing Account (for year ending December 31, 19. .)

*(Prime cost section)*

| Raw materials | £ | | £ |
|---|---:|---|---:|
| Opening stock at | | Prime cost c/d | 39 165 |
| January 1 | 2 100 | | |
| Purchases | 31 250 | | |
| | 33 350 | | |
| *Less* Closing stock | 7 250 | | |
| Cost of raw materials used | 26 100 | | |
| Wages | 12 250 | | |
| Power | 815 | | |
| | £39 165 | | £39 165 |

*(continued overleaf)*

(*Cost of manufactured goods section*)

| | | £ | £ | | £ |
|---|---|---|---|---|---|
| Prime cost | b/d | 39 165 | | | |
| *Overheads* | | | Cost of finished goods | | |
| Factory salaries | | 8 500 | (transferred to Trading | | |
| Factory rent and rates | | 750 | A/c) | | 50 640 |
| Factory lighting | | 800 | | | |
| Factory repairs | | 1 200 | | | |
| Factory depreciation | | 1 275 | | | |
| Sub-total | | 51 690 | | | |
| *Work-in-progress* | | | | | |
| Stock at Jan. 1 | 3 500 | | | | |
| *Less* Stock at | | | | | |
| December 31 | 4 550 | | | | |
| | | − 1 050 | | | |
| | | £50 640 | | | £50 640 |

Trading Account (for year ending December 31, 19. .)

| *Finished goods* | £ | | £ |
|---|---|---|---|
| Opening stock at Jan. 1 | 7 250 | Sales | 84 275 |
| Cost of finished goods | 50 640 | *Less* Returns | 405 |
| | 57 890 | | 83 870 |
| *Less* Closing stock | 8 500 | | |
| Cost of goods sold | 49 390 | | |
| Warehouse wages | 8 625 | | |
| Warehouse rates | 1 100 | | |
| Cost of sales | 59 115 | | |
| Gross profit | 24 755 | | |
| | £83 870 | | £83 870 |

Profit and Loss Account (for year ending December 31, 19. .)

| | | £ |
|---|---|---|
| | Gross profit | 24 755 |

*Fig. 5.1 A manufacturer's accounts*

*Notes:*
(i) In the prime cost section the accountant has to decide which costs he will regard as prime costs. Raw materials and wages are always embodied in the finished product. Some accountants would regard power for machines as a prime cost, as in this example.
(ii) Work-in-progress presents difficulties. If the opening stock of work-in-progress is greater than the closing stock, the effect will be an increase in the cost of manufactured goods. If the closing stock of work-in-progress is greater than the opening stock there will be a decrease in the total cost of finished goods. In the latter case, more work-in-progress has been held back — to be passed on to the next year's accounts — than was

handed on to this year from the previous year, on January 1.

You will see that the total cost of the manufactured goods is found by the formula:

Total cost = Prime costs *plus* Overheads *plus* or *minus* Net work-in-progress

(iii) In a normal Trading Account, a trader enters his purchases, and sets them against sales to find his gross profit. A manufacturer does not have purchases in this way. His main purchases are raw materials which appear in the Manufacturing Account. In his Trading Account, however, it is the finished goods carried forward from the Manufacturing Account which are set against sales to find the profits. In Fig. 5.1, the finished goods have been carried forward at their manufactured cost, and the gross profit is the difference between this cost price and the sales figure.

**Finding a manufacturing profit.** As described in Note (iii) to Fig. 5.1, when the manufacturer transfers his goods to the warehouse at manufactured cost, the gross profit is found by deducting this cost price (or, rather, the cost of sales based upon it) from the selling price. Unfortunately this procedure is not entirely satisfactory, because it does not give any indication of the profitability of the factory. The gross profit achieved is the result of two processes: the manufacturing process and the trading process. If the results of these two activities can be separated to show their respective results, we improve our control of the business. Suppose a factory is efficient, but the sales manager is lax, and negotiates sales at too low a price. The profit made from the factory will be lost by his weak policies. In contrast, a very efficient sales manager, striking good bargains with customers, can bring no benefit if the factory is inefficient and its running costs are too high. Where it is possible to bring out a manufacturing profit it is desirable to do so. This can be achieved by comparing the factory cost of our goods with the current market price of similar goods on the open market. Where such a figure can be obtained, a revised Manufacturing Account can be prepared, with the 'cost of manufactured goods' section showing a manufacturing profit. Fig. 5.2 illustrates the effect of this on the profit figures calculated in Fig. 5.1. The market value of the goods manufactured, i.e. the total we would have to pay to buy them from an outside firm, is taken as £60 000.

*(Cost of manufactured goods section)*

| | | £ | | £ |
|---|---|---|---|---|
| Prime cost | b/d | 39 165 | Market value of finished | |
| *Overheads* | | | goods (transferred to | |
| Factory salaries | | 8 500 | Trading A/c) | 60 000 |
| Factory rent and rates | | 750 | | |
| Factory lighting | | 800 | | |
| Factory repairs | | 1 200 | | |
| Factory depreciation | | 1 275 | | |
| | | 51 690 | | |
| *Work-in-progress* | £ | | | |
| Stock at Jan. 1 | 3 500 | | | |
| *Less* Stock at | | | | |
| Dec. 31 | 4 550 | | | |
| | | −1 050 | | |
| | | 50 640 | | |
| Manufacturing profit | | 9 360 | | |
| | | £60 000 | | £60 000 |

Trading Account (for year ending December 31, 19. .)

| *Finished goods* | £ | | £ |
|---|---|---|---|
| Opening stock at | | Sales | 84 275 |
| Jan. 1 | 7 250 | *Less* Returns | 405 |
| Market value of goods | | | 83 870 |
| manufactured | 60 000 | | |
| | 67 250 | | |
| *Less* Closing stock | 8 500 | | |
| Cost of goods sold | 58 750 | | |
| Wages | 8 625 | | |
| Rates | 1 100 | | |
| Cost of sales | 68 475 | | |
| Gross profit | 15 395 | | |
| | £83 870 | | £83 870 |

Profit and Loss Account (for year ending December 31, 19. .)

| | £ |
|---|---|
| Manufacturing profit | 9 360 |
| Gross profit | 15 395 |
| | £24 755 |

*Fig. 5.2 Bringing out a manufacturing profit*

*Notes to Fig. 5.2:*
(i) The total profit from Fig. 5.1 is unchanged, but now the portion attributable to the factory can be seen. It leads us to conclude that the factory is earning profits and manufacturing is therefore worth while.
(ii) If, for example, the market value had been only £45 000, not £60 000, this would have meant that there would be a manufacturing loss of £5 640, instead of a profit of £9 360. This loss would be hidden by the Trading Account which would show a £30 395 profit (£83 870 sales less £53 475 cost of sales). Under these circumstances, the goods would be uncompetitive and the factory ought to be closed.

## 5.4   Exercises

1.   What are *prime costs*? What are *overheads*? Give three examples of each.

2.   Gorleston Ltd is a manufacturing company and the following details for the year 19.. were extracted from its books:

|  | £ |
|---|---|
| Stock of raw materials at January 1, 19.. | 25 265 |
| Stock of raw materials at December 31, 19.. | 23 181 |
| Stock of manufactured goods at January 1, 19.. | 45 284 |
| Stock of manufactured goods at December 31, 19.. | 37 259 |
| Work-in-progress at January 1, 19.. | 14 258 |
| Work-in-progress at December 31, 19.. | 16 359 |
| Purchases of raw materials | 376 258 |
| Manufacturing wages | 188 950 |
| Sales | 895 726 |
| Factory expenses | 24 825 |
| Rent and rates of factory | 13 000 |
| Rent and rates of office | 7 500 |
| General administration expenses | 34 260 |
| Salesmen's salaries | 18 590 |
| Motor expenses | 15 250 |
| Other selling expenses | 14 950 |
| Depreciation of plant (Manufacturing Account) | 10 000 |
| Depreciation of motor vans | 3 000 |

You are asked to prepare Gorleston Ltd's Manufacturing Account and a Trading and Profit and Loss Account for the year 19...

## Unit Six

# Applying Basic Concepts:
# 4. The Accounts of Limited Companies

### 6.1 Elementary Company Final Accounts

In the earlier book, *Success in Principles of Accounting*, the routine aspects of company accounts were considered, and the preparation of the Final Accounts of limited companies described. The set of exercises in this Unit is a recapitulation of the earlier work, but first we must summarize the *Companies Act 1981*.

**The Companies Act 1981.** The passage of this Act was preceded by a period of discussion about the presentation of company accounts. The purpose of the Act was to implement the *European Economic Community Fourth Directive on Company Law* which was approved in 1978 and was required to be implemented to harmonize accounting arrangements within the EEC. This Directive included clear formats for the preparation of company accounts, and similar formats have now been reproduced in the 1981 Companies Act. Some of these are shown in full in this Unit and in Unit 7.

The chief feature of the 1981 Companies Act is that it restores to supreme importance in the preparation of the accounts of companies the requirement that every Profit and Loss Account shall give a 'true and fair view' of profit, or loss, and every balance sheet shall give a 'true and fair view' of the state of affairs of the company. This requirement—first introduced in the 1948 Companies Act—had been increasingly disregarded in recent years, and Section 1 of the 1981 Act restores it to its former place of importance. Accountants must stick to the spirit of the law, rather than the letter of the law, and if a set of accounts prepared in accordance with the requirements of the Companies Acts does not result in a 'true and fair view' the necessary additional information to give a 'true and fair view' must be provided.

**The formats for preparing company accounts.** The formats given in the Act include four possible formats for Profit and Loss Accounts and two for balance sheets. For the purpose of this Unit we shall look at Format 3 for the Profit and Loss Account and the vertical style for the balance sheet.

Profit and Loss Account
Format 3

| A | Charges | B | Income |
|---|---------|---|--------|
| 1 | Cost of sales | 1 | Turnover |
| 2 | Distribution costs | 2 | Other operating income |
| 3 | Administrative expenses | 3 | Income from shares in group companies |
| 4 | Amounts written off investments | 4 | Income from shares in related companies |
| 5 | Interest payable and similar charges | 5 | Income from other fixed asset investments |
| 6 | Tax on profit or loss on ordinary activities | 6 | Other interest receivable and similar income |
| 7 | Profit or loss on ordinary activities after taxation | 7 | Profit or loss on ordinary activities after taxation |
| 8 | Extraordinary charges | 8 | Extraordinary income |
| 9 | Tax on extraordinary profit or loss | 9 | Profit or loss for the financial year |
| 10 | Other taxes not shown under the above items | | |
| 11 | Profit or loss for the financial year | | |

*Notes:*

(i) A1 and B1 are the Trading Account, where sales (turnover) are set against the cost of sales to produce the gross profit.

(ii) The gross profit brought down on to the credit side of the account is followed by B2, B3, B4, B5 and B6. These are simply other sources of income not connected with trading (sales).

(iii) Against the profits earned as shown on the credit side of the account, B1–6, we have the expenses, listed in the order A2, distribution costs; A3, administrative expenses; A4, amounts written off investments; A5, interest payable and similar charges. This is a rather incomplete list of expenses, but all expenses incurred must ultimately be added to it.

(iv) Item A6 then asks us to deduct the tax due on profits made. It actually says 'tax on losses' as well, but this is clearly not sensible. The deduction of tax on profits treats it as a charge against the profits and not an appropriation of them. This is not sound in theory, but many accountants argue that it does make practical sense, reflecting the fact that the Government wants its share of the income as a first claim on the profits.

(v) A7 and B7 are exactly the same. In practice it means that if we have a profit after taxation we shall enter it as net profit on the debit side and bring it down as net profit on the credit side. On the other hand, if we have a loss we shall enter it as a loss on the credit side and bring it down as a balance on the debit side.

(vi) B8 tells us to add to the profit after tax, which we have carried down on the credit side, any 'extraordinary income' for the year. This means income arising not from our ordinary trading activities but from some other source, like the sale of a capital asset at a profit. Against this extraordinary income we are allowed to set A8, any extraordinary charges, and must also set A9, the tax on the extraordinary profit.

(*continued overleaf*)

(vii) We are then asked to deduct A10 (any other taxes not shown under the above items).

(viii) We finish up, A11 and B9, with a profit or loss for the financial year. Once again, all it means is that the balance of profit (or loss) will be entered on one side and brought down to the other side. If it is a profit we can proceed to appropriate it to the shareholders in the way decided by the directors. If it is a loss it will be carried forward to the next year.

The formats for the balance sheet are discussed more fully in Unit 7. Here we shall consider the vertical style, the most popular presentation today; it is given in Schedule 1 of the Act as shown below. There are some anomalies and inconsistencies in this presentation, and these are discussed in the Notes below the format.

**Balance sheet**

**Format 1**

A Called-up share capital not paid

B Fixed assets
   I Intangible assets
      1 Development costs
      2 Concessions, patents, licences, trade marks and similar rights and assets
      3 Goodwill
      4 Payments on account
   II Tangible assets
      1 Land and buildings
      2 Plant and machinery
      3 Fixtures, fittings, tools and equipment
      4 Payments on account and assets in course of construction
   III Investments
      1 Shares in group companies
      2 Loans to group companies
      3 Shares in related companies
      4 Loans to related companies
      5 Other investments other than loans
      6 Other loans
      7 Own shares

C Current assets
   I Stocks
      1 Raw materials and consumables
      2 Work-in-progress
      3 Finished goods and goods for resale
      4 Payments on account

II Debtors
  1 Trade debtors
  2 Amounts owed by group companies
  3 Amounts owed by related companies
  4 Other debtors
  5 Called-up share capital not paid
  6 Pre-payments and accrued income
III Investments
  1 Shares in group companies
  2 Own shares
  3 Other investments
IV Cash at bank and in hand

D Pre-payments and accrued income

E Creditors: amounts falling due within one year
  1 Debenture loans
  2 Bank loans and overdrafts
  3 Payments received on account
  4 Trade creditors
  5 Bills of exchange payable
  6 Amounts owed to group companies
  7 Amounts owed to related companies
  8 Other creditors including taxation and social security
  9 Accruals and deferred income

F Net current assets (liabilities)

G Total assets less current liabilities

H Creditors: amounts falling due after more than one year
  1 Debenture loans
  2 Bank loans and overdrafts
  3 Payments received on account
  4 Trade creditors
  5 Bills of exchange payable
  6 Amounts owed to group companies
  7 Amounts owed to related companies
  8 Other creditors including taxation and social security
  9 Accruals and deferred income

I Provisions for liabilities and charges
  1 Pensions and similar obligations
  2 Taxation, including deferred taxation
  3 Other provisions

(*continued overleaf*)

J  Accruals and deferred income

K  Capital and reserves
    I  Called-up share capital
    II  Share Premium Account
    III  Revaluation reserve
    IV  Other reserves
       1  Capital redemption reserve
       2  Reserve for own shares
       3  Reserves provided for by the articles of association
       4  Other reserves
    V  Profit and Loss Account

*Notes:*
(i) In vertical style balance sheets the assets are listed first, in the order of permanence. In a preliminary note the Act says that fictitious assets (such as preliminary expenses, costs of research, etc. may never be shown as assets in any company's balance sheet. We therefore start with intangible assets, followed by tangible assets, etc. Item A is a special case and is discussed below.

(ii) A note in the Schedule referring to 'A' states that called-up share capital not paid may be shown in either position A or position CII5. This is an anomaly because when capital is called up, the posting of the call letter makes a binding contract with the shareholder who becomes a debtor for the capital called. This is therefore a current asset and the item should appear in position CII5 and not in position A.

(iii) Fixed assets are divided into intangible assets and tangible assets, arranged in the 'order of permanence'. The 'order of permanence' means that the most permanent assets are placed first — thus goodwill cannot be disposed of until the business is sold (and is consequently very permanent). We can sell premises fairly easily, and tools and equipment even more easily. These are tangible assets, physically available for sale, and not intangibles which are inseparable from the sale of the business.

(iv) Investments are assets which may be acquired for trade purposes (trade investments), because we wish to acquire control of subsidiary companies. If we do that we cannot sell the investments without losing control, and consequently they are fixed assets and appear at BIII. Other investments are not acquired for trade purposes but to earn income from a temporary surplus of cash. Such investments are current assets, and are shown in position CIII.

(v) The presentation of the remaining items is excellent, particularly D, which is shown as even more liquid than cash. You might ask how anything could be more liquid than cash. The answer is that cash which has already been spent for next year is so liquid that we have already spent it. It is therefore the least permanent, and most liquid, item in the presentation.

(vi) We now come to the first of the anomalies in the presentation of the balance sheet in Format 1. It is at the point where all the assets have been presented and we deduct the liabilities (creditors etc.) listed in item E. Clearly, although omitted from the Act, we cannot leave out the word 'Less' in our published accounts, because only if E is deducted can we have F as the 'Net current assets', or G as the 'Total assets less current liabilities'.

(vii) The second anomaly is that the rest of the presentation is in reverse order to the order of permanence. Another point is that we must link the two halves of the balance sheet by inserting the words 'Financed by'. The net assets in the upper part of the presentation have been financed by the funds made available in the rest of the presentation, the long-term creditors and the shareholders.

(viii) Finally, item K, 'capital and reserves', is the most important source of the finance, and although Parliament has not specified it, we can separate the preference shareholders' interest from the ordinary shareholders' interest.

We can now attempt some simple Company Final Accounts with these new presentations in mind, but before doing so, we shall summarize the general requirements of the Companies Acts.

### (a) Types of Company

At present there are two chief types of company—*private limited companies* and *public limited companies*. Formerly both types of limited companies, whether or not their shares were quoted on the Stock Exchange, had titles ending with the word 'limited', signifying that the proprietors have limited liability and are only liable to the extent of the value of the shares which they have purchased. The name itself gives no clue as to the total capital available to meet a claim upon the company. In Great Britain, to discover what this value is we must carry out a search at Companies House (see p. 69 for address).

Since the Companies Act 1980 was passed, however, public limited companies are being renamed to include the words 'public limited company', to distinguish them from private limited companies. The capital of a public limited company cannot be less than the authorized minimum (currently £50 000), a figure which may be revised from time to time by Statutory Instrument, by the Secretary of State (Companies Act 1980, Section 85).

### (b) A Set of Final Accounts

A full set of Final Accounts might include a Manufacturing Account, a Trading Account, a Profit and Loss Account, an Appropriation Account (where the profits are appropriated to the various groups of shareholders) and a balance sheet. Not all of these accounts have to be published, however, so that a set of published accounts usually starts with a statement of the turnover, followed by an abbreviated Profit and Loss Account and a balance sheet. Only certain details of the Profit and Loss Account need to be published—hence the reference above to an *abbreviated* Profit and Loss Account.

*Note:* The word *published* in this context means that copies of the accounts must be submitted to the Registrar of Companies so that they may be filed at Companies House. The public may inspect these copies for a small fee and may copy any pages of information. The accounts are therefore a matter of public record and, as such, may be said to be published. Since all members and debenture holders have the right to receive a copy of the balance sheet and any other document annexed thereto by law—Profit and Loss Account, Auditor's Report and Directors' Report—it may be necessary to have quite a large number of copies printed.

Under the 1981 Act certain companies are designated 'small' and 'medium', and these companies are excused from supplying copies of full 'published' accounts to the Registrar. *Small* companies are those which:

(a) have a turnover of less than £1 400 000;
(b) have balance sheet totals less than £700 000;
(c) have less than 50 employees.

These companies need not provide a Profit and Loss Account and need only provide a very abbreviated balance sheet (Section 6(2) 1981 Act).

*Medium-sized* companies are those which:

(a) have a turnover of less than £5 750 000;
(b) have balance sheet totals of less than £2 800 000;
(c) have less than 250 employees.

These companies need not reveal turnover, and only rudimentary profit figures (Section 6(8) 1981 Act).

#### (c) Rights of Investors

In order to attract capital from as wide a range of investors as possible, various classes of security are issued by companies. The rights they confer vary.

(i) **Debentures** are issued to debenture holders who do not become members of the company but are usually secured creditors of the company. The debenture may be supported by a trust deed, which is usually lodged with a debenture trustee who studies the company's affairs from the point of view of the debenture holders to ensure that any covenants in the trust deed are properly observed. In certain circumstances the trustee may take over the assets of the company and run it in the interests of the debenture holders.

(ii) **Preference shares** are issued to preference shareholders who are members of the company and who hold shares which have preferential rights to profits (when available) and possibly also preferential rights in the distribution of any assets on dissolution. Usually, preference shareholders receive a fixed percentage return on their investment (for example, the shares may be 7 per cent Preference Shares) and are cumulative unless the terms of issue or the Articles of Association state otherwise. This means that a dividend missed one year, because of a failure to make profits, accumulates and can be claimed the following year. There are also *participating preference shares*, the holders of which also receive their preference dividend and then may participate in any residue of profits to be shared among the ordinary shareholders.

(iii) **Ordinary shares** are issued to ordinary shareholders, who are members of the company prepared to invest without being given any preferential treatment. They are entitled to take an equal share of any profits left after the preference shareholders have received their proper allocation and run an equal risk of losing their capital on dissolution of the company. For these reasons ordinary shares are often referred to as *equity* or *risk* shares.

Since both debentures and preference shares are rewarded by a fixed rate of interest or dividend, it follows that once this is paid these investors are not entitled to any further share in the profits of the company. Usually at least some of the profits are retained for future use in the company; these are *revenue reserves* and are the property of the ordinary shareholders only. Similarly, should a revaluation of the assets for any reason produce a *capital reserve*, this also belongs to the ordinary shareholders, not to the preference shareholders, whose only claim on the assets of the company in any dissolution is for the sums they originally invested in the company. On the accounts, it is desirable to show both types of reserves as part of the ordinary shareholders' interest in the company, and not confuse the ownership by displaying the preference share capital with the ordinary share capital.

### (*d*) The Liabilities of a Company

The liabilities shown on the balance sheet of a limited company include the ordinary shareholders' interest in the company, the preference shareholders' interest in the company, the debentures and any current liabilities outstanding. There is often an item called deferred taxation, but a full discussion of this is not possible here.

### (*e*) The Assets of a Company

Schedule 1 of the 1981 Act and Schedule 2 of the Companies Act 1967 give a host of detailed requirements about balance sheet presentation. Many of these details are explained more fully later in this Unit. Here we note only that the assets should be divided into fixed and current assets. Other classes of assets are also referred to.

Within this group, there are three types of assets: *fictitious, intangible* and *trade investments*. Fictitious and intangible assets do not represent anything real. For example, preliminary expenses, which are incurred in connection with any issue of shares or debentures, or any discount given on the issue of shares represent completely *fictitious assets*. The only evidence that a company has to show for preliminary expenses is that it has come into existence and may begin trading. All it has to show for expenses incurred on the issue of shares or debentures, in the form of underwriting payments, for example, is that funds for use by the company have been collected. Out of £1m shares issued, we may actually only have £975 000 in cash, the remaining £25 000 having been 'lost' to pay the underwriters and their costs of issue.

Goodwill is an example of an *intangible asset*. It is, perhaps, more real than the fictitious assets described above, as it may exist in the minds of customers, but it is certainly intangible.

The third type of asset which is neither fixed nor current is a *trade investment*. It often happens that a company wishes to gain effective control of other companies. Perhaps they supply raw materials or components which are vital to the parent company or they may be part of the parent company's marketing organization—wholesale or retail outlets for its products. In these cases the parent company is known as a *holding company*, the company that is controlled is a *subsidiary* and the whole enterprise is called a *group*. The parent company keeps control of its subsidiaries by securing 51 per cent of the voting shares. These shares are known as trade investments, being investments in other companies in the same trade as the parent company. It is this type of trade investment which may be described as *assets which are neither fixed nor current*.

The shares may be sold on the Stock Exchange (if they are shares in public companies) or privately (if they are shares in private companies). To this extent the shares are current assets. However, a holding company does not hold trade investments in order to sell them again but in order to retain control of the subsidiary. It therefore will not sell them and they are — to that extent — fixed. The requirement to show trade investments as a separate item on the balance sheet is useful to people thinking of investing in a company, since it helps them to judge its financial position. Under the 1981 Act, trade investments are displayed on the balance sheet as part of the fixed assets. Note that it is now possible in certain circumstances, and subject to certain controls, for a company to purchase its own shares.

(i) **Net current assets.** It is frequently the case that companies prepare their balance sheets in such a way as to bring out the net current assets; in other words, the current liabilities do not appear in the liabilities section of the balance sheet, but are deducted from the current assets in the assets section of the balance sheet. This has the advantage of bringing out the excess of current assets over current liabilities, which is often called the *net working capital* of the business, or, as in our sub-heading, the *net current assets.*

(ii) **Treatment of fictitious assets on the balance sheet.** The system of showing fictitious assets as deductions from the ordinary shareholders' interest in the company is similar to the net current assets presentation described in (i) above. Since the fictitious assets are really losses of the business, the inclusion of these items as assets is misleading and is now specifically forbidden by the Companies Act 1981. (See Unit 7 for a discussion of this section of the 1981 Act.) As the Companies Acts require the accounts to show a 'true and fair view' of the affairs of the company, a truer picture is presented if we do not show these assets as 'assets' at all, but instead deduct them from the liabilities part of the balance sheet to show the ordinary shareholders' interest in the company net of these items. This is illustrated in Fig. 6.1 (pp. 61–4).

We shall now attempt some simple Company Final Accounts using the new styles of presentation. The examples are intended to provide a link with elementary accounts. The detailed layout for dealing with taxation is disregarded: this will be dealt with in Unit 7.

## 6.2  An Example of Simple Company Final Accounts

The following trial balance was extracted from the books of Clear-as-Crystal Ltd on December 31, 19... The company's authorized capital is £200 000, divided in the following way: ordinary capital £150 000; 9% preference capital £50 000.

## Trial balance (as at December 31, 19. .)

|  | £ | £ |
|---|---|---|
| Issued share capital 80 000 ordinary shares of £1 each |  | 80 000 |
| 9% preference shares of £1 each |  | 50 000 |
| Profits prior to incorporation |  | 25 000 |
| Premium on preference shares |  | 2 000 |
| 8% debentures (issued January 1, 19. .) |  | 40 000 |
| Freehold buildings at cost | 90 000 |  |
| Plant at cost | 40 000 |  |
| General reserve |  | 15 000 |
| Plant replacement reserve |  | 12 000 |
| Motor vehicles at cost | 16 500 |  |
| Provision for depreciation on plant at start |  | 15 000 |
| Provision for depreciation on motor vehicles at start |  | 4 800 |
| Provision for depreciation on furniture at start |  | 5 000 |
| Sales |  | 363 984 |
| Purchases | 216 500 |  |
| Returns in | 4 250 |  |
| Returns out |  | 5 500 |
| Debtors | 18 750 |  |
| Creditors |  | 27 260 |
| Bad debts | 320 |  |
| Provision for doubtful debts January 1, 19. . |  | 1 200 |
| Motor expenses | 1 895 |  |
| Rent and rates | 4 350 |  |
| Insurances | 720 |  |
| Salaries | 49 800 |  |
| Trade investments | 32 500 |  |
| Other investments (short-term) | 60 000 |  |
| General administration expenses | 5 840 |  |
| Stock-in-trade at January 1, 19. . | 28 549 |  |
| Bank balance | 50 000 |  |
| Furniture and fittings at cost | 10 000 |  |
| Directors' fees | 22 000 |  |
| Balance on Appropriation Account as at January 1, 19. . |  | 9 790 |
| Cash in hand | 125 |  |
| Discount received |  | 480 |
| Discount allowed | 550 |  |
| Preliminary expenses | 1 365 |  |
| Patent rights | 3 000 |  |
|  | £657 014 | 657 014 |

You are given the following additional information:

(a) Stock-in-trade at December 31, 19. . was £32 979.
(b) Rent owing at December 31, 19. . was £550.
(c) Insurance in advance at December 31, 19. . was £140.
(d) Provision for doubtful debts is to be increased to £1 685.
(e) Debenture interest is payable annually on December 31, and the amount due is to be provided for.
(f) A reserve for corporation tax of £18 000 is to be created.
(g) Trade investments are valued by the directors at £35 000.
(h) The market value of the other investments is £64 550.
(i) A sum of £365 is to be written off the preliminary expenses.
(j) Depreciation on plant is to be provided for at 10 per cent of cost; on motor vehicles at 25 per cent of cost and on furniture at 10 per cent of cost.
(k) A sum of £5 000 is to be transferred to general reserve and £4 000 to plant replacement reserve.
(l) A dividend at the rate of 10 per cent on the ordinary share capital and a dividend on the preference shares are to be provided for.

You are asked to prepare a Trading and Profit and Loss Account and an Appropriation Account for 19. . and a balance sheet as at December 31, 19. . . These are shown in Fig. 6.1 (pp. 61–4). (Taxation is ignored.)

Trading and Profit and Loss Account (for year ending December 31, 19. .)

| | £ | | £ |
|---|---|---|---|
| Opening stock | 28 549 | Sales | 363 984 |
| Purchases | 216 500 | *Less* Returns in | 4 250 |
| *Less* Returns out | 5 500 | Net turnover | 359 734 |
| | 211 000 | | |
| | 239 549 | | |
| *Less* Closing stock | 32 979 | | |
| Cost of sales | 206 570 | | |
| Gross profit | c/d 153 164 | | |
| | £359 734 | | £359 734 |
| Motor expenses | 1 895 | Gross profit | b/d 153 164 |
| General | | Discount received | 480 |
| administration | | | 153 644 |
| expenses | 5 840 | | |
| Rent and rates | 4 350 | | |
| *Add* Amount due | 550 | | |
| | 4 900 | | |
| Insurances | 720 | | |
| Amount in advance | 140 | | |
| | 580 | | |
| Bad debts | 320 | | |
| Salaries | 49 800 | | |
| Directors' fees | 22 000 | | |
| Discount allowed | 550 | | |
| Bad debts provision | 485 | | |
| Depreciation | | | |
| Plant | 4 000 | | |
| Motor vehicles | 4 125 | | |
| Furniture | 1 000 | | |
| | 9 125 | | |
| Debenture interest due | 3 200 | | |
| | 98 695 | | |
| Net profit | c/d 54 949 | | |
| | £153 644 | | £153 644 |

*(continued overleaf)*

## Appropriation Section

| | | £ | | | £ |
|---|---|---|---|---|---|
| Reserve for corporation tax | | 18 000 | Balance at January 1 | b/d | 9 790 |
| Profit after tax | c/d | 46 739 | Net profit for year | | 54 949 |
| | | 64 739 | | | 64 739 |
| | | | | | |
| Preliminary expenses | | 365 | Profit after tax | b/d | 46 739 |
| General reserve | | 5 000 | | | |
| Plant replacement reserve | | 4 000 | | | |
| Preference share dividend | | 4 500 | | | |
| Ordinary share dividend | | 8 000 | | | |
| | | 21 865 | | | |
| Balance | c/d | 24 874 | | | |
| | | £46 739 | | | £46 739 |
| | | | | | £ |
| | | | Balance | b/d | 24 874 |

Clear-as-Crystal Ltd
Balance sheet (as at December 31, 19. .)

| | £ | £ Less depreciation to date | £ Present value |
|---|---|---|---|
| *Fixed assets* | At cost | | |
| *Intangible assets* | | | |
| Patent rights owned | 3 000 | — | 3 000 |
| *Tangible assets* | | | |
| Land and buildings | 90 000 | — | 90 000 |
| Plant and machinery | 40 000 | 19 000 | 21 000 |
| Furniture and fittings | 10 000 | 6 000 | 4 000 |
| Motor vehicles | 16 500 | 8 925 | 7 575 |
| | 159 500 | 33 925 | 125 575 |
| *Investments*: Shares in related companies | | | 32 500 |
| (valued by the directors at £35 000) | | | |
| *Current assets* | | | |
| Stock | | 32 979 | |
| Debtors | 18 750 | | |
| *Less* Provision for bad debts | 1 685 | | |
| | | 17 065 | |
| Other investments (market value £64 550) | | 60 000 | |
| Cash at bank | | 50 000 | |
| Cash in hand | | 125 | |
| Insurance in advance | | 140 | |
| | | 160 309 | |
| *Less current liabilities* | | | |
| Creditors | 27 260 | | |
| Ordinary dividend | 8 000 | | |
| Preference dividend | 4 500 | | |
| Debenture interest due | 3 200 | | |
| Rent due | 550 | | |
| | | 43 510 | |
| | Net current assets | 116 799 | |
| | Total assets less current liabilities | £274 874 | |

**Financed by:**
*Debenture holders' interest in the company*

| | | |
|---|---|---|
| 8% Debentures (issued January 1, 19. .) | | 40 000 |
| Reserve for corporation tax | | 18 000 |
| *Preference shareholders' interest in the company* | | |
| | Authorized | |
| 9% Preference shares of £1 | £50 000 | 50 000 |
| | c/fwd | 108 000 |

|  | b/fwd | 108 000 |
|---|---|---|

*Ordinary shareholders' interest in the company*

|  | £ | |
|---|---|---|
|  | Authorized | |

| £1 Ordinary shares fully paid | | |
|---|---|---|
| (80 000 issued) | 150 000 | 80 000 |

*Capital reserves*

| Profits prior to incorporation | 25 000 | |
|---|---|---|
| Premium on preference shares | 2 000 | |
|  |  | 27 000 |

*Revenue reserves*

| General reserve | 15 000 | |
|---|---|---|
| *Add* Additions | 5 000 | |
|  | 20 000 | |

| Plant replacement | | | |
|---|---|---|---|
| reserve | 12 000 | | |
| *Add* Additions | 4 000 | | |
|  |  | 16 000 | |

| Balance on | | | |
|---|---|---|---|
| Appropriation A/c | | 24 874 | |
| *Less* Fictitious assets | | | |
| Preliminary | | | |
| expenses | 1 365 | | |
| *Less* Amount | | | |
| written off | 365 | | |
|  |  | 1 000 | |
|  | | 23 874 | |
|  | | | 59 874 |

| Ordinary shareholders' equity | 166 874 |
|---|---|
|  | £274 874 |

*Fig. 6.1 Simple company final accounts*

## 6.3   Exercises

1.   The following trial balance was extracted from the books of Golden Chrysanthemum Ltd as at December 31, 19.0. You are asked to produce a full set of Company Final Accounts based on this trial balance and the notes below it.

## Trial balance

| | £ | £ |
|---|---:|---:|
| Ordinary share capital, authorized and issued shares of £1 each | | 150 000 |
| Premium on shares | | 28 000 |
| 8% Preference shares of £1 authorized and issued | | 75 000 |
| 7% Debentures (2 500 debentures of £10) | | 25 000 |
| Sales | | 429 256 |
| Purchases | 238 060 | |
| Sales returns and purchases returns | 1 256 | 1 060 |
| Carriage in | 500 | |
| Bad debts | 1 380 | |
| Provision for bad and doubtful debts | | 860 |
| Rates and insurance | 3 425 | |
| Light and heat | 2 860 | |
| Salaries | 49 356 | |
| General expenses | 28 432 | |
| Debtors and creditors | 12 660 | 4 845 |
| Freehold buildings at cost | 180 000 | |
| Furniture and equipment at cost | 12 500 | |
| Provision for depreciation on furniture as at January 1 | | 4 325 |
| Stock-in-trade, at January 1, 19.0 | 26 240 | |
| Balance at bank | 67 258 | |
| Cash in hand | 485 | |
| Debenture interest | 875 | |
| Balance of Appropriation Account at January 1, 19.0 | | 14 621 |
| Preliminary expenses | 1 800 | |
| General reserve | | 20 000 |
| Reserve for future taxation | | 12 480 |
| Commission received | | 1 640 |
| Trade investments | 100 000 | |
| Other investments | 40 000 | |
| | £767 087 | £767 087 |

The following information is available:

(a) Closing stock at December 31, 19.0 was £35 000.
(b) The rest of the debenture interest is due and is to be allowed for.
(c) Half the preliminary expenses are to be written off.
(d) Appraisal of the debtors reveals bad debts to the further sum of £160. These are to be written off and the provision for bad debts is to be raised to 10 per cent of the outstanding debtors.
(e) Rates and insurances paid in advance amount to £225.

(*f*) An employee on assignment in Saudi Arabia is owed salary of £2 834.

(*g*) Trade investments are valued by the directors at £135 000.

(*h*) The market value of other investments is £49 725.

(*i*) The directors recommend that the preference dividend is paid in full and that £20 000 be placed in general reserve. The reserve for future taxation is to be increased by £50 000 and a dividend of 15 per cent is to be paid on ordinary shares.

(*j*) Depreciation of 10 per cent is to be written off the Furniture and Equipment Account.

# Unit Seven

## The Published Accounts of Limited Companies

### 7.1 The Published Accounts of Companies

Although a full set of accounts (i.e. Manufacturing Account, Trading and Profit and Loss Account, Appropriation Account and balance sheet) are necessary to calculate the profit for the period and the state of a business on the last day of the accounting period, it is not necessary for companies to publish the full details of their accounts. The shareholders and other interested parties must take the auditor's word that the routine accounts have been checked; publication is required only of those items of expense which are really significant and throw light on the general conduct of the affairs of the company. Naturally companies hesitate to reveal every detail of their affairs to rivals and often only publish the minimum required by the Companies Acts.

The Acts of Parliament now controlling companies are the Companies Acts 1948–81 which include the following statutes: the Companies Act 1948, the Companies Act 1967, the Companies Act 1976, the Companies Act 1980 and the Companies Act 1981, as well as parts of one or two other Acts. This rather confusing pattern of Acts reflects the British Parliament's attempts to control companies and the European Economic Community's attempts to harmonize European accountancy regulations.

These European regulations were mentioned earlier and reference was made in Unit 6 to the new formats for published accounts given in Schedule 1 of the 1981 Act, which this Act makes Schedule 8 of the 1948 Act. This rather unusual procedure, implanting part of a later Act into an Act published 30 years earlier, simply recognizes that the 1948 Act is still the major statute. It is not possible to reproduce all four of the Profit and Loss Account formats here; the one reproduced in Unit 6 is adequate for our purpose. However, it is desirable to reproduce the non-vertical style of the balance sheet, because it does resolve the ancient problem about the traditional style of the British balance sheet.

An account of the historical development of the British style balance sheet and the errors made in the Companies Act of 1856 is given on page 65 of *Success in Principles of Accounting*. The horizontal style of balance sheet, shown below, follows the European style of having the assets stated first (on the left-hand side of the page) and the liabilities second (on the right-hand side of the page). It is now, therefore, correct to abandon the traditional British style and produce balance sheets with assets on the left-hand side and liabilities on the right-hand side. This is, of course, an alternative to, and an improvement upon, the vertical style which has recently been more commonly used in the United Kingdom (but not in Europe).

Balance sheet
Format 2

| *Assets* | *Liabilities* |
|---|---|

*Assets*

A Called-up share capital not paid
    (see CII5 below)

B Fixed assets
    I Intangible assets
        1 Development costs
        2 Concessions, patents,
            licences, trade marks and
            similar rights and assets
        3 Goodwill
        4 Payments on account
    II Tangible assets
        1 Land and buildings
        2 Plant and machinery
        3 Fixtures, fittings, tools
            and equipment
        4 Payments on account and
            assets in course of
            construction
    III Investments
        1 Shares in group
            companies
        2 Loans to group companies
        3 Shares in related
            companies
        4 Loans to related
            companies
        5 Other investments other
            than loans
        6 Other loans
        7 Own shares

C Current assets
    I Stocks
        1 Raw materials and
            consumables
        2 Work-in-progress
        3 Finished goods and goods
            for sale
        4 Payments on account

*Liabilities*

A Capital and reserves
    I Called-up share capital
    II Share Premium Account
    III Revaluation reserve
    IV Other reserves
        1 Capital redemption
            reserve
        2 Reserve for own shares
        3 Reserves provided for by
            the articles of association
    V Profit and Loss Account

B Provisions for liabilities and
charges
    1 Pensions and similar
        obligations
    2 Taxation including
        deferred taxation
    3 Other provisions

C Creditors
    1 Debenture loans
    2 Bank loans and overdrafts
    3 Payments received on
        account
    4 Trade creditors
    5 Bills of exchange payable
    6 Amounts owed to group
        companies
    7 Amounts owed to related
        companies
    8 Other creditors including
        taxation and social
        security
    9 Accruals and deferred
        income

D Accruals and deferred income

II Debtors
   1 Trade debtors
   2 Amounts owed by group
     companies
   3 Amounts owed by related
     companies
   4 Other debtors
   5 Called-up share capital
     not paid
   6 Pre-payments and accrued
     income
III Investments
   1 Shares in group
     companies
   2 Own shares
   3 Other investments
IV Cash at bank and in hand

D Pre-payments and accrued
  income

We have already commented on the headings in Unit 6. One point is worth mentioning. Section 3(2) of Section A of Part 1 of Schedule 1 states that fictitious assets such as 'preliminary expenses' may not appear as assets on any company's balance sheet. This is sound, since they are not in any sense 'real' assets, and should be deducted from the ordinary shareholders' interest in the company. Section 84 of the Act states that such development costs must be set off against the company's distributable profits. This is shown in Fig. 6.1.

As described in Unit 6.1(*b*), the term *published accounts* implies that the information required for businesses in Great Britain must be made available to the Registrar of Companies and is then incorporated in the company's file at Companies House. (The Registrar of Companies has two addresses: Companies House, 55 City Road, London EC1Y 1BB and the Head Office at Crown Way, Maindy, Cardiff CF4 3UZ.)

The documents comprise:
  (*a*) an abbreviated Profit and Loss Account;
  (*b*) a balance sheet;
  (*c*) an auditor's report;
  (*d*) a directors' report.

In the sections which follow references to relevant parts in the Companies Acts are given at the end of each sub-paragraph.

## 7.2 The Statutory Requirements for Published Profit and Loss Accounts

The following matters must be disclosed in the published Profit and Loss Account:

(i) **Turnover.** The turnover for the financial year must be disclosed, also the method used to arrive at the figure. This figure need not be revealed if it does not exceed £5 750 000 unless the company is a holding company, or the subsidiary of another body corporate (2 Sch.13A (2, 4 and 5) 1967 and S6(7)(b) 1981).

The requirement to disclose turnover has proved controversial since 1967 when the threshold for disclosure was set at £50 000 per annum. This made it possible for large companies to discover the turnover of rival smaller firms and it proved to be detrimental to the small firms. In the 1981 Act the limit was raised to £5 750 000.

Statement of Standard Accounting Practice No. 5 requires that turnover shall be shown net of value added tax, which must accordingly be deducted from the total sales figure if the records have been kept inclusive of VAT.

The 1981 Act requires that if a company has different classes of business the turnover in each class and the profit attributable to each class shall be shown separately (1 Sch.55 1981). There is a proviso that if the declaration is likely to be detrimental, turnover need not be disclosed, but a note to that effect must appear.

(ii) **Rents received.** If rents received are a substantial part of revenue, their value (less outgoings) must be shown (2 Sch.12(1)(ga) 1967). This is repeated in 1 Sch.53(5) 1981.

(iii) **Income from listed and unlisted investments.** The income received from these investments must be shown separately. A listed investment is one for which a quotation or permission to deal has been given on a recognized Stock Exchange. SSAP 8, *The Treatment of Taxation under the Imputation System in the Accounts of Companies*, states that incoming dividends from United Kingdom resident companies should be included at the amount of cash received or receivable, plus the tax credit (2 Sch.12(1)(g) 1967 as amended by the 1976 Act and the 1981 Act (1 Sch.53(4) 1981)).

(iv) **Prior-year items.** Sometimes a profit or loss occurs because of an event in a preceding financial year. It may be appropriate to include such items under another heading, but if they are not included in this way, they should be stated separately. The opening balance on the Appropriation Account should be adjusted accordingly (2 Sch. 12A 1967).

(v) **Auditor's remuneration including expenses.** All such expenditure must be grouped together under a separate heading (2 Sch. 13 1967). This is repeated in 1 Sch. 53(7) 1981.

(vi) **Depreciation and the method of provision.** The amount charged to revenue by way of provision for depreciation, renewals or diminution in value of fixed assets must be shown. If the calculation has been based upon any other value than the asset values shown in the balance sheet this must be stated. If depreciation is not provided, or if it is provided in some other way than a depreciation charge or a provision for renewals, this must be stated in a note (2 Sch. 12(1)(a), 12(4) and 14(2) 1967). Note 14 of Schedule 1 of the 1981 Act requires that cost of sales, distribution costs and administrative expenses must take account of depreciation or diminution in value of assets.

(vii) **Interest payable.** The amounts payable on bank loans, overdrafts and other loans repayable within five years, whether on the security of debentures or not, and the amounts payable on all other loans must be shown (1 Sch. 53(2) 1981). Amounts payable to group companies must be shown separately.

(viii) **Hire of plant and machinery.** The amount of such hire charges, if material, must be shown separately (2 Sch. 12(1)(gb) 1967). This is repeated in 1 Sch. 53(6) 1981.

(ix) **Transfer to provisions (other than depreciation) or withdrawals for another purpose.** Sometimes a transfer to a provision may be made for a valid purpose and subsequently withdrawn for a different purpose. This must be shown. Section 12.2 of the Companies Act 1967 provides that if certain information is revealed, which might prejudice a company's position, it may be included under another heading (for example, a provision to meet a lawsuit might reveal that a company expected to lose the case concerned) (2 Sch. 12(1)(f) 1967).

(x) **Unusual, exceptional or non-recurrent transactions.** Where a profit, or loss, is the result of an unusual event, such as a change in the basis of accounting, or a transaction not usually undertaken by the company, this should be made clear in an explanatory note (2 Sch. 14(6) 1967).

(xi) **Directors' emoluments.** The Acts contain various requirements about the emoluments of directors to be shown in the Profit and Loss Account. They include in Section 196 of the Companies Act 1948:

(*a*) the aggregate amount of the directors' emoluments;
(*b*) the aggregate amount of the directors' or past directors' pensions;
(*c*) the aggregate amount of any compensation to directors or past directors for loss of office. These sums must distinguish between emoluments as a director and other emoluments as an employee. Companies which are neither holding companies nor subsidiaries, and whose aggregate directors' emoluments are less than £40 000 do not need to divulge the ranges of directors' emoluments shown below, but other companies must show, under Sections 6 and 7 of the Companies Act 1967 and S.I. (1979) 1618:

(*a*) the chairman's emoluments, or the emoluments as chairman of each person so acting;
(*b*) the emoluments of the highest paid director, or directors if equal, if in excess of the chairman's emoluments;
(*c*) the numbers of directors (with comparisons with the previous period) whose emoluments fall within bands of £5 000;
(*d*) the numbers of directors (with comparisons with the previous period) who have waived emoluments, and the amount thereof.

(xii) **Emoluments of employees.** The number of employees whose emoluments exceed £20 000 should be shown in bands of £5 000 above that figure (S8, 1967 and S.I. (1979) 1618).

(xiii) **UK corporation tax and related matters.** Under 2 Sch. 12(1)(c) 1967 the amount of the charges to revenue for United Kingdom corporation tax, taxation relief for double taxation, the charge for overseas taxation and (so far as charged to revenue) capital gains, should be stated. Under 2 Sch. 14(3) 1967 the basis for computation must also be revealed, and under 2 Sch. 14(3A) 1967 any special circumstances affecting taxation liability must also be stated in a note to the accounts. 1 Sch. 54(3) 1981 also requires details of double taxation relief.

(xiv) **Redemption of share capital and loans.** The amounts provided for the redemption of share capital or loans must be stated (2 Sch. 12(1)(d) 1967).

(xv) **Transfers to and from reserves.** Any material amounts to be set aside to reserves, or proposed to be set aside (subject to the approval of the shareholders at the Annual General Meeting) or to be withdrawn from reserves, should be stated (2 Sch. 12(1)(e) 1967).

(xvi) **Dividends paid or proposed.** Under 2 Sch. 12(1)(h) 1967 the aggregate amount of dividends must be stated. SSAP 8 lays down that these shall be stated net of advance corporation tax under the imputation system. This system requires the company to deduct tax at the standard income tax rate from all dividends paid, and pay it over to the Inland Revenue authorities. The shareholder actually receives a dividend net of standard-rate tax and a tax credit for the tax paid, which can be set off against the tax payable. It brings the tax to the Exchequer rather more quickly, which helps the Exchequer cash flows, and gives the shareholders a dividend on which the tax liability has already been met.

*Note:* Under the Companies Act 1980 EEC restrictions on the distribution of profits have been implemented. These make it illegal to distribute dividends if the net assets of the company are less than the aggregate of the share capital and the non-distributable reserves.

(xvii) **Comparative figures.** This section provides that comparative figures for the preceding year must be shown (2 Sch. 14(5) 1967). The 1981 Act requires that comparative figures for previous years should be adjusted (for inflation) so that they do in fact give a true comparison.

The style of published Profit and Loss Accounts is illustrated in Fig. 7.1 opposite. Alternative formats are also given in the Companies Act 1981.

(xviii) **Number of employees.** Particulars of the number of employees in each category and the aggregate cost of salaries, social security contributions and pensions must be given.

Profit and Loss Account of XYZ Ltd
(for year ended December 31, 19..)
*(Based on Format No. 1, Companies Act 1981)*

£

Turnover: this need not be shown if the company is neither a
holding company, nor a subsidiary, and the amount does not
exceed £5 750 000 or such other amount as the Minister may
publish in a statutory instrument. Companies with a turnover
of less than £1 400 000 need not publish a Profit and Loss
Account.

| | |
|---|---:|
| Cost of sales (after taking depreciation into account) | *x* |

| | | |
|---|---:|---:|
| Gross profit or loss | | *x* |
| *Less* | £ | |
| Distribution costs | *x* | |
| Administrative expenses | *x* | |
| (Depreciation need not be shown except as a note in the accounts, it having been taken into account above) | | *(x)* |
| *Add* | | *x* |
| Other operating income | | *x* |
| Income from shares in related companies | | *x* |
| Income from other fixed investments | | *x* |
| Other interest receivable and similar income | | *x* |
| | | *x* |
| | | *x* |
| *Less* | | |
| Amounts written off investments | *x* | |
| Interest payable and similar charges | *x* | |
| Tax on profit or loss on ordinary activities | *x* | |
| | | *(x)* |
| (This line may now be labelled 'Profit or loss on ordinary activities after taxation') | | *x* |
| Extraordinary income | *x* | |
| *Less* Extraordinary charges | *(x)* | |
| Extraordinary profit or loss | *x* | |
| *Less* Tax on extraordinary profit or loss | *(x)* | |
| | | *x* |
| | | *x* |
| Other taxes not shown under the above items | | *(x)* |
| Profit or loss for the financial year | | £ *x* |

*Fig. 7.1 Published Profit and Loss Account – a suggested format*

*Notes:*
(i) ( ) denotes deduction.
(ii) It is permissible to give more than the minimum information required by the format.

## 7.3    The Published Balance Sheet of a Company

We shall now consider the chief features of the balance sheet which the United Kingdom statutes require:

(*a*) **Assets**
(i) The assets shall be summarized with such particulars as are necessary to disclose their general nature (2 Sch.2 1967). Particulars shall be given of the value of the asset at the start of the year, any disposals or acquisitions during the year, the accumulated provision for depreciation to date and the value at the balance sheet date (1 Sch. Part III 42 (1–3) 1981).

(ii) They shall be classified under headings appropriate to the company's business, except where the amount is immaterial and they may then be included under some other class (2 Sch.4(1) 1967).

(iii) Fixed assets, current assets and assets which are neither fixed nor current shall be separately identified (2 Sch.4(2) 1967). They shall be displayed in one of the formats shown in the 1981 Act, the items referred to as 'neither fixed nor current' in the 1967 Act now appearing as 'fixed assets' under the sub-heading 'investments' (1 Sch. Part I(1)(a) 1981).

(iv) The methods used to arrive at the amount of the fixed assets under each heading shall be stated (2 Sch.4(3) 1967).

(v) Freehold land and leasehold land should be distinguished from each other, and short leases distinguished from long ones (2 Sch.11(6C) 1967).

(vi) Additions and disposals of fixed assets (except investments) during the year should be shown (2 Sch.11(6B) 1967).

(vii) The amounts of any asset at the date of the balance sheet should be shown. The value should be found by taking the aggregate cost (or, in certain cases, valuation) less the aggregate depreciation to date since acquisition. Exceptions are provided for certain classes of assets, notably investments valued by directors and goodwill, patents and trade marks (2 Sch.5 1967).

The value of current assets is to be their production cost or their purchase price, but if the net realizable value is less than either of these they shall be stated at the net realizable value (1 Sch. Part II 22–3 1981).

(viii) The aggregate amount of goodwill, patents and trade marks not written off should be shown (2 Sch.(1)(b) 1967). They must have been acquired for valuable consideration or created by the company itself.

(ix) The value of shares held in subsidiary companies (or in fellow subsidiaries of a holding company) and the amounts due from subsidiaries (or from the holding company and fellow subsidiaries) should be shown (2 Sch.15(2) 1967).

(x) The amount of quoted investments and their market value must be shown (2 Sch.8(1)(a) 1967 and 2 Sch.11(8) 1967).

*Note:* Article 35 of the Companies Act 1980 made it illegal for companies to buy their own shares. The 1981 Act permits companies to buy their own shares, both as trade investments and current assets. They must be shown separately and the sums used must be distributable profits of the company. The nominal value of the shares held must be shown separately.

(xi) The amount of unquoted investments and the directors' valuation must be shown. If the directors' valuation is not given there are strict requirements about the cost, depreciation and revenue received from the investments, etc. (2 Sch.5(2)(c) and 2 Sch.5A 1967).

(xii) Where debentures of the company are held by a nominee or trustee for the company, the nominal amount of the debentures and the amount at which they are stated in the books of the company should be disclosed (2 Sch.10 1967).

(xiii) Where any loans to employees for the purpose of buying shares in the company have been made the aggregate amount should be shown (2 Sch.8(1)(c) 1967).

(xiv) Fictitious assets, such as preliminary expenses, expenses incurred in connection with the issue of shares and debentures, discount on shares and debentures or commission on shares and debentures or development costs of any kind shall be shown to the extent that they have not been written off (2 Sch.3 1967). The reasons for capitalizing these costs, and the period over which they are to be written off, shall be stated (1 Sch. Part II 20(2) 1981).

(xv) Comparative figures for the preceding year should be shown (2 Sch.11(11) 1967).

## (b) Liabilities

(i) **The share capital and reserves.** The share capital and reserves are owed to the shareholders who contributed the original capital and may therefore be regarded as internal liabilities (to members of the firm). Other liabilities to debenture holders and other creditors are external liabilities.

1. The authorized share capital and issued share capital must be summarized, with such particulars as are necessary to disclose the general nature of the liabilities of the company to the shareholders (2 Sch.2 1967 and 1 Sch. Part III 38(1) 1981). Any shares allotted during the year should be shown, giving their number, value and the consideration received. Any contingent right to the allotment of shares in a company should be stated.

2. The amounts of any redeemable preference shares must be shown with details of the dates and terms of the redemption, premium payable, etc. (2 Sch.2(a) 1967 and 1 Sch. Part III 38(2) 1981).

3. In rare cases it is permitted for a dividend to be paid on shares out of capital. In such cases, the amount of capital and the rate of interest paid must be stated (2 Sch.2(b) 1967).

4. The amount of the Share Premium Account, if any, must be stated (2 Sch.2(c) 1967).

5. The aggregate amount of reserves, classified under headings appropriate to the company's business must be shown (2 Sch.4(1) 1967 and 2 Sch.6 1967). Movements in the reserves since the previous accounting period with the source of increases or the application of sums deducted from the reserves, must also be shown (2 Sch.7(a and b) 1967 and 1 Sch. Part III 46(2) 1981).

*Note:* In 2 Sch.27 1967 the expression 'reserve' specifically excludes any amount written off or retained to provide for depreciation, renewals or diminutions in value of assets or to provide for any known liability, disputed liability or contingent liability.

6.   The Capital Redemption Reserve Fund established under Section 58A of the 1948 Act as a permanent reserve when redeemable preference shares are redeemed, must be shown (S58(1)(d) 1948). It has a special place in the formats prescribed in the 1981 Act.

7.   The name of the company's ultimate holding company and its country of incorporation must be shown, unless the Department of Trade has given permission for these details to be withheld for reasons it considers sound (S5(1) 1967).

(ii) **External liabilities and provisions.** The term 'provision' is defined in 2 Sch.27 1967 as any amount written off or retained by way of providing for depreciation, renewals or dimunition in value of assets, or retained by way of providing for any known liability of which the amount can be determined with substantial accuracy. The section also provides that the term 'liability' shall include all liabilities in respect of expenditure contracted for, and all disputed or contingent liabilities.

1.   The liabilities and provisions shall be classified under headings appropriate to the company's business. But, if they are very small, they may be included under any relevant heading (2 Sch.4(1)(a and b) 1967). Where the publication of the provision would prejudice the company, and is not required in the public interest, the Department of Trade may allow the company not to produce a separate statement (2 Sch.6(b) 1967). Any debentures issued during the year should be shown, including the reasons for making the issue, the class of debenture and the number, value and consideration received (1 Sch. Part III 41(1) 1981).

2.   The aggregate amount of provisions (other than depreciation provisions which are shown as a deduction from the asset heading) should be shown, with the movements during the year (increases or decreases) and the source of the increase or the application of the funds causing the decrease (2 Sch.7 1967). The amount of any provisions for taxation other than deferred taxation shall be stated (1 Sch. Part III 47 1981).

3.   Particulars should be given of any redeemed debentures which the company has power to reissue (2 Sch.2(d) 1967).

4.   The aggregate amount of bank loans and overdrafts should be shown (2 Sch.8(1)(d) 1967).

5.   The aggregate amount of loans made to the company should be shown, other than bank loans and overdrafts, any part of which has more than five years to run (2 Sch.8(1)(d) 1967). There are rules for deciding repayment dates (2 Sch.30 1967). The terms on which any loan is repayable and the rate of interest must also be given (but not for bank loans and overdrafts) (2 Sch.8(4) 1967 and 1 Sch. Part III 48 1981).

6.   If a liability of the company is secured on assets otherwise than by operation of the law this must be stated (2 Sch.9 1967). Also, particulars of any charges on the assets of the company to secure the liabilities of any other person should be given (2 Sch.11(4) 1967).

7.   Any amounts due to subsidiaries should be set out separately from all other liabilities (2 Sch.15(2) 1967).

8.   If a company is itself a subsidiary, amounts due to the holding company or to fellow subsidiaries must be shown, separating debentures from other loans (2 Sch.16 1967).

9.   The aggregate amount of recommended dividends must be shown (2 Sch.8(1)(e) 1967). Arrears of cumulative dividend in any class of shares must be shown (1 Sch. Part III 49 1981).

10.   The amount of any sums set aside to prevent undue fluctuations in charges for taxation shall be stated (2 Sch.7A 1967) and any sums used from this provision for another purpose must be declared (2 Sch.11(8A) 1967).

11.   The basis on which any amount set aside for corporation tax has been computed must be stated (2 Sch.11(10) 1967). It is not possible in this book to deal with the current regulations for the treatment of taxation in the balance sheet of companies. It is essential to refer to a manual such as *Croner's Guide to Corporation Tax* which is available from Croner House, 173 Kingston Road, New Malden, Surrey KT3 3SS. Subscribers receive revision pages with up-to-date information on regulations.

12.   Comparative figures must be given for the preceding financial period.

The style of published balance sheets is illustrated by Fig. 7.2 (pp. 78–9). It is based on Format No. 1 in the Companies Act 1981.

Balance sheet of XYZ Ltd
(as at December 31, 19..)
*(Based on Format No. 1, Companies Act 1981)*

| *Fixed assets* (see Note i) | At cost (or valuation) | Depreciation to date | £ |
|---|---|---|---|
| *Intangible assets* | | | |
| Development costs | x | x | x |
| Concessions, patents, etc. | x | x | x |
| Goodwill | x | x | x |
| Payments on account | x | x | x |
| *Tangible assets* | | | |
| Freehold land and buildings | x | x | x |
| Leasehold property (long lease) | x | x | x |
| Leasehold property (short lease) | x | x | x |
| Plant and machinery | x | x | x |
| Other | x | x | x |
| | x | x | x |

| *Investments* (investments not held as trade investments should be shown as current assets) | £ | |
|---|---|---|
| Shares in group companies | x | |
| Loans to group companies | x | |
| Shares in related companies | x | |
| Loans to related companies | x | |
| Other investments (note of market value) | x | |
| Unlisted investments (note of directors' valuation) | x | |
| Own shares (note of nominal value) | x | |
| | | x |

| *Current assets* | £ | |
|---|---|---|
| *Stocks* | | |
| Raw materials | x | |
| Work-in-progress | x | |
| Finished goods | x | |
| *Debtors* | | |
| Trade debtors | x | |
| Amounts owed by group companies | x | |
| Amounts owed by related companies | x | |
| Other debtors | x | |
| Called-up share capital not yet paid | x | |
| *Investments* | | |
| Shares in group companies | x | |
| Own shares | x | |
| Other investments | x | |
| Cash at bank or in hand | x | |
| Pre-payments and accrued income | x | |
| *Less* Creditors' amounts due in less than one year | x | |
| Creditors | x | |
| Dividends proposed | x | |
| Loans and overdrafts | x | |
| Tax currently due | x | |
| | | (x) |

Net working capital (Net current assets)     x

Net assets    £ x

| | | £ |
|---|---|---|
| *Financed by:* | | |
| Debentures | | *x* |
| Other long-term liabilities (see Note ii) | | *x* |
| Indebtedness to holding company or subsidiary (under current liability if short-term) | | *x* |

| | *Authorized* | |
|---|---|---|
| *Preference shareholders' interest in the company* | | |
| Preference shares of (give nominal value per share) (see Note iii) | *x* | *x* |

| | *Authorized* | | |
|---|---|---|---|
| *Ordinary shareholders' interest in the company* | £ | £ | |
| Ordinary shares of (give nominal value per share) (see Note iv) | *x* | *x* | |

| | | £ | |
|---|---|---|---|
| Reserves (list capital reserves before revenue reserves) | | £ | |
| Profits prior to incorporation (if any) | | *x* | |
| Share Premium Account (if any) | | *x* | |
| Capital redemption reserve fund (if any) | | *x* | |
| Property Revaluation Account (if any) | | *x* | |

| | £ | £ | *x* |
|---|---|---|---|
| Plant replacement reserve | | *x* | |
| General reserve | *x* | | |
| Additions in year | *x* | | |
| | | *x* | |
| Balance on Appropriation Account | *x* | | |
| *Less* Fictitious assets (see Note v) | *(x)* | | |
| | | *x* | |
| | | | *x* |

| | | |
|---|---|---|
| Ordinary shareholders' interest | | *x* |
| | | £ *x* |

*Fig. 7.2 Published balance sheet — a suggested format*

*Notes:*
(i) The word valuation may refer to an original value placed on the asset in 1948 (when the main Act became law) or a more recent valuation. If valued in the last year the names of the valuers, or their qualifications and the bases used, must be disclosed.
(ii) A reserve for corporation tax may well appear at this point.
(iii) Full details of the earliest and latest dates for redemption, premium on redemption, etc. must be given.
(iv) If Section 65 of the Companies Act 1948 (permission in major construction works to pay interest on capital out of capital) applies, the full details must be explained.
(v) In so far as they have not been written off, it is necessary to show the following fictitious assets: (*a*) preliminary expenses; (*b*) expenses of issuing shares and debentures; (*c*) commission paid in respect of shares and debentures; (*d*) discount on debentures; (*e*) discount on shares. If deducted at this point it ensures that the true value of the shareholders' interest is disclosed. Under the 1981 Companies Act these items may not appear as assets, but must be shown as a set-off against distributable profits.

## 7.4  The Directors' Report

The directors' report has to be attached to the balance sheet, but does not form a part of it. The details which have to be stated include the names of the directors, the principal activities of the company and its subsidiaries and any significant changes in those activities during the year.

The Companies Act 1981 (Section 13) requires the report to give 'a fair review of the development of the business of the company and its subsidiaries during the financial year'. It then requires:

(*a*) an account of any relevant post-balance sheet developments;
(*b*) an indication of likely future developments; and
(*c*) an indication of the activities of the company and its subsidiaries in research and development.

The directors must give details of any 'own share' transactions (Section 14) and the auditors must check the consistency of the directors' report with the accounts (Section 15).

The chief points to be mentioned in the report are:

(i) the proposed dividend;
(ii) the proposed transfers to reserves;
(iii) the market value of land in so far as it differs to any extent from the book value as shown in the balance sheet;
(iv) an explanation of any issue of shares during the year;
(v) an explanation of the issue of any debentures during the year;
(vi) any interests of any director in the contracts engaged in by the company during the year;
(vii) if the company engages in different classes of activities, the division of turnover and profits between or among the various activities must be shown;
(viii) the average number of employees per week must be disclosed, and their aggregate remuneration in the year;
(ix) contributions to political and charitable bodies, where these exceed £50;
(x) particulars of exports, where the company total turnover exceeds £5 750 000.

**Post-balance sheet events (SSAP 17).** Anticipating the changes recommended in the 1981 Act the accountancy bodies issued a Statement of Standard Accounting Practice (SSAP 17) in August 1980. This requires that events occurring after the balance sheet date which refer to the position of the business before that date should be revealed in a financial statement where adjustment to the Final Accounts may be necessary. No disclosure is required if the post-balance sheet event does not affect the circumstances at the balance sheet date.

All post-balance sheet events are divided into *adjusting* and *non-adjusting* events. Thus the bankruptcy of a major debtor would be an adjusting event, as also would be a valuation report that revealed a permanent diminution in the value of property. SSAP 17 recommends that the information to be disclosed should include

(a) the nature of the event, and

(b) an estimate of the financial effect or a statement to the effect that it is not practicable to make such an estimate.

## 7.5 Exercises

1. (a) Define the terms 'provision' and 'reserve' as used in the Companies Acts 1948–1981. What is the difference between these and a liability?

(b) State under which of these three classes you would list the following items:

   (i) amounts written off for depreciation of machinery;

  (ii) amounts put away to equalize dividends;

 (iii) the credit balance left in Appropriation Account;

 (iv) rent due;

  (v) subscriptions in advance to a club;

 (vi) Share Premium Account;

(vii) profits prior to incorporation;

(viii) a sum set aside for possible bad debts in the future;

 (ix) sums set aside on the redemption of preference shares;

  (x) amounts set aside to replace assets at an expected higher price than the cost of assets in use at present.

# Introduction to Cost and Management Accounting

## 8.1 Relationship between Financial and Cost Accounts

Accounting is a term which refers to the numerous record-keeping activities carried out as a result of business transactions. It deals with the collection and recording of business facts and figures and is an information system reporting to a wide variety of individuals and interested parties.

Accounting is concerned with business transactions and the exchange or transfer of value in respect of goods and services. These transactions involve transfers which are either internal or external and are recorded at *historical cost*. This means that items are valued at what they cost when they were purchased or manufactured internally at some past time. There are many forms of business ownership such as sole traders, partnerships, limited companies and public sector enterprises responsible to the government and public authorities. There are also non-profit-making organizations and co-operative societies. The accounting systems found in these organizations vary considerably, depending on the demands of management and the legal requirements which have to be met.

Many people are confused by the titles given to accountants and systems of accounting. They are familiar with the term *financial accounting*, relating it to book-keeping which produces a profit statement and a balance sheet, but are unsure of the function of *cost accounting* and *management accounting*.

### (a) Financial Accounting

Book-keeping systems and methods can be adapted to suit a particular form of business enterprise; in the first instance they are concerned with *stewardship* and are designed to comply with the law. Stewardship means that the business must account to the owners for the activities carried out in their names. To a large extent, financial accounts are concerned with external affairs and relationships, that is with individuals and organizations outside the business.

The increasing size of business units, the advent of limited companies, and more recently, of holding companies and multi-national corporations, has resulted in large and very complex organizations. There is also the effect of economic conditions which have caused rapid inflation and the distortion of profits shown in company accounts. The financial accounts record the results of transactions and transfers carried out, so that at the end of a period, the Trading and Profit and Loss Account, the Appropriation Account and the balance sheet can be produced. The company books show the amount invested in the business and the amount withdrawn by the owners. The accounts are classified as *Real Accounts*, showing the value of the fixed assets; *Personal*

*Accounts* recording transactions with debtors and creditors connected with the activities of the business; and *Nominal Accounts*, showing the expenses and losses incurred and any gains or profits made. There are also the Cash Account and Bank Account entries to record receipts and payments.

The draft final accounts may, in the first instance, by drawn up for internal use and after any necessary adjustments have been made, they will be prepared (as far as companies are concerned) as published accounts to comply with the legal and taxation requirements of the various Companies and Finance Acts. They will take account of any recommendations by the directors on the payment of dividends and similar matters.

There is no strict borderline between financial, cost, and management accounts, and in some organizations integration may take place. Any statistics or other statements prepared depend on the type, size and nature of the business and the requirements of management.

Three organizations or institutions have exerted a great influence on the way in which financial accounts are produced.

(i) **The law.** The accounting requirements for companies are clearly laid down in the Companies Acts 1948–1981. Every company balance sheet must give a true and fair view of the state of affairs of the company as at the end of its financial year, and every Profit or Loss Account must give a true and fair view of the profit or loss of the company for the financial year. There are many other matters in the Companies Acts which have to be complied with, including requirements in connection with income and corporation tax, value added tax and so on.

(ii) **Professional bodies.** Accountancy organizations now exert considerable influence on the way in which accounts are laid out. As we saw in Unit 2.3, the accountancy bodies issue Statements of Standard Accounting Practice (Accounting Standards) which describe methods of accounting approved by their various governing councils. Members of these bodies are obliged to observe accounting standards or justify departures from them.

(iii) **The Council of the Stock Exchange.** This organization is chiefly concerned with the protection of the shareholder, and any company which wishes to make a public issue of its shares must submit financial information covering many years and must comply with the rules issued by the Council.

#### (*b*) Cost Accounting

Cost accountancy is 'the application of accounting and costing principles, methods and techniques in the ascertainment of costs: it then proceeds to analyse savings and/or excess expenditures where actual costs differ from previous experience, or from standards'. It is an essential aid to management in establishing selling prices and providing information for the day-to-day control of operations. It helps management in the decision and policy-making processes and in determining future policies in respect of operations and plans for further capital expenditure. The form of costing used depends on many factors, and in the small business may be merely an estimation using certain details from the financial books. In other organizations the system may be very sophisticated, using standard costing, budgetary control and other modern techniques, which form the subject-matter of this book.

Cost accounting uses basically the same information as is shown in the financial books, but in the process of costing, through the analysis and classification of accounts, it reveals the costs of departments, processes, products and units; it also shows selling, distribution and administrative costs by departments, functions and services. Costing indicates inefficiencies, waste of materials and wages and analyses losses caused by idle time of machinery and plant. It classifies expenses as direct and indirect costs and charges these at each stage of manufacture to the product. Cost accounting records the actual cost which can be compared with estimates or standard costs. It can provide a perpetual inventory of stores and other materials. In summary, costing uses book-keeping procedures to classify and record expenditure so as to allow accumulation of cost information in order to be able to measure managerial efficiency. All these methods are explained in the Units which follow.

#### (c) Management Accounting
Management accountancy provides management with accounting information for the purpose of planning and running a business. It developed because of management's demands for information on past and present operations and future trends. It integrates cost and financial accounting — analysing and interpreting past and present results and providing forecasts for the future. It is also concerned with alternative methods of production and operational procedures and is mainly concerned with financial planning.

Thus it can be seen that financial, cost, and management accounting are interrelated. Financial accounting has limitations because insufficient information is made available for management to be able to identify and forecast major trends and problems. Financial accounting can only show the results that have been achieved, but this may be too late for events to be controlled or changed. Management must identify the need for change in advance of any emergency and detect problems in time to take corrective action. In this respect, cost and management accounting must supplement the information provided by financial accounting so that management can develop, interpret and achieve overall policies and objectives.

### 8.2    Elements of Cost

The cost of a particular item or service is the amount spent on labour, materials and expenses (Fig. 8.1). These three groups of costs may be divided into direct and indirect costs.

#### (a) Direct Costs
These costs consist of materials, wages and expenses which can easily be identified with a particular unit, a product or a service which a business or organization sells. For example, if a customer orders a piece of mahogany

furniture which is to be made to a special design, the direct costs would include the main material (mahogany), the wages of the cabinet-maker and other workers, and the charge made by the designer. These costs are directly related to the goods being manufactured, and collectively make up what is known as the *prime cost* of the product.

### (b) Indirect Costs

These are costs which are added to the prime cost in order to obtain the total cost. They are overhead costs because they cannot be allocated directly to the unit or service, but have to be apportioned or absorbed by *cost units* (see Unit 8.6) or *cost centres*.

**Cost centres.** Administrative departments are not usually suitable as units for determining production costs, and therefore the organization is divided into cost centres. Other natural divisions would be groups of similar machines, similar processes or operations to which costs can be charged.

Using furniture again as an example, the indirect materials could include the glue which could not be measured as a charge to a particular piece of furniture, but would be included in the costs of the department where the furniture was made. The wages of the foreman would have to be charged to the cost of running the department and his wages would be apportioned to the products of that department, so that each product would bear a share of that cost. An example of indirect expense of this type of department would be the maintenance cost of machinery used by the employees.

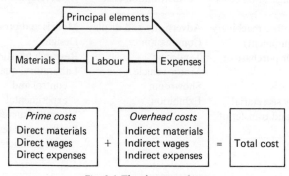

*Fig. 8.1 The elements of cost*

## 8.3 Classification of Overhead Costs

Cost classification is the process of grouping costs according to their common characteristics. This is a very important procedure in respect of overhead expenses as it is essential that each unit of production or service bears its fair share of indirect costs (see Table 8.1). There are five major functions of a business to which costs are allocated.

**Table 8.1    Examples of overhead costs**

*Production department (factory)*

Rent and rates
Insurance of premises, plant, employees, etc.
Indirect wages and salaries (i.e. wages and salaries not attributable directly
    to a particular unit of production)
Heating and lighting
Indirect power (i.e. power not attributable to a particular unit or process of
    production)
Depreciation
Repairs to plant, buildings, etc.
Indirect materials (i.e. materials not attributable to a particular unit or
    process of production)
Personnel expenses

*All other departments*

*Note:* The costs of all other departments will be overhead costs. These will include many
general costs (for example, all departments will have to pay rent, rates, lighting and
heating, wages and salaries, etc.). Some of the more specialized departmental costs are
shown below.

| Administration costs | Selling and distribution costs | Research and development costs |
|---|---|---|
| Service (office machinery and equipment) | Advertising and display Commission | Models and prototype Design |
| Computer purchase or hire | Tendering Motor vehicle | Research questionnaire Laboratory, quality |
| Legal | Showroom | control and |
| Company secretarial (issue and transfer of shares) | Exhibition | experimental Literature survey Purchase and testing of |
| Personnel | | rival products |
| Pension | | |

*(a)* **Production**
This department produces or prepares the goods or service sold, and its
involvement ends when these are complete after the primary packing of the
product.

*(b)* **Administration**
This is the function of controlling the operations of a business, formulating the
policy and directing the activities, but it is not directly related to the functional

activities of production, selling, distribution or research. However, the production and marketing divisions need the service of administrators and this is classified separately, although the benefit derived from the administrative service may be charged separately to production and marketing at a later stage.

(c) **Selling**
This is the operation of the sales department in securing orders and retaining customers and includes the costs incurred in promoting sales.

(d) **Distribution**
This process begins with making the product ready for dispatch and is completed when it is delivered to the customer and the returned container or empty package is made ready for further use. The selling and distribution functions are sometimes combined and costs applied as a single charge.

(e) **Research and Development**
This function may only exist in large organizations and covers research for new or improved methods and the development of new or improved products. Allocation of the cost is a policy decision made by management, normally including the chief accountant and the managing director.

## 8.4 How Total Cost is Made Up

How do we identify cost? It may be thought that cost is the price paid, the value of the goods, or the outlay. In fact, it is the amount of expenditure incurred on a given item. In cost accounting we use certain procedures *in order to ascertain each outlay incurred on particular items*. Total cost includes several elements which have to be added together. This accumulation can be done after each operation or after each stage of assembly, but for administrative purposes it is usually shown on a cost sheet as direct and indirect expenditure. We start with the prime or direct costs and finish with the indirect costs. For purposes of control, details can be shown by breaking down the cost into classes of direct material and labour and of indirect or overhead costs (Fig. 8.2).

## 8.5 The Costing Department

The costing department, which is supervised by the chief cost accountant, has the following objectives:

(a) the analysis and classification of all expenditure so that the cost of operations, units, processes and products can be ascertained;

(b) where appropriate, developing cost standards, reporting variances and indicating waste of materials, wages and resources;

(c) provision of *actual costs* for comparison with *estimates*, as an aid in price fixing, and for use in the preparation of quotations and tenders;

(d) provision of information to enable Profit and Loss Accounts and balance sheets to be prepared at suitable intervals;

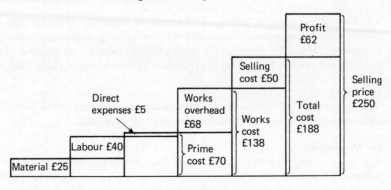

Cost Sheet

| | £ | £ |
|---|---|---|
| *Materials* | | |
| Steel | 5 | |
| Brass | 20 | |
| | | 25 |
| *Labour* | | |
| Machining | 30 | |
| Assembly | 10 | |
| | | 40 |
| *Direct expenses* | | |
| Patterns | | 5 |
| Prime cost | | 70 |
| *Works overhead* | | |
| Machining (200% on labour) | 60 | |
| Assembly (80% on labour) | 8 | |
| | | 68 |
| Works cost | | 138 |
| Selling cost | | 50 |
| Total cost | | 188 |
| Profit | | 62 |
| Selling price | | £ 250 |

*Fig. 8.2 How total cost is made up*

*Note:* In this example the cost of administration is included in works overhead and selling costs.

(e) maintenance of adequate records so that information can be provided quickly and efficiently to all who may need assistance in the control of the organization;

(f) operation of a system of perpetual inventory for raw materials, finished parts, components, and finished goods;

(g) collection of data for the preparation of *budgets* and for use in cost control accounts and budgetary control procedures;

(h) designing and installing new methods and systems so that effective information can be given promptly to other departments.

## 8.6 Methods of Cost Accounting

Various *basic costing methods* have **been** established to suit the kind of goods manufactured or the type of services provided. For purposes of control there are different ways in which cost information may be given to management. In order to present this information in the most suitable way, superimposed principles and techniques are applied and used in the costing system. The basic costing methods are either *specific order costing* or *operation costing* (Fig. 8.3).

### (a) Specific Order Costing

This method applies to production which is authorized by a special order or contract and the work consists of separate *jobs*, *batches* or *contracts*. An order number is issued to collect the elements of cost for goods manufactured for stock or to the requirements of a customer, or when the specific order is a contract (usually concerned with constructional or civil engineering activities).

(i) **Job costing.** This applies to goods manufactured for stock or to customers' special requirements. It also applies when capital expenditure is made and the fixed asset is manufactured internally instead of being purchased. When repairs are exceptional and not regarded as normal maintenance, the work is carried out and the costs are charged to a job order number. A characteristic of job costing is that the job moves through the processes or operations as a continuously identifiable unit.

(ii) **Batch costing.** This is similar to job costing and applies when similar articles are manufactured in batches either for sale or for stock or when units from a batch are required for use or assembly on other specific orders. The batch of items is costed as a job and as the parts are identical the *unit cost* is obtained by dividing the batch cost by the quantity produced.

(iii) **Contract costing.** This form of specific order costing is usually applied to work which extends over a long period and, consequently, the cost is considerable. It is work undertaken to customers' special requirements and applies particularly to construction work such as ship-building, bridge-building, and civil engineering.

The term *unit costs*, used in (ii) above, is a unit of quantity of product or service, or time, in relation to which costs may be ascertained or expressed. Examples of typical units are:

| Industry | Operation or product | Unit used: cost per |
|---|---|---|
| Automotive | stampings | 100 stampings |
| Brewing | beer | kilolitre |
| Brickmaking | bricks | 1 000 bricks |
| Fertilizer | acid phosphate | tonne |
| Pharmaceutical | tablets | 1 000 tablets |
| Transport | heavy goods movements | tonne/kilometre |

(b) **Operation Costing**

This basic costing method applies to operations of a process or service nature where standardized goods or services result from a sequence of repetitive and more-or-less continuous operations or processes. The average cost per unit is obtained by taking the total cost which applies and averaging this over the units produced during the period.

(i) **Process costing.** Manufacture which is continuous or where production is on a mass production basis, causing a loss of identity of individual items or materials uses process costing. It is assumed that similar amounts of material, labour and overhead will be charged to each process. It is an averaging technique where the process cost per unit is obtained by finding the average cost per unit for the period. Production may be of a single process or several processes, where the completed units are transferred from one process to the next. Among the industries using process costing are breweries, paint factories, cement production and food products.

(ii) **Service costing.** This is operation costing where a standardized service is provided by a service cost centre or an undertaking. Average costs per unit are calculated per period and costs can be ascertained in relation to the standardized unit or measurement. Services using this method include transport, canteens, power, heating, personnel and welfare.

(c) **Superimposed Principles and Techniques**

The costing system uses the basic costing method appropriate to the way in which goods are manufactured or the services provided, and it is then adapted so that the routine system will supply information which can be presented in a particular manner. The main principles and techniques which may be *superimposed* consist of:

    (i) absorption costing;
    (ii) marginal costing;
    (iii) actual cost ascertainment;
    (iv) variance accounting;
    (v) standard costing;
    (vi) budgetary control;
    (vii) uniform costing.

(i) **Absorption costing.** This is a principle whereby *fixed* as well as *variable* costs are allotted to cost units. The object is to ensure that, as far as is possible, all the costs of operating a business are charged to the cost units. The problem is that although variable costs tend to vary in direct proportion to changes in the volume of output or turnover, fixed costs accrue in relation to the passage of time. As the level of activity and the overhead absorption rates are estimated and predetermined, any variation in activity or overhead costs results in an over- or under-absorption of overhead costs. This is more fully explained in Unit 12.9.

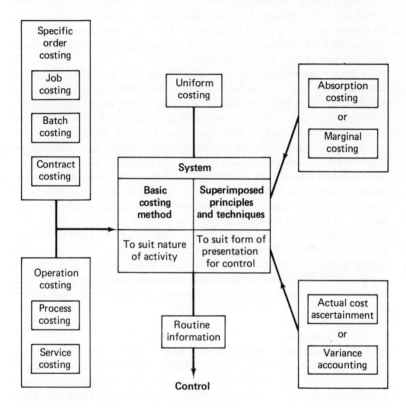

*Fig. 8.3 Management accounting: methods, principles and techniques related to the routine system* (reproduced by courtesy of the Institute of Cost and Management Accountants)

*Notes:*
(i) The chart displays the chief methods of cost accounting, which are described in the Units that follow.
(ii) Exact terminology is very important in accounting for costs (management accounting). The recognized definitions are published in *Terminology of Management and Financial Accountancy* which is obtainable from the ICMA.
(iii) Variance accounting also includes standard costing and budgetary control.

(ii) **Marginal costing.** This technique is used in the routine costing system which ascertains the variable (marginal) cost of cost units. The margin or difference between the variable cost and the selling price is known as the *contribution* and the fixed costs for the relevant period are written off in full against the contribution for that period (see Unit 15).

(iii) **Actual cost ascertainment.** This is the principle whereby the costs of cost centres and cost units are ascertained and, subject to certain approximations, are then assumed to represent actual costs. The term *historical cost* is generally used to indicate actual cost but the term is not recommended because the word historical applies also to other concepts.

(iv) **Variance accounting.** This technique is concerned with *standard costing* and *budgetary control*. Standard costs and budgeted cost allowances are established and the difference between these and the actual costs are variances which are recorded and studied in order to find out why there is a difference between planned and actual performance (see Units 16 and 17).

(v) **Standard costing.** This is the method of costing in which the standard costs (predetermined costs) of products and services are prepared (see Unit 16).

(vi) **Budgetary control.** This is a method which relates to the establishment of budgets for responsibility centres. These centres are the responsibility of executives and their performance is assessed by a continuous comparison of actual with budgeted results (see Unit 17).

(vii) **Uniform costing.** Trade associations often adopt and recommend this system to their members so that all members of the association can use the same principles and/or practices. This system can also be used by a group of companies so that useful comparisons of detailed costs which have been prepared using the same costing principles and practices can be made within the group.

(*d*) **Other Techniques**

(i) **Differential costing.** This refers to the manner in which alternative courses of action are examined. It is a technique which studies the behaviour of costs at different volumes of output and sales and the relationship between contribution and sales value which is the contribution/sales ratio (see Unit 15.8).

(ii) **Incremental costing.** This is used in the preparation of special information where consideration is given to a range of graduated changes in the level or nature of activity. The additional costs and revenues likely to result from each degree of change are presented.

Costing and pricing are interrelated. Costing is invaluable in the formulation and approval of policies; the information it provides enables expenditures to be controlled and prices to be established.

In general, selling prices are determined by competition and the effect of supply and demand. In this respect operating efficiency is of paramount importance. It is essential to maintain a high level of activity with volumes of output which will result in low unit costs. There are occasions when prices are set below the full cost, in order to retain regular customers, and when new products are introduced. When there is no established price structure, goods are sometimes priced on cost, plus an agreed percentage to cover the profit. When this applies to large contracts, it is sometimes a condition that an auditor's certificate is sent with the invoice stating that the price is correct within the terms of the contract. Contracts on a *cost-plus* basis are not always favourable to the customer because:

the cost tends to be higher than when there is a fixed price;

manufacturers have little incentive to reduce costs as they would receive a smaller return;

dishonest contractors may increase the actual cost by fraudulently including amounts which are not applicable to the contract.

This demonstrates the need for an auditor's certificate which, in some cases, is supplied by the customer's auditor after inspection of the documents and cost sheets.

## 8.7  Value Analysis

This is a management technique for reducing or eliminating items of cost, by questioning the need to use the particular materials, labour or services specified in the original process. *Value engineering* is the application of the value analysis techniques to new products in the development or prototype stage, but often there is insufficient time at this stage to investigate, compare and secure the cost of alternatives as required by the application of value analysis.

This procedure is designed to improve profitability by cutting out unnecessary costs, while maintaining the quality and usefulness of the product. A check list is used which presents a series of questions with the object of encouraging an individual or members of a team to produce ideas which will lead to a reduction in cost and/or an improvement in design. The following list gives an indication of the kinds of questions which can be asked during the value analysis of any component, product, item of equipment or service.

(i)  Does it serve a useful purpose?

(ii)  Can the design be simplified?

(iii)  Does its use justify the expenditure involved?

(iv)  Can the item be replaced by something better or less costly?

(v)  Can a cheaper or different grade of material be used?

(vi)  Can the item be replaced by a standard product?

(vii)  Can it be produced more cheaply using a different process?

(viii)  Is there another supplier who can provide it for less?

A value analysis team may consist of people from departments such as design, methods, production, sales, purchasing and costing. Considerable savings and improvements can be made by companies using this technique. In particular, savings can be made in raw materials costs, production time taken, and in reducing the weight of the product.

## 8.8 Quality Circles

The idea of quality circles came from Japan and they have now spread to many other countries. The aim of the circles is to improve efficiency in an organization, to reduce its costs and increase competitiveness by allowing employees to participate in the running of an organization and to help contribute to its success. The procedure is concerned with analysing problems and solving them by using the knowledge and experience of small groups of workers.

The quality circle is a voluntary body which meets fortnightly or monthly. A departmental group may consist of the foreman, usually the leader, and several workers. Shop-floor workers have a special contribution to make, as they are in daily contact with the products and manufacturing operations and are aware of many problems and uneconomic methods which management may not have noticed. Problems may concern complaints from customers, difficulties arising in the engineering or design department, imperfect processing and planning, excessive scrap, unsuitable tools or equipment, product quality and reliability, and progressing of materials.

In the course of their deliberations, members may have to seek advice from specialists and experts within the organization. The company appoints a *facilitator* to co-ordinate the affairs and activities of the group and to contact other individuals in the company when information and help is needed. The facilitator must be carefully selected for his or her ability to obtain the respect of others by listening, consulting and communicating, in order to motivate the group and maintain morale.

The leader of the circle may receive training in the organizational aspects of group activities such as how to obtain, select and interpret information, constructive discussion, and how to respond usefully to the contributions of others. There may also be instruction in statistical methods and other problem-solving techniques such as Pareto analysis which pays attention to key areas and which uses the more or less constant relationship between quantity and value. Graphs may be used to illustrate the items or areas where the greatest losses appear or to indicate the possible causes of failure.

When recommendations are made to management, they must be implemented, but if the suggestions are unacceptable, clear reasons must be given for the rejection otherwise there is a collapse of confidence in the use of quality circles as an aid to management.

## 8.9 Personnel

In different organizations, the staff of a costing department varies widely and the duties and responsibilities of individuals depend on those given to the head of the department. The staff may consist of a chief cost accountant or controller with assistants, time clerks, wages clerks and cost clerks. Or it may be organized into separate sections such as timekeeping, wages, costing, stores control accounting and similar activities.

It is the duty of the chief cost accountant to maintain and improve the system at all times, especially when changes are taking place within the organization or when new techniques become available outside the business. He or she must have close contact with the executives of other departments, determining their needs and presenting information promptly.

## 8.10  Cost Accounting Manual

A manual or set of standard practice instructions should be drawn up by the chief cost accountant to outline the system in detail so that misunderstandings can be avoided. This is most useful to new employees, since, among other things, it indicates the forms to be used and the routes they will travel. It will also give detailed information on the various procedures; on the coding and classification of accounts and the reports to be issued.

## 8.11  Relationship with Other Departments

In order to carry out this work, the cost department must co-operate with the other departments in a business. It processes a vast amount of data which is received from the following departments:

| | | |
|---|---|---|
| Engineering | Progress | Sales |
| Planning | Inspection | Purchasing |
| Production control | Storekeeping | Accounts |
| Work study, Method study and Rate fixing | Dispatch and packing | |

In addition, the cost department gives and receives advice from many individuals in the firm, from general management to superintendents and foremen.

### Transfer Pricing

Transfer pricing is a device which seeks to measure departmental performance. Each department is expected to earn a profit therefore an arbitrary selling price or value is fixed when work is transferred to other departments. The system is not widely used. As an example, in the manufacture of a mixing drum:

Department 1 (the plate department) draws out a steel plate, cuts it to size and trims the material. This cost, material, wages and overhead is collected and a percentage is added for the profit element for the department. This is a notional profit. The plate department transfers this blank plate at the agreed price to:

Department 2 (the press department) which presses the plate in the press, by the use of dies, to the shape of the mixing drum. This department records its costs for power, overheads and notional profit. The total cost, that is the original transfer cost plus the costs of Department 2, decides the new transfer price to Department 3. The process continues through the departments until the drum is a finished good.

Every individual and every process or department contributes towards the performance and profitability of an organization. If this is to be measured to assess the degree of efficiency of managers or divisions of a business, what method of pricing is to be used as output is transferred? The use of market price is satisfactory in theory, but the transfer of work or units of production at intermediate stages in a manufacturing process generally cannot be related to market prices, since none exist. This is because values have to be assigned to operations on a product which is incomplete or which is special and not produced elsewhere.

Within a group or in one particular factory it is sometimes possible to establish a market price by inviting quotations for the work before deciding where the work is to be carried out. Management needs to be assured that the quality of the work and the rate of delivery is up to company standards.

The *transfer price* is the minimum price quoted, whether internally or by another business. When a market price is unobtainable the usual procedure is to charge cost plus a percentage. Cost must include the full outlay, including any extra costs such as packing and carriage when the work is dispatched to another part of the group. Alternatively, the price can be based on a variable cost plus an addition for fixed cost, and a profit which is related to the overall profit of the organization. The expected return on capital employed will be known, and if the different segments of the business are allocated their share of this, the profit expected from each segment can be calculated and a percentage established for use in transfer pricing.

## 8.12    Coding

The costing system needs symbols, codes and account numbers in order to facilitate the collection and processing of a wide variety of data. Coding is essential when computers and other office machines are used, as it aids the sorting and tabulation of data into groups of similar items. It also enables accounts to be located quickly, aids the memory and helps clerical work to be carried out speedily and efficiently.

A coding system should be simple, easily remembered and flexible so that expansion can take place without the need to reorganize the entire system. The following items need codes and account numbers:

| | | |
|---|---|---|
| Raw material, parts and finished goods | Overhead expenses | Fixed assets |
| Direct and indirect labour operations | Customers' orders | Tools and equipment |
| | Stock orders | |
| | Jobs and processes | |

**Standing Order Numbers**

Expenses are classified, and each type of expense is given a *standing order number*, or code, to which costs are charged as they occur. These numbers or codes are shown in the manual of accounts, and probably lists of expense orders will be posted up in each department to guide those involved with expense costs. For example, a number could be issued for charging the cost of repairs, which would be used by all departments. It would be followed, however, by additional figures, representing the number of the department where the cost occurred and the type of asset repaired (e.g. desk or machine).

Items in a numerical code can be issued in sequence, in *blocks of numbers* or in *groups of related items* so that a coding system may be drawn up using one or more of the following methods:

(i) **Sequence coding.** On the establishment of a coding system, similar or related items can be grouped together in the classification and given numbers in sequence. However, this does not allow for the introduction at a later date of extra items into a group of related items as each new item has to take the next number in the series. New items have to take a number at the end of the list and to overcome this a *block code* can be used whereby a block of numbers can be used for similar types of expenses with spare numbers for use in the future when new types of expenses arise.

(ii) **Block coding.** For example, if the main classification number for 'repairs' is 27 and there are 12 departments, the numbers for repairs will extend from 2701 to 2712 in a sequence coding, but in a block coding the numbers for repairs could range from 2701 to 2720. This allows for expansion as numbers 2713 to 2720 would be reserved for future use.

(iii) **Group classification.** This is a numerical classification where the first figure is the major classification and the succeeding digits are minor classifications. If the major classification for heating is 21 the next digit could represent the type of heating and the next one or two digits would indicate the department.

> 21  *Heating*
> 211  Gas        2116 (6 representing tool room)
> 212  Solid fuel  2126 (6 representing tool room)

(iv) **Mnemonic codes.** Letters can be used to designate the various items such as 'R' for repairs (R27). They can also be used for part numbers or codes to represent the type of material used in the manufacture of a component. For example 'B' could be brass, 'CS' could be cast steel and 'MS' could be mild steel.

(v) **Decimal coding.** This is a system where important items in a classification can be combined in a code number, for example, 21 heating, 01 gas, 06 tool room, as 21.01.06.

There are other special or proprietary systems in use. One is based on the shape of a component and the class of material used. This groups together all items of a similar shape, size and material and encourages standardization and the reduction of the variety of stocks held.

Standing orders or codes are appropriate in many cases but for customers' orders, stock orders, jobs and processes, a sequence code is usually adopted as the numbers are assigned at the date of issue.

## 8.13  Exercises

1. What do you understand by the terms (*a*) financial accounting, (*b*) cost accounting and (*c*) management accounting?

2. What do you consider to be the objects of costing?

3. Write an essay on the methods of cost accounting.

4. Explain what you understand by (*a*) classification of costs and (*b*) coding.

5. Why is it desirable to classify overhead costs?

# Unit Nine
# Recording Material Costs

## 9.1 Types of Materials

In the process of production the following materials are required:

### (*a*) Direct Materials

The term *direct* means materials which are actually embodied in the finished product. Examples are raw materials, manufactured items, components and other purchased items such as steel, timber, castings, nuts and bolts, engines and electric motors.

### (*b*) Indirect Materials

There are also indirect materials or consumables which do not enter into the product, but are needed during the course of manufacture. Examples are oil and cleaning materials for machines, fluorescent tubes for lighting the factory, polish and stationery for works' offices, and batteries for electric trucks. When certain direct materials cannot be accurately or economically charged direct to the product because the quantities are small, they are treated as indirect material costs.

## 9.2 Basic Documents

In the process of accounting for cost there is a number of basic documents which are used in the recording procedures, and there are at least three essential forms used for materials.

### (*a*) Specification or Bill of Materials

The specification or parts list shows the direct materials required in the production process and indicates the quality and quantity of the materials and components to be used. The list shows the code or item number of the parts specified, and these materials will be held in stock until required or they will be purchased and charged direct to the job or account number. In many industries a large number of the items will be manufactured on the premises and held in stock until required for assembly.

### (*b*) Materials Requisition

This is a stores requisition which authorizes the stores department to issue the specific items of material written or listed on the requisition form. Various departments or officials may be authorized to requisition materials, but normally requisitions are prepared by the production department. There may be several copies of the same requisition but one of these will be priced by the stores ledger clerk and sent to the cost office. In a modern organization the stores ledger clerk will probably be the person who operates a stores accounting machine or computer. Examples of materials requisition notes are given in Fig. 9.1.

| MATERIALS REQUISITION | | | No. *G.294* | | |
|---|---|---|---|---|---|
| Bin no. | Drawing no. *72 491* | Code no. *46* | Group *6* | Order no. *X.20 798* | |
| | Description | | Quantity | Unit price £ | Value £ |
| | | | | | |
| *X.284* | *Crawler Pad* | | 1 | *30.85* | *30.85* |
| | | | | | |
| | | | | | |
| | | | | | |
| | | | | | |

| Authorized by: *J.Brown* | Date *September 7* | Stores ledger *I. P.* | Cost ledger *H. F.* | *30.85* |
|---|---|---|---|---|
| | | | | Total |

| MATERIALS REQUISITION    No. *296* | | |
|---|---|---|
| Stores code | Bin no. | Material group | Account no. |
| *D.142* | *A.164* | *7* | *JP. 20496* |
| Quantity | Description | Value |
| *20 litres* | *Engine Oil* | £ *25.00* |
| Authorized | Priced by | Stores ledger | Cost ledger |
| *R.Gregg* | *P.S.* | *S.C.* | *R.F.* |

*Fig. 9.1 Examples of materials requisitions*

(c) **Materials Return Note**

After the items have been issued, it is sometimes discovered that some are faulty or incorrect. For example, if a component such as a water pump is found to be of the wrong type, it is returned to the stores with a materials return note, and a materials requisition for the correct type of pump.

If more material is issued than is actually used, as in the case of steel plate, tubes or bricks, which come in stock sizes or large quantities, the excess material is returned to stores, together with a materials return note which is, in effect, a credit note. Three or more copies may be issued, of which one is retained by the factory department, one is sent to the storekeeper and a third copy is priced by the stores ledger clerk and sent to the cost office. A materials return note is shown in Fig. 9.2.

| MATERIALS RETURN NOTE | | Cost code 5 | Order no. B. 3. 879 |
|---|---|---|---|
| Quantity | Description | | Condition |
| 1 | Water Pump | | New |
| Date of return | Water pump G.307 was issued instead of G.309. The incorrect item has been examined and is to be taken into stock. | | |
| Sept. 8 | Signature: J. Brown | Date: Sept. 8 | |
| Material code | Description | Quantity | Value |
| G. 307 | Water Pump | 1 | £ 18 | 38 |
| Posted to stock records ✓ | | Total | 18  38 |
| Credited to Cost Account ✓ | | | |

Fig. 9.2 A materials return note

#### (d) Materials Transfer Note

This form records the transfer of material from one store, department or cost centre to another. Double-entry accounting must be supplied so that Stores Control Accounts are adjusted and debited and credited with the value transferred. On receipt of the materials transfer note the cost office will make the necessary entries in the Cost and Stores Accounts. A materials transfer note is shown in Fig. 9.3.

### 9.3  Purchasing Procedure

The purchasing department receives purchase requisitions and procures raw materials and finished goods of the correct quality and type, and at the lowest possible cost for delivery on the date required by the stores department or production department. The purchase requisition may be issued by a materials controls section from the storekeeper, production controller, foreman or

| MATERIALS TRANSFER NOTE | | No. *708* | |
|---|---|---|---|
| Date *October 6.*   To Order no. *G. 3293.* | | From Order no. *G. 1765.* | |
| From *Fitting department* | To *Erecting department* | Requisition issued | ✓ |
| Drawing no. *76408* | Code no. *32* | | Material group  *9* |
| Description | Quantity | Unit price | Value |
| *Spindle* | 2 | £ *15.00* | £ *30.00* |
| Authorized by: *J. Brown* | Received by: *W. Jones* | Cost ledger | *M. Y.* |

*Fig. 9.3 A materials transfer note*

similar official. The stores ledger clerk is probably authorized to prepare purchase requisitions when the stock of particular items falls to the re-order level, as indicated on the stock card. The purchasing department is aware of prices and delivery times for many of the items required but where this information is not available a request for a quotation is sent to the suppliers. In due course, a *purchase order* is prepared and sent to the supplier. There may be several copies of this order with the original going to the supplier, the second retained by the purchasing department for filing and other copies going to the stores department, accounts department, etc.

### (a) Receipt of Purchases

Procedures vary considerably in different businesses but usually goods are checked for quality and quantity. The arrival of goods is recorded by the issue of a *goods received note* by the receiving department, usually the stores department (Fig. 9.4). The supplier sends an advice note in respect of the goods, and after noting the number of this and the number of the purchases order, the goods received note is prepared. Where there is no separate receiving department this will be made out by the stores department and copies are needed for:

(i) the purchasing department, to enable their copy of the purchases order to be checked with the goods received note and the invoice, when the copy of the purchases order is transferred to the completed file. If the order is incomplete, a note is made and the order held until final delivery.

(ii) the accounts department, to enable payment to be made after checking with the supplier's invoice. This copy is then passed to the cost department for updating the stock records card, where appropriate.

(iii) the requisitioning department, as notification that the material has arrived.

| GOODS RECEIVED NOTE | | | No...*368*... | | |
|---|---|---|---|---|---|
| | | | Date...*Sept. 9*.. | | |
| Order no. | | Supplier | | Carrier | |
| *B. 40 826* | | *XY Manufacturing Co.* | | *B.R.* | |
| No. of packages | Particulars | | Quantity | Unit price | £ |
| *2* | *Diesel Engines* | | *2* | *926  00* | *1 852  00* |
| Received by: *J. Pells* | | Approved by: *N.Smith* | | Bin no. *E. 28* | |
| Stores ledger *B. M.* | | Cost ledger *J. V.* | | Invoice no. *G. 1 058* | |

*Fig. 9.4 A goods received note*

When goods are returned to a supplier a debit note is sent and the copy of the note is retained by the accounts department for checking against the credit note which is expected in due course.

### (b) Purchases Invoices

The procedure for recording invoices and accounting for materials may be comparatively simple where a small quantity of materials is purchased or where only one product is made. Where there are many different products and large amounts of materials, however, the procedure is more complex because of the amount of analysis required. The procedure depends, therefore, on the way in which costs are controlled or recorded, and the reconciliation which may be necessary between the cost and financial accounts. Essential information has to be extracted from the invoices for entry into the financial accounts and the costing system, and this may be entered on a posting slip or on the invoice itself using a rubber stamp. Each posting slip or invoice is given a reference number and in the process of accounting for purchases it is necessary to record the liability arising from the purchase, and the quantity and value of the materials for the stock records and cost accounts. The stamp on an invoice or the slip may include the following:

   (i) date invoice received;
  (ii) goods received note number;
 (iii) buying office approval;
 (iv) extensions and totals checked;
  (v) cash discount terms;
 (vi) charged to ... (standing order no., job no., stock, etc.);
(vii) date paid ....

Invoices for materials and goods supplied are entered in a purchases journal and other items or services are recorded in an expense journal. Suppliers' accounts are credited, and debit is made to a Purchases or Materials Control Account. When separate totals of purchases have to be obtained for different stores, departments or products, a columnar purchases journal can be used, or the invoices can be listed and shown on a purchases analysis sheet (see Fig. 9.5, where the sheet is shown in two halves).

| | | | | PURCHASES | | |
| | | | | | Debits | |
| Date | Invoice number | Capital expend- iture | Overhead expenses | Stores department | | |
| | | | | 1 | 2 | 3 |
| | | £ | £ | £ | £ | £ |

| ANALYSIS | | | January 19. . | | | |
| | | | | | | Credits |
| Customers' orders | | | Stock orders | | | Accounts payable |
| Product group | | | Product group | | | |
| A | B | C | A | B | C | |
| £ | £ | £ | £ | £ | £ | £ |

Fig. 9.5 A purchases analysis sheet

The whole procedure for procuring goods and materials, recording and paying for them is shown diagrammatically in Fig. 9.6.

## 9.4   Adjusting Invoice Costs

In arriving at the cost of materials and supplies it is necessary to ensure that the value charged to stock and cost accounts is the total cost of the items at the point of usage. The net amount on the invoice represents the list or catalogue price less the seller's trade discount and, where appropriate, includes value added tax. When we determine the cost we must see that the correct trade discount is given, that the VAT is deducted and that a deduction has been made for any other allowances which are in the terms of the contract.

If a cash discount is allowed for prompt payment, this is usually deducted, when payment is made, from the net amount on the invoice. Cash discount is

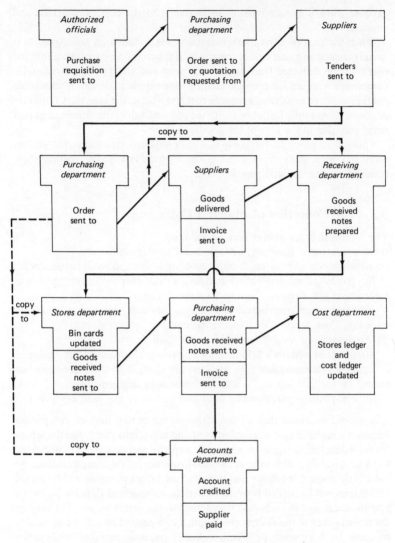

*Fig. 9.6 Procedure for procuring goods and materials*

generally excluded from the cost accounts as the gain is attributed to good financial management. The cost of transport or carriage inwards is another item which has to be accounted for. Sometimes this is shown on the invoice or sometimes a charge for carriage will follow later, unless the price shown includes the cost of carriage. When the purchaser arranges his own transport by using a contractor, it is important to see that the charge is added to the cost of the goods. The cost of carriage inwards is treated only as an overhead expense when it is inconvenient to charge it to the cost of materials and supplies.

When the cost of unreturnable containers is included on an invoice, it is usually treated as a part cost of the goods. If the containers are returnable, the cost must be deducted from the invoice price and charged to a Returnable Containers Account for eventual credit by the supplier. However, sometimes containers are returnable at a reduced cost and if this is the case, the Containers Account should only be debited with the reduced value, the difference in cost being included in the cost of the goods.

You will see from the foregoing that material costs are collected in various ways but principally from invoices, goods received notes, posting slips, material requisitions and transfer notes.

## 9.5    The Collection of Material Costs

The following types of cost may be collected.

(a) *From invoices, goods received notes and posting slips:*

   (i) all goods and materials purchased for stores and recorded as stock;

   (ii) goods and materials purchased for a special purpose and chargeable to a particular job, Cost Account or Expense Account;

   (iii) components from outside the business for stock or as a special purchase for a job, Cost Account or Expense Account.

(b) *From material requisitions and transfer notes:*

   (i) goods or materials held in stock and required for jobs, Cost Accounts or Expense Accounts, and materials already charged to these accounts but needed on another job, or for another account or department;

   (ii) components purchased or produced internally and held as stock.

It should be noted that an internally manufactured item or component becomes a material cost when completed and taken into stock. The document for recording this charge to stores may be a special *posting slip* or in some cases, the *final route slip* which follows the final inspection of the completed item. As there is no invoice, it follows that manufactured stock items have to be costed and entries will be needed between Materials, Labour and Expense Accounts and the total cost in each case transferred to the stores ledger. The various documents used in the system are designed and printed to suit the particular business. In this respect, differently coloured paper or coloured bands at the top of sheets of paper can be used to indicate the different groups or classes of materials.

Cost sheets also vary widely between businesses and industries but it is usually convenient to show material costs in groups or classes as this makes comparison and control of costs much easier. The cost of cast steel, plates and sections, non-ferrous materials, timber, special purchases, etc. can then be checked and compared.

## 9.6    Exercises

1.    What basic documents are used for materials issued from, or returned to, the stores department and for those materials moved between departments? Design one of these documents.

2.    Describe the procedure which follows the receipt of a purchase requisition by the purchasing department, up to the time when the invoice is received and passed for payment, and the cost of the goods is recorded in the accounts of a business.

3.    Purchases invoices have to be posted to creditors' accounts, but they also have to be dealt with in the Cost and Stores Accounts. Describe the routine for dealing with invoices from the time of receipt until they are charged to the Cost or Stores Accounts.

4.    Material costs have to be collected and charged to Cost and Stores Accounts. Explain in detail the kinds of material involved and the documents which record the costs to be debited to the Cost or Stores Accounts.

5.    In a large manufacturing company it is often necessary to analyse the purchases invoices as they arrive, in order to provide essential information. State why a purchases analysis is essential and show the layout of a purchases analysis sheet.

# Unit Ten

# Stores Control and the Pricing of Requisitions

## 10.1 Stock Control

It is necessary for a business to hold stocks of materials, whether they are used regularly or infrequently, and, as far as possible, deliveries should be matched with usage. Stockholding is an expensive business. The costs have to be weighed against losses which may occur if the company is unable to supply customers or the operational needs of the factory. Storage costs include the loss of interest, the overhead costs of the stores and possibly loss due to obsolescence or deterioration. The practice of storekeeping varies widely but material control is concerned with the following:

(*a*) deciding on the items to be held in stock and the requirements to meet planned production;

(*b*) ensuring that material of the correct quality and quantity is available as and when required;

(*c*) providing information for the purchasing department on future requirements together with the expected delivery dates;

(*d*) the provision of records of movements into and out of stores and of materials used for each order;

(*e*) economy in storage and ordering costs and the effect of price reductions for bulk purchases.

A general stock list should be maintained for the use of stores staff and for production control, purchasing and technical requirements. This list should provide the description, the code numbers, dimensions and units of issue (litres, grammes, for example).

## 10.2 Levels of Stock

The fixing of stock levels is difficult and frequent revision is necessary due to changing conditions. Where information and facilities are available, statistical and scientific methods can be used, but these methods are outside the scope of this book.

For most purposes the following system is appropriate. A material record card should be kept for each item of stock on which is listed:

(i) location symbol and bin number;

(ii) description and code number of the item;

(iii) maximum, minimum, re-order level and re-order quantity;

(iv) quantity reserved for specific jobs;

(v) quantity on order still awaiting delivery.

There may also be a record of receipts, issues and balance in hand, although this may be recorded on a separate sheet.

### (a) Re-order Level

The object of this stock level is to prevent stock falling below the minimum. In this calculation it is necessary to assume that there will be maximum consumption and that the supplier will take the maximum period to supply the goods. If the maximum consumption is 250 units per week and the supplier takes two to four weeks to deliver, then the calculation is as follows:

$$\text{Maximum consumption} \times \text{Maximum delivery period}$$
$$= 250 \times 4 = \underline{\underline{1\,000 \text{ units}}}$$

### (b) Minimum Stock Level

This is the lowest level to which the balance can be allowed to fall, and is a danger signal, indicating that action must be taken to avoid a *stock out*. In this calculation it is assumed that there will be normal consumption during the normal waiting period. If consumption is 150 units per week for a period of three weeks the minimum stock level is calculated as follows:

$$\text{Re-order level } less \text{ Normal consumption during normal re-order period}$$
$$= 1\,000 \text{ units } less\ (150 \times 3) = \underline{\underline{550 \text{ units}}}$$

### (c) Maximum Level

This is the highest permitted stock level, and is set with the object of restraining excessive investment in stocks, economizing in storage space and avoiding losses in perishable goods.

This method of calculation begins with the quantity at re-order level and expects minimum consumption during the shortest delivery time.

$$\text{Re-order level } less \text{ (Minimum consumption} \times \text{Minimum re-order period)}$$
$$plus \text{ Re-order quantity of, say, 250}$$
$$= 1\,000 \text{ units } less\ (100 \text{ units} \times 2 \text{ weeks}) \ plus\ 250$$
$$= 800 + 250 = \underline{\underline{1\,050 \text{ units}}}$$

### (d) Re-order Quantity

This is the standard quantity to order in normal circumstances. The re-order quantity has to be reviewed from time to time and amended where necessary, and consideration should be given to the rate of consumption and the delivery time.

### (e) Economic Order Quantity (EOQ)

The most favourable ordering quantity can be calculated by using a formula, although applying this to each item held in stock would be quite a task. It is easier to prepare a table based on the formula to show the optimum ordering quantity for various amounts of consumption.

The object of the EOQ is to show in particular circumstances the size of the order which provides the lowest stockholding cost per item purchased. The problems involved in this exercise are connected with:

  (i) storage accommodation available;
  (ii) the expenses incurred when placing orders;
  (iii) the cost of storage.

These problems are difficult to solve because of the many variable factors. Storage accommodation may be adequate, for example, but if the effect of EOQ is to increase stocks considerably, then extra costs may be incurred if extra space has to be acquired or rent has to be paid for storage. The cost of placing an order must also account for items such as the cost of stationery, and postage, and the expenses of operating the purchasing department. Records of the transactions will have to be made, the invoices will have to be checked and paid, and the receiving department may incur greater or lesser expenses for storage, stock, management, etc.

The cost of storage includes the cost of running the stores department, as well as the cost of transport and insurance, and costs connected with interest on capital invested in stocks. Stocks may, of course, deteriorate or become obsolete, and you have to allow for any reductions in cost which may result from the receipt of quantity discounts. It will be seen that storage costs increase in direct proportion to the quantities ordered, and in proportion to the average level of materials stored, whereas the cost of re-ordering is reduced as the quantities are increased or as a result of a smaller number of orders placed. This is shown diagrammatically in Fig. 10.1.

A formula for establishing the economic order quantity is as follows:

$$EOQ = \sqrt{\frac{2CO}{S}}$$

where $C$ = Consumption per annum (i.e. usage in units)
      $O$ = Order cost (of placing one order)
      $S$ = Storage and holding of one unit for one year (usually expressed as a percentage of the cost per unit)

**Example 10.1**
Annual consumption     = 1 200 units
Cost of re-ordering     = £5.00
Storage and holding costs = 20% of £1.50 = 30p (unit cost price = £1.50)

$$EOQ = \sqrt{\frac{2CO}{S}} = \sqrt{\frac{2 \times 1\,200 \times £5}{£0.30}} = \sqrt{\frac{12\,000}{0.30}}$$
$$= \sqrt{40\,000}$$
$$= \underline{\underline{200}} \text{ (6 orders per annum)}$$

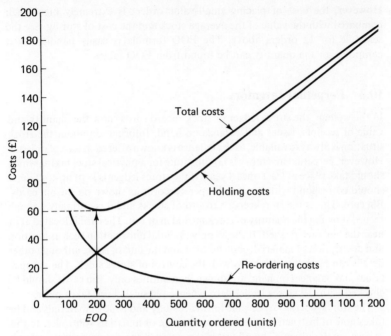

*Fig. 10.1 Economic order quantity*

*Notes:*
(i) Holding costs are low when the quantity ordered is small and high when the quantity ordered is large.
(ii) Re-ordering costs are high when the quantity ordered is small and low when the quantity ordered is large.
(iii) Total costs are lowest at £60, when the quantity ordered is 200 units. This is therefore the *economic order quantity*.

---

This can be illustrated further in the following schedule:

| Orders placed during the year | 1 | 2 | 3 | 4 | 5 | 6 | 10 | 12 |
|---|---|---|---|---|---|---|---|---|
| Quantity re-ordered | 1 200 | 600 | 400 | 300 | 240 | 200 | 120 | 100 |
| Average stock | 600 | 300 | 200 | 150 | 120 | 100 | 60 | 50 |
| | £ | £ | £ | £ | £ | £ | £ | £ |
| Value of average stock @ £1.50 | 900 | 450 | 300 | 225 | 180 | 150 | 90 | 75 |
| Storage and holding cost 20% | 180 | 90 | 60 | 45 | 36 | 30 | 18 | 15 |
| Cost of placing orders | 5 | 10 | 15 | 20 | 25 | 30 | 50 | 60 |
| Total cost per annum | 185 | 100 | 75 | 65 | 61 | 60 | 68 | 75 |

From the formula, it can be seen that when 1 200 units are ordered annually and consumed, 200 is the size of the order which produces the lowest cost per item purchased. When placing six orders during the year, the total cost is estimated at £60. The cost of ordering has little effect on large-value orders.

However, the cost·of placing small-value orders is extremely high when compared with the value of the average stock and the cost of storing. See the schedule for 12 orders above. The EOQ formula is easily handled by a computer, or the quantity can be found from EOQ tables.

## 10.3  Perpetual Inventory

In this system, the stores ledger or stock record cards show the quantity and value of receipts, issues and balance on hand. Information about the stock situation is always available, as the balance is known after each receipt or issue. However, perpetual inventory is no substitute for a physical stocktaking which should take place at least once a year. If the stores ledger is kept up-to-date, it should correspond with the storekeeper's records as shown on the bin cards.

**Bin card.** This is the storekeeper's record of stocks and it is normally a rough record showing the quantity of stock moved in or out. The card is located at or near the bin, rack or shelf. It shows only essential information such as location and description of material, code number and the unit of issue, although other details can be shown if it helps with the control of stores stock. The receipts, issues and balances on hand are shown in quantities only. Bin cards should be checked with the stores ledger card when a physical check takes place.

The storekeeper is responsible for the custody and issue of materials and he takes note of instructions from the production or materials controller. In this respect, materials may be allocated or reserved for future orders and this information, which can be shown on a bin card, shows the *free balance* or stock available for other purposes (Fig. 10.2).

## 10.4  Annual Stocktaking

Stocktaking involves counting, weighing, measuring, listing and valuing raw materials, work-in-progress and finished goods. It is a physical inventory which takes place annually or at other dates during the year. The annual stocktake fits in with the preparation of the final accounts and balance sheet and the requirement that the accounts show a true and fair view. The object is also to verify the accuracy of stock records and to reveal any losses resulting from pilferage, fraud or any other cause. The stocktake shows up any problems or weaknesses in the system or caused by the action of employees. The annual stocktaking usually means that the production departments have to be closed, but this can be avoided if continuous stocktaking is carried out instead.

The plans and procedure for stocktaking should be made in advance by selecting personnel and instructing them in their duties, and arranging for the printing of stock sheets. Information and instructions should also be given to the production and service departments, so that preparations can be made for stocktaking to operate in an orderly manner. If possible, the stock sheets should be written up in advance with the basic information such as description, code number, etc.

| BIN CARD | | | | | | |
|---|---|---|---|---|---|---|
| Description . . . . . . . . . . . . . . | | | Bin number . . . . . . . . . . . . . | | | |
| Maximum stock . . . . . . . . . . | | | Code number . . . . . . . . . . . | | | |
| Minimum stock . . . . . . . . . . . | | | Re-order qty. . . . . . . . . . . . | | | |
| Re-order level . . . . . . . . . . . . | | | Unit of issue . . . . . . . . . . . . . | | | |
| Received | | | Issued | | | Balance |
| Date | Ref. | Quantity | Date | Ref. | Quantity | Quantity |
| | | | | | | |
| | | | | | | |
| | | | | | | |
| | | | | | | |
| | | | | | | |

*Fig. 10.2 A bin card*

Work-in-progress is usually dealt with by taking cost as shown in the cost ledger for each of the unfinished jobs. If the cost is not available through the costing system, a physical check is necessary to determine this, either by a technical estimate or on the basis of a percentage of the materials, labour and other expenses which are relative to the work already carried out. The valuation of work-in-progress will be dealt with in later Units but it should be noted that stocks and work-in-progress normally need to be stated at cost, or if lower, at net realizable value, and reference should be made to SSAP 9. The valuation of work-in-progress should include the prime cost plus a fair share of overheads. Fair overheads include production overheads and those incurred in bringing the product to its present location and condition (see Unit 12).

## 10.5   Stocktaking Procedure

(a) A senior member of the staff should be in control. In many companies stocktaking and investigations into discrepancies would be under the supervision of the internal auditor who is a member of the company staff, and is responsible either to the chief accountant or directly to the management. He works in accordance with an audit programme, and also deals with special assignments on behalf of the management. He surveys the accounting system, makes investigations, suggests improvements and reports generally.

(b) The stocktake should take place during a slack period and, as far as possible, stores departments and storage sections should be closed to normal operations.

(c) When certain items belong to customers or suppliers the items should be distinctly labelled by attaching labels to parts or complete products with string or wire. Labelled items should be kept in a separate area of the stores.

(d) Strict instructions should be issued to the effect that no records of receipts or issues made after stocktaking begins should be entered until the stocktaking is complete. Receipts should be held in the receiving department or in a special storage area and exceptional issues should be noted on the bin card. To avoid unauthorized entries the stock record cards can be ruled off as the stocktaking begins.

(e) Stocks are counted, weighed or measured and when this is not convenient an estimate will be made by someone qualified to make such calculations. The auditor's permission must be received if it is essential to use an estimate instead of an exact amount.

(f) Before a reconciliation can be made between the value of physical stocks and book figures, certain matters have to be dealt with:

(i) materials may have been recorded but the invoice may not have been received, or vice versa;

(ii) goods may have been drawn from the bins and held in containers ready for assembly but they may not have been charged to the accounts;

(iii) account will have to be taken of materials in service vans, on constructional sites or away from the factory being processed or repaired.

There is a variety of different ways of recording the inventory and the example in Fig. 10.3 shows that it should be possible to write up the first three columns before the beginning of the stocktaking.

## 10.6   Investigating Discrepancies and Adjusting the Stock Control Account

The stock discrepancy report shows the difference between the number of items counted in the physical check, and the number shown on the bin card and on the stock record card. It provides information to enable the auditor or selected employees to examine all the records (bin cards, stock record cards, materials requisitions, goods received notes) and to reconcile the quantities indicated, by establishing the cause of the variances (Fig. 10.4).

Clerical or arithmetical errors may be responsible for discrepancies, and requisitions may have been lost, mislaid or posted more than once. It may be necessary to check the basic documents connected with the receipt and issue of materials or to seek explanations from the storekeeper and other people. Perhaps the issue or receipt was entered on the wrong card or the error might

| | INVENTORY SHEET | | | | | | |
|---|---|---|---|---|---|---|---|
| Department .............. | | | | Sheet no. ...... | | | |
| | | | | Date ......... | | | |
| Stocks recorded by ......... | | Checked by ........ | | Priced by ........ | | | |
| Bin no. | Description | Code no. | Quantity | Unit | Unit price | Value |
| | | | | | | |
| | | | | | | |
| | | | | | | |
| | | | | | | |
| | | | | | | |

Fig. 10.3 An inventory sheet

| | INVENTORY | | | | | | | | |
|---|---|---|---|---|---|---|---|---|---|
| | Stock Discrepancy Report | | | | | | | | |
| | | | | | | Sheet no ........ | | | |
| | | | | | | Date .......... | | | |
| Department .............. | | | | | Investigated by ............. | | | | |
| | | | | Bin card | | Stock record card | | | |
| Bin no. | Description | Code no. | Actual quantity | Quantity | | | | Value | | Remarks |
| | | | | + | − | + | − | + | − | |
| | | | | | | | | £ p | £ p | |
| | | | | | | | | | | |
| | | | | | | | | | | |
| | | | | | | | | | | |

Fig. 10.4 A stock discrepancy report

date from the last stocktake. If pilferage or fraud is the cause, improved security arrangements will be needed.

When the stocktaking and investigations are complete, there will be a list of two columns, one of items and values which have to be added (stock surpluses and revaluations) and the second column which reduces the quantity and value of stocks (stock deficiencies and items written off as depreciated or obsolete). The Stock Account or Stock Control Account will have to be debited with the surpluses and credited with the deficiencies.

## 10.7    Obsolete, Slow Moving and Dormant Stocks

In Statement of Standard Accounting Practice No. 9 it is recommended that stocks should be valued at cost or net realizable value, whichever is lower, and the items should be reviewed in order to deal with those that are obsolete, slow moving or dormant.

Obsolescence is the decline in value of an asset as a result of new inventions or improved designs. The slow movement or dormancy of an item may be related to obsolescence, or may be caused by over-stocking, made by mistake, or because of unforeseen changes since the time when the purchases or manufacturing requisition was issued. When it is established that some or all of a particular item is no longer usable or it is doubtful whether it will be required in future, this should be written off or written down (reduced in value).

One method of dealing with the slow movement of stocks is to fix a period when it is considered that their value will be a nil value, and to write off a proportion or percentage of the cost each year. For example, if a five-year period was chosen, and provided the item has not moved during the past year, then 20 per cent of the value is written off. This continues year by year and if the inventory list has five columns, one for each year, to show the value written off at each stage of the non-movement, it provides useful information on the real value of stocks and acts as a signal to the relevant department to investigate the possibility of using the items in some other way. Materials may also be dormant due to deterioration caused by bad storage conditions or faulty handling. Items may be damaged, or rusty, or in a dirty condition, or may be useless because of storage in damp conditions. They should be written down or written off, and steps taken to avoid future losses of this kind.

## 10.8    Continuous Stocktaking

The time between successive annual stocktakings is a long one and it may be advisable to check certain types of materials more frequently. This applies where there is a breaking of bulk causing losses or where there is a large quantity of off-cuts, such as with steel and timber. More frequent checking is required in these circumstances. Continuous stocktaking is a system which proceeds throughout the year, with the object of checking each item at least once during the year. It has the advantage of using experienced stocktakers who check a certain number of items each day. The shutdown of production departments is avoided, while those who might carry out frauds or falsify records can be deterred by changing each day the area where the checking takes place. Continuous stocktaking helps the stores manager to be kept informed more frequently of any problems and discrepancies found by the auditors.

## 10.9   Stores Layout and Methods of Storage

The stores department should be located somewhere close to, and with easy access to, the production departments. There may be a large central stores or a number of smaller stores. The business may commence with a large central stores but as expansion proceeds it is more difficult to situate the stores close to the production departments.

The stores department may be sectionalized, with a raw material store for primary materials such as iron, steel and timber, and a general store for other purchases and items manufactured by the factory and held for subsequent assembly or for sale as spare parts. There may be sub-stores where it is more convenient to hold certain stock adjacent to a production centre. Sub-stores can be used for partly-finished stock and sub-assemblies which are not due for final assembly until a later date. Finished stocks awaiting sale and dispatch may also be held in a separate store.

When materials arrive, they must be identified, labelled and kept in a place where they can easily be found. Goods of particular classes should be stored in their respective sections. Firms need either a good coding system or well-displayed signs, on or over the aisles and at the bins or shelves. In a large store, the floor plan should be posted in various parts of the building and location lists should be prepared to enable staff to find the various types of goods.

The following matters have to be considered when establishing a new store or expanding an existing one:

(a)  the size and location of the site and the services available, such as water, gas and electricity;

(b)  ease of access to rail, road, inland waterways and possibly sea-borne traffic;

(c)  the amount and type of materials to be stored and the handling requirements;

(d)  the kind of building needed (single- or multi-storey) or modifications necessary to enable the use of fork-lift trucks, conveyors, hoists, overhead cranes, lifts, etc.;

(e)  the type of lighting and amount of heating required;

(f)  the space needed for the receiving and issuing sections, and the accommodation necessary for office staff;

(g)  the quantity and type of fixtures, fittings and equipment needed, such as bins, racks, shelving, cupboards, pallets, etc. and any special flooring requirements;

(h)  the size of doors, aisles and platforms, for easy access;

(*i*) the storage of any special materials requiring security or safety precautions, including additional ventilation;
(*j*) the provision of firefighting equipment, hydrants, sprinklers, etc.;
(*k*) the provision of toilet, cloakroom and welfare facilities.

## 10.10  Recording of Receipts and Issues

The stores ledger consists of the stock record cards which are basic records in accounting for materials and supplies. The ledger is a perpetual inventory showing the materials received into stock, materials issued and the balance on hand, and sometimes includes other information such as material reserved. The cards are also referred to as stores ledger cards or the stock control cards. The kind of information shown on the card includes the name of the item and its code or part number, and its location in the stores, showing the bin, shelf or rack where the item can be found. The card may also show the unit in which the item is purchased, or issued and a record of purchases, with the source of supply and possibly the maximum, minimum, re-order level and re-order quantity. A typical form is shown in Fig. 10.5.

## 10.11  Material Costing

When materials and supplies are issued, the material requisition has to be priced and details of the issue are entered on the stores ledger card. Materials which are purchased for particular orders are kept in a separate section of the stores and are not usually priced from the stores ledger as they are charged direct to the Cost Account when the invoice is received. This method is known as the *specific cost method* and it means that the actual cost of goods purchased specially is charged to a specific Cost Account.

There is no one method of valuing stores issues which can be used under all conditions, but the accountant and the management must select the method(s) which they consider appropriate and must use them consistently when pricing material requisitions.

When goods are perishable or liable to deteriorate the physical stock should be issued on a FIFO basis. With non-perishable goods this does not matter, and it is important to appreciate that there is no connection between the order of issue of the physical stock and the method of pricing, which is a bookkeeping procedure.

The usual methods adopted for the pricing of issues are as follows:

(*a*) first in, first out (FIFO);
(*b*) last in, first out (LIFO);
(*c*) simple average cost;
(*d*) weighted average cost (AVCO);
(*e*) standard cost;
(*f*) replacement cost;
(*g*) base stock.

STOCK LEDGER CARD

Location . . . . . . . . . . . . . . .
Code number . . . . . . . . . . . .
Description . . . . . . . . . . . . .

Unit . . . . . . . . . . . . . . .
Delivery time . . . . . . . . . . .
Re-order level . . . . . . . . . . .

Re-order quantity . . . . . . . . .
Maximum stock . . . . . . . . .
Minimum stock . . . . . . . . .

| | Receipts | | | | Issues | | | | | Balance | | |
|---|---|---|---|---|---|---|---|---|---|---|---|---|---|
| Date | Ref. | Quantity | Price £ | Value £ | Date | Ref. | Quantity | Price £ | Value £ | | Quantity | Price £ | Value £ |
| | | | | | | | | | | | | | |
| | | | | | | | | | | | | | |

Fig. 10.5 A stock ledger card

## (a) First In, First Out

In this method, the price of the oldest stocks is used, regardless of the order in which the goods leave the store. The most recent purchases have to be accumulated until they equal the new quantity balance, then the previous price or prices can be used to calculate the value of the issue.

**Example 10.2**

The stores ledger card shows a stock of 65 items at a total value of £539.50 and a requisition is received for 15 items. The receipts were as follows:

| Ref. | Quantity | Price each £ | Value £ |
|------|----------|--------------|---------|
| A | 10 | 7.000 | 70.000 |
| B | 15 | 8.000 | 120.000 |
| C | 20 | 8.500 | 170.000 |
| D | 20 | 8.975 | 179.500 |
| | 65 | | £539.500 |

The entries are shown in Fig. 10.6.

The new balance is 50 (65 *less* 15) items, and to select the price on a FIFO basis, work backwards using the most recent purchases to accumulate stocks, until 50 is reached. This consists of D 20 + C 20 + 10 of B. The prices to be used for pricing the requisition include the remaining 5 of B at £8.00 each and 10 of A at £7.00 each, which is a total of £110.00.

The advantages are:

(i) prices are based on cost and no profit or loss can arise in the accounts when this method of pricing is used;

(ii) the inventory value which results from the method of pricing is normally a fair representation of current commercial values as the inventory value shown represents the most recent purchases;

(iii) the method is well-founded as it assumes that goods are issued in order of receipt;

(iv) it is an easy method to operate.

The disadvantages are:

(i) issue prices may not be equivalent to current values;

(ii) clerical errors may be made because of having to select the appropriate prices for issues and the correct quantities and prices when valuing the stock;

(iii) with changing prices, a comparison of the cost of one job with another can be misleading;

(iv) when prices are increasing, the charge to production will be low, and the replacement cost will probably be much higher. This tends to overstate the profits and reduces the amount of working capital if the profits are paid out as dividends.

## (b) Last In, First Out

In this method of pricing, issues are priced using the cost of the most recent

STOCK LEDGER CARD                                    (FIFO)

Location......... A.10
Code number...... 21c
Description...... Pinion, R.H.

Unit........... 1
Delivery time... 2-4 weeks
Re-order level... 100

Re-order quantity ..... 120
Maximum stock ..... 200
Minimum stock ..... 40

| Receipts | | | | | Issues | | | | | Balance | | |
|---|---|---|---|---|---|---|---|---|---|---|---|---|
| Date | Ref. | Quantity | Price £ | Value £ | Date | Ref. | Quantity | Price £ | Value £ | Quantity | Price £ | Value £ |
| 19.. | | | | | 19.. | | | | | | | |
| JAN. 1 | S.387 | 10 | 7.000 | 70.00 | | | | | | 10 | | 70.00 |
| " 7 | " | 15 | 8.000 | 120.00 | | | | | | 25 | | 190.00 |
| " 10 | " | 20 | 8.500 | 170.00 | | | | | | 45 | | 360.00 |
| " 17 | " | 20 | 8.975 | 179.50 | | | | | | 65 | | 539.50 |
| | | | | | JAN.19 | 21 942 | 15 | | | | | |
| | | | | | | | 10 | 7.000 | 70.00 | | | |
| | | | | | | | 5 | 8.000 | 40.00 | | | |
| | | | | | | | | | | 50 | | 429.50 |

Fig. 10.6 A FIFO stock ledger card

purchases. When further issues are made, the latest price is taken from the stock which remains, and each time a new batch is received, the price changes to the value of the most recent purchase. This may result in several receipts being only partly issued on the stock card.

The advantages are:

(i) issues are priced at cost and no profits or losses arise;

(ii) the price of issues is fairly close to current values;

(iii) the charge to production is close to current values and replacement costs;

(iv) the information to management is an indication of current costs and is more realistic.

The disadvantages are:

(i) inventory values are based on the oldest stocks and may not correspond to current prices;

(ii) clerical errors can arise as the records are somewhat involved, with different quantities and prices on a stock card which have to be kept and used when pricing issues or valuing the inventory;

(iii) a comparison of the costs of different jobs may be misleading.

The entries are shown in Fig. 10.7.

### (c) Simple Average Cost

The simple average cost method is easy to operate and may be satisfactory when prices are stable but it often gives ridiculous results and has not much to recommend it. Issues are not based on actual cost, and a profit or loss may arise because of the use of fictitious prices which are calculated by averaging the prices instead of using a weighted average, by taking into account quantities and values. The price is fixed by adding the prices of receipts represented by the stock-in-hand and dividing by the number of receipts. For example, two receipts with unit prices of £7 and £8 are added together and divided by two, giving a simple average of £7.50. This method ignores the quantities and when these differ, discrepancies arise in the accounts. For general use it cannot be recommended, but an example is given in Fig. 10.8 to illustrate these discrepancies. The simple average prices are shown with the balance on hand, and 50 at £8.492 is £424.60, compared with the value of £417.715, giving an error of £6.885.

The advantage is that the system is simple to operate.

The disadvantages are:

(i) profits or losses may arise from its use;

(ii) it gives inaccurate figures when pricing issues or valuing stocks and cost sheets can present misleading information.

### (d) Weighted Average Cost

The weighted average cost method requires a calculation each time an invoice is received for the receipt of goods. The quantity purchased is added to the present stock-in-hand and the invoice value is added to the present value. The

## STOCK LEDGER CARD                                      (LIFO)

Location ........ A.10
Code number ...... 21c
Description ...... Pinion R.H.

Unit ............ 1
Delivery time .... 2-4 weeks
Re-order level .... 100

Re-order quantity ... 120
Maximum stock ...... 200
Minimum stock ...... 40

| Receipts | | | | | Issues | | | | | Balance | | |
|---|---|---|---|---|---|---|---|---|---|---|---|---|
| Date | Ref. | Quantity | Price £ | Value £ | Date | Ref. | Quantity | Price £ | Value £ | Quantity | Price £ | Value £ |
| 19.. | | | | | 19.. | | | | | | | |
| JAN. 1 | S.387 | 10 | 7.000 | 70.000 | | | | | | 10 | | 70.000 |
| " 7 | " | 15 | 8.000 | 120.000 | | | | | | 25 | | 190.000 |
| " 10 | " | 20 | 8.500 | 170.000 | | | | | | 45 | | 360.000 |
| " 17 | " | 20 | 8.975 | 179.500 | | | | | | 65 | | 539.500 |
| | | | | | JAN. 19 | 21 942 | 15 | 8.975 | 134.625 | 50 | | 404.875 |

Fig. 10.7 A LIFO stock ledger card

STOCK LEDGER CARD                    (SIMPLE AVERAGE COST)

Location ........... A.10
Code number ....... 21c
Description ....... Prior R.H.

Unit ............... 1
Delivery time ..... 2-4 weeks
Re-order level .... 100

Re-order quantity .. 120
Maximum stock ..... 200
Minimum stock ..... 40

| Receipts | | | | | Issues | | | | | Balance | | |
|---|---|---|---|---|---|---|---|---|---|---|---|---|
| Date | Ref. | Quantity | Price £ | Value £ | Date | Ref. | Quantity | Price £ | Value £ | Quantity | Price £ | Value £ |
| 19.. | | | | | 19.. | | | | | | | |
| JAN. 1 | 5.387 | 10 | 7.000 | 70.000 | | | | | | 10 | 7.000 | 70.000 |
| " 7 | " | 15 | 8.000 | 120.000 | | | | | | 25 | 7.500 | 190.000 |
| " 10 | " | 20 | 8.500 | 170.000 | | | | | | 45 | 7.835 | 360.000 |
| " 17 | " | 20 | 8.975 | 179.500 | | | | | | 65 | 8.119 | 539.500 |
| | | | | | JAN. 19 | 21.942 | 15 | 8.119 | 121.785 | 50 | 8.492 | 417.715 |

Fig. 10.8 A simple average cost stock ledger card

new quantity is then divided into the new value to obtain the weighted average. This involves a greater amount of clerical labour, but this method has much to recommend it, especially where the materials are subject to wide price fluctuations, and where they are carried in stores for a relatively long period. When using the weighted average price, the larger the multiplier the greater the error, and it may be necessary to use five places of decimals in the unit prices so as to avoid a discrepancy between the balances on the stores cards and the balance shown in the Stores Control Account.

In costing exercises, whenever materials are returned to stock, they should be valued at the price of issue, in order to cancel out and credit the Cost Account with the original amount charged. When using the weighted average method a new unit price has to be calculated when materials are returned. Unit prices are also calculated each time there is a receipt of materials. The entries are shown in Fig. 10.9.

The advantages are:

(i) the price is based on cost, and the method is generally accurate, provided the unit price is carefully set. With this method, no profits or losses arise.

(ii) it is a sensible system which operates on the basis that if parts are identical the prices should also be the same;

(iii) it avoids the involved calculations and records which occur with FIFO and LIFO, and as prices are only fixed on receipts, it simplifies the procedure.

The disadvantage is that there is usually a need to fix unit prices to several decimal places.

### (e) Standard Cost

This method uses a predetermined cost and can be applied whether or not a system of standard costing is used. A standard cost is not a rough estimate, but a cost fixed after a careful study of all the factors involved in purchasing and producing the goods. As a fixed price is used for issues during the period of account, it is only necessary to keep a record of quantities. The variance which is found when comparing actual cost with standard cost is written off to a Material Price Variance Account, either when the item is taken into stock or at the date of issue.

The advantages are:

(i) there is a reduction in clerical costs, as the continual calculations and recording of unit costs is avoided; it is therefore simple to operate;

(ii) the system eliminates the variations in cost which occur with other methods and makes cost comparisons much easier;

(iii) it indicates to what extent the purchasing department is operating efficiently and securing supplies at the recognized prices.

The disadvantages are:

(i) standard prices have to be set carefully when the system is installed or a new price is fixed and revisions are necessary from period to period;

STOCK LEDGER CARD   (WEIGHTED AVERAGE COST)   AVCO

Location ........ A.10 ........
Code number ...... 21c ......
Description ...... Pinion R.H. ......

Unit ............ 1 ............
Delivery time ...... 2-4 weeks ......
Re-order level ...... 100 ......

Re-order quantity ...... 120 ......
Maximum stock ...... 200 ......
Minimum stock ...... 40 ......

| | Receipts | | | | | Issues | | | | | Balance | | |
|---|---|---|---|---|---|---|---|---|---|---|---|---|---|---|
| Date | Ref. | Quantity | Price £ | Value £ | | Date | Ref. | Quantity | Price £ | Value £ | | Quantity | Price £ | Value £ |
| 19.. | | | | | | 19.. | | | | | | | | |
| JAN. 1 | S.387 | 10 | 7.000 | 70.000 | | | | | | | | 10 | 7.000 | 70.000 |
| " 7 | " | 15 | 8.000 | 120.000 | | | | | | | | 25 | 7.600 | 190.000 |
| " 10 | " | 20 | 8.500 | 170.000 | | | | | | | | 45 | 8.000 | 360.000 |
| " 17 | " | 20 | 8.975 | 179.500 | | | | | | | | 65 | 8.300 | 539.500 |
| | | | | | | JAN. 19 | 2196 21742 | 15 | 8.300 | 124.500 | | 50 | 8.300 | 415.000 |

Fig. 10.9 A weighted average cost stock ledger card

(ii) profits and losses arise due to the variations in prices;

(iii) when prices change, the issues do not represent current values until the standard prices are revised.

### (f) Replacement Cost

In this method, the intention is to price issues at the current buying price, with the object of showing product costs at the replacement or current cost. This may be a practical method when the item to be sold is almost entirely made up of raw material, but the maintenance of a list of current prices for masses of different items and a large variety of raw materials is a considerable problem. This method not only involves raw materials, but also the cost of labour and expenses for the manufactured items which are held in stock.

The advantages are:

(i) the method used and calculations are comparatively simple;

(ii) the value of the issues are at current prices.

The disadvantage is that when there are frequent price changes, it is difficult to maintain price lists which record the current costs.

### (g) Base Stock

It is assumed that a minimum amount of raw materials or items should be carried in stock as a reserve or buffer stock in case of emergencies. Such stock is treated in a similar manner to fixed assets, as it is held at the original cost, but stock above the base may be priced on some other basis.

There are one or two other methods. One is the *highest in, first out* (HIFO) where the most costly items are disposed of first, but it is a difficult method to operate. Then there is *next in, first out* (NIFO) which charges the price of materials ordered but not yet received. It too is difficult to administer as future prices may have to be estimated and problems arise when reconciling the stock valuations and the accounts at the end of the period.

The object of material costing is to recover costs and there are certain kinds of materials which are subject to losses, such as evaporation during storage or at the time of issue, when breaking bulk or cutting off. In order to credit the stores ledger with the amount debited, an attempt is made to do this by fixing an *inflated price* which allows for the wastage.

For example, assuming there is an estimated loss of 10 per cent and the material cost is £9 per kilogramme, the inflated price is:

$$\frac{100}{90} \times £9 = \underline{\underline{£10 \text{ per kg}}}$$

## 10.12  Scrap Material

In many manufacturing processes a certain amount of scrap such as turnings and borings is anticipated, and there is also scrap consisting of defective items caused by poor workmanship, bad design, faulty tools or equipment or the use of sub-standard materials.

*Waste* is generally taken as having no value, whereas *scrap* is considered to have some value, although the material cannot be used for its original purpose. It is necessary to place a fair value on scrap, although this may be difficult because of market fluctuations. The value of scrap taken into stock should take account of the market price and should allow for the cost of handling and disposal. Depending on the procedure adopted, the following entries should be made.

> *Debit*  Scrap Sales Account
> *Credit* Original Cost Account
>               or
>           Overhead Expenses Account
> *or*
> *Debit*  Scrap Materials Account
> *Credit* Original Cost Account
>               or
>           Overhead Expenses Account

Whenever possible or convenient, the original job or process should be credited with the value of scrap but if it is impracticable the credit should be set off against the Overhead Expenses Account.

If materials purchased for a specific job prove to be defective, the rectification cost should be charged to that job as a direct expense, and credit should be given for any allowance made by the supplier. In other cases, the cost of rectification should be charged to a Spoilage Account and treated as an overhead expense. The Spoilage Account should be credited with any sales of defective materials.

Scrap may be collected or may be allowed to accumulate in the stores before being sold at a convenient date or at an advantageous price.

If any profits are shown in the accounts for the sale of scrap or defective work, they should be treated as *other income*.

## 10.13   Exercises

1.  Your company operates a large engineering company with a department which is concerned with stock control. What are the functions of the stock controller and why is it essential that this department is operated efficiently?

2.  In periods of (*a*) rapidly rising prices and (*b*) rapidly falling prices, state which of the following methods you would recommend for pricing material requisitions and valuing stocks at the end of the financial year:

   (i)  First in, first out method;
   (ii) Average cost method;

   (iii)  Last in, first out method;

   (iv)  Standard cost;

    (v)  Replacement cost.

In your answer, briefly describe the characteristics of each method and make your recommendations.

# Unit Eleven

# Accounting for Labour Costs

## 11.1 Direct and Indirect Labour

(a) **Direct Labour**

Labour cost may be *direct* or *indirect*. Direct labour cost is the wages paid to employees who are working directly on the material and altering its form or construction. *Conversion costs* in the manufacturing departments include direct labour costs, direct expenses as well as absorbed production overheads (see Unit 12.3). Direct wages are the cost of time spent in actual production or the (wages) cost of performing the main task or service which can be measured and charged to a cost unit. The employee on direct labour produces for stock or for a particular customer, and his wages are charged direct to a *stock order number* or *code*, or to the customer's order number.

(b) **Indirect Labour**

Indirect labour cost is the wages cost of employees whose time cannot be measured or identified with specific items or products. The indirect worker does not change the form or construction of a product or perform a main service chargeable to a cost unit. The salary of a superintendent or inspector and the wages paid to a maintenance engineer or truck driver in a factory are examples of indirect labour costs. The employee on indirect labour earns a salary or wage which is classed as an *overhead expense* and is chargeable to a *standing order number* or *code*. These expenses are then analysed and shown either as departmental overhead expenses or service department expenses.

With the advance of technology, it is becoming more difficult to identify labour as direct or indirect, and when there are difficulties it is necessary to apply the *test of convenience*. If it is possible to measure the time spent, labour can be classified as direct. For example, it may be very inconvenient to measure and record short operations: in this case it would be easier to treat the wages for such workers as indirect costs and charge them to an Overhead Expense Account. The spray-painting of a large number of small, but different, items every hour of the working day is an example of this problem.

## 11.2 Methods of Labour Remuneration

There are many different methods of paying for work, based broadly on time or production, and the elaborate nature of some schemes makes the subject a complicated one. Wages calculated on time tend to be independent of production, whereas wages based on production usually involve some form of incentive scheme, and tend to be independent of time.

*Remuneration* is the reward for labour and service, and *incentive* is the stimulation of effort and effectiveness by offering monetary inducement or enhanced facilities. We shall consider labour remuneration and incentive systems under the following headings:

time rates;

piece rates;

bonus systems.

## (a) Time Rates

**1. Time rates at ordinary wage levels.** This system operates by paying labour for the time spent rather than the work produced. The employee is paid on a time rate, generally referred to as a *day rate*, and payment is by the hour, day or week. Wages are calculated by taking the rate per hour and multiplying this by the total hours worked as shown on the clock card or time sheet. Any premium due for overtime or any allowance for shiftwork is added on.

Some occupations are unsuitable for payment on the basis of output produced, especially those requiring a high degree of skill or when the output or degree of efficiency is difficult to measure. Examples are work in process industries, such as chemical and oil refining, where the operator has little or no control over the rate of production. The day rate method is also favoured where a worker is learning a job or trade.

**2. Time rates at high wage levels.** This method provides a high day rate payment for a continuously high standard of performance and productivity. Because payments are well above the normal rates paid to workers elsewhere, labour is attracted to the firm. This factor enables the firm to select good employees, but supervision has to be carefully organized in order to maintain output at a high level. Like the time rates at ordinary wage levels this system is simple to operate, but in return for a much higher day rate, it demands a much higher standard of performance and output from workers. This method can result in lower unit costs and a reduction in fixed overhead cost per unit as against the time rate at ordinary wage levels because of the possibility of greater production.

**3. Measured day-work.** During the last thirty years, schemes have been introduced which pay employees above the time rate at ordinary wage levels by measuring their output over a period of time, say three months, and paying them on the basis of their efficiency and performance during that time. An assessment is therefore made of each employee's performance during the previous period and the payment made is related to the level of performance. This system replaces the piece-work systems described below. The main reason for the introduction of this method of remuneration was that workers found their earnings fluctuated widely from week to week because of incorrect estimates or bad rate fixing. Arguments and disputes frequently arose as new piece-work prices were fixed and new work was issued. At the end of each period, the worker's efficiency is reviewed and, if necessary, the rate is adjusted for payment during the next quarter.

This system benefits an organization because it reduces paperwork, saves clerical work and means less time will be spent in calculating wages. Calculating the payment for each job or operation under piece-work conditions is a costly business especially for machining jobs where the time spent on each item is very short. Furthermore there is a better atmosphere on the shop floor because no time is lost disputing who will do which job, and what time should be allowed. Although payment is based on output of a previous period the system is referred to as day-work because the employee receives a regular rate per hour for a fairly long period.

### (b) Piece Rates

This method of remuneration is related to effort, and varies with the rate of production, so payment depends on results, and inducements are offered to the worker to increase output. The aim is to reduce the works cost per article by spreading the total overhead cost of the factory over a greater number of articles.

Monetary incentives for extra output are either *individual*, when a worker receives a reward for personal effort, or *collective*, when the employees share a bonus earned in a group scheme.

Collective schemes should be:
  (i) fair both to employer and employee;
  (ii) simple for clerical staff and employees to operate and understand;
  (iii) in conformity with any national, local or trade agreements;
  (iv) clearly defined, with worthwhile and attainable objectives, and with regulations which cannot be misunderstood;
  (v) carefully prepared, with allowances being set only after the job or work has been properly assessed. The piece rates or time allowance per job once fixed, should remain unchanged unless methods or conditions change.

The *piece rate* system of payment can be considered under three headings:
  (i) straight piece rate;
  (ii) piece rates with guaranteed day rates;
  (iii) differential piece rates.

**1.   Straight piece rate.** A straight piece rate is the payment of a fixed sum per fixed unit produced, regardless of the time taken. Piece-work conditions provide for payment on the basis of jobs completed, units produced or operations performed, and the straight piece rate enables a worker to receive a wage in direct relation to the amount of work completed. Under ordinary day rate methods of payment, a fast worker receives only the rate of pay of a slow worker, so there is little incentive for workers to do more than is necessary. A variation of the straight piece rate is the standard time system based on the *standard hour*, which allows a worker a fixed time for each operation: it is a hypothetical unit, to represent the amount of work which should be performed in one hour at standard performance.

**Example 11.1**

| Piece rate | 10 pieces at 20p per piece = £2 |
| --- | --- |
| Standard time rate | Standard time for 10 pieces = 1 hour |
| | Standard rate for 1 hour = £2 |

If 10 pieces are made in 45 minutes, instead of one hour, the worker would earn £2.

The advantages of a straight piece rate are:
  (i) it is simple to understand and to calculate;
 (ii) there is a direct incentive to increase output;
(iii) individual output can be easily and quickly determined;
(iv) unit costs are reduced.

The disadvantages are:
  (i) no payment or allowance is normally made for unsuitable materials, variations in the efficiency of tools and machinery, or production delays, which are matters outside the control of the worker;
 (ii) varying rates of output between different workers may result in labour troubles.

**2.  Piece rates with guaranteed day rates.** Incentive schemes should not be affected by matters outside the employees' control, but there are a number of factors which restrict the output and earnings of those on piece rates. These include shortage of materials, unsuitable materials, power failures, machine breakdowns and delays caused by inefficient planning and progressing. It was, in fact, the loss of earnings of those on straight piece rates that led to the introduction of piece rates with guaranteed day rate.

Straight piece rates have mainly been superseded by piece rates with guaranteed day or guaranteed weekly wages. The following examples illustrate the working of piece rates with guaranteed weekly wage and the standard time rate system.

**Example 11.2**

Day rate and guaranteed weekly wage of £2 per hour for 40 hours gives £80 per week;

piece rate of £1.25 per unit, with guaranteed weekly wage of £80;

standard time rate of an allowance of $37\frac{1}{2}$ minutes per piece with guaranteed weekly wage of £80;

the rate of £1.25 per piece and $37\frac{1}{2}$ minutes per piece are equivalent allowances, but in the following examples the rate paid is £1.25 per piece.

| | Workman A | Produces 80 pieces in 40 hours | |
| --- | --- | --- | --- |
| | | Earnings = 80 × £1.25 = £100 (paid) | |
| | | *Less* Day rate wages | £ 80 |
| | | Bonus earned | £ 20 |

Workman B    Produces 70 pieces in 40 hours
Earnings = 70 × £1.25 = £87.50 (paid)
*Less* Day rate wages    £80.00

Bonus earned    £  7.50

Workman C    Produces 55 pieces in 40 hours
Earnings = 55 × £1.25 = £68.75
Day rate wages    £80.00 (paid)

Addition to earnings
to reach £80    £11.25 (deficit)

Incentive schemes are introduced for two main reasons:
   (i) to enable employees to earn extra wages for increased output;
   (ii) to increase the level of output thereby reducing unit costs.

Table 11.1 shows how unit cost is reduced as the level of output rises.

**Table 11.1 The effect of fixed overhead on the cost per unit**

| Workman | Units produced | Price per unit | Time taken | Direct material cost (50p per unit) | Direct labour cost | Variable overhead cost | Fixed overhead cost | Total cost | Cost per unit |
|---|---|---|---|---|---|---|---|---|---|
|  |  | £ | hours | £ | £ | £ | £ | £ | £ |
| A | 80 | 1.00 | 40 | 40.00 | 80.00 | 60.00 | 180.00 | 360.00 | 4.50 |
| B | 64 | 1.00 | 40 | 32.00 | 64.00 | 48.00 | 180.00 | 324.00 | 5.06 |
| C | 53 | 1.00 | 40 | 26.50 | 60.00 | 39.75 | 180.00 | 306.25 | 5.78 |

*Notes:*
(i) Workmen are on straight piece-work with a guaranteed weekly wage of £60.
(ii) A earns £80; B earns £64 and C earns £53 but receives an extra £7 to reach the guaranteed wage of £60.
(iii) Fixed costs included in the cost per unit are A £2.25; B £2.81 and C £3.40, an increase of 56p between A and B and 59p between B and C.
(iv) The difference in *cost per unit* is the extra share of fixed cost of 56p between A and B, and between B and C it is an extra share of fixed cost of 59p per unit, plus 13p, which is the addition (£7 ÷ 53) for guaranteed wage.

**3.   Differential piece rates.** This is the *Taylor* system which fixes a standard price or time for doing a job, but there are two piece rates, a *low rate* for output below standard and a *high rate* for production above standard. This incentive method was later modified by Gantt and Merrick.
   The advantages of the differential piece rate system are:

(i) it provides a very strong incentive to fast workers;
(ii) it is simple to understand and work;
(iii) only the best workers are attracted to the firm.

The disadvantages are:
(i) the beginner or slow learner is penalized;
(ii) the quality of the work may suffer as workers strive to reach high output.

### (c) Bonus Systems

**1. Premium bonus schemes** (individual bonus systems). These are incentive systems which allow for the payment of day rate plus a proportion of the time saved when the worker performs the task in less than the time allowed. Thus any gain from increased output is shared between the employee and the employer. The employer is protected against high rate-fixing and has the advantage of diminishing labour cost. Premium bonus schemes also have the following features:

(i) basic time rate is usually guaranteed;
(ii) the hourly rate of workers increases but not in proportion to output;
(iii) as a result of the above, rate-fixing which is set too high does not have the same effect as it would with piece rates;
(iv) the employer is given an incentive to improve methods and equipment in order to encourage increased output.

Examples of premium bonus systems are:
*Halsey and Halsey–Weir system.* The percentage of time saved, which is paid, varies from 30 per cent to 70 per cent, with 50 per cent being the most popular. Although the harder an employee works, the less he gets per piece, it is possible for him to more than double his earnings. However, an exceptional amount of time saved may indicate bad rate-fixing. With 50–50 sharing, the employee is paid for the time taken plus 50 per cent of the time saved. The time rate is then multiplied by the total hours in order to arrive at the wages to be paid.

### Example 11.3

Time allowed, 60 hours; time taken, 40 hours
(40 hours + 50% of 20 hours) × £2.00 = (40 hours + 10 hours) × £2.00
Wages paid = 50 hours × £2.00 = £100

*Rowan system.* This is similar to the Halsey–Weir system with a standard time and a bonus for time saved. The bonus is a percentage or proportion of the time rate. This is calculated by relating the *time saved* to the standard time allowed and working this as a percentage of the time rate.

### Example 11.4

Time rate £2.00 per hour; time allowed (TA), 30 hours; time taken (TT), 21 hours; time saved (TS), 9 hours.

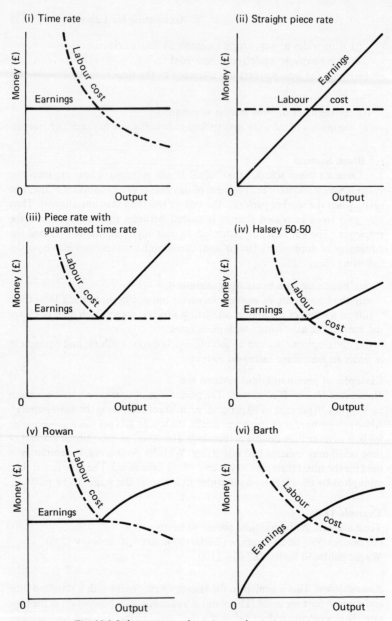

Fig. 11.1 Labour costs and earnings under various systems

*Notes:*

(i) With a time rate, cost per unit falls as output rises. The problem is to keep output high since there is no incentive to raise it.

(ii) Straight piece-work provides a constant rate of pay and constant cost per unit of output.

(*continued opposite*)

Bonus as a *percentage* of the time rate $=\dfrac{TS}{TA}$ per cent

$$=\dfrac{9}{30} \times 100 \text{ per cent} = 30 \text{ per cent}$$

$$30 \text{ per cent of } £2.00 = \underline{60 \text{ pence}}$$

Rate for time taken $= £2.60$ per hour
21 hours @ $£2.60 = £54.60$ or
21 hours @ $£2.00$ plus $30\% = £42.00 + £12.60 = £54.60$

Bonus as a *fraction* of the time rate $=\dfrac{TS}{TA} \times £2.00$

$$=\dfrac{9}{30} \times £2.00 = \underline{60 \text{ pence}}$$

With the Rowan system, the earnings are better than with Halsey 50–50 until the time saved is 50 per cent of the time allowed. After this point, however, the earnings rate declines, and the Rowan system gives a smaller return than Halsey. Earnings can never be doubled under this scheme.

*Barth variable sharing plan.* This method was introduced to encourage people learning a job and slow workers. It does not guarantee a time rate, but earnings are higher than under a straight piece-work system.

**2. Group or collective bonus systems.** Sometimes it is easier to measure the output of a group of workers, instead of the output of individuals, or there may simply be a preference for a group system. In order to provide an incentive to a group, a collective payment is made on an agreed basis for any savings in cost, or for output above an agreed minimum. This collective payment is then shared among the group in an agreed way.

## 11.3   Costs and Earnings under Different Systems

Incentive schemes are introduced with the object of increasing the rate of production, reducing labour costs per unit of output where possible, and minimizing fixed overhead cost per unit. Fig 11.1 shows the earnings and labour cost curves under various systems to illustrate the effect of increased output on remuneration and costs. Table 11.2 shows costs and earnings under different systems.

---

(iii) The guaranteed wage reduces the power of the incentive. Up to the point where the employee starts to earn a bonus, any gains or losses arising from variations in output are taken by the employer.

(iv) Labour cost falls sharply as output increases up to standard and above this standard, labour costs continue to fall at a reducing rate.

(v) Labour cost decreases as output increases up to task level.

(vi) Labour cost decreases rapidly for low production but not so rapidly when production increases.

**Table 11.2    Comparison of costs and earnings under various systems**

| | Time rate Hour £ (a) | Week £ (b) | Time allowed per unit (hours) (c) | Units produced (d) | Total time allowed (e) (c×d) | Time taken (hours) (f) | Time saved (hours) (g) (e−f) | Bonus hours paid (h) | Total hours paid (i) (f+h) | Gross wage £ (j) (a×i) | Labour cost per hour £ (k) (j÷f) | Labour cost per unit £ (l) (j÷d) |
|---|---|---|---|---|---|---|---|---|---|---|---|---|
| Day rate | 1.50 | 60.00 | — | 15 | — | 40 | — | — | 40 | 60.00 | 1.500 | 4.00 |
| Piece rate with guaranteed weekly rate | 1.50 | 60.00 | 2 | 18 | 36 | 40 | — | — | 40 | 60.00 | 1.500 | 3.33 |
| Straight piece-work rate | 1.50 | 60.00 | 2 | 30 | 60 | 40 | 20 | 20 | 60 | 90.00 | 2.250 | 3.00 |
| Halsey 50–50 | 1.50 | 60.00 | 2 | 30 | 60 | 40 | 20 | 10 | 50 | 75.00 | 1.875 | 2.50 |
| Rowan | 1.50 | 60.00 | 2 | 30 | 60 | 40 | 20 | 13⅓ | 53⅓ | 80.00 | 2.000 | 2.67 |
| High rate of efficiency: | | | | | | | | | | | | |
| Halsey 50–50 | 1.50 | 60.00 | 2 | 50 | 100 | 40 | 60 | 30 | 70 | 105.00 | 2.625 | 2.10 |
| Rowan | 1.50 | 60.00 | 2 | 50 | 100 | 40 | 60 | 24 | 64 | 96.00 | 2.400 | 1.92 |

*Note:* The Table shows that the day-worker costs an employer most, followed by the piece-worker with guaranteed weekly rate, but they both receive the same gross wage of £60. With straight piece-work, labour cost per unit is lower than the day rate, or piece rate with guaranteed weekly rate, and the gross wage is the highest among the first five examples. Halsey 50–50 shows a lower unit cost and labour cost per hour than Rowan, but the relationship changes as efficiency improves and ouput increases. At higher levels of output, the labour cost per unit is reduced considerably and the Rowan cost falls below the Halsey 50–50 cost.

## 11.4 The Personnel Department

Co-operation between the wages department and the personnel department is essential as new employees arrive and others leave. The personnel office should inform the wages office on matters such as dismissals, retirement, and changes in rates of pay caused by promotion or demotion. Sometimes wages are related to age, and increments may be awarded on birthdays. The wages office should be told about special deductions from pay and of changes in local or national rates of pay. For its part the wages office provides information and prepares reports for the personnel office on matters such as time-keeping, absenteeism, sickness, earnings in respect of claims for compensation and similar matters.

Labour costs can be expensive if there is a high labour turnover which results in high costs of recruitment, re-training costs and heavy costs of spoilage.

Losses may also occur as a result of inexperience in the handling of tools, equipment and machinery. Delays, machine damage and injury to workers may occur.

The *percentage rate of labour turnover* can be measured as follows:

$$\frac{\text{Total number of people leaving in the year}}{\text{Average number of people employed in the year}} \times 100$$

Thus if 100 staff out of 500 leave in the year, the rate of labour turnover is:

$$\frac{100}{500} \times 100 = 20\% \text{ per annum}$$

## 11.5 Time Recording

Most organizations use some form of time-keeping to provide a record of time spent in the factory or department and to record the time spent on a job or operation.

**Methods of Recording Attendance and Time Spent on Jobs**

*(a)* **Time Sheets or Attendance Books**
Time sheets are usually for the week, although daily sheets are issued where it is more convenient. In wages and costing offices the use of coloured paper or coloured bands is a convenient device for indicating occupations, classes of materials, or whether a job is a piece-work or day-work job. This system can be used with time sheets where, for example, a red band across the top of a job card could indicate a day-work job and a blue one, a piece-work job. Time sheets are not entirely satisfactory because of the time spent recording the information and the illegibility of some of these records. Some firms use attendance books for employees to sign in and out as a way of recording attendance and absence.

## (b) Time Recorders for Attendance Time

Dial time recorders or card time recorders are situated at the gate or outside the departmental office. In the dial recorder, a radial arm is pressed into holes on a clock face to register the time against the employee's number on a paper roll. Card time recorders are more common but they need *in* and *out* racks to contain the cards. The employee takes the card from the *out* rack and inserts it in the recorder to register the time, and then places it in the *in* rack. The cards which remain in the *out* rack are evidence of absentees.

## (c) Time Recorders for Process Time

These record operation or activity time on the back of job cards or tickets. The time taken, *elapsed time*, has to be calculated from the start and finish times. This method is useful when workers are paid by results. At the end of the week the total time shown on the individual tickets or cards has to be reconciled with the attendance time. A typical job card is shown in Fig. 11.2.

| Description: | 20 Gear wheels | | | Charge to : Order no.  X.71492 | | |
|---|---|---|---|---|---|---|
| Drg. no. 50719 | Code no. 01C746 | | M/c sect.  3 | Payroll no.  608 | | |
| Dept. no.  5 | Oper. no.  4 | Machine casting | | Time allowed | | |
| | | | | Each 2 hrs. | Total 40 hrs. | |
| Send to | | | | Time taken | Time saved | |
| Dept. no  8 | Oper. no.  5 | | | | | |
| | | | | 30 hrs. | 10 hrs. | |
| Replaced:    Nil | | | | Wages cost | | |
| Qty. scrapped   Nil | | Qty. passed  20 | Initials  AN | Hrs. 40 | Rate 1.50 | Total 60.00 |

*Fig. 11.2 Job card*

*Note:* This job card illustrates the fourth operation in the production of a gear wheel. It has to be machined in Department 5 and then sent to Department 8 for the next operation. The complete sequence of operations will be shown on an operation layout sheet.

## (d) Monitel Time Systems

A recent development (devised by Shaw & Sons Ltd in collaboration with Monitel Ltd) enables costs to be allocated to particular jobs or account numbers without any tedious calculation. Using a special punched card an electric clock can be programmed with an employee's time cost. When starting a job, the hourly rate key on the Monitel unit is depressed, followed by a start–stop button. The digital clock ceases to show the time and, instead, displays the cost of the employee's time being used on a client's business. This cost is not just the employee's wage, but includes overheads; it is better to use an hourly rate. This system also has applications in the professions. Thus a solicitor's time at £8.00 per hour might be increased to £18.00 per hour when all overheads and so forth have been built into the hourly rate. A ten-minute period spent reviewing a client's problem would therefore be charged to the client's account as £3.00. One added advantage of such a system to accountants, solicitors and professional consultants is that the system offers a package of costing sheets.

## 11.6 The Wages Department

The functions of the wages department are as follows:

(i) to calculate the day rate wages and all bonuses earned;

(ii) to calculate overtime and shift premiums;

(iii) to reconcile the clock card total with the total of hours shown on the job tickets for each employee;

(iv) to check the wage rates and total computation on job tickets, and enter gross wages;

(v) to deal with payroll deductions, including PAYE, and calculate net pay.

(vi) to record details of individual earnings and deductions on personal record cards;

(vii) to arrange for payment by cash, cheque or credit transfer.

## 11.7 Preparation of Wages

### (a) Calculation of Wages

Time sheets, clock cards and job tickets have to be sent to the wages office at the end of each week, although finished job tickets can be sent daily. This enables the clerks to calculate earnings as each finished job ticket is received. Duplicate job tickets are written out by the time-keepers for unfinished jobs at the end of the week, and the wages office has to keep a record of time taken to date, for use in calculating the bonus earned when the job is completed.

When calculations are complete, a reconciliation is made between the total hours shown on each employee's clock cards and the total hours shown on his job tickets. Next, the overtime premium or shift time allowances have to be calculated. The final computation may be as follows:

Total clock hours 48 (Monday to Friday 40 hours; Sunday 8 hours)
Day rate £60 per week (£1.50 per hour)
Double time for Sunday work

|  | Hours | Wages earned £ |  |
|---|---|---|---|
| Day-work | 7 | 10.50 | (7 × £1.50) |
| Piece-work | 41 | 75.00 | (Time allowed 50 hours 50 × £1.50) |
| Overtime premium | 8 | 12.00 | (Allowance for Sunday work, paid at day rate) |
|  | 56 | £97.50 |  |

### (b) Preparation of Payroll

Once the job tickets have been collected and calculated, in order to find the gross wages for each worker, it is necessary to refer to the schedule or list of deductions. There are *standard* deductions and *variable* or *special* deductions in respect of PAYE, National Insurance contributions and so on, and these must be recorded in order to find the net pay. The payroll can then be prepared and the cash analysis made, but in certain cases payment is by cheque or credit transfer.

One of the most important documents in a wages office is the earnings record or personal record card of each employee. At the same time as tabulating the wages, the details of earnings and deductions can be entered on the personal record cards. At the end of the year these records will provide information about total wages paid, tax deducted and superannuation contributions.

### (c) Book-keeping Entries for Wages and Deductions

The cost of employing labour consists of gross wages plus employer's contributions to social security payments, pensions schemes and holiday pay. Large manufacturing companies usually have a separate payroll for each manufacturing unit. Total wages paid to employees are called *gross wages* but the total expense incurred by a firm on the Wages Account includes other expenses such as employer's National Insurance contributions.

The entries in the financial books might appear as given below:

Gross wages £40 000; Deductions: PAYE £9 700; National Insurance £4 000; Recreation Club £300. Employer's National Insurance Contribution £5 000.

|  | Debit £ | Credit £ |
|---|---|---|
| Wages Account (£40 000 + £5 000) | 45 000 |  |
| Social Security Account (National Insurance: |  |  |
|                   Employees' £4 000 |  | 9 000 |
|                   Employer's £5 000) |  |  |
| Income Tax Account (PAYE) |  | 9 700 |
| Recreation Club Account (Employees' |  |  |
|   contributions) |  | 300 |
| Wages Payable Account (Cash required) |  | 26 000 (net pay) |
|  | £45 000 | £45 000 |

(d) **Wages Analysis**

After the completion of the payroll, the next step in costing is to analyse the wages in order to arrive at the labour cost chargeable to each of the cost accounts. The way in which the analysis is carried out varies between different organizations because of the method of costing used and the size of the business. For example, a company manufacturing machinery and equipment may be producing five different product groups. It manufactures both for stock and to customers' requirements and has ten production departments and three service departments. It also produces a large proportion of the components for fitting and setting up the products.

The gross wages of the employees are recorded on a large number of job cards, each of which shows a number representing a standing order, a stock order or a customer's order. These cards are sorted into numerical order for each department, and the stock and customers' numbers are sorted into product groups. They are then listed to provide a total for each of the service departments and other departments in respect of indirect labour. For direct labour, totals are provided for the stock and customers' orders under each of the five product groups.

The next step is to calculate, for each department, the overhead chargeable to each cost account, by using the appropriate recovery rate (see Unit 12). The wages analysis provides the figures which are debited to the Work-in-progress Control Account and the various Overhead Accounts and credited to the Wages and Salaries Control Account. A Control Account in the cost ledger, as in the financial accounts, is an account which controls a subsidiary ledger. The transactions which are recorded in detail in individual accounts within the subsidiary ledger are entered in summary form in the Control Account. The balance of the account should always equal the total of the balances on the individual accounts in the subsidiary ledger.

Each department has its own overhead rate and this is used to calculate the overhead expenses chargeable to each cost account. The total expense charged against the department or cost centre will have to be reconciled with the total of the individual calculations. The layout of a wages analysis is indicated in Fig. 11.3.

| Wages analysis and overhead recovery<br>Department no. 1 | | |
|---|---|---|
| Order no. | Wages<br>£ | Overhead<br>£ |
| 58742 | 121.50 | 243.00 |
| 58903 | 64.38 | 128.76 |
|  | etc. | etc. |
|  | £5 602.00 | £11 204.00 |

*Fig. 11.3 Wages analysis and overhead recovery*

Note: This indicates that the direct wages charged to stock orders in Department 1 is £5 602. It also shows that the overhead recovery rate for this department is 200 per cent on direct wages, giving £11 204.

## 11.8   Exercises

1. The managing director of a group of companies requested the group personnel manager to prepare a report on the labour situation in each of its factories. This report indicated that the situation within the group was satisfactory with the exception of one factory where a considerable amount of time was spent in advertising for and recruiting labour. The managing director has now written to you, as chief cost accountant, asking for information which will enable him to become acquainted with the problem of high labour turnover in this factory and to take effective action to correct the situation. You are required to send him a report which:

(a) gives details of the effect of high labour turnover on costs;
(b) shows the steps that could be taken in an effort to reduce costs; and
(c) explains how the rate of labour turnover is calculated.

2. Calculate the labour cost chargeable to Order number 2075 in respect of an employee machining a casting, under (a) the Halsey 50–50 scheme, and (b) the Rowan scheme.

> Rate of pay:     £2.25 per hour
> Time taken:     9 hours 30 minutes
> Time allowed:   12 hours 30 minutes

# Unit Twelve
# Accounting for Overhead Costs

## 12.1 Introduction: Accumulation of Expenses

Indirect costs are expenses incurred in the performance of a service, not as a result of changing the form of the product. In the process of identifying and classifying these costs and services, standing expense orders and codes are used. The symbols or codes which may be used are in the form of numbers, decimals and letters, to assist memory. The standing order number or code is a permanent feature of the costing system, and exists for a long time, so that new orders do not have to be issued each time an expense is incurred.

The collection of overhead expenses takes place under the standing order code numbers and these expenses consist of:

  (i) materials as shown on stores requisitions;
 (ii) wages as analysed and charged to expense codes;
(iii) invoices for materials and services chargeable as expenses;
(iv) chargeable expenses made by journal entry for costs incurred internally, and those requiring allocation for a particular period of account, e.g. depreciation and insurance.

An analysis of standing order costs is made in order to assemble the expenses under the various production departments, service departments and cost centres.

### (a) Cost Centres
A cost centre may be a department, a group of machines, a method, a process or an operation for which costs may be ascertained. A power plant, a steam plant, a machine shop, material store or repair and maintenance department, and hand labour are examples which may be classified as either *production cost centres*, *process cost centres* or *service cost centres*.

### (b) Overhead Groups
There are four distinct groups of overhead costs, each of which is usually dealt with separately when collecting the expenses and computing the product costs, as goods are taken into stock or dispatched to the customer. These groups form an important part of the cost control procedures:

  (i) factory or works expenses;
 (ii) administrative and office expenses;
(iii) selling and distribution expenses (marketing expenses);
(iv) research and development expenses.

Overhead costs have to be established for each type of expense and as they are indirect costs they have to be *absorbed* by production and sales. The costs of overhead expenses are kept and recorded in a manufacturing expense, or overhead expense, ledger, where the standing orders and their costs are shown.

### (c) Budget Centres

For the purposes of budgetary control, the organization is divided into units known as *budget centres*. These are natural divisions of the organization to which costs are charged and, for control purposes, they are the responsibility of an individual such as a foreman or works manager who is, therefore, responsible for organizing and controlling the expenditure which relates to his own department or budget centre.

## 12.2    Types of Overhead Expense

### (a) Fixed Costs

These remain unchanged within the short term and are not related to the volume of production. They are constant costs over a period of time and include, rent, rates, depreciation, insurance and salaries.

### (b) Variable Costs

These are directly related to the volume of output and consist of items such as fuel, lubricants, power, spoilage, royalties, compressed air, small tools.

### (c) Semi-variable Costs

These are partly fixed and partly variable. They change as production facilities are utilized above or below normal levels. Examples are the cost of supervision, clerical labour, telephone charges, electricity and gas.

## 12.3    Allocation, Apportionment and Absorption

### A Service Department

This is one which provides services and facilities which are ancillary to the production departments and other service or administrative departments. Indirect costs occur within production and service departments and a considerable amount of overhead costs occur where the actual or specific expenditure is charged direct to the department. Each industry has its own problems of selecting an appropriate basis for apportionment. This may be by man or machine hour, or on the basis of labour costs, mileage run, and other methods as mentioned later in this Unit.

It is comparatively simple to apportion fixed costs, but complications arise with variable costs which result from activities within a department, such as overtime and shift working which changes from time to time. The technical expert generally uses activity or operating time when making his estimate. Each of the production and service departments has its own set of standing orders to which indirect costs are charged. For example, the cost of operating and running the overhead cranes in a machine department would be charged to the standing order number of that department. Charging the wages of the crane-driver is a simple matter but other costs such as power are more difficult to allocate and may have to be shared out and apportioned on some other basis. The following terms are used in the process of charging and distributing overhead expenses to departments, cost centres, cost units, jobs and processes.

*Allocation* is the allotment of whole items of cost to cost centres or cost units.

*Apportionment* is the allotment to two or more cost centres of proportions of common items of cost on the estimated basis of benefit received.

*Absorption* is the allotment of overhead to cost units by means of rates separately calculated for each cost centre. In most cases the rates are predetermined.

## 12.4   Bases for Apportioning Indirect Expenditure to Production and Service Departments

Special principles have to be followed in determining the method of sharing indirect expenditure items, incurred for the benefit of more than one department. Alternative bases are:

(i) **Effective floor area.** Expenses shared include rent, rates, building expense, fire precautions.

(ii) **Effective cubic capacity.** Space or volume costs apply to heating and sometimes for building depreciation, industrial cleaning and decorating costs.

(iii) **Capital value of buildings and plant.** The book value can be used for insurance and depreciation.

(iv) **Volume or weight of materials.** In some industries, storekeeping and material handling costs can be charged out on this basis.

(v) **Number of employees.** Some expenses can be shared pro rata on the basis of the number of employees in each department, or on the number who benefit from the expenditure. This basis applies to personnel and welfare costs, such as canteen costs, first aid costs, wages of gatemen, and administration costs.

(vi) **Metered consumption.** This includes items such as electricity, gas, compressed air, steam, water.

(vii) **Average inventory values.** This includes fire protection and insurance.

(viii) **Points wired.** This is for telephones.

(ix) **Technical estimate.** This is used where it is impossible to apply more exact methods. This may be necessary in the case of electricity, gas, compressed air, steam, hydraulic power, laboratory and telephone costs.

### Apportionment Rates

Records are kept in order that expenses can be shared out on the appropriate basis. These include the area and cubic capacity of each centre, the number of employees in each department, the number of items or weight of materials handled and the capital value of buildings and plant, and so on. This enables percentages to be fixed for each department. A simple example is given below using the area of five departments for the apportionment of rent. Having calculated the area used by each department as well as the total area, percentages can be fixed. One per cent is represented by £50.

| | % | Rent £ |
|---|---|---|
| Machine shop | 45 | 2 250 |
| Welding shop | 21 | 1 050 |
| Assembly department | $24\frac{1}{2}$ | 1 225 |
| Tool room | $4\frac{1}{2}$ | 225 |
| Power and general services department | 5 | 250 |
| | 100 | £5 000 |

## 12.5   Factory or Works Expenses

The costs recorded in a manufacturing organization relate to:

(a) materials, wages and expenses in respect of jobs and products;
(b) similar costs in respect of all other work.

The costs under (b) may consist of:

(i) expenditure on capital goods or extensions;
(ii) expenditure on research and development;
(iii) the overhead costs of the organization.

The costs as divided in (a) and (b) above can be classified as:

(i) direct costs relating to jobs and products [in (a)];
(ii) indirect costs relating to all other work [in (b)].

The capital expenditure of materials, wages and direct expenses, plus a fair share of overheads will be transferred and debited to the appropriate Asset Account. If the cost of research and development is fairly stable from year to year it will be written off by a transfer to the Profit and Loss Account. If the cost is exceptionally large in a particular year, and benefit from the research will accrue later, some of the costs may be carried forward and written off at a later date. In some cases it may be possible to recover these costs by a direct allocation to the products identified with the research. The indirect costs of the organization mentioned in (iii) above are those charged to the standing order numbers of the manufacturing, service and administration departments. They are the overhead expenses of the organization as charged to budget centres.

### Procedures for Allocating and Apportioning Overhead Costs
Indirect costs are charged to budget and cost centres by allocation or apportionment. The *allocation* is a straightforward procedure because by charging the cost to a standing order number, it becomes identified with a particular budget centre. For example, the salary of a machine shop

superintendent is allocated from the staff payroll to the machine shop by charging it to the standing order number for that particular expense. Such costs are peculiar or exclusive to a particular budget centre but where these costs are closely related to other budget or cost centres, they are known as common costs.

Common costs are distributed by *apportioning* them so that other budget or cost centres are charged a sum equivalent to the benefit received. For example, in an organization where there are no separate meters the invoice for electricity would be charged by allocating it to a budget centre. As it is a common cost, it is then apportioned and charged to other budget and cost centres. The salary of a production controller would likewise be allocated to the service department where he or she works and then the amount would be apportioned by charging other budget and cost centres with the amounts attributable to them. This apportionment is known as a *primary distribution*. This is followed by a secondary distribution when the costs of the service departments are charged to the production departments.

In some systems the service department costs are charged entirely to the production departments, but in others, some of these costs are charged to the production departments and other service departments before a final distribution is made to the production departments.

There are therefore two stages in the distribution of expenses. They are explained more fully in the next section.

## 12.6    Overhead Distribution

Overheads have to be distributed in two stages, a *primary distribution* and a *secondary distribution*. The first distributes the costs collected under various standing order headings (electricity, telephone expenses, etc.) on some fair basis to *all* departments and service departments. Then, since all overheads must in the end be borne by the units of production, and included in the charges made to the customer, the total costs of the service departments have to be distributed among the production departments in some fair proportion. This is the second stage of distributing overheads.

### (a)  Primary Distribution

This method allocates or apportions expenses to the standing orders of the production and service departments. Primary distribution takes place when it is possible to allocate, measure exactly or apportion a fair amount. A typical distribution is shown in Table 12.1 (p. 150).

**Table 12.1    Primary distribution**

| Expense | Basis | Factory overhead analysis | | | | |
| | | Production departments | | | Service departments | |
| | | Machine shop | Welding shop | Assembly department | Tool room | Power and general services |
|---|---|---|---|---|---|---|
| | | £ | £ | £ | £ | £ |
| Rent | Area | 2 250 | 1 050 | 1 225 | 225 | 250 |
| Rates | Area | 1 125 | 525 | 613 | 112 | 125 |
| Heat | Cubic capacity | 1 400 | 1 050 | 1 225 | 225 | 200 |
| Light | Area | 450 | 210 | 245 | 45 | 50 |
| Indirect labour | Allocation | 670 | 250 | 780 | 90 | 210 |
| Indirect material | Allocation | 110 | 90 | 80 | 700 | 900 |
| Insurance | Book value | 170 | 100 | 80 | 50 | 200 |
| Canteen | Employees | 270 | 150 | 180 | 60 | 90 |
| etc. | etc. | etc. | etc. | etc. | etc. | etc. |
| Totals | | £8 000 | £9 400 | £12 600 | £4 000 | £7 000 |

**(b) Secondary Distribution**

The costs of a *service department*, such as the tool room, have to be distributed among the production departments and other user/service departments. This is done successively with the various service department costs, in some cases reactivating the costs of a department which have already been written off. Thus the tool room department costs already written off may be reactivated because the power and general service department costs, when apportioned, mean that the tool room has to bear its fair share of general service costs. These reactivated costs will then have to be re-apportioned. This is illustrated in Table 12.3.

To make the final distribution on the basis of services received, the proportion chargeable to each department is reduced to a percentage of the total. For example, the services of the maintenance department could be shared out on the basis of man hours of service rendered, with the man hours of each department being reduced to percentages. The cost of a stores department could be distributed by using the number of requisitions or the value of the requisitions and fixing percentages for each department using the service.

An example is given below of apportionment percentages used to eliminate the service department costs of a tool room and a power and general services department. The first service department, the tool room, is to be closed off, first, by apportioning the tool room costs to the other service department and to the manufacturing departments as follows:

30% to power and general services; 20% to machine shop; 10% to welding shop; and 40% to the assembly department.

Thus the tool room costs can be eliminated by being transferred to the other departments, both service and manufacturing. Although there are now no tool room costs, the costs of the power and general services department have increased by the 30% of the tool room costs which were charged to that department. The cost of the power and general services department (the original cost plus the 30%) are now apportioned to the first service department, the tool room, and the manufacturing departments by charging 20% to tool room; 40% to machine shop; 30% to welding shop; and 10% to the assembly department. This process is continued until all the service department costs have been eliminated by transferring them to the manufacturing departments.

*Apportionment percentages of reciprocal services and manufacturing departments*

|  | Manufacturing departments | | | Service departments | |
|---|---|---|---|---|---|
|  | Machine shop | Welding shop | Assembly department | Tool room | Power and general services |
|  | % | % | % | % | % |
| Tool room costs shared as : | 20 | 10 | 40 | — | 30 |
| Power and general services costs shared as : | 40 | 30 | 10 | 20 | — |

*Reciprocal service*

The easiest method is to charge service department costs direct to the producing departments but this ignores the fact that generally services rendered by service departments apply to both producing and other service departments, because the services are reciprocal.

There are three usual methods of secondary distribution.

(i) **Distribution on a non-repetitive basis.** When using this method of transferring expenses there is only one distribution of the expenses of each service department. All the expenses of a service department are spread over the producing and other service departments, and from then on, no further expenses are received or distributed by that service centre. The distribution should be carried out in a specific order by first taking the service department which carries out work for the greater number of other service departments. Where two or more departments service the same number of departments, you should commence with the department with the largest cost. In Table 12.2 this means that the power and general services costs must be distributed first.

**Table 12.2  Overhead distribution on a non-repetitive basis**

|  | Production departments | | | Service departments | | |
|  | Machine shop | Welding shop | Assembly department | Tool room | Power and general services | Total |
|---|---|---|---|---|---|---|
|  | £ | £ | £ | £ | £ | £ |
| Primary distribution | 8 000 | 9 400 | 12 600 | 4 000 | 7 000 | 41 000 |
| Service department distributions: | | | | | | |
| Power and general services | 2 800 | 2 100 | 700 | 1 400 | (7 000) | |
| Tool room | 1 543 | 771 | 3 086 | (5 400) | — | |
| Totals | £12 343 | £12 271 | £16 386 | — | — | £41 000 |

*Notes:*
(i) It will be seen that the power and general service costs are distributed in the normal way using 40%, 30%, 10% and 20%.
(ii) The tool room cost of £5 400 is distributed only to the producing departments in the proportion of 2:1:4.

(ii) **Repeated or continuous distribution.** This is the reciprocal basis of allotment whereby the service department account is closed, and is reopened and closed again as successive distributions take place. There may be several apportionments until finally all the service costs are distributed. Under this method there is no particular arrangement or order of distribution. A typical distribution is shown in Table 12.3.

(iii) **Algebraic method using simultaneous equations.** This method uses simultaneous equations to solve the problem of distributions. However, the solutions by this method become difficult with a large number of service departments, and a computer may be needed to arrive at the correct answers. The calculations are given on p. 154.

**Table 12.3   Repeated distribution of reciprocal services**

| | Production departments | | | Service departments | | |
| | Machine shop | Welding shop | Assembly department | Tool room | Power and general services | Total |
|---|---|---|---|---|---|---|
| | £ | £ | £ | £ | £ | £ |
| Direct expenses | 8 000 | 9 400 | 12 600 | 4 000 | 7 000 | 41 000 |
| Service department distributions: | | | | | | |
| Tool room | 800 | 400 | 1 600 | (4 000) | 1 200 | |
| Power and general services | 3 280 | 2 460 | 820 | 1 640 | (8 200) | |
| Tool room | 328 | 164 | 656 | (1 640) | 492 | |
| Power and general services | 197 | 148 | 49 | 98 | (492) | |
| Tool room | 20 | 10 | 39 | (98) | 29 | |
| Power and general services | 11 | 9 | 3 | 6 | (29) | |
| Tool room | 2 | 1 | 3 | (6) | — | |
| Totals | £12 638 | £12 592 | £15 770 | — | — | £41 000 |

*Notes:*

(i) The tool room costs are distributed among the other departments 2:1:4:3.

(ii) The increased power and general services charges are then distributed 4:3:1:2, thus reopening the Tool Room Account.

(iii) The tool room share of the power and general distribution is then re-allocated 2:1:4:3, thus reopening the Power and General Account, which is then redistributed, and so on.

(iv) Finally, the residue is allocated from the tool room to the producing departments, in the ratio 2:1:4.

Using the same data as in Tables 12.2 and 12.3:

Let £x be the total overhead of the tool room after apportioning y.

Let £y be the total overhead of the power and general services department after apportioning x:

$$x = 4\ 000 + 0.2y\ (20\%)$$
$$y = 7\ 000 + 0.3x\ (30\%)$$

Multiply by 10 to eliminate decimals:

$$10x = 40\ 000 + 2y$$
$$10y = 70\ 000 + 3x$$

Rearrange

$$10x - 2y = 40\ 000 \quad (1)$$
$$-3x + 10y = 70\ 000 \quad (2)$$

Multiply (1) by 5 and add (2) to eliminate y:

$$50x - 10y = 200\ 000$$
$$-3x + 10y = \ \ 70\ 000$$

Total                                    $47x = 270\ 000$

Divide by 47                       $x = £5\ 744.68$

Substituting 5 744.68 for x in (1):

$$57\ 447 - 2y = 40\ 000$$

Rearrange                 $57\ 447 - 40\ 000 = 2y$

$$y = £8\ 723.50$$

The total overhead of the power and general services department is £8 723.50. When this is distributed it gives the results shown in Table 12.4.

## 12.7    Recovery of Factory or Works Expenses

Production costs comprise *prime cost plus production overhead* but as overhead expenses cannot be specifically related to any particular item of output they have to be spread over production. The expenses are *absorbed* by production, and rates for recovering these costs have to be established. It is inconvenient to charge actual costs because you have to wait until the end of an accounting period. So before the actual costs are ascertained, an estimate is made of future costs and *predetermined rates* are fixed. To decide on the method of recovering costs, the production, the raw materials used and the type of labour employed have to be examined. Other factors to take into account are seasonal working, shift work, etc.

## 12.8    Application of Overhead to Production

The methods used include the following:

(i) percentage of prime cost;

(ii) percentage of direct material cost;

**Table 12.4  Apportionment of repeated distribution totals obtained by algebraic methods**

| | Repeat distribution total £ | Amount apportioned % | £ | Production departments | | | | | | Total £ |
|---|---|---|---|---|---|---|---|---|---|---|
| | | | | Machine shop % | £ | Welding shop % | £ | Assembly department % | £ | |
| Original overhead cost | | | | | 8 000 | | 9 400 | | 12 600 | 30 000 |
| Value of x (tool room) | 5 745 | 70 | 4 021 | 20 | 1 149 | 10 | 574 | 40 | 2 298 | 4 021 |
| Value of y (power and general services) | 8 724 | 80 | 6 979 | 40 | 3 490 | 30 | 2 617 | 10 | 872 | 6 979 |
| Totals | | | | | £12 639 | | £12 591 | | £15 770 | £41 000 |

(iii) percentage of direct labour cost;
(iv) rate per direct labour hour;
 (v) rate per machine hour;
(vi) rate per unit of product.

The rate of absorption is found by using the following formula:

$$\frac{\text{Estimated overhead expenses of the cost centre}}{\text{Estimated total production in terms of units or value}}$$

This is multiplied by 100 to obtain the percentage for (i), (ii) and (iii).

(i) **Percentage of prime cost**

$$= \frac{\text{Overhead expenses}}{\text{Direct material} + \text{Direct wages} + \text{Direct expenses}} \times 100$$

This is a simple method to apply, but as many overhead costs are related to time, and because materials usually form a large part of the total prime cost, it has no logical basis. It can only be used satisfactorily where one standard product is made which uses a fixed quantity of material at a constant price, and where the time taken in production is constant. An example illustrates the problem:

|                      | Product A | Product B |
|----------------------|-----------|-----------|
|                      | £         | £         |
| Direct materials     | 5.00      | 15.00     |
| Direct wages         | 10.00     | 10.00     |
| Direct expenses      | 1.00      | 1.00      |
| Prime cost           | 16.00     | 26.00     |
| Works overhead 100%  | 16.00     | 26.00     |
| Total cost           | £32.00    | £52.00    |

For the same period of time both products use the facilities of the factory, including lighting, heating, and the cost of supervision and administration. Product B, however, is expected to contribute an extra £10 towards overhead costs. In a competitive market where other producers are using a more scientific method of absorbing overheads, orders might be lost for product B because it costs more. Product A may be underpriced but lack of orders for B might require a higher rate of overhead for A which would increase its cost.

(ii) **Percentage of direct material cost** $= \dfrac{\text{Overhead expenses}}{\text{Total direct material cost}} \times 100$

This method is also simple to compute but has no logical basis. The costs of materials may fluctuate from one supplier to another and at different periods of the year. Some materials are cheap and others expensive. This method ignores all such problems and is therefore unlikely to produce accurate production costs.

(iii) **Percentage of direct labour cost** $= \dfrac{\text{Overhead expenses}}{\text{Total direct labour cost}} \times 100$

Overheads can be absorbed by using a single rate for the whole factory or by having separate rates for each department. The single or blanket rate is not usually suitable as the time spent on each operation varies within the different departments. It is usually necessary to have separate rates for each department.

The percentage on direct labour is a simple method to use and the details required are usually available without having to keep extra records. The direct labour cost of each department is found in the wages analysis. Although it is more accurate than the other methods mentioned, it ignores the fact that expensive machinery may be contributing considerably towards the value of the output. Also, goods produced by highly skilled and highly paid workers carry more of the burden. Another example would be where a low earner occupies a large floor area for a considerable time on a process or job, which requires a large amount of supervision. The space and other overhead costs will be high for the area used, yet the overhead recovery will be small because of the low wages.

(iv) **Rate per direct labour hour** $= \dfrac{\text{Overhead expenses}}{\text{Total direct labour hours}}$

This method is considered fair where cost centres are not extensively mechanized and where most of the overhead expense is incurred on a time basis. Records of direct labour hours have to be kept. This method overcomes the main objection of the direct labour cost, as jobs taking the same time are charged with the same amount of overhead, whereas with direct labour cost, the high rate wages carry a disproportionate amount of overhead.

(v) **Rate per machine hour**
$$= \dfrac{\text{Total overhead expenses applicable to the machine}}{\text{Total operating hours for the period}}$$

This is more difficult to compute but is a very accurate and logical method of allocating overhead expenses to each job. It is suitable for a department which is extensively mechanized but care will be needed when fixing the rates. Details of the effective floor space occupied have to be recorded, in order to charge rent (or the cost of space) and rates, and reference has to be made to the plant register to obtain the amount of depreciation. The estimated cost of power and sundry materials such as oil and cleaning materials used in the previous period must be calculated. A charge is usually made for the cost of supervision and any other salaries which may be applicable. Repairs and maintenance, lighting, insurance and other relevant items must be included in the total cost.

An example of computing the costs to establish a machine hour rate is given on p. 158.

*Machine no. 273*
*Costs for a period of 48 weeks*

|  | £ |
|---|---|
| Rent, rates and insurance | 467.10 |
| Lighting | 48.00 |
| Heating | 42.00 |
| Power (metered consumption) | 570.10 |
| Consumable materials based on past records | 120.20 |
| Repairs and maintenance estimated by manager | 466.10 |
| Service department charge | 124.00 |
| Supervision | 338.70 |
| Indirect labour | 314.00 |
| Depreciation | 1 340.20 |
|  | £3 830.40 |

Total hours for 48 weeks at 38 hours per week $= 38 \times 48 = 1\ 824$

Rate per hour $= \dfrac{£3\ 830.40}{1\ 824} = £2.10$

(vi) **Rate per unit of product** $= \dfrac{\text{Overhead expenses}}{\text{Number of units of product}}$

This is a simple, direct and equitable method for uniform products where weight or size of product can be used to calculate the rate of charge for overhead expenses.

There is another method but it is seldom used. A *blanket rate* is a single rate which is used for all the production departments. To be of any value at arriving at the correct cost, it would be used where one product is made in a continuous process or where several products pass through all departments, spending the same time in each.

## 12.9    Over- and Under-absorbed Overhead

Overhead absorption rates are calculated using either actual or predetermined rates. The use of predetermined rates will avoid the large variation in unit costs which occur when actual costs are used.

If the rates are established on actual expenses incurred, no costs can be completed until the close of the accounting period and this delay is very unsatisfactory. By using actual costs, the total cost of overheads is charged to production and there is no balance on the Overhead Accounts. During the year, however, this generally results in a large variation in the unit costs because of holidays, seasonal activity and other factors which affect the use of capacity. The absorption rates change considerably from one month to the next, but if these rates are estimated in advance, costing can proceed as work is completed and a uniform rate can be used which is an estimate of actual costs for the year.

Because of the variation in activity caused by seasonal factors and for other reasons, there is likely to be a difference between the cost of overheads and the total amount absorbed at the end of each period of account. However, if the rates are reasonably accurate the costs and absorptions level out over the year. In some months there may be a large amount of overhead cost under-absorbed and in others there may be an over-absorption. When an overhead cost absorbed by production is greater than the actual cost, it is called *over-absorbed overhead*, but if it is less, it is called *under-absorbed overhead*. Many factors are responsible for this situation, but the main causes are the following:

(*a*) **Over-absorption**

   (i) an increase in activity resulting in greater use of factory capacity—for example, increase in overtime, extra shifts, additional employees on direct labour—means that more overhead will be absorbed than planned;

   (ii) an increase in direct wage rates—when overhead is absorbed on a basis of direct wages.

(*b*) **Under-absorption**

   (i) a decrease in activity caused by less overtime, reduced shifts or short-time working as a result of lack of orders, strikes, etc. The decrease in activity means that less overhead will be absorbed than planned.

   (ii) a reduction in the number of direct workers;

   (iii) the introduction of machines or improved factory services when predetermined rates of absorption are being used and before absorption rates have been adjusted to meet the new conditions.

There are several ways of disposing of the balance on the overhead accounts:

   write off to Profit and Loss Account;
   transfer to a Reserve Account;
   adjust the cost of sales and inventories.

**Normal Capacity**
This is the capacity to manufacture and sell, based on anticipated sales and allowing for limiting factors and normal problems which occur from time to time. Normal capacity is used as a basis for fixing overhead rates and stock levels and also in the planning of production and sales, including price fixing. When overheads are over- or under-absorbed, normal capacity has to be kept in mind, because the way it was determined may be the cause of the variances. The fixed, variable and semi-variable overheads must be examined and the apportionments and calculations must be checked carefully. If the differences are not variable overheads but fixed costs or expenditure variances then they should be written off to Costing Profit and Loss Account.

**Example 12.1** (Absorption of overhead)
A manufacturing company has four production departments engaged on the production of three groups of products. The methods used for the absorption of overhead expenses are as follows:

Department 1: rate per direct labour hour;
Department 2: rate per machine hour;
Department 3: rate per direct labour hour;
Department 4: percentage on direct wages.

Additional information is as follows:

| Dept. | Direct wages | Direct labour or machine hours | Percentage on direct labour | Rate per direct labour or machine hour |
|---|---|---|---|---|
| | £ | | % | £ |
| 1 | 1 200 | 980 | — | 1.10 |
| 2 | 2 875 | 2 390 | — | 3.00 |
| 3 | 8 960 | 6 800 | — | 1.60 |
| 4 | 6 284 | 4 880 | 150 | — |
| | £19 319 | £15 050 | | |

Production overhead costs are as follows:

| Indirect materials | | Indirect wages | | Expenses | |
|---|---|---|---|---|---|
| | £ | | £ | | £ |
| Purchases | 1 248 | Wages | 11 099 | Expense creditors | 4 135 |
| Stores Ledger | 9 606 | | | Fixed costs | 2 973 |

### Absorption of production overheads

| Dept. | Direct labour | Rate of absorption | Direct labour/ machine hours | Overhead absorbed |
|---|---|---|---|---|
| | £ | | | £ |
| 1 | 1 200 | £1.10 per hour | 980 | 1 078 |
| 2 | 2 875 | £3.00 per hour | 2 390 | 7 170 |
| 3 | 8 960 | £1.60 per hour | 6 800 | 10 880 |
| 4 | 6 284 | 150 per cent | 4 880 | 9 426 |
| | | | | £28 554 |

The Factory Production Overhead Account is as shown below:

### Factory Production Overhead Account

| | £ | | £ |
|---|---|---|---|
| *Indirect materials* | | | |
| Purchases | 1 248 | Transfer to Work-in-progress | |
| Stores ledger | 9 606 | Account | 28 554 |
| *Indirect wages* | 11 099 | Production overhead under- | |
| | | absorbed (Profit and Loss | |
| | | Account) | 507 |
| *Expenses* | | | |
| Expense creditors | 4 135 | | |
| Fixed costs | 2 973 | | |
| | £29 061 | | £29 061 |

A diagrammatic display of the collection, distribution and absorption of overhead costs is given in Fig. 12.1.

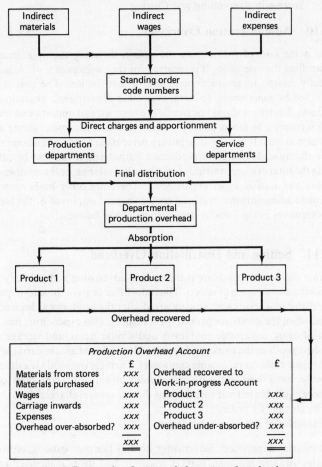

*Fig. 12.1 Collection, distribution and absorption of overheads*

Notes:
(i) Overhead (indirect) costs are collected under appropriate headings, using the standing order code numbers, to which are charged the costs and expenses incurred.
(ii) These indirect manufacturing expenses are accumulated on a functional basis for costs charged direct or allocated to the producing and service cost centres. When certain expenses have to be shared, they are apportioned, by transferring proportions of the cost to those departments or cost centres using the service.
(iii) The next stage is the distribution on some fair basis of the cost of each service department, either directly to the production departments or to both producing and servicing departments, until all the service department costs have been transferred.
(iv) The departmental production overheads are then absorbed by the various products by charging these overheads to the products on the most appropriate basis, using predetermined rates of absorption. For example, they could be based on a percentage of direct wages, a rate per direct labour hour or machine hour, or some similar method.
(v) At the end of each cost period we strike a balance between the actual cost of overhead in each department and the amount of overheads absorbed by production. This indicates over- or under-absorption on the Production Overhead Account.

## 12.10 Administration Overhead

This is the cost of formulating the policy, directing the organization and controlling the operation. It is incurred for the business as a whole and is not directly related to production, selling or distribution. The cost is usually absorbed by *apportioning* the total over other departments, or sections of the business. Each item should be carefully examined and apportioned on a basis which ensures, as far as possible, a charge which is commensurate with the service received. It may be an arbitrary percentage figure, or an amount based on a sliding scale related to productive output and it can also be calculated using the total of direct and indirect wages and salaries, or the number of work people and staff in other departments. There are other bases on which to calculate administrative overhead such as capital employed or the time spent by executives in the various departments of the business.

## 12.11 Selling and Distribution Overhead

*Selling overhead* expenditure is incurred in advertising and publicity and the soliciting and securing of orders; it includes office costs of the sales department. The *distribution* costs are those incurred after the product has been manufactured when the goods are packed for transport. This expenditure includes the cost of cases, collapsible containers and similar items, and storage costs of finished goods at the works and depots. Also included are the carriage charges and repair costs on returnable containers. Carriage outwards is a distribution expense, but if these costs vary considerably on individual customers' orders, it is more equitable to treat such costs as direct expenses chargeable to the job or to the customer's order.

Examples of selling overheads are:

rent of sales department; advertising; cost of samples; catalogues; royalties; salaries and commissions; market research; bad debts if incurred regularly during the year.

Costs may be recovered as follows:

(*a*) Costs varying directly with the value of the articles or the quantity sold may be recovered as a direct charge to the works or production cost.

(*b*) Costs which are not related to particular items sold, and which can be classified as fixed costs, may be recovered by:

(i) *Percentage of invoice value.* The selling price of each item is a suitable method where standard selling prices are used and where the sale of each type of product is fairly constant during the year.

(ii) *Rate per article.* The estimated fixed expenses are apportioned fairly to each product group. The total charged to each product group is then divided by the estimated sale of each type to give the rate chargeable.

(iii) *Percentage on works cost.* This is sometimes used because of its simplicity, but generally it is an inaccurate method except in cases where only one type of product is made. Works cost does not usually reflect the proportion of selling costs which should be chargeable.

The rates of absorption in respect of selling and distribution costs are predetermined in a similar manner to those relating to works' expenses by using past records and taking into account future activities and estimated costs.

## 12.12    Exercises

1.   State what you understand by the following terms used in a costing system: (a) allocation; (b) apportionment; (c) absorption.

2.   (a) What are the main groups of overhead expenses?

(b) What bases can be used for apportioning indirect expenses to production and service departments?

3.   What is meant by primary and secondary distribution? Explain fully and indicate in your answer how secondary distribution can be carried out.

# Unit Thirteen
# Job and Contract Costing

## 13.1 Main Characteristics

Manufacturing is initiated by:

(*a*) receipt of a customer's order;
(*b*) issue of an internal production order.

The costs are recorded on a *job cost sheet* (discussed in Unit 13.3) which is designed to record the factual information of all items of expenditure and charges incurred, in order to ascertain the total cost. The job cost sheet is prepared in order to find the amount of profit, and to be used when comparing costs with estimates. It is also used as a comparison with previous costs of similar work and when the contract or order is placed on a *cost plus* basis.

When orders are received for standard products, they are normally taken from stock but when an order is for a standard product modified to a customer's requirements, then the job cost sheet is charged with the cost of the standard product plus the cost of modifications carried out. In other cases, the work is for whatever the customer has ordered and a manufacturing or job order number will be issued to collect the costs. Internal orders may be issued for individual items, batches of components and units for eventual assembly into finished products. *Job costing* is concerned with the costing of individual orders or contracts. The *contract* may be for items such as the construction of an hotel, a bridge or an oil rig, whereas jobs include the production of tractors, truck mixers, furniture, castings and repair work. With either jobs or contract work, it is possible to follow the work through the factory or on the site from the raw material to the completion of the job or contract.

## 13.2 Estimating

This relates to forecasting the cost of contracts, jobs, standard products and repair work. The function of the estimating department is to estimate, for the purpose of fixing selling prices, for setting standards and for providing information which can be used for comparison with actual costs. The information is also used to determine whether or not to quote or tender for certain kinds of work.

When an order or an inquiry is received there will probably be a preliminary meeting of the sales department and the design department to suggest improvements or modifications to the order where they consider it necessary. The cost estimator needs to be a person with experience and with a knowledge of plant layout, production methods, machines, equipment and tools. When dealing with tenders and quotations, the estimator must establish the expected factory cost, and allow for selling costs and other factors such as royalties, transport, special packing, value added tax (always treated separately since it may be recoverable) and terms of payment, which may increase the total outlay. He often works from preliminary designs or plans as there may not be sufficient time to prepare detailed drawings. The estimate may consist of a series of estimates based on different rates for different classes of work, such as drilling, machining or welding, rather than fixing the cost of many different items which may not be a feasible proposition because of a shortage of time.

A material schedule is then prepared by the drawing office to show the total weight of each type of raw material. This office also lists the purchased components which will be priced by the purchasing department. In many cases it will be necessary to refer to the chief engineer or drawing office manager for the drawing office costs.

It is necessary to establish the requirements and the grades of labour, with the current rates of pay in each case.

Direct expenses such as transport, insurance, and possibly the cost of outside erection, have to be allowed for, and charges have to be made for the cost of works overhead, administration costs and selling expenses.

## 13.3  Job Cost Sheets

These are designed to supply the information required and are tailor-made to suit the particular organization. There may be one cost sheet for all the details or a master sheet or summary with supporting sheets for each department.

The cost sheet may include a section which lists the main items of cost as estimated by the estimating department, so that comparisons can be made when the work is completed.

### Information Shown on Cost Sheets

The details must be properly arranged and tabulated so that management and others can grasp the important facts quickly. The following information can be provided:
- (a) the job order number for internal or customers' orders;
- (b) name of customer;
- (c) the general description of the product to be supplied or the work to be carried out;
- (d) price quoted;
- (e) delivery date;
- (f) weight of goods dispatched;
- (g) terms or conditions of sale;
- (h) selling price;
- (i) commission payable;
- (j) sub-contractors;
- (k) direct materials classified as required;
- (l) direct labour cost in each department or cost centre;
- (m) direct expenses classified for each type of expense;

| Order no. | | | | | | | | Front | |
|---|---|---|---|---|---|---|---|---|---|
| INTERMEDIATE COST SHEET | | | | | | | | | |
| GROUP | MATERIALS | Month £ p | | Month £ p | | Total £ p | | Month £ p | | Total £ p |

| GROUP | MATERIALS | Month £ | p | Month £ | p | Total £ | p | Month £ | p | Total £ | p |
|---|---|---|---|---|---|---|---|---|---|---|---|
| 1 | General stores | | | | | | | | | | |
| 2 | Bolts and nuts | | | | | | | | | | |
| 3 | Iron castings | | | | | | | | | | |
| 4 | Steel castings | | | | | | | | | | |
| 5 | Non-ferrous castings | | | | | | | | | | |
| 6 | Plates and sections | | | | | | | | | | |
| 7 | Welding | | | | | | | | | | |
| 8 | Tubes and pipes | | | | | | | | | | |
| 9 | Paint | | | | | | | | | | |
| 10 | Timber | | | | | | | | | | |
| 11 | Packing | | | | | | | | | | |
| 12 | Direct purchases | | | | | | | | | | |
| | | | | | | | | | | | |
| 1 | Drawing office | | | | | | | | | | |
| 2 | Carriage | | | | | | | | | | |
| 3 | Freight and insurance | | | | | | | | | | |
| 4 | Outside erection | | | | | | | | | | |
| 5 | Outside erection overhead | | | | | | | | | | |
| 6 | Travelling | | | | | | | | | | |
| | Carried forward | | | | | | | | | | |

*Fig. 13.1 Intermediate cost sheet (front)*

| Order no. | | | | | | | | | | | | | Back | | |
|---|---|---|---|---|---|---|---|---|---|---|---|---|---|---|---|
| INTERMEDIATE COST SHEET | | | | | | | | | | | | | | | |

| DEPT. | Month | | | Month | | | Total | | | Month | | | Total | | |
|---|---|---|---|---|---|---|---|---|---|---|---|---|---|---|---|
| | Hours | £ | p | Hours | £ | p | Hours | £ | p | Hours | £ | p | Hours | £ | p |
| b/f | – | | | – | | | – | | | – | | | – | | |
| Wages | | | | | | | | | | | | | | | |
| 1 | | | | | | | | | | | | | | | |
| 2 | | | | | | | | | | | | | | | |
| 3 | | | | | | | | | | | | | | | |
| 4 | | | | | | | | | | | | | | | |
| 5 | | | | | | | | | | | | | | | |
| 6 | | | | | | | | | | | | | | | |
| 7 | | | | | | | | | | | | | | | |
| 8 | | | | | | | | | | | | | | | |
| 9 | | | | | | | | | | | | | | | |
| 10 | | | | | | | | | | | | | | | |
| 11 | | | | | | | | | | | | | | | |
| 12 | | | | | | | | | | | | | | | |
| 13 | | | | | | | | | | | | | | | |
| Totals | | | | | | | | | | | | | | | |
| Works o/h | % | | | % | | | % | | | % | | | % | | |
| 1 | | | | | | | | | | | | | | | |
| 2 | | | | | | | | | | | | | | | |
| 3 | | | | | | | | | | | | | | | |
| 4 | | | | | | | | | | | | | | | |
| 5 | | | | | | | | | | | | | | | |
| 6 | | | | | | | | | | | | | | | |
| 7 | | | | | | | | | | | | | | | |
| 8 | | | | | | | | | | | | | | | |
| 9 | | | | | | | | | | | | | | | |
| 10 | | | | | | | | | | | | | | | |
| 11 | | | | | | | | | | | | | | | |
| 12 | | | | | | | | | | | | | | | |
| 13 | | | | | | | | | | | | | | | |
| Totals | | | | | | | | | | | | | | | |
| Admin. o/h | | | | | | | | | | | | | | | |
| Totals | | | | | | | | | | | | | | | |

*Fig. 13.2 Intermediate cost sheet (back)*

| Order no. | | | | | | Front | |
|---|---|---|---|---|---|---|---|
| **FINAL COST SHEET** | | | | | | | |
| Date order booked | | | Customer | | Order no. | | |
| Delivery date | | | Details | | | | |
| Date begun | | | Price | | Terms | | |
| Date dispatched | | | Remarks | | | | |
| **Estimate** | | | | **Materials** | | | |
| Weight | £ | p | Group | | Weight | £ | p |
| | | | 1 | General stores | | | |
| | | | 2 | Bolts and nuts | | | |
| | | | 3 | Iron castings | | | |
| | | | 4 | Steel castings | | | |
| | | | 5 | Non-ferrous castings | | | |
| | | | 6 | Plates and sections | | | |
| | | | 7 | Welding | | | |
| | | | 8 | Tubes and pipes | | | |
| | | | 9 | Paint | | | |
| | | | 10 | Timber | | | |
| | | | 11 | Packing | | | |
| | | | 12 | Direct purchases | | | |
| | | | Allocations: | From order no. | | | |
| | | | 1 | Parts common | | | |
| | | | 2 | Parts peculiar | | | |
| | | | 3 | Engine unit | | | |
| | | | 4 | Wheel unit | | | |
| | | | 5 | Jib | | | |
| | | | 6 | Jib extension | | | |
| | | | 7 | Erection | | | |
| | | | Direct expenses | | | | |
| | | | 1 | Drawing office | | | |
| | | | 2 | Carriage | | | |
| | | | 3 | Freight and insurance | | | |
| | | | 4 | Outside erection | | | |
| | | | 5 | Outside erection overhead | | | |
| | | | 6 | Travelling | | | |
| — | | | Total carried forward | | — | | |

*Fig. 13.3 Final cost sheet (front)*

| Order no. | | FINAL COST SHEET | | Cost brought forward | | Back |
|---|---|---|---|---|---|---|
| | | | | | | £    p |
| Estimate | | | | | | |
| Hours | Wages | | | Hours | £    p | |
| | £    p | Wages | | | | |
| | | 1    Foundry | | | | |
| | | 2    Pattern makers | | | | |
| | | 3    Girder and platework | | | | |
| | | 4    Forging | | | | |
| | | 5    Turning and machining | | | | |
| | | 6    Welding | | | | |
| | | 7    Fitting | | | | |
| | | 8    Erection | | | | |
| | | 9    Tooling | | | | |
| | | 10    Painting | | | | |
| | | 11    Packing | | | | |
| | | 12    Maintenance | | | | |
| | | 13    Carpenters | | | | |
| | | | | | | |
| | | Works overhead | % | | | |
| | | 1    Foundry | | | | |
| | | 2    Pattern makers | | | | |
| | | 3    Girder and platework | | | | |
| | | 4    Forging | | | | |
| | | 5    Turning and machining | | | | |
| | | 6    Welding | | | | |
| | | 7    Fitting | | | | |
| | | 8    Erection | | | | |
| | | 9    Tooling | | | | |
| | | 10    Painting | | | | |
| | | 11    Packing | | | | |
| | | 12    Maintenance | | | | |
| | | 13    Carpenters | | | | |
| | | ADMINISTRATION OVERHEAD | | | | |
| | | SELLING AND DISTRIBUTION OVERHEAD | | | | |
| | | | | Cost £ | | |
| | | Invoice price £ . . . . . . . | Profit  £ . . . . . . . | | | |
| | | | Loss  £ . . . . . . . | | | |

Fig. 13.4 Final cost sheet (back)

(n) works overhead for each department;
(o) administration overhead;
(p) selling and distribution overhead;
(q) outside erection costs;
(r) profit and loss;
(s) retention percentage.

Figs. 13.1, 13.2, 13.3 and 13.4 are examples of job cost sheets. Many jobs extend over a long period and the value of the work-in-progress accumulates over many months. If the job is incomplete at the end of the first month, the various classes of costs have to be accumulated at the end of the second month, and so on, until the work is complete. This is shown on the intermediate cost sheet in Figs. 13.1 and 13.2. When the job is complete the costs can be summarized by transferring the figures to the final cost sheet shown in Figs. 13.3 and 13.4.

Whether computers are used or the work is carried out manually, this information is needed in order to control and report on the progress of job orders. Another type of cost sheet is shown in Figs. 13.5 and 13.6.

## 13.4  Work-in-progress

Many factors determine how the costs are entered on the cost sheets. The costs may be posted weekly or monthly and the sheets may be filed in one ledger, or there may be several ledgers representing different product groups for customers' orders and work-in-progress. At the end of each cost period, the accumulated costs represent the value of work-in-progress, which is really a book inventory of work that is incomplete and of orders that have not yet been invoiced to the customer.

For example, a manufacturing company may have five product groups, and in each group, machines are produced in a variety of sizes. The company is engaged on the batch production of these machines and in the manufacture of components and spare parts which are taken into stock as they are completed. There will be five job ledgers containing the work-in-progress for the internal production orders and five job ledgers containing the work-in-progress in respect of customers' orders.

Production orders are issued for the manufacture of parts which are common to the machines of a particular group and for parts which are peculiar to different sizes and types of machines. There are also erection orders for the batches of machines. As the work is completed, transfers are made to the stores ledger and finished stock ledger and allocations are made to customers' orders in the job ledger (customers'). The sales analysis, dispatch reports and similar documents indicate the customers' orders which are complete, and transfers are made from the finished stock ledger to the job ledger (customers'). If production is continuous, with machines being allocated direct from the job ledger (stock) to the job ledger (customers'), then reference is made to erection or assembly sheets to find the orders which have to be allocated. The cost department costs the parts and components which are taken into stock, and transfers are made in total at the end of each month.

In batch production it frequently happens that some machines are completed and sold before the batch is complete. In this case an estimate is made of the eventual cost per machine when allocating costs to the customers' ledger, and this amount is adjusted when the batch order is complete. After all the postings, transfers and allocations have been made, the value on the cost sheets, after deducting the cost of goods already sold, represents the work-in-progress. The value shown on cost sheets in the job ledger (stock) represents the work-in-progress on internal jobs and production orders, and the job ledger (customers') shows the invoice values, the cost of any items and work-in-progress at the end of the month.

In order to ensure that postings, transfers and allocations agree with the original records, and as a reconciliation with the figures posted to the cost ledger, a summary is prepared for each of the job ledgers. This is necessary and is a check on the correctness of the value of work-in-progress carried forward at the end of each month. Examples are given in Figs. 13.7 and 13.8 (pp. 174 and 175).

## 13.5  Special Job Costs

Many jobs incur special costs which are essential expenses in the manufacture of the product and in the successful completion of the order to the satisfaction of the customer. Some of these special costs are described below, with an explanation of their treatment in the costing process.

(i) **Patterns.** Patterns produced specially for a particular job are chargeable to that job and may be retained for repeat orders or dispatched to the customer when the job is completed. Any repairs during the progress of the job should be charged to the job rather than to overheads.

(ii) **Jigs, tools and dies.** A similar procedure applies to these items when specially produced.

(iii) **Estimating costs.** These costs should be examined carefully and if they apply both to the production and selling function, they can be apportioned and recovered in works overhead and selling overhead. Only where these costs are exceptionally high should they be considered as a direct expense. If the estimating function comes under the control of the sales manager and the expenses are incurred with the object of acquiring orders, it is a selling overhead.

(iv) **Consultant's fees and inspection costs.** These costs are direct expenses for outside charges for advice and special inspection.

(v) **Overtime premium.** When this is requested by the customer, it can be treated as a direct expense; otherwise it is treated as an overhead expense.

(vi) **Hire of special machinery and equipment.** The cost is a direct expense chargeable to the job.

(vii) **Defective work.** The treatment of waste and scrap has already been mentioned under stores control (see Unit 10.12), but it is important to take

| Estimate | | Date | MATERIALS | | | | | | | | | Front |
| Weight | Cost £ p | | Cast iron £ p | Cast steel £ p | Plates and sections £ p | Non-ferrous £ p | Timber £ p | General stores £ p | Direct purchases £ p | Weight | Total £ p | Order no........ |
| --- | --- | --- | --- | --- | --- | --- | --- | --- | --- | --- | --- | --- |
| | | | | | | | | | | | | |
| | | | | | | | | | | | | |

Fig. 13.5 Job cost sheet (front)

JOB COST SHEET    Back

Customer . . . . . . . . . . . . . . . . . .
Particulars of order . . . . . . . . . . . . . . . . . .

Order no . . . . . . . . . .    Date . . . . . . . . . .
Estimated weight . . . . . . . . . .

**DIRECT WAGES AND OVERHEADS**
Departments

| Week ending | Foundry | | Platework | | Welding | | Machine | | Erection | | Painting | | Weekly totals | | Cumulative cost | |
|---|---|---|---|---|---|---|---|---|---|---|---|---|---|---|---|---|
| | Wages | O/h | Wages | O/h | Wages | O/h | Wages | O/h | Wages | O/h | Wages | O/h | Wages | O/h | Wages | O/h |
| | £ p | £ p | £ p | £ p | £ p | £ p | £ p | £ p | £ p | £ p | £ p | £ p | £ p | £ p | £ p | £ p |
| | | | | | | | | | | | | | | | — | — |

**DIRECT EXPENSES**

| Drawing office | | Outside erection | | Carriage | Freight and insurance |
|---|---|---|---|---|---|
| Salary | O/h | Wages | O/h | | |
| £ p | £ p | £ p | £ p | £ p | £ p |

**ESTIMATE**

| Weight | £ p |
|---|---|
| | |

**SUMMARY**

Materials
Wages
Manufacturing overhead
Direct expenses
Administration overhead
Selling and distribution overhead
Total cost

| COST | |
|---|---|
| £ | p |

Invoice price £
Profit
Loss

Fig. 13.6 Job cost sheet (back)

WORK-IN-PROGRESS (STOCK ORDERS)          Month. . . . . . . . . . . . . .  19 . . .

| Order no. | Description | Materials | Direct expenses | Wages | Works overhead | Administration overhead | Allocations | Work-in-progress |
|---|---|---|---|---|---|---|---|---|
|  |  |  |  |  |  |  |  |  |
|  | Totals |  |  |  |  |  |  |  |

*Fig. 13.7 Work-in-progress (stock orders)*

*Note:* This is a summary of the balances and final costs on the job cost sheets for stock orders.

| Order no. | Description | Materials | Allocation | Direct expenses | Wages | Works overhead | Administration overhead | Selling expenses | Cost of sales | Work-in-progress |
|-----------|-------------|-----------|------------|-----------------|-------|----------------|-------------------------|------------------|---------------|------------------|
|           |             |           |            |                 |       |                |                         |                  |               |                  |
| Totals    |             |           |            |                 |       |                |                         |                  |               |                  |

WORK-IN-PROGRESS (CUSTOMERS' ORDERS)    Month . . . . . . . . . . . . . . . 19 . . .

*Fig. 13.8 Work-in-progress (customers' orders)*

*Note:* This is a summary of the balances and final costs on customers' orders.

into account the difference between the terms scrap, waste and spoilage. Waste usually refers to material which has no value, whereas items spoiled or scrapped may have some value which can be recovered by sale or by use in some other form. Spoilage generally refers to damage resulting from manufacturing operations which is of such a nature that the work and material has to be scrapped.

Defective work, however, is faulty work or material which does not meet the standard of workmanship or quality desired, but which can be brought up to the standard desired by the use of additional materials or labour. The cost of the additional materials or labour is known as *re-operation cost*.

When the selling price of spoiled and scrapped work is significant, the value can be credited to the job or process. A similar procedure can be used if defective work is sold as scrap or re-used in some other way. If re-operation takes place with defective work, the extra costs can be charged to a standing order as production overhead, since they cannot be charged a second time to the job or contract. This applies to the cost of materials and labour up to the point or operation where the work became defective. If the defective work was caused by another department, then it can be charged to that department. A typical report is given in Fig. 13.9.

(viii) **Interest.** Where the job extends over a considerable period there may be a justifiable case for charging the cost of interest. This may apply when there is no agreement for payments on account, and where the value of work-in-progress during the period of the job is of great value. The selling price will allow for this special cost, and if cash is borrowed to finance the contract, the expense can be charged as a direct expense.

(ix) **Travelling expenses.** If expenditure on visits to site is heavy and relates to a particular job, then it is chargeable as a direct expense.

## INSPECTION DEPARTMENT

### SPOILAGE AND DEFECTIVE WORK REPORT

No. 206

Date Jan 2 19..

Cost Office copy

| Drawing no. | Part no. | Qty. | Order no. |
|---|---|---|---|
| 39798 | 3 | 10 | B. 10274 |

| Quantity | | | |
|---|---|---|---|
| Passed | Scrapped | To be replaced | Re-operation |
| 7 | 3 | 3 | — |

**DESCRIPTION**

PINS

| | Responsible for rejection | | |
|---|---|---|---|
| Man no. | Dept. | Supplier |
| 179 | 5 | — |

Reason for rejection: UNDER SIZE

Signed H.J. Inspector

Work to be carried out

PRODUCE 3 PINS FROM OPERATION 1 TO 5

| DESCRIPTION | Department | Operation no. | Material | Wages | Overhead | Total cost |
|---|---|---|---|---|---|---|
| | | | | | Cost | |
| SAW PIN 9cm × 30cm | 7 | 1 | 2.50 | 1.00 | 1.00 | 4.50 |
| CENTRE AND SPOT FACE | 4 | 2 | | 1.50 | 2.25 | 3.75 |
| TURN, GROOVE AND FINISH TAPER | 4 | 3 | | 4.00 | 6.00 | 10.00 |
| SCREW | 4 | 4 | | 1.25 | 1.87 | 3.12 |
| DRILL AND TAP | 5 | 5 | | 2.80 | 3.50 | 6.30 |
| | | | | | | |
| Totals | | | 2.50 | 10.55 | 14.62 | 27.67 |

Chargeable to:
Defective Work Account

*Fig. 13.9 A spoilage and defective work report*

*Note*: The cost of these items has already been charged to the job order number and the excess costs of replacement are treated as overhead expenses.

## 13.6    Job Costing for Parts and Components

The following is an example of a cost sheet for parts manufactured for stock, and on completion debited to the account in the stores ledger. For instance, the production department of a manufacturing company issues an order (no. 29374) for the manufacture of 10 pulley wheels, part number 72948/3. The job cost is prepared from the following information:

Material requisition no. 547 shows that 10 castings (material group 1) were issued from the stores at £5.75 each.

The job cards received by the cost department recorded the following details:

| Cost centre | Hours worked | Wages paid |
|:---:|:---:|:---:|
| | | £ |
| 1 | 8 | 11.80 |
| 2 | 10 | 18.45 |
| 3 | 4 | 6.30 |
| 4 | 3 | 5.25 |

The Works Overhead rates are as follows:

| Cost centre | Percentages on direct wages |
|:---:|:---:|
| 1 | 110 |
| 2 | 160 |
| 3 | 200 |
| 4 | 180 |

Administration costs are applied to total direct wages at the rate of 200 per cent. As this is a new part, produced to meet customers' requirements for spare parts, it is necessary to fix the selling price, which allows for a profit of 40 per cent on selling price, in accordance with the company's normal policy.

The 40 per cent margin is needed in order to cover the cost of packing and carriage charges, the incidental expenses of operating the spares and sales department, and the net profit which is required.

The selling price of the spare part is based on the estimated cost so that customers can be quoted a firm price. Should the estimated cost vary considerably from the actual cost, then the spares price on future orders will have to be revised.

The estimating department stated that the estimated unit cost of these pulley wheels was as follows:

Materials £5.75

| Cost centre | Wages | Works overhead | Administration overhead |
|:---:|:---:|:---:|:---:|
| | £ | £ | £ |
| 1 | 1.19 | 1.31 | |
| 2 | 1.83 | 2.93 | |
| 3 | 0.63 | 1.26 | |
| 4 | 0.50 | 0.90 | |
| 1–4 | | | 8.30 |

The cost sheet is shown in Fig. 13.10.

### Cost sheet

Description 10 pulley wheels                     Order no.: 29374
Part no. 72948/3                                 Date: January 23, 19..

| Unit cost | | | | | Total |
|---|---|---|---|---|---|
| Estimated cost | Actual cost | Direct materials | | | cost |
| £ | £ | | | | £ |
| 5.75 | 5.750 | Group 1 | | | 57.50 |
| | | Direct wages | | | |
| | | | Hours | £ | |
| 1.19 | 1.180 | Cost centre 1 | 8 | 11.80 | |
| 1.83 | 1.845 | Cost centre 2 | 10 | 18.45 | |
| 0.63 | 0.630 | Cost centre 3 | 4 | 6.30 | |
| 0.50 | 0.525 | Cost centre 4 | 3 | 5.25 | |
| £4.15 | £4.180 | | | | 41.80 |
| | | Works overhead | % | | |
| 1.31 | 1.298 | Cost centre 1 | 110 | 12.98 | |
| 2.93 | 2.952 | Cost centre 2 | 160 | 29.52 | |
| 1.26 | 1.260 | Cost centre 3 | 200 | 12.60 | |
| 0.90 | 0.945 | Cost centre 4 | 180 | 9.45 | |
| 6.40 | 6.455 | | | | 64.55 |
| | | Administration | % | | |
| 8.30 | 8.360 | Overhead: | 200 | | 83.60 |
| £24.60 | £24.745 | Total cost | | | £247.45 |

Selling price of pulley wheel, 72948/3
                Selling price = 100%
        Profit margin = 40% of Selling price
        Cost price = 60% of Selling price

$$\text{Selling price} = \frac{\text{Estimated cost}}{\text{Cost price \%}} \times \text{Selling price \%}$$

$$= \frac{£24.60}{60} \times 100$$

$$= £41.00$$

*Fig. 13.10 Example of a cost sheet*

*Note:* When these items are sold there will be further costs for packing, carriage, etc., as well as a charge for selling and distribution overheads.

## 13.7    Job Costing of Batch Production and Customers' Orders

The next example concerns a cost sheet for the sale of a product composed of parts and units manufactured under job costing methods. The details of these costs are shown in the job ledger (stock and work-in-progress), and on the sale of machines a transfer is made of the value of the units which make up a complete machine.

**Example 13.1**

The sales department of a manufacturing company issued an order (No. 3126) for the preparation and dispatch of a machine ordered by a customer, XY Contracting Co Ltd. The machine is to be modified and painted to the customer's requirements, and the production department has already issued various orders to manufacture, for stock, parts and units for these machines, and instructions have been given for the erection of a batch of twelve standard machines. These are still in the process of being erected and the first machine has been completed, modified, dispatched and invoiced to the customer at £10 150 plus £100 for the cost of modifications. The following information enables the cost sheet (see Fig. 13.11) to be prepared:

Units and orders allocated from the job ledger (stock and work-in-progress) to the customer's ledger:

|  |  | £ |
|---|---|---|
| Order number 30562 | One set of parts common | 3 483 |
| Order number 30563 | One set of parts peculiar | 2 987 |
| Order number 29578 | One petrol unit | 1 298 |
| Order number 31123 | Erection | 432 |

Modification costs and other expenses charged to the customer's order:

*Direct expenses* are as follows:

| *Materials* | £ | | £ |
|---|---|---|---|
| Mild steel | 15.88 | Drawing office | 15 |
| General stores | 10.76 | Carriage outwards | 174 |
| Timber | 15.04 | Royalty | 100 |
| Packing materials | 12.49 | Cost of travelling and expenses | |
| Paint | 23.06 | of operating instructor | 35 |

*Wages paid*

| Fitting shop 17 hours | 26.98 |
|---|---|
| Painting shop 8 hours | 14.63 |
| Packing shop 4 hours | 6.38 |

*Works overhead* Rate per direct labour hour

| Fitting shop | 2.25 |
|---|---|
| Painting shop | 1.50 |
| Packing shop | 1.45 |

Administration costs are included in works overhead and selling expenses. Sales expenses are applied at 6 per cent of invoice value.

Cost sheet

Customer: XY Contracting Co Ltd          Order no.: 3126

                                         Date: June 10, 19..

Description of order: One machine, modified and painted to requirements

| *Materials* | | £ | £ |
|---|---|---|---|
| Mild steel | | 15.88 | |
| General stores | | 10.76 | |
| Timber | | 15.04 | |
| Packing materials | | 12.49 | |
| Paint | | 23.06 | |
| | | | 77.23 |
| *Allocations* | | | |
| One set parts common | Order no. 30562 | 3 483.00 | |
| One set parts peculiar | Order no. 30563 | 2 987.00 | |
| One petrol unit | Order no. 29578 | 1 298.00 | |
| Erection | Order no. 31123 | 432.00 | |
| | | | 8 200.00 |
| *Direct expenses* | | | |
| Drawing office | | 15.00 | |
| Carriage outwards | | 174.00 | |
| Royalty | | 100.00 | |
| Travelling costs and expenses | | | |
| of operating instructor | | 35.00 | |
| | | | 324.00 |
| *Direct labour* | *Hours* | | |
| Fitting shop | 17 | 26.98 | |
| Painting shop | 8 | 14.63 | |
| Packing shop | 4 | 6.38 | |
| | | | 47.99 |
| *Works overhead* | *Per direct* | | |
| | *labour hour* | | |
| Fitting shop | 2.25 | 38.25 | |
| Painting shop | 1.50 | 12.00 | |
| Packing shop | 1.45 | 5.80 | |
| | | | 56.05 |
| *Selling expenses:* 6% of £10 250 | | | 615.00 |
| | | Total cost: | £9 320.27 |
| *Invoice price:* | | | 10 250.00 |
| | | Profit/(Loss) | £  929.73 |

*Fig. 13.11 Cost sheet for machine ordered by XY Contracting Co Ltd*

## 13.8    Contract Costing

Companies engaged in the building, civil engineering and heavy engineering industries use job costing in the form of contract accounts, because the contracts tend to last for a fairly long time. The terms of the contract therefore usually allow for progress payments to be made during the course of the contruction. At the end of the financial year, an assessment is made of the amount of work completed, and when it is clear that a profit is being made, credit can be taken for ascertainable profit while the contract is in progress, subject to certain limitations.

If the outcome cannot reasonably be assessed before the conclusion of the contract, then it is not prudent to take any profit at that stage. When a loss is expected, then provision should be made for the whole of the loss as soon as it is recognized, and this reduces the value of the work done to date to its net realizable value.

### Interest on Borrowed Money
It is not normally appropriate to include interest; however, where sums borrowed can be identified as financing long-term contracts, interest can be included, but the facts should be clearly stated.

### Attributable Profit
When the outcome of the contract can be assessed with reasonable certainty then it may be possible to calculate that part of the total profit currently estimated to arise over the duration of the contract. But the likely increases in cost so far not recoverable under the terms of the contract, which fairly reflect the profit attributable to that part of the work performed at the accounting date, must be allowed for.

### Foreseeable Losses
An estimate of foreseeable losses has to be made, irrespective of whether or not the work has started, or of what proportion of the work has been carried out, or of whether profits are expected to arise on other contracts.

### Disclosure in Accounts
A long-term contract can be described as 'at cost plus attributable profit (if any) less foreseeable losses (if any) and progress payments received and receivable'. An adequate explanation of the policy followed in arriving at the value of work-in-progress should be set out in a note.

### Items included in Contract Accounts
(i) **Materials.** These are sent to site by the stores department or they may be ordered as direct purchases and delivered to site by the supplier. At the end of the year, unused materials are credited to the Contract Account and carried down as a debit in this account on the first day of the following period. During the year, materials are sometimes returned to suppliers or to stores and may also be transferred to, or received from, other sites.

(ii) **Wages and salaries.** These are prepared at the company's head office or on large contracts by the site accountant or cashier. When wages are outstanding at the end of the year, the accrued amount should be debited to the Contract Account and carried down as a credit on the first day of the next period.

(iii) **Plant and equipment.** The value of fixed assets sent to site can be charged to the Contract Account or retained on the books at head office. If the book value is charged to the Contract Account, at the year end this must be depreciated in the normal way and the new book value carried down. The account is credited with the written down value of the asset on the last day of the year, and the same figure is debited to the account when brought down on the first day of the new year.

### Contract Account

| 19.. | | £ | 19.. | | £ | £ |
|---|---|---|---|---|---|---|
| Feb. 7 | Plant sent to site | 20 000 | Dec. 31 | Plant | 20 000 | |
| | | | | *less* | | |
| | | | | depreciation | 2 000 | |
| | | | | Amount carried down | | 18 000 |

If plant is purchased specially for the contract, it should be registered in the plant register in the usual way but posted to the Contract Account, not to the Plant Account. If plant is sold when the work is finished, the value of the sale should then be credited to the Contract Account and no posting is needed in the Plant Account. The wear and tear on plant used on contracts is often very great, and at the end of each accounting period it is valued and this amount is credited to the Contract Account. Any charges for transport, erection, dismantling and repairs and maintenance are charged to the Contract Account. Plant is frequently hired, and in this case the cost is a direct charge to the account.

When a large company has a number of contracts proceeding at the same time, with plant being used on several jobs, then it may be possible to use an hourly, daily or weekly rate for the use of the plant. A Plant Repairs and Maintenance Account is used for collecting the costs and the appropriate amounts are credited to this account and charged to the Contract Accounts.

(iv) **Head office overheads.** This expense is debited to the Contract Account, but the method used for charging depends on the circumstances. The costs are mainly estimating and administration which should be charged in proportion to the services provided by the headquarters staff.

(v) **Sub-contracts.** This expense may form a substantial part of the total cost and is a direct charge to the account. At each stage of the contract as the value of the completed work is certified, it is essential to include an amount to cover the cost of sub-contract work completed but not yet invoiced.

(vi) **Retention money.** The method of payment is set out in the contract and normally allows for progress payments at suitable intervals. These payments are made on the authority of certificates issued by the customer's engineer, architect or surveyor stating what he considers to be the value of work completed to the standard required. To ensure that the work is completed on time, so-called *penalty clauses* are often included in contracts. These set agreed *liquidated damages* which are payable by the contractor if he fails to complete on time, and entitle the customer to retain part of the payment, the *retention money*, to cover the so-called penalty, or the correction of the faulty work. This is a percentage of the value of the work certified or of the contract price. Usually, the full value of the order is invoiced on completion of the work but a certain amount will not be due for payment until a specified date.

(vii) **Profit taken during the progress of the contract.** As already explained under attributable profit earlier in this section, it may be possible to take a reasonable proportion of the profit during the process of the contract. To allow for contingencies and to take a fair amount of profit it is necessary to examine the contract in respect of the proportion of the work which has been completed and the time which has elapsed since the work began, as well as the value of the work certified, the amount of cash received and the total value of the contract. SSAP 9 makes some suggestions about work-in-progress in this type of situation.

We have to arrive at the notional or apparent profit and then to take a proportion of this to the Profit and Loss Account and to reserve or hold in suspense the remainder of the notional profit. The profit taken and the profit reserved are debited to the Contract Account and the amount reserved is carried down as a credit to the next period. After taking into account the above factors it is usual to apply an arbitrary fraction of, say, two-thirds or three-quarters when calculating the amount of profit to take to the Profit and Loss Account.

**Example 13.2**

| | | |
|---|---|---|
| (a) | Cost of work certified | £325 000 |
| (b) | Value of work certified | £400 000 (proportion of contract price) |
| (c) | Notional profit $(b-a)$ | £75 000 (estimated or apparent profit) |
| (d) | Cash received (85% of $b$) | £340 000 (allowing for 15% retention) |
| (e) | Cost of work not yet certified | £75 000 |
| (f) | Profit taken to Profit and Loss Account | A proportion of $\frac{2}{3}$ of notional profit |
| (g) | Proportion of $\frac{2}{3}$ taken | A fraction $(d)/(b)$ represented by the cash received over the work certified (because it would be imprudent to take the profit on the retention money as being earned until it is actually paid under the terms of the contract) |

The above information can now be shown as:

$$\frac{2}{3} \times \text{Notional profit} \times \frac{\text{Cash received}}{\text{Value of work certified}}$$

$$= \frac{2}{3} \times £75\,000 \times \frac{£340\,000}{£400\,000} = £42\,500 \text{ to Profit and Loss Account}$$

and £75 000 − £42 500 = £32 500 Profit reserved and carried forward.

The Contract Account for the next period of account will show *debit* items for values brought down such as materials on site, plant at written-down value, and the cost of work not yet certified. On the *credit* side will be shown the profit held in reserve, and accrued expenses such as wages, direct expenditure, and the value of work not yet invoiced by the sub-contractors.

If the work is near completion it may be considered reasonable to take three-quarters of the notional profit instead of two-thirds as shown above.

Another formula which can be used is

$$\text{Proportion taken} = \text{Notional profit} \times \frac{\text{Value of work certified}}{\text{Contract price}}$$

(viii) **Work-in-progress.** There are alternative methods of showing the closing entries in Contract Accounts. In the first method, there are credit entries for the *cost* of the work not yet certified and the *value* of the work certified. The value represents the sales value of the work completed at the date of the certificate, and this amount is debited to the contractee in the customer's account. Foreseeable losses which are estimated to arise during the duration of the contract should be credited to the Contract Account. The work-in-progress should be stated in the balance sheet at cost plus attributable profit or less a foreseeable loss, and a deduction must be made for cash received at the accounting date. (In examinations, unless there are instructions to the contrary, the method shown in Fig. 13.12 should be followed.)

The alternative method ignores the cost of work certified, work not yet certified and the profit reserved. The Contract Account is balanced by a credit entry in respect of work-in-progress, and this is carried down as a debit entry which opens the account for the next period. It is shown in the balance sheet at this figure, less the cash received. An example of the alternative method is given later in this Unit. First, we must look at a Contract Account which shows the value of work certified and not yet certified.

## 13.9 An Example of a Contract Account

A building company is working on a contract for extensions to factory buildings. The contract with F and C Contruction Co Ltd is valued at £720 000 and began on September 1, 19.6. The balances shown at January 1, 19.7 were as follows:

*Debit balances*

|  | £ |
|---|---|
| Work-in-progress at cost | 70 000 |
| Materials on site | 32 000 |
| Plant at cost | 33 000 |

Other accounts and details appropriate to the contract for the year 19.7 are as follows:

|  | £ |
|---|---|
| Materials issued to site | 134 000 |
| Wages paid | 129 000 |
| Plant sent to site during the year at cost | 95 000 |
| Materials returned to headquarters | 6 000 |
| Head office overheads | 24 000 |
| Sub-contractor's charges not yet received | 90 000 |
| Accrued wages | 3 000 |
| Plant hire | 8 000 |
| Cash received | 432 000 |
| Cost of work not yet certified | 73 000 |
| Value of work certified as complete | 480 000 |
| Materials on site at December 31, 19.7 | 29 000 |
| Plant on site at December 31, 19.7 at valuation | 114 000 |

The Contract Account is shown in Fig. 13.12 opposite.

Contract for Extension of Factory Buildings Account

| 19.7 | | £ | 19.7 | | £ |
|---|---|---|---|---|---|
| Jan. 1 | Work-in-progress at cost b/d | 70 000 | Jan./Dec. | Materials returned to stores | 6 000 |
| Jan. 1 | Materials on site b/d | 32 000 | | Materials on site c/d | 29 000 |
| Jan. 1 | Plant at site at cost b/d | 33 000 | | Plant at valuation c/d | 114 000 |
| Jan./Dec. | Materials issued to site | 134 000 | | Cost of work not yet certified c/d | 73 000 |
| Jan./Dec. | Wages paid | 129 000 | | | 222 000 |
| Jan./Dec. | Plant sent to site at cost | 95 000 | | Value of work certified | |
| Jan./Dec. | Plant hire | 8 000 | | (Customer's | |
| Jan./Dec. | Head office overheads | 24 000 | | A/c) | 480 000 |
| Jan./Dec. | Sub-contractor's charges not yet received c/d | 90 000 | | | |
| Dec. 31 | Wages accrued c/d | 3 000 | | | |
| | | 618 000 | | | |
| Dec. 31 | Profit on contract (to Profit and Loss A/c) | 50 400 | | | |
| Dec. 31 | Profit reserved c/d | 33 600 | | | |
| | | £702 000 | | | £702 000 |
| 19.8 | | | 19.8 | | |
| Jan. 1 | Materials on site b/d | 29 000 | Jan. 1 | Sub-contractor's charges b/d | 90 000 |
| Jan. 1 | Plant at valuation b/d | 114 000 | Jan. 1 | Wages accrued b/d | 3 000 |
| Jan. 1 | Cost of work not yet certified b/d | 73 000 | Jan. 1 | Profit reserved b/d | 33 600 |

*Fig. 13.12 Example of a Contract Account*

*Note:* The account in Fig. 13.12 shows that the total expenditure to December 31, 19.7, as represented by the *debits*, is £618 000, and the *credits*, including the cost of work not yet certified, is £222 000. This enables a figure to be obtained which provides the cost of work certified. The apparent or notional profit can be found by subtracting this from the value of work certified and a calculation can then be made to find the amount of profit to take to the Profit and Loss Account.

*(continued overleaf)*

Cost of work certified = £618 000 *less* £222 000 = £396 000

Notional profit = Value of work certified *less* Cost of work certified
$$= £480 000 \text{ } less \text{ } £396 000 = £84 000$$

Profit taken to Profit and Loss Account

$$= \frac{2}{3} \times \text{Notional profit} \times \frac{\text{Cash received}}{\text{Work certified}}$$

$$= \frac{2}{3} \times £84 000 \times \frac{£432 000}{£480 000} = £50 400$$

Profit reserved and carried forward
$$= \text{Notional profit } less \text{ Profit to Profit and Loss A/c}$$
$$= £84 000 \text{ } less \text{ } £50 400 = £33 600$$

The Customer's Account appears in Fig. 13.13.

### F and C Construction Co Ltd Account

| | £ | | | £ |
|---|---|---|---|---|
| Value of work certified | | Cash | | 432 000 |
| (Contract A/c) | 480 000 | Balance | c/d | 48 000 |
| | £480 000 | | | £480 000 |
| | | | | |
| Balance | b/d  48 000 | | | |

*Fig. 13.13 Example of a Customer's Contract Account*

It should be noted that the balance of £48 000 is retention money and at this stage of the contract the customer is not a debtor for £48 000. The amount should be included with work-in-progress.

| *Work-in-progress* | (workings) |
|---|---|
| | £ |
| Cost of work not yet certified | 73 000 |
| Debit balance on Customer's Account | 48 000 |
| | 121 000 |
| *Less* Profit reserved | 33 600 |
| | 87 400 |

The other balances in the Contract Account will appear under their respective headings in the balance sheet.

The following calculation should be made to obtain the figures for inclusion in the balance sheet:

|                              | £       |
|------------------------------|---------|
| Cost of work certified       | 396 000 |
| Cost of work not certified   | 73 000  |
| Contract value at cost       | 469 000 |
| *Add* Profit taken           | 50 400  |
|                              | 519 400 |
| *Less* Cash received         | 432 000 |
|                              | 87 400  |

Items in the above exercise would appear in the balance sheet as follows:

### Balance sheet (Part only)

| Fixed assets | £ | £ | Profit and Loss | £ | £ |
|---|---|---|---|---|---|
| Plant at site | | | Account | | 50 400 |
| (at cost) | 128 000 | | *Current liabilities* | | |
| *Less* Depreciation | 14 000 | | Creditors— | | |
| | | 114 000 | Sub-contractor | 90 000 | |
| | | | Wages accrued | 3 000 | |
| *Current assets* | | | | | 93 000 |
| Work-in-progress | 519 400 | | | | |
| *Less* Cash | | | | | |
| received | 432 000 | | | | |
| | | 87 400 | | | |
| Materials on site | 29 000 | | | | |

Plant depreciation is calculated as shown below.

| 19.8 | | | £ |
|---|---|---|---|
| Jan. 1 | Balance at cost | b/d | 33 000 |
| Jan./Dec. | Plant sent to site | | 95 000 |
| | | | 128 000 |
| Dec. 31 | Plant at valuation | | 114 000 |
| | *Depreciation* | | 14 000 |

**Alternative method.** The work-in-progress is £519 400 and this balances the account. It is shown above as cost to date £469 000 plus profit taken £50 400, and is stated in the balance sheet at £519 400 less cash received £432 000 (£87 400).

The Contract Account in abbreviated form is shown in Fig. 13.14 (p. 190).

### Contract for Extension of Factory Buildings Account

| | £ | | £ |
|---|---|---|---|
| Total expenditure to date | 618 000 | Materials returned to stores | 6 000 |
| Profit to Profit and Loss | | Materials on site | c/d 29 000 |
| A/c | 50 400 | Plant at valuation | c/d 114 000 |
| | | | 149 000 |
| | | Work-in-progress | c/d 519 400 |
| | £668 400 | | £668 400 |
| Materials on site | b/d 29 000 | Sub-contractor's | |
| Plant at valuation | b/d 114 000 | charges | b/d 90 000 |
| Work-in-progress | b/d 519 400 | Wages accrued | b/d 3 000 |

*Fig. 13.14 Abbreviated Contract Account*

The Customer's Account would show a credit balance for the cash received on account. On the balance sheet this would be shown as a reduction from the work-in-progress figure of £519 400 to give a figure of £87 400.

## 13.10 Exercises

1. A medium-sized engineering company produces standard products by batch production. It also makes large machines which are job-costed on a contract basis and erected at the customer's site. Production of these takes from one to three years. You are asked to:

(a) State the functions of an estimating department and explain the services which it will provide to a business similar to the above;

(b) Prepare an estimate for a machine designed to customer's requirements, manufactured and assembled at the company's works, but erected at the customer's site.

2. Draw up a cost sheet for use in a field with which you are familiar.

# Unit Fourteen
# Process Costing

## 14.1 A Comparison of Job Order Costing and Process Costing

The production or manufacture of specific orders is known as the job order system. In order to find the production cost, each of the elements of cost for the operations to be carried out and for the components of the finished product are accumulated separately. There is a continuous collection of different manufacturing costs and each part of the order can be identified as production proceeds. The cost of the job is found when the order is complete. In comparison, production which is evaluated by using process costing is a continuous flow of the same kind of units passing through one or more processes, and the accumulation of the elements of cost is collected from process to process. This continues until instructions are given to stop or reduce production. The cost of each department or process is found at the end of each cost period, and costs accumulate as they are transferred from process to process, or the processes themselves are operations which are added together to find the total cost.

## 14.2 Equivalent Production

With production by processes, costing is carried out at the end of each cost period, and usually some unfinished units remain in process when the costs are taken. It is therefore necessary to have a report on the stage of completion and to calculate what is known as *equivalent units*. *Equivalent production* represents fully completed units and when dealing with work in process, information is needed on the degree of completeness so that a correct valuation can be made in the Process Accounts. An estimate of the degree of completion is made on a percentage basis. For example, 100 units which are 50 per cent complete are equivalent to 50 complete units. This type of information is needed so that the correct values can be applied to units transferred to other processes, to the finished units and to the units still in process.

## 14.3 Process Costing Procedure

Job costing usually incurs a lot of detail, and costs are computed from day to day whereas process costs tend to be computed at the end of the month. Process costing is carried out, to a large extent, on the basis of average costs and overall this leads to less work and smaller clerical expenses, although average costs often provide misleading results.

When there is more than one process, costs flow from one process to the next until production is complete. The units are then transferred to a Finished

Goods Account. Between processes, the finished output of each process becomes the raw material of the next process in the production programme. The costing procedure is as follows:

(a) direct and indirect costs are collected in accounts and at the end of the cost period they are charged to processes;

(b) daily and weekly records are made of quantities of production such as units, kilogrammes, etc. The monthly figures of each process are drawn up and recorded in the form of a report.

(c) the average cost per unit is obtained for each process by dividing the total cost of each process by the normal output of each process;

(d) at the end of the period, a calculation is made to obtain the equivalent production for each process;

(e) the cost of units normally lost is borne by the units completed;

(f) where joint products are manufactured, the process costs should be apportioned on a fair and acceptable basis (see Unit 14.6);

(g) when costs are computed, it is necessary to deal with normal losses, abnormal losses, spoilage and by-products.

On the assumption that all finished products are transferred at the end of a period, the following information is needed for each process:

(i) the quantity of units in process at the beginning of the period and their stage of completion in the form of a percentage;

(ii) the quantity received from the preceding process;

(iii) the quantity transferred to the next process;

(iv) the quantity of finished units at the end of the period;

(v) the units still in process and their stage of completion at the end of the period.

**Example 14.1** (Equivalent units, unit costs and a Process Account)

(a) *Process costs*

| Process A | £ | £ | |
|---|---|---|---|
| Opening stock (950 units 40% complete) | | 1 292 | *Opening stock and costs in the current period* |
| Material | 9 143 | | |
| Wages | 4 600 | | |
| Overheads | 6 900 | | |
| Debited to Process Account | | 20 643 | |
| | | £21 935 | |

*(b) Details of production in current period*

| | Actual units | Equivalent units |
|---|---|---|
| Opening stock (40% complete) | 950 | 380 |
| Units introduced | 6 000 | |
| Units transferred to Process B | 5 900 | |
| Closing stock (36% complete) | 1 050 | 378 |

| *(c) Equivalent production* | Units |
|---|---|
| Incomplete units at beginning of period (60% of 950) | 570 |
| Units introduced | 6 000 |
| Incomplete units in process | 6 570 |
| *Less* Closing stock (incomplete 64% of 1 050) | 672 |
| Equivalent production | 5 898 |

| *Proof:* | Units |
|---|---|
| Units introduced and completed (6 000 − 1 050) | 4 950 |
| Opening stock completed (60% of 950) | 570 |
| Closing stock (equivalent units = 36% of 1 050) | 378 |
| | 5 898 |

*(d) Unit cost in current period*

$$\frac{\text{Current cost}}{\text{Equivalent production}} = \frac{\text{Materials} + \text{Wages} + \text{Overheads}}{5\ 898}$$

$$= \frac{£9\ 143 + £4\ 600 + £6\ 900}{5\ 898} = \frac{£20\ 643}{5\ 898} = £3.50$$

| *(e) Transfer value of completed units* | £ |
|---|---|
| Process costs (£1 292 + £9 143 + £4 600 + £6 900) | 21 935 |
| *Less* Value of closing stock (36% of 1 050 × £3.50) = 378 × £3.50 | 1 323 |
| Value of units transferred to Process B | £20 612 |

*Proof:*

| Units | | £ |
|---|---|---|
| 950 | { Cost charged in previous period | 1 292 |
| | { Cost charged in current period (570 × £3.50) | 1 995 |
| 4 950 | Introduced and completed in current period (4 950 × £3.50) | 17 325 |
| 5 900 | Units transferred | £20 612 |

(f)

## Process A Account

| | Units | £ | | Units | £ |
|---|---|---|---|---|---|
| Opening stock (40% | | | Transfer to | | |
| complete) | 950 | 1 292 | Process B | 5 900 | 20 612 |
| Materials | 6 000 | 9 143 | Closing stock (36% | | |
| Wages | | 4 600 | complete) balance | | |
| Overheads | | 6 900 | carried down | 1 050 | 1 323 |
| | 6 950 | £21 935 | | 6 950 | £21 935 |
| Balance b/d | | | | | |
| (36% complete) | 1 050 | 1 323 | | | |

## 14.4    Normal Losses and Abnormal Losses or Gains

The nature of operations in the process industries usually includes wastage of materials as a result of evaporation, spillage, handling and other causes. The loss or wastage may be perceptible, but frequently it is invisible and unavoidable. In most factories, conditions and circumstances are seldom ideal and a measure of loss has to be accepted as normal. The materials which emerge from a process can be subjected to a quantity and a quality control. Under normal conditions the input of materials will be expected to produce a certain yield. Operating efficiency can be measured by calculating a yield percentage, and comparing this with a percentage which indicates the output expected. The estimated output may be fixed by the use of a formula or may be based on expert judgment. It is often fixed following tests carried out over a short period when the plant is operating under normal conditions. It is useful to remind ourselves of the terminology used for losses and gains (see Unit 13.5).

*Waste* is discarded substances having no value.

*Scrap* is discarded material having some recovery value.

*Spoilage* is units of output which fail to reach the required standard of quality or specification. Such faulty units may be capable of rectification, and this can be done if the cost of doing so is less than the loss in value from allowing the fault to remain uncorrected. When it is uneconomic to rectify a fault, the article may be sold as sub-standard if it is still functionally sound; otherwise it may be disposed of as scrap.

*By-product* is a product which is recovered incidentally from the material used in the manufacture of recognized main products. A by-product might have either a net realizable value or a usable value, such value being relatively unimportant in comparison with the saleable value of the main products.

### Example 14.2

A new process is to receive 1 000 units of material, and it is estimated that there will be a process loss of 5 per cent, and an output of 950 units. During the first period of production the actual output amounted to 945 units. Calculate the yield on output expected and the yield from actual output.

*Output expected*

$$\text{Yield} = \frac{\text{Estimated output}}{\text{Weight or units entering process}} \times 100$$

$$= \frac{950}{1\ 000} \times 100 = \underline{\underline{95\%}}$$

*Actual output*

$$\text{Yield} = \frac{\text{Actual output}}{\text{Weight or units charged to process}} \times 100$$

$$= \frac{945}{1\ 000} \times 100 = \underline{\underline{94.5\%}}$$

In job costing, it is usually easy to trace the source of the loss, but, when material goes through a process, it is much more difficult as wastage may occur throughout the process or at the beginning or end of it. If it occurs throughout the process, one might assume that all the units or materials should bear the loss, but general practice is to make the completed units only bear the loss. A loss which is visible and accumulates during the process may be in the form of waste, which has no value, or scrap material, which can be used in future processes or may be sold. If it has a value, the normal loss which is borne by the good units will be smaller by that amount.

*Abnormal loss* is the loss caused by inefficiency, unsuitable and low standard material, and any conditions which arise during the process which are not acceptable in normal circumstances. An abnormal loss should not be charged to production but credited to the Process Account and debited to an Abnormal Loss Account, before being charged to the Profit and Loss Account.

## 14.5  Treatment in the Accounts of Normal and Abnormal Output

### Normal Output

Producers will want to know the cost per unit of normal output, which is the yield expected from a given quantity of material or units of input. If no loss is expected during processing, the normal output is the quantity of material or units introduced. In other cases, a calculation has to be made by using the yield percentage to find the units of normal output and normal loss.

**Example 14.3**

Yield expected 95%
Costs of materials and conversion costs £9 500
Units of materials introduced 1 000

$$\text{Normal output} = \frac{95}{100} \times 1\ 000 = 950 \text{ units}$$

Normal loss (1 000 − 950) = 50 units

$$\text{Cost per unit} = \frac{£9\ 500}{950} = \underline{\underline{£10}} \quad \left( \frac{\text{Processing costs}}{\text{Normal output}} \right)$$

In this example it is assumed that the normal loss has no scrap value, and therefore the good units bear the whole of the cost, including the normal loss. When the scrap has a value, the cost per unit is reduced by taking the scrap value into account. Suppose, for example, scrap is sold at £0.95 per unit.

Cost of processing = £9 500 − (50 × £0.95) = £9 500 − £47.50 = £9 452.50

$$\text{Cost per unit} = \frac{£9\ 452.50}{950} = \underline{\underline{£9.95}} \quad \left( \frac{\text{Net processing cost}}{\text{Normal output}} \right)$$

**Abnormal Loss and Abnormal Gain**
When there is a difference between the actual output and the normal (estimated) output there is either an abnormal gain or an abnormal loss. Provided the abnormal units pass through the complete process, thereby incurring the same materials and conversion costs as the other units, then the cost per unit is the same for both normal and abnormal units. The following accounts may be required:

(i) **Normal Loss Account.**
(ii) **Abnormal Loss Account.** This is required when the actual number of units lost is greater than the normal (estimated) loss in units. The loss in abnormal units is found when, after allowing for incomplete units, the units of input exceed the good units produced *plus* the units of normal loss.
(iii) **Abnormal Gain Account.** This is required when, after allowing for incomplete units, the good units produced *plus* the loss in normal units is greater than the units of input.

When an abnormal gain occurs, the real loss in units is the difference between the number of units of normal loss and the number of abnormal units, as the abnormal gain appears on the debit side of the Process Account and the normal loss is shown on the credit side.

When the normal loss is sold as scrap, the amount recovered is shown with the units of normal loss on the credit side of the Process Account. There is a confused situation when an abnormal gain occurs, because the normal loss in units and the scrap value of those units appears on the credit side of the Process Account in the usual way, but an adjustment is made in the Normal Loss Account to reduce the units to the actual number lost. This procedure is necessary in order to record the correct unit cost in the Process Account and the actual amount recovered for scrap is shown in the Normal Loss Account.

The balance on the Abnormal Gain Account or on an Abnormal Loss Account is transferred to the Profit and Loss Account.

The book-keeping entries are as follows:

Normal loss
    *Debit* Normal Loss A/c    *Credit* Process A/c (with units and scrap value)
    *Debit* Debtor's A/c      *Credit* Normal Loss A/c (with sale of scrap)

Abnormal gain
    *Debit* Process A/c        *Credit* Abnormal Gain A/c (with units and
                                   production cost of units)
Reduce the credit amount in the Abnormal Gain A/c by transferring the units at the scrap value to the Normal Loss A/c. This reduces the units in the Normal Loss A/c, to the actual number sold.
    *Debit* Abnormal Gain A/c   *Credit* Normal Loss A/c (with units at scrap
                                   value)

Abnormal loss
    *Debit* Abnormal Loss A/c   *Credit* Process A/c (with units and production
                                   cost of units)
    *Debit* Debtor's A/c      *Credit* Abnormal Loss A/c (with sale of scrap)

These entries are illustrated in Example 14.4.

**Example 14.4** (Entries for an abnormal gain)

| | | |
|---|---|---|
| Units produced | 4 850 | |
| Units of normal loss (5% of input) | 250 | (5% of 5 000) |
| | 5 100 | |
| *Less* | | |
| Units introduced into process | 5 000 @ £1.00 each | |
| Units of abnormal gain | 100 | |
| Normal loss: sold as scrap at £0.10 per unit | | |
| Normal recovery 250 @ £0.10 | £25 | |
| *Less* | | |
| Reduction in scrap units sold due to 100 units of | | |
|   abnormal gain | £10 | |
| Value of scrap sold | £15 | |
| Direct labour | £1 900 | |
| Overheads | £3 100 | |

### Process Account 1

| | Units | Per unit | Value | | Units | Per unit | Value |
|---|---|---|---|---|---|---|---|
| | | £ | £ | | | £ | £ |
| Materials | 5 000 | 1.00 | 5 000 | Normal loss | 250 | 0.10 | 25 |
| Direct labour | | | 1 900 | Process 2 | 4 850 | 2.10 | 10 185 |
| Overheads | | | 3 100 | | | | |
| Abnormal gain | 100 | 2.10 | 210 | | | | |
| | 5 100 | | £10 210 | | 5 100 | | £10 210 |

The cost per unit is calculated as follows:

Normal output = 95% of 5 000 = 4 750 units

Actual output = 4 850 units

Abnormal gain    100 units

Normal loss = 5 000 units − 4 750 units = 250 units

Scrap value of normal loss = 250 × £0.10 = £25

Process cost = Total cost − Cost of normal loss

= (Materials + Direct labour + Overheads) − Normal loss

= (£5 000 + £1 900 + £3 100) − £25

= £10 000 − £25 = £9 975

$$\text{Cost per unit} = \frac{\text{Process cost}}{\text{Normal output}} = \frac{£9\ 975}{4\ 750} = £2.10$$

The 4 850 units transferred to the next process and the *debit* for 100 units of abnormal gain are priced at £2.10 per unit and these entries close the Process Account.

### Normal Loss Account

| | Units | Per unit | Value | | Units | Per unit | Value |
|---|---|---|---|---|---|---|---|
| | | £ | £ | | | £ | £ |
| Process 1 A/c | 250 | 0.10 | 25 | Abnormal Gain | | | |
| | | | | A/c | 100 | 0.10 | 10 |
| | | | | Debtor's A/c | 150 | 0.10 | 15 |
| | 250 | | £25 | | 250 | | £25 |

The real loss in units equals 250 units of normal loss *less* 100 units of abnormal gain and 150 units are sold for £15. Under normal conditions, £25 is received and the loss of £10 is chargeable against the abnormal gain (*Debit* — Abnormal Gain A/c, *Credit* — Normal Loss A/c).

Abnormal Gain Account

| | Units | Per unit £ | Value £ | | Units | Per unit £ | Value £ |
|---|---|---|---|---|---|---|---|
| Normal Loss A/c | 100 | 0.10 | 10 | Process 1 A/c | 100 | 2.10 | 210 |
| Profit and Loss A/c | | | 200 | | | | |
| | 100 | | £210 | | 100 | | £210 |

The actual gain resulting from the abnormal units is £200.

Journal entries for these transfers would appear as follows:

Journal

| | | £ | £ |
|---|---|---|---|
| Normal Loss A/c | Dr. | 25 | |
| Process 1 A/c | | | 25 |
| Transfer of normal loss of (5% of 5 000 units) 250 units at £0.10 per unit | | | |
| Process 2 A/c | Dr. | 10 185 | |
| Process 1 A/c | | | 10 185 |
| Transfer of 4 850 units at £2.10 per unit to the next process | | | |
| Process 1 A/c | Dr. | 210 | |
| Abnormal Gain A/c | | | 210 |
| Transfer of a gain of 100 units at £2.10 per unit | | | |
| Abnormal Gain A/c | Dr. | 10 | |
| Normal Loss A/c | | | 10 |
| Adjustment of normal loss (250 units at £0.10) to actual loss of 150 units at £0.10 | | | |
| Debtor's A/c | Dr. | 15 | |
| Normal Loss A/c | | | 15 |
| Sale as scrap of 150 units at £0.10 per unit | | | |
| Abnormal Gain A/c | Dr. | 200 | |
| Profit and Loss A/c | | | 200 |
| Transfer of gain during process after adjusting for a reduction of 100 normal loss units at £0.10 per unit | | | |

## 14.6   Joint Products

### (a) Examples of Joint Products
The term *joint products* refers to two or more products which are the result of

processing operations. The items produced are separated during the process but they may need further processing before they are in a saleable condition. Joint products occur in such industries as oil refining (petrol and fuel oils), agriculture (wool and mutton) and in chemical processing. Applying or assigning costs to joint products is a difficult problem.

### (b) By-products

In addition to the main or joint products, there may be a by-product which arises from the residue or is recovered during or after the processing. By-products are saleable and although in certain cases they may be sold in their original form without further expenditure, there are often further charges for labour and materials when the by-product is prepared for sale. The net realizable value of a by-product is the estimated selling price (net of trade discounts) less all attributable costs incurred, after separation from the main product or joint products. The value is relatively small compared to the saleable value of the main or joint products. After fixing the value of a by-product up to the point of separation, it is apportioned by crediting the Process Account.

The ICMA publication *Terminology of Management and Financial Accountancy* refers to the problem of defining the terms by-product, joint products, waste and scrap, and states that a clear distinction between these terms is not always possible or even necessary. A product regarded as a by-product in one factory may be termed as a joint product or scrap in another. However, the term applied is less important than the use of common sense in valuing the item and in treating it in the accounts.

### (c) Valuation of Joint Products

It is essential to make a profit on the processing and to obtain an adequate amount of cash for each joint product, and a method has to be found which can be used in apportioning and allocating costs to them. Management has to make this policy decision, but because of the many changes which take place in demand, technology and marketing, there is no question of methods being fixed, and modifications to the accounting procedures have to take place whenever conditions change.

### (d) Apportionment of Joint Costs

The costs up to the point of separation or split-off are common costs, and after this point, expenses arise which are peculiar to each of the joint products. These extra costs may have an important influence on the method adopted for apportioning the common costs. Common costs can be dealt with in the following ways:

(i) **Average unit cost.** When the output of a process emerges at the split-off point in units which are similar and which can be expressed in units of the same type, then the average cost per unit can be calculated for the entire output. When the units are not similar, it may be possible to convert them to other, common units which are, for example, litres, kilogrammes or metres. But the type, grade or quality of the product may be different.

This method is not particularly good as it is usually difficult to establish whether the cost of production is the same for each of the products.

(ii) **Apportionment by using physical units.** At the separation point, proportions of the total cost are given to each product on the basis of physical output. The proportion may be in the form of percentages or in volume, weight, etc. of the raw material contained in each product.

(iii) **Apportionment by market price.** This is an apportionment on the basis of sales value and is a popular method of arriving at costs, although selling prices are not necessarily based on cost, but are often determined by market forces. The sales value at the separation point is used if the selling prices of joint products are available for production up to this point, but as this is seldom the case the apportionment has to be based on the selling prices of the completed product (final sales value), or on what is referred to as the *net sales value*, which is the sales value less the costs after separation. Examples are given below:

Cost of production of joint Products A and B before separation: £54 000
Costs after separation: Product A: £6 000
Product B: £9 000
Units produced and selling prices:
  Product A: 6 000 units at £5.00 each = £30 000
  Product B: 8 000 units at £7.50 each = £60 000

(iv) **Apportioning on final sales value.**

$$\text{Apportionment} = \frac{\text{Product sales value}}{\text{Total sales value}} \times \text{Joint cost}$$

Product A

$$\frac{£30\ 000}{£90\ 000} \times £54\ 000 = £18\ 000 \ (60\% \text{ of sales value})$$

Product B

$$\frac{£60\ 000}{£90\ 000} \times £54\ 000 = £36\ 000 \ (60\% \text{ of sales value})$$

$$\underline{\underline{£54\ 000}}$$

| Product | A | | B | |
|---|---|---|---|---|
| | £ | % of sales value | £ | % of sales value |
| Joint cost | 18 000 | 60 | 36 000 | 60 |
| Cost after separation | 6 000 | 20 | 9 000 | 15 |
| *Total cost* | 24 000 | 80 | 45 000 | 75 |
| Profit | 6 000 | 20 | 15 000 | 25 |
| Sales value | £30 000 | 100 | £60 000 | 100 |

The above example shows that if an apportionment is made on sales value and the additional costs are ignored, A and B each show a margin of 40 per cent of sales value. The variation of 5 per cent in profit to sales (A20%, B25%), is caused by the additional costs which bear more heavily on A at 20 per cent of sales value than on B at 15 per cent of sales value or selling price, and indicates that post-separation costs must be taken into account when apportioning joint cost.

(v) **Apportioning on net sales value.**

Net sales value = Sales value − Further costs

Product A: £30 000 − £6 000 = £24 000

Product B: £60 000 − £9 000 = £51 000

Total net sales value                £75 000

$$\text{Apportionment} = \frac{\text{Product net sales value}}{\text{Total net sales value}} \times \text{Joint costs}$$

Product A

$$\frac{£24\,000}{£75\,000} \times £54\,000 = £17\,280$$

Product B

$$\frac{£51\,000}{£75\,000} \times £54\,000 = £36\,720$$

£54 000

| Product | A | % of selling price | B | % of selling price |
|---|---|---|---|---|
| | £ | | £ | |
| Joint cost | 17 280 | 57.6 | 36 720 | 61.2 |
| Cost after separation | 6 000 | 20.0 | 9 000 | 15.0 |
| Total cost | 23 280 | 77.6 | 45 720 | 76.2 |
| Profit | 6 720 | 22.4 | 14 280 | 23.8 |
| Selling prices | £30 000 | 100 | £60 000 | 100 |

For Product A, a comparison of the two methods shows that the amount of the joint cost when using the sales value method is £18 000, and this is reduced to £17 280 when applying the net sales value, increasing the profit by £720. The post-separation cost of A is greater in proportion to cost and sales than that of B, and by extracting the separation costs from the sales value we arrive at a more accurate proportion of the joint costs chargeable to each product.

(e) **Valuation of By-products**

When the value of the by-product is relatively small, the revenue obtained from its sale is treated as other income and the sales value is credited to the Profit and Loss Account, but no cost is transferred to this Account from the Process Account. In this method, the major or joint products bear the full cost of the process, and the Profit and Loss Account is debited with any disposal costs. If a large number of transactions occur from by-product sales, it may be convenient to open a By-product Account in order to record these sales and attributable costs incurred after separation, and at the end of the period to transfer the profit or loss to the Profit and Loss Account.

When by-products are given a value, one of the following methods may be used:

(i) **Sales revenue or market value.** The estimated cost is based on the sales value less any costs incurred up to the time of delivery, and this is the net realizable value mentioned earlier in this Unit (see Unit 14.4).

(ii) **Standard cost.** As the selling prices of by-products often fluctuate considerably, a standard value may be established. This is a convenient way of avoiding the continual changes in the price set for the by-product and the effect these have on the main product. The standard cost may be fixed by calculating an average of the prices obtained over a short period of time, or an arbitrary figure may be used.

(iii) **Transfer value.** By-products are sometimes used internally in manufacturing or servicing and the market value or standard cost method can be used.

(iv) **Accounting for a by-product.** When a value is given to a by-product, the cost is credited to the Process Account and debited either to a By-product Account or direct to the Profit and Loss Account. In the case of internal usage, it is credited to the Process Account and debited to a Manufacturing or Service Account.

It is necessary to charge against the revenue received any appropriate administrative costs and the cost of packing and carriage.

## 14.7 Conversion Costs

Conversion costs include all production costs of converting the raw materials (or other materials which are direct) into the finished or partly-finished product, but the cost of direct material is excluded. In process costing conversion costs refer to the cost of direct labour and production overhead charged to the Process Account.

## 14.8 Process Accounts

**Example 14.5**

On January 1, a company starts to make a new product which has to be processed three times before it can be transferred to the Finished Stock Account. The production and costing records at December 31 disclosed the following information for Process 1. Show the Process 1 Account.

Materials issued             1 500 @ £3.60 per unit
Direct wages                   £2 250
Production overhead          £3 750
Normal loss is set at 5%
Actual output = 1 400 units        (no work-in-progress)
The normal loss and abnormal units have no scrap value.
The actual output is transferred to Process 2.

### Process 1 Account

| 19.. | | Per unit £ | Amount £ | 19.. | | Per unit £ | Amount £ |
|---|---|---|---|---|---|---|---|
| | Units | | | | Units | | |
| Jan. 31 Materials | 1 500 | 3.60 | 5 400 | Jan. 31 Normal | | | |
| Jan. 31 Direct | | | | loss | 75 | — | — |
| wages | | | 2 250 | Jan. 31 Abnormal | | | |
| Jan. 31 Production | | | | Loss or | | | |
| overhead | | | 3 750 | Yield | | | |
| | | | | Account | 25 | 8.00 | 200 |
| | | | | Jan. 31 Output | | | |
| | | | | transferred | | | |
| | | | | to second | | | |
| | | | | process | 1 400 | 8.00 | 11 200 |
| | 1 500 | | £11 400 | | 1 500 | | £11 400 |

*Workings*
Normal loss = 5% of 1 500 = 75 units
Normal output = 1 500 − 75 = 1 425 units
Actual output              = 1 400 units
Abnormal loss 1 500 − (1 400 + 75) =    25 units
                                 1 425 units

$$\text{Cost of normal output} = \frac{\text{Cost of processing}}{\text{Normal output}} = \frac{£11\ 400}{1\ 425} = £8.00 \text{ per unit}$$

*Note:* Normal loss only has a value when it can be sold as scrap.

**Example 14.6**
Example 14.5 shows a Process Account with an abnormal loss. Occasionally an abnormal gain may occur. Assuming that the actual output transferred was 1 435 units, the account would appear as follows:

### Process 1 Account

| 19.. | Units | Per unit £ | Amount £ | 19.. | Units | Per unit £ | Amount £ |
|---|---|---|---|---|---|---|---|
| Jan. 31 Materials | 1 500 | 3.60 | 5 400 | Jan. 31 Normal loss | 75 | — | — |
| Jan. 31 Direct | | | | Jan. 31 Output | | | |
| wages | | | 2 250 | transferred | | | |
| Jan. 31 Production | | | | to second | | | |
| overhead | | | 3 750 | process | 1 435 | 8.00 | 11 480 |
| Jan. 31 Abnormal | | | | | | | |
| Loss or | | | | | | | |
| Yield A/c | 10 | 8.00 | 80 | | | | |
| | 1 510 | | £11 480 | | 1 510 | | £11 480 |

*Workings*

$$\text{Cost per unit} = \frac{\text{Cost of processing}}{\text{Normal output}} = \frac{£11\,400}{1\,425} = \underline{£8.00 \text{ per unit}}$$

Output transferred = 1 435 @ £8.00 per unit = £11 480
Abnormal gain = 10 @ £8.00 per unit = £80
The normal loss is set at 75 units but as 10 are gained only 65 are actually lost.

**Example 14.7**
In Examples 14.5 and 14.6 the value per unit is the same for both the units transferred and units of abnormal loss and abnormal gain. In this example the units of normal loss are sold at a scrap price of £0.95 per unit.

### Process 1 Account

| | Units | Per unit £ | Amount £ | | Units | Per unit £ | Amount £ |
|---|---|---|---|---|---|---|---|
| Jan. 31 Materials | 1 500 | 3.60 | 5 400 | Jan. 31 Normal loss | 75 | 0.95 | 71.25 |
| Jan. 31 Direct | | | | Jan. 31 Abnormal | | | |
| wages | | | 2 250 | loss or yield | 25 | 7.95 | 198.75 |
| Jan. 31 Production | | | | Jan. 31 Output | | | |
| overhead | | | 3 750 | transferred | | | |
| | | | | to second | | | |
| | | | | process | 1 400 | 7.95 | 11 130.00 |
| | 1 500 | | £11 400 | | 1 500 | | £11 400.00 |

*(continued overleaf)*

*Workings*
Cost of processing = £11 400 *less* Value of scrap sold
$$= £11\ 400 - 75 \text{ units @ £0.95} = £11\ 400 - £71.25$$
$$= £11\ 328.75$$

$$\text{Cost of normal output} = \frac{\text{Cost of processing}}{\text{Normal output}} = \frac{£11\ 328.75}{1\ 425} = \underline{\underline{£7.95 \text{ per unit}}}$$

Value of output transferred and abnormal loss charged at £7.95 per unit.

**Example 14.8**
The previous examples have assumed that there is no work-in-progress at the beginning or end of the manufacturing period. To take a simple example where work in process is involved, let us assume that production takes place in two processes.

*Process 1*

| | |
|---|---:|
| Manufacturing cost | £12 600 |
| 2 400 units in process | |
| Units completed and transferred to Process 2 | 1 800 units |
| 600 units 50% complete | 300 units |
| Equivalent production | 2 100 units |

$$\text{Cost of each completed unit} = \frac{\text{Cost of processing}}{\text{Equivalent production}} = \frac{£12\ 600}{2\ 100}$$
$$= \underline{\underline{£6.00 \text{ per unit}}}$$

| | |
|---|---:|
| 1 800 units transferred to Process 2, at £6.00 per unit | = £10 800 |
| 600 units (50% complete = 300 at £6.00 each) work in process | = £ 1 800 |
| | £12 600 |

*Process 2*

| | | |
|---|---:|---:|
| 1 800 units received from Process 1, at £6.00 | | = £10 800 |
| Manufacturing cost: Direct materials | £600 | |
| Direct labour | £2 100 | |
| Works overhead | £3 300 | |
| | | = £ 6 000 |
| | | £16 800 |

| | |
|---|---:|
| Units completed and transferred to Finished Stock A/c | 1 560 units |
| 240 units 50% complete | 120 units |
| Equivalent production | 1 680 units |

$$\text{Cost of each completed unit} = \frac{\text{Cost of processing}}{\text{Equivalent production}} = \frac{£16\ 800}{1\ 680}$$
$$= \underline{\underline{£10.00 \text{ per unit}}}$$

| | |
|---|---:|
| 1 560 units transferred to Finished Stock A/c at £10.00 per unit | = £15 600 |
| 240 units (50% complete = 120 at £10.00 per unit) work in process | = £1 200 |
| | £16 800 |

Process 2 Account

| | Per Units | unit £ | Amount £ | | Per Units | unit £ | Amount £ |
|---|---|---|---|---|---|---|---|
| Transfer from | | | | Transfer to | | | |
| Process 1 | 1 800 | 6.00 | 10 800 | Finished | | | |
| Direct materials | | | 600 | Stock A/c | 1 560 | 10.00 | 15 600 |
| Direct labour | | | 2 100 | Balance (work | | | |
| Works overhead | | | 3 300 | in process) c/d | 240 | | 1 200 |
| | 1 800 | | £16 800 | | 1 800 | | £16 800 |
| Balance b/d | 240 | | 1 200 | | | | |

This example is a simplification because it has been assumed that production has proceeded evenly with the application of materials and labour, with work in process at the 50 per cent completion stage. In practice, this does not apply and there are variations in the stage of completion of materials, labour and overheads, and therefore each element has to be dealt with separately.

Calculations will be needed to establish the equivalent production and value for units of materials, labour and overhead, and these may be worked out on the basis of the average cost method or the FIFO method.

*(a)* **Average Cost Method**
In this system, average unit costs are calculated by adding the opening work in process cost to the process costs of the current period and dividing this total cost by the equivalent production for the period. In many process industries production tends to proceed at a steady pace, with similar stocks and volumes of production from one period to the next. There is little variation and generally costs do not change to any great extent. The system is easy to understand and to operate and if prices and costs fluctuate, the calculation of an average evens out the fluctuations. The objections to this method of unit cost valuation are that exceptional changes in operating costs may be hidden by a system that damps down the fluctuations, and cost control may not be as effective as it is intended to be. Average unit costs for materials can be calculated as shown on p. 208.

$$\text{Unit cost} = \frac{\text{Opening work-in-progress} + \text{Process costs for period}}{\text{Completed units transferred} + \text{Equivalent units at close of period}}$$

*Process 1*                          *Materials*
                          *Unit costs in January*
January 1      Opening work-in-progress (100% completed) 200 units £200
January 1–31   Materials charged                                £2 100
January 31     Units transferred                                 1 500
January 31     Closing work-in-progress (100% completed)       700 units
     *Calculation of equivalent production*

|                               | Units |
|-------------------------------|-------|
| Units transferred January 31  | 1 500 |
| Closing work-in-progress      |   700 |
|                               | 2 200 |

*Cost of equivalent production*

|                                     | £     |
|-------------------------------------|-------|
| Opening work-in-progress on January 1 |   200 |
| Materials charged in January        | 2 100 |
|                                     | £2 300 |

$$\text{Average unit cost of material} = \frac{£2\ 300}{2\ 200} = £1.045\ 45$$

A calculation would also be made to find the average unit cost of conversion, i.e. wages and overhead. The average unit costs would then be used to calculate the transfer values which are required in order to close the Process Account. Materials included in the transfer values would be as follows:

|                                                        |         | £ |
|--------------------------------------------------------|---------|-----|
| Units of material transferred to Process 2             | 1 500 × £1.045 45 = | 1 568 |
| Work-in-progress carried down in Process 1 on February 1 |         |     |
|                                 700 units at £1.045 45 = |         | 732 |
|                                                        |         | £2 300 |

## (b) FIFO Method

This method enables cost control to be exercised because costs of the current period are disclosed and a comparison can be made with the cost in the previous period. The calculations are necessary to find the unit cost in each period, but variations in unit cost are not overlooked as may happen when an average is obtained.

*Calculation of equivalent production*
*Materials*

|  | *Units* |
| --- | ---: |
| Units completed and transferred January 31 | 1 500 |
| *Less* Opening work-in-progress completed | 200 |
| Units completed and processed entirely in January | 1 300 |
| *Add* Units of closing work-in-progress | 700 |
|  | 2 000 |

For purposes of valuation on a FIFO basis, unit costs are calculated as follows:

*Materials*

$$\frac{\text{Closing work-in-progress in December}}{\text{Equivalent units}} = \frac{£200}{200} = £1.00 \text{ per unit}$$

$$\frac{\text{Material cost in January}}{\text{Units charged and completed in January}} = \frac{£2\ 100}{2\ 000} = £1.05 \text{ per unit}$$

*Cost of equivalent production*

|  |  | £ |
| --- | --- | ---: |
| December | 200 units @ £1.00 | 200 |
| January | 1 300 units @ £1.05 | 1 365 |
|  | 1 500 units transferred | 1 565 |
| January | 700 units @ £1.05 | 735 |
|  | 2 200 units | £2 300 |

The following illustration shows how the three elements of cost are dealt with on a FIFO basis in process costing.

**Example 14.9**

The Process Account on January 1 shows that the balance brought down consists of 200 units at various stages of completion, the value of which is £1 100.

*Work in process brought forward*

|  |  | £ |
|---|---|---|
| Materials | 100% completed | 200 |
| Wages | 50% completed | 500 |
| Works overhead | 50% completed | 400 |

At January 31 the situation is as follows:

*Work in process carried forward 700 units*

| Materials | 100% completed |
|---|---|
| Wages | 50% completed |
| Works overhead | 50% completed |

During January, 1 500 units were completed and transferred to the next process. The costs charged to the process were as given below:

|  | £ |
|---|---|
| Materials | 2 100 |
| Wages | 8 925 |
| Works overhead | 7 210 |

Units of output and unit cost are as shown in Table 14.1.

**Table 14.1    Calculating for the current period, the units produced and unit costs on a FIFO basis**

| | Units transferred (a) | Equivalent units carried down (b) | Units completed (c) (a+b) | Deduct equivalent units brought down (d) | Units produced this period (e) (c−d) | Period costs (f) £ | Unit cost (g) (f÷e) £ |
|---|---|---|---|---|---|---|---|
| Materials | 1 500 | 700 | 2 200 | 200 | 2 000 | 2 100 | 1.05 |
| Wages | 1 500 | 350 | 1 850 | 100 | 1 750 | 8 925 | 5.10 |
| Overheads | 1 500 | 350 | 1 850 | 100 | 1 750 | 7 210 | 4.12 |

*Workings*
*Equivalent production* (Work in process)

Brought forward
Materials 200 × 100% = 200 for £200 = £1 per unit
Labour    200 × 50% = 100 for £500 = £5 per unit
Overhead 200 × 50% = 100 for £400 = £4 per unit

Carried forward
£
Materials 700 × 100% = 700 at £1.05 per unit =   735
Labour    700 ×  50% = 350 at £5.10 per unit = 1 785
Overhead 700 ×  50% = 350 at £4.12 per unit = 1 442
                                              £3 962

*Value of units transferred*

| | | £ | £ | £ |
|---|---|---|---|---|
| Materials: | 200 @ £1.00 per unit | 200 | | |
| | 1 300 @ £1.05 per unit | 1 365 | | |
| | 1 500 | | 1 565 | |
| Labour: | 100 @ £5.00 per unit | 500 | | |
| | 1 400 @ £5.10 per unit | 7 140 | | |
| | 1 500 | | 7 640 | |
| Overhead: | 100 @ £4.00 per unit | 400 | | |
| | 1 400 @ £4.12 per unit | 5 768 | | |
| | 1 500 | | 6 168 | |
| | | | | 15 373 |

*Add* Work in process carried forward                3 962
Total charged to Process Account                  £19 335

Process 1 Account

| 19.. | | Units | £ | 19.. | | Units | £ |
|---|---|---|---|---|---|---|---|
| Jan. 1 | Balance b/f | 200 | 1 100 | Jan. 31 | Transfer to | | |
| Jan. 31 | Materials | 2 000 | 2 100 | | Process 2 | 1 500 | 15 373 |
| Jan. 31 | Labour | | 8 925 | Jan. 31 | Balance b/d | 700 | 3 962 |
| Jan. 31 | Overhead | | 7 210 | | | | |
| | | 2 200 | £19 335 | | | 2 200 | £19 335 |
| Feb. 1 | Balance b/d | 700 | 3 962 | | | | |

## 14.9    Exercises

1.   Explain how by-products should be dealt with in process costing (*a*) where they are very small in total value, (*b*) where they are of substantial value, and (*c*) if they need further processing before they can be sold.

2.   The following terms are used in the cost department of a company where the operations of the factory are conducted by a continuous flow of materials and units of output from one process to another:

   (*a*)   equivalent units;
   (*b*)   normal losses;
   (*c*)   abnormal losses and gains;
   (*d*)   by-products;
   (*e*)   joint products.

Define each of these terms and explain how these would be dealt with in Process Accounts.

# Unit Fifteen
# Marginal Costing

## 15.1  Marginal Costing Technique

Marginal costing is the ascertainment of costs by differentiating between *fixed costs* and *variable costs* and bringing out clearly the effect on profit of changes in volume or type of output. This is a technique of management accountancy which recognizes the nature of cost and its behaviour under varying conditions. The Institute of Cost and Management Accountants, in its publication *Terminology of Management and Financial Accountancy*, recommends that the term *marginal costing* should be applied only where the routine system incorporates the marginal principle.

Marginal costing is concerned with the effect of *fluctuating volumes* on costs, and assesses the change in profitability which may occur under certain conditions. Although volume is significant in the improvement of profitability, capacity must also be taken into account. There are different definitions of normal capacity, but it usually means the capacity *both to make and sell* for a reasonable period in the future. Profitability can be affected by a change in normal capacity, as well as by a change in the type of product being made and sold. Efficient management searches for ways of improving the return on capital employed, and an understanding of marginal costing enables them to achieve greater effectiveness because they are aware of the contribution which their products are making or can make towards the fixed costs and profits of their organization. The following terms are used in connection with this technique:

(i) **Marginal cost.** This is the variable cost of one unit, or the amount at any given volume of output by which aggregate costs are changed if the volume of output is increased or decreased by one unit.

(ii) **Fixed costs.** These costs tend to be unaffected by variations in volume of output. They are costs such as rent, rates, insurance, executive salaries, etc. which have no relationship to volume, but accumulate over a period of time.

(iii) **Variable costs.** These costs tend to change directly with variations in the volume of output. Examples are raw materials, electrical power, fuel, spoilage and so forth.

(iv) **Semi-variable costs.** These costs contain a fixed element and a variable element, and apply to expenses where there is a fixed charge and a cost per unit such as gas, electricity and telephone charges.

Within certain limits, variable costs alter in accordance with activity but fixed costs remain the same. There are circumstances when fixed costs have to be reduced or increased at various stages of expansion, but in the short term they remain constant. Even when fixed costs change they are not *variable* in the costing sense of *variable with output*. For example, a factory manager's salary does not vary with output, but if the firm grows, he may need an assistant. When presented with overhead costs at different levels of activity, the variable element can be separated and the fixed cost determined by deducting the cost at one rate of activity from the cost at a higher level of activity.

**Example 15.1**

|  | Activity 60% £ | Activity 70% £ | Activity 80% £ |
|---|---|---|---|
|  | 64 000 | 70 500 | 77 000 |
| *Less* 60% Activity |  | 64 000 |  |
| Variable cost |  | 6 500 |  |
| *Less* 70% Activity |  |  | 70 500 |
| Variable cost |  |  | 6 500 |

A 10% change in activity costs £6 500 in variable cost. The fixed cost is found by taking the total cost and deducting the variable cost for the level of activity.

|  | £ |
|---|---|
| Cost at 60% | 64 000 |
| *Less* Variable cost | 39 000 (6 × £6 500) |
| Fixed cost | £25 000 |

At a level of 80% activity £77 000 *less* (8 × £6 500) = £25 000 fixed cost.
Some typical cost graphs are shown in Fig. 15.1, and described in the notes below the diagrams.

(v) **Contribution.** This term is used in profit planning and refers to the difference between sales revenue and variable cost. The variable cost here is also known as the *marginal cost* and consists of the prime cost plus the variable overheads.

Imagine a case where goods costing £2 000 for direct wages, direct materials and variable overheads are sold for £3 000. The difference between this sales revenue and the variable costs is £1 000. This is the *contribution*. To what does it contribute? It contributes to the only part of the costs of the enterprise not yet covered — the fixed costs (fixed overheads). Once these have been totally covered the firm has *broken even* and will, from this point, make a profit. If, in the example chosen, fixed overheads were £800 then the contribution covers all the fixed costs and contributes £200 to the profits of the business. Had the fixed overheads been £1 300 the firm would not have broken even and an overall loss of £300 would have been sustained.

When marginal costs are truly variable, the marginal cost per unit and the contribution per unit remain unchanged regardless of the level of activity. Under such circumstances marginal costing can be used with advantage as long as it is used after carefully considering all the factors involved.

The contribution per unit of output and sales accumulates as sales are made, and this provides a fund which pays for the fixed expenses and then gives a profit. The point at which total contribution equals total fixed cost is known as the *break-even point*. The different levels of activity have an effect on unit costs because of the burden of fixed costs which, in the short term, are the same at any volume of output. The charts in Fig. 15.2 (p. 218) illustrate the effect of volume.

## 15.2  Marginal Costing and Absorption Costing Compared

Total costing is the traditional way of arriving at and presenting the cost of jobs. Another name for it is absorption costing and as its name implies, an attempt is made to absorb and recover all the costs of the enterprise, including the fixed overheads. The conventional way of showing the cost of a product is to take the marginal costs and to add an on-cost (see *Success in Principles of Accounting*, Unit 29.2) for fixed expenses in an endeavour to present unit or product costs so that the degree of profitability can be seen. The charge for fixed expenses, however, is set at the beginning of the trading period when the fixed costs and the volume of production can only be based on estimates. There may be errors in estimating the costs, incorrect methods of apportionment and mistakes made in arriving at the expected volume of output. In these circumstances, the costs and results shown by total costing can be misleading. The fixed expenses are incurred over a period of time and have no connection with volume, and to include an amount for fixed expenses in the cost of a product is considered by the advocates of marginal costing to be incorrect, as the effect of volume changes the amount of fixed cost per unit, as shown in Fig. 15.3 (p. 220).

(i) Factory rent

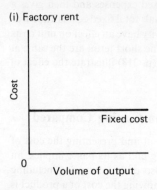

Fixed cost

0   Volume of output

(ii) Direct wages

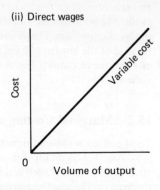

Variable cost

0   Volume of output

(iii) Materials A: Quantity discount;
      B: Shortages developing

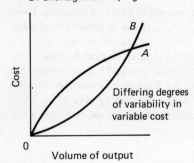

B

A

Differing degrees
of variability in
variable cost

0   Volume of output

(iv) Running motor vehicles

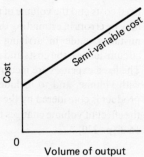

Semi-variable cost

0   Volume of output

Fig. 15.1 Behaviour of costs (i–iv)

Notes:

(i) The first graph shows a fixed cost (rent) which is fixed over a given period of time. There is a wide range of activity shown as the volume of output. The cost of rent remains the same whatever the volume of output during the set period of time.

(ii) A variable cost (direct wages) is shown on this graph. It illustrates that the cost varies in direct proportion to the volume of output. As the volume of output increases, so does the cost of direct wages.

(iii) This diagram shows two curves each representing a different variable cost. Costs sometimes behave differently as volume changes and, if the cost of a particular item is plotted on a chart, it may rise steeply at low volume whereas another item may rise less steeply. Graph (ii) is a linear situation (cost varying in direct proportion to output). Curve A in graph (iii) illustrates a reduction in unit cost as the output increases as a result of quantity discounts. Curve B illustrates an increase in material costs as the demand for material grows and shortages develop.

(iv) This graph shows a semi-variable cost (of running motor vehicles) which consists of a fixed cost (the purchase of the vehicle) and variable costs (petrol, oil, etc.) incurred in running the vehicles.

(v) Supervisory labour

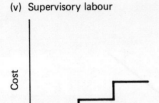

(vi) Salesman's salary and commission

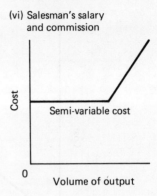

(vii) Maintenance

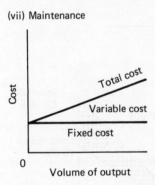

(viii) Production cost

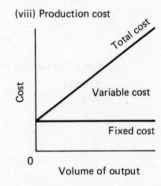

*Fig. 15.1 Behaviour of costs (v–viii)*

Notes:

(v) This is a stepped graph for semi-variable costs which shows the cost behaviour pattern for supervisors' wages. There is a fixed cost and as the output increases there may be overtime payments and perhaps an increase in supervisory staff as extra workers are taken on.

(vi) This graph illustrates another example of fixed and variable costs where a salesman receives a fixed salary and commission once he has achieved a particular volume of sales.

(vii) This is a semi-variable chart which shows the planned cost of maintenance as fixed cost (preventive maintenance) and a variable cost arising from changes in output.

(viii) This is similar in design to the previous graph but shows the total cost of products (fixed costs plus variable costs) at each level of activity. For example, if a factory with a fixed cost of £4 000 per month produces 250 chairs, with a variable cost of £48 each (£12 000 total), the total cost is £16 000. This represents a cost of £64 per chair, if production and costs proceed according to plan.

(a)  Production cost

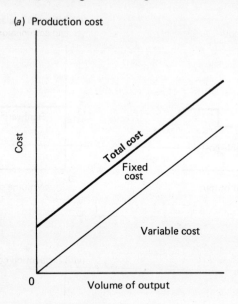

(b)  Production cost and sales

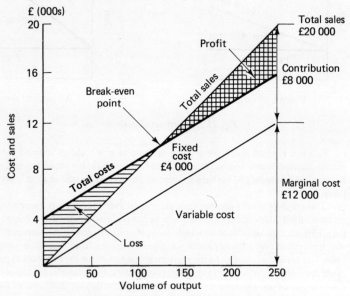

*Fig. 15.2 Contribution, total cost, break-even and profit*

*Notes to Fig. 15.2:*

(i) These graphs show the same information as Fig. 15.1(viii) but the fixed cost and variable cost are shown in reverse order with fixed cost above the variable cost. In addition, the second graph shows the line of total sales, from which can be read the total sales income at any volume of output, assuming all goods are sold. It is also possible to find, at any volume of output, the total variable cost, total fixed cost and total cost. The purpose of showing graph (b) in this form is to illustrate the marginal cost area and the components of contribution. The variable item of cost is the marginal cost and the contribution consists of fixed cost recovered plus profit beyond the break-even point. The profit area is the shaded section between total cost and total sales, beyond break-even point.

(ii) Fig. 15.2 (b) uses the information already given in Fig. 15.1(viii) for the production of 250 chairs. It is planned to sell the chairs at £80 each (total £20 000). It can be seen that the total profit is £4 000 (£20 000 *less* £16 000) giving a profit of £16 per chair. The profit of £16 only applies if the whole of the production is sold and the costs are as planned for that production period. The contribution is that part of the sales income which recovers the fixed costs and produces the profit. For example, at an output of 200 chairs, the income of £16 000 (200 chairs at £80 each) covers variable costs of £48 per chair (£9 600), leaving a contribution of £6 400 (£16 000 *less* £9 600). This covers fixed costs of £4 000 and a profit of only £2 400.

|  | Sales of 250 chairs | | Sales of 200 chairs | |
|---|---|---|---|---|
|  | Total | Per chair | Total | Per chair |
|  | £ | £ | £ | £ |
| Variable cost | 12 000 | 48 | 9 600 | 48 |
| Fixed cost | 4 000 | 16 | 4 000 | 20 |
| Total cost | 16 000 | 64 | 13 600 | 68 |
| Profit | 4 000 | 16 | 2 400 | 12 |
| Sales | 20 000 | 80 | 16 000 | 80 |
| Contribution: |  |  |  |  |
| Fixed cost | 4 000 |  | 4 000 |  |
| Profit | 4 000 |  | 2 400 |  |
| Total | 8 000 |  | 6 400 |  |
| Contribution per chair | £32 |  | £32 |  |

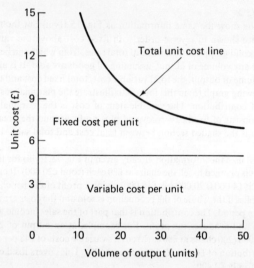

*Fig. 15.3 The effect which volume of output has on fixed cost per unit and total unit cost*

The values below indicate how unit costs are reduced when the volume of output increases as shown in Fig. 15.3. Fixed cost is taken as £100 and the cost of one unit amounts to £105.

| Volume of output | Variable cost per unit £ | Fixed cost per unit £ | Total unit cost £ |
|---|---|---|---|
| 1 | 5.00 | 100.00 | 105.00 |
| 10 | 5.00 | 10.00 | 15.00 |
| 20 | 5.00 | 5.00 | 10.00 |
| 30 | 5.00 | 3.33 | 8.33 |
| 40 | 5.00 | 2.50 | 7.50 |
| 50 | 5.00 | 2.00 | 7.00 |

You can see that while variable cost per unit remains constant at £5.00, the fixed cost per unit is reduced from £100 to £2.

This not only illustrates how volume affects unit costs, but also shows that volume affects the overhead expenses because absorption rates are pre-determined and this results in the under- or over-absorption of overheads which do not arise under marginal costing.

The marginal costing technique is of special importance to the price estimator who, while remaining conscious of the burden of fixed costs, can use *contribution* when deciding on the level of prices. Initially contribution pays for the fixed costs and once these are accounted for profits can occur. It may be necessary to increase turnover in order to reach the production target set by normal capacity decisions and the estimator may have scope for varying the prices so that the overall profit is improved.

When marginal cost statements are presented, management is assisted in its decision-making as it now knows which products provide the greatest contribution. Management is therefore in a better position to decide how surplus capacity can be utilized, where expansion is possible, which factories are to manufacture which products and whether expenditure on advertising should be concentrated on selected products.

The measurement of profit is the same under total and marginal costing, although the presentation of the cost information may be displayed differently. As far as the accounts are concerned, it is merely a question of when the profit is taken. At the end of the trading period there will normally be work-in-progress and finished stocks which are carried forward, and in absorption costing these are valued at full cost of production, whereas in marginal costing they are priced at variable cost. This affects the profits, as, under marginal costing, the fixed cost element is written off in the period when it is incurred, while in total costing some of the fixed cost of the period is carried forward.

## 15.3   Marginal Cost Statements

In order for management to measure the performance, statements which show the contribution provided by different products are very important. The following statements show how costs are provided which indicate the total cost and the marginal cost.

| Total cost | £ | % | Marginal cost | £ | % |
|---|---|---|---|---|---|
| Direct material | 30 000 | 30 | Direct material | 30 000 | 30 |
| Direct wages | 20 000 | 20 | Direct wages | 20 000 | 20 |
| Overheads | 30 000 | 30 | Variable overhead | 14 000 | 14 |
| Total cost | 80 000 | 80 | Marginal cost | 64 000 | 64 |
| Profit (net) | 20 000 | 20 | Contribution | 36 000 | 36 |
| Sales | £100 000 | 100 | | £100 000 | 100 |

The marginal cost statement shows that 36% of sales value is *contribution* and this fund pays the fixed costs; the balance is profit.

| Cost statement | £ | % |
|---|---|---|
| Contribution | 36 000 | 36 |
| *Less* Fixed cost | 16 000 | 16 |
| Profit (net) | £20 000 | 20 |

On the assumption that marginal cost has been correctly assessed, the contribution percentage can be used to estimate future profits, provided fixed costs remain unchanged and there are facilities and capacity to expand sales.

For example if sales can be increased without increasing fixed costs to a sales turnover of £130 000, the contribution at 36% would be £46 800. As fixed cost has already been covered, the extra contribution would be further profit of £10 800.

*Marginal cost statement*

|  | £ | % |
|---|---|---|
| Direct material | 39 000 | 30 |
| Direct wages | 26 000 | 20 |
| Variable overhead | 18 200 | 14 |
| *Marginal cost* | 83 200 | 64 |
| Contribution | 46 800 | 36 |
| *Sales* | £130 000 | 100 |
| Contribution | 46 800 | 36.0% |
| *Less* Fixed cost | 16 000 | 12.3% |
| *Profit* | £30 800 | 23.7% |

This indicates that fixed cost as a percentage of sales is reduced from 16% to 12.3% and profit is increased from 20% to 23.7% of sales.

The marginal costing technique is a good investigatory procedure as it provides information on the behaviour of costs and greatly helps marketing. Trading results are normally presented in the form of total costs but if marginal accounts are drawn up, the final figures could be shown as in the example below:

| Opening stock | 1 800 units at £35 each |
|---|---|
| Closing stock | 1 500 units at £40 each |
| *Production* | |
| Direct material | 8 700 units at £25 each |
| Direct labour | 8 700 units at £10 each |
| Variable overhead | 8 700 units at £5 each |
| Fixed expenses | £137 000 |
| *Selling expenses* | |
| Variable | 10% of selling price |
| Fixed | £25 000 |
| *Administration expenses* | |
| Fixed | £45 000 |
| Sales | 9 000 units at £80 each |

Trading and Profit and Loss Account

|  | £ | £ | £ |
|---|---|---|---|
| Sales (9 000 units @ £80) |  |  | 720 000 |
| *Less* Variable costs |  |  |  |
| Direct materials (8 700 @ £25) |  | 217 500 |  |
| Direct labour (8 700 @ £10) |  | 87 000 |  |
| Variable overhead (8 700 @ £5) |  | 43 500 |  |
|  |  | 348 000 |  |
| *Add* Opening stock (1 800 @ £35) | 63 000 |  |  |
| *Less* Closing stock (1 500 @ £40) | 60 000 |  |  |
|  |  | 3 000 |  |
|  |  | 351 000 |  |
| *Add* Variable selling expenses (10% of £720 000) |  | 72 000 |  |
| Marginal cost |  |  | 423 000 |
| Contribution   41.2% |  |  | 297 000 |
| *Less* Fixed cost |  |  |  |
| Fixed production cost |  | 137 000 |  |
| Fixed administration expense |  | 45 000 |  |
| Fixed selling expense |  | 25 000 |  |
|  |  |  | 207 000 |
| Net profit   12.5% |  |  | £ 90 000 |

## 15.4   Contribution/Sales Ratio (C/S Ratio)

This ratio shows the relationship between contribution and sales value and is usually expressed as a percentage. It is reached by a calculation similar to the one in the last section where the contribution as a percentage of sales is 36%. The formula is as follows:

$$\frac{\text{Contribution}}{\text{Sales}} \times 100 = \frac{\text{£46 800}}{\text{£130 000}} \times 100 = \underline{\underline{36\%}}$$

This ratio used to be called the Profit/Volume ratio, but as profit only begins when the break-even point has been reached, this term tends to be misleading because it refers to the volume of sales above the break-even point where a percentage of the sales revenue represents profit.

The ratio applies to the sales revenue below, as well as above, the break-even point. It is really a *Contribution/Sales ratio*, which indicates the proportion of sales revenue which contributes to fixed costs and to profit.

The sales and contribution are in direct proportion to each other, whatever the sales value, and an increase in sales value results in an increase in the value of the contribution by the same percentage that applied to the percentage increase in sales value. The ratio can be used in profit planning to calculate the contribution provided at any level of sales.

The ratio applies if fixed costs remain the same and there are no limiting factors to restrict expansion of production or sales, or to increase marginal costs. This can be shown by using the figures in the above statements.

Sales of £100 000 were increased to £130 000, which is equivalent to a *30% increase*. Contribution of £36 000 was increased to £46 800, which is equivalent to a *30% increase*.

It is useful to know the value of the contribution per unit as this figure can be used to work out how many extra units need to be sold to provide extra profits. If the selling price of one unit is £10, the volume of sales shown in the examples above are 10 000 and 13 000 and the unit cost is:

*Unit cost*

|  | £ |
|---|---|
| Direct material | 3.00 |
| Direct wages | 2.00 |
| Variable overhead | 1.40 |
| *Marginal cost* | 6.40 |
| Contribution | 3.60 |
| Selling price | 10.00 |

The contribution per unit can be used in the following way:

If fixed costs are £16 000 and the profit required is £30 800, the contribution required is £46 800 (£16 000+£30 800) and the number of units to be sold is as follows:

$$\frac{\text{Total contribution}}{\text{Contribution per unit}} = \frac{£46\ 800}{£3.60} = 13\ 000 \text{ units}$$

The type of information given above can be shown on a contribution chart or profit graph (Fig. 15.4).

The horizontal axis of a profit graph shows either the volume of output or the sales value, and the vertical axis shows contribution. The diagonal line is plotted using the contribution. It begins at the value of total fixed costs below the horizontal axis and finishes at the value of total contribution above the axis, corresponding to an output of 10 000 units, which has a sales value of £100 000. A loss is shown below the horizontal axis and a profit is shown above. Contribution is needed to provide the revenue to pay the fixed expenses, and if there is no production and no sales, the business will make a loss of £16 000. The point at which the diagonal line crosses the horizontal is the *break-even point* or position where the contribution from a certain volume of output and sales equals the fixed cost. The following statement shows the results at various levels of activity.

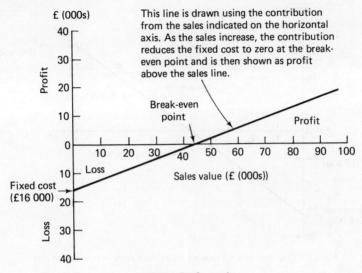

£ (000s)

This line is drawn using the contribution from the sales indicated on the horizontal axis. As the sales increase, the contribution reduces the fixed cost to zero at the break-even point and is then shown as profit above the sales line.

Break-even point

Profit

Fixed cost (£16 000)

Loss

Sales value (£ (000s))

*Fig. 15.4 Profit graph*

| | *Marginal cost statement* | | | | | | | |
|---|---|---|---|---|---|---|---|---|
| Output (units) | 4 000 | | 4 445 | | 8 000 | | 10 000 | |
| | £ | % | £ | % | £ | % | £ | % |
| Sales | 40 000 | 100 | 44 450 | 100 | 80 000 | 100 | 100 000 | 100 |
| | £ | | £ | | £ | | £ | |
| Direct material | 12 000 | | 13 335 | | 24 000 | | 30 000 | |
| Direct wages | 8 000 | | 8 890 | | 16 000 | | 20 000 | |
| Overheads | 5 600 | | 6 223 | | 11 200 | | 14 000 | |
| Marginal cost | 25 600 | 64 | 28 448 | 64 | 51 200 | 64 | 64 000 | 64 |
| Contribution | 14 400 | 36 | 16 002 | 36 | 28 800 | 36 | 36 000 | 36 |
| *Less* Fixed cost | 16 000 | 40 | 16 000 | 36 | 16 000 | 20 | 16 000 | 16 |
| Profit | (£ 1 600) | ( 4) | £ 2 | B/E* | £12 800 | 16 | £20 000 | 20 |

\* Break-even point.

This statement shows that the break-even point is at approximately 4 445 units. Alternatively, this result can be obtained from the graph by interpolation, as shown in Fig. 15.4.

The break-even point is also the stage where the income from sales exactly equals the total costs or expenditure and is the point where the contribution from sales equals the fixed cost and where there is neither a profit nor a loss. This is illustrated in Fig. 15.5.

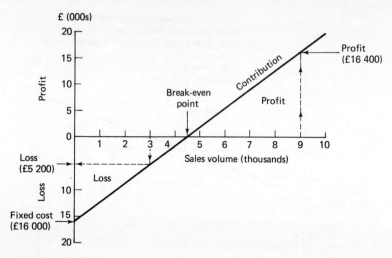

*Fig. 15.5 How contribution reaches break-even point and goes into profit*

*Note:* At various levels of output (assuming all output is sold) we can see what the profit or loss situation will be, by drawing in perpendiculars from the horizontal axis to the graph. Thus, at sales of 3 000 units the loss is seen to be £5 200 and at sales of 9 000 units the profit will be £16 400. The point where the graph crosses the horizontal line is the break-even point. At this output — just below 4 500 units — the contribution achieved by the output is sufficient to cover all the fixed costs and we are about to move into a profitable situation. From now on the contribution from further sales will be a contribution to profits.

## 15.5　Break-even Analysis

Profit can be measured by analysing costs into fixed and variable categories, and determining profit or loss at varying levels of activity. Break-even analysis operates by furnishing details of the contribution which the various products or processes are making to the profitability of the enterprise. Such analysis helps management to formulate its policy in deciding what products to manufacture and the prices at which they should be sold. It helps in 'make or buy' decisions, in problems connected with conditions of slump and seasonal trading and when closure is under consideration.

**Margin of Safety**

This is illustrated in Fig. 15.6. It is the amount by which sales exceed the break-even point of sales. If there is excess capacity, it could represent the maximum degree of security which the business could provide if the full capacity was utilized. A fairly wide margin is needed in order to cope with competition and changes in demand, and the extent of the margin indicates the amount of turnover which, if lost, would place the business in an insecure position.

The width of the margin depends on the amount of fixed cost and contribution, and the turnover achieved. Each of these factors can affect the degree of safety. For example, an increase in selling price increases the contribution and improves the margin of safety, whereas a reduction in selling price has the opposite effect, by reducing the contribution/sales ratio and requiring additional volume or a reduction in costs to maintain the margin of safety. If fixed costs are increased while contribution and sales volume remain stable, the break-even point moves to the right and reduces the margin of safety.

## 15.6 Break-even Point

At break-even point we are interested in three aspects: (i) sales value; (ii) sales volume; (iii) the margin of safety.

(i) **Sales value at break-even point (BEP)**. This can be expressed as being equal to:

$$\frac{\text{Fixed cost}}{1 - \dfrac{\text{Variable cost (Marginal cost)}}{\text{Total sales value}}}$$

Taking total sales at £100 000, for 10 000 units, marginal cost at £64 000, and fixed cost at £16 000, we find:

$$\text{Sales value at BEP} = \frac{£16\,000}{1 - \dfrac{£64\,000}{£100\,000}} = \frac{£16\,000 \times £100\,000}{£36\,000}$$

$$= £44\,444$$

An alternative formula derived from the above is:

$$\text{Sales at BEP} = \text{Fixed cost} \times \frac{\text{Total sales}}{\text{Contribution}}$$

$$= £16\,000 \times \frac{£100\,000}{£36\,000} \left( \begin{array}{l} \text{Contribution} = £100\,000 - £64\,000 \\ \phantom{\text{Contribution}} = £36\,000 \end{array} \right)$$

$$= £44\,444$$

The sales value at break-even point can also be found by using the contribution/sales ratio.

$$\text{Sales at BEP} = \frac{\text{Fixed cost}}{\text{C/S ratio}} \left( \text{C/S ratio} = \frac{£36\,000}{£100\,000} \times 100 = 36\% \right)$$

$$= \frac{£16\,000}{36} \times 100 = £44\,444$$

or, taking 36% as 0.36:

$$\frac{£16\,000}{0.36} = £44\,444$$

(ii) **The number of units sold at break-even point.** This can be calculated by dividing the fixed cost by the contribution per unit.

The contribution per unit is $\dfrac{\text{Contribution}}{\text{Units sold}} = \dfrac{£36\,000}{10\,000} = £3.60$

Therefore:

$$\text{Number of units sold at break-even point} = \frac{\text{Fixed cost}}{\text{Contribution per unit}}$$

$$= \frac{£16\,000}{£3.60} = 4\,444 \text{ units at £10 each}$$

(iii) **The margin of safety.** This can be calculated by dividing the profit by the contribution/sales ratio.

$$\frac{\text{Profit}}{\text{C/S ratio}} = \frac{£20\,000}{0.36} \qquad \left( \frac{£20\,000}{36} \times 100 \right)$$

= Sales value of £55 556 (Sales *less* Sales at break-even point)

## 15.7  Marginal Costing and Break-even Analysis

In the break-even charts shown in Figs. 15.6 and 15.7 the graphs of costs and revenues have been shown as straight lines for simplicity. In real life the graphs of costs and revenues might be curved slightly because, for example, discounts may be offered to customers placing bulk orders. The sales revenue and costs are shown on the vertical axis and the volume of sales, or units sold, or activity expected is shown on the horizontal axis. The sales revenue graph shows the income from sales. It starts at 0 on both scales, since there is no income when there are no sales, and rises uniformly as the volume of sales rises. In Fig. 15.6, variable costs do not begin at the origin of the graph, since fixed costs have already been incurred. The variable costs, therefore, start above the fixed costs, and rise uniformly as the volume of sales rises. If we plot these variable costs we can draw in the total cost line. We can now indicate the profit, loss, break-even point, and margin of safety. The break-even chart then appears as shown in Fig. 15.6.

Another type of break-even chart is one which has the variable cost at the base, showing more clearly the marginal cost and the contribution (see Fig. 15.7).

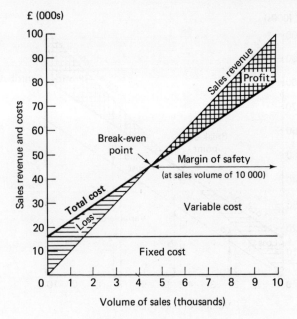

£ (000s)

*Fig. 15.6 A break-even chart*

## The Limitations of Break-even Charts

Cost behaviour is the response of cost to a variety of influences. Therefore when working out a cost–contribution–sales analysis, we must take into account any factors which may have an effect on the results, and realize that the break-even graph is only a pictorial expression which relates costs and profit to activity. The graph tends to over-simplify the real situation as there are other effects besides volume.

(*a*) Costs and revenues are shown as straight lines, but selling prices are not necessarily fixed, and the revenue may change depending on the quantities of goods sold direct, sold through agents and sold at a discount. The slope of the graph will not be constant but will vary according to the circumstances.

(*b*) Variable costs may not be proportional to volume because of overtime working, reductions in the price of materials when bulk discounts are negotiated, or because of an increase in the price of materials when demand outstrips supply. If sales are made over a wider area, distribution costs tend to rise considerably.

(*c*) Fixed costs do not always remain constant during the period of activity.

(*d*) The efficiency of production or a change in production methods has an effect on variable costs.

(*e*) The various quantities of different goods sold (the *sales mix*) may not change the total sales value to any great extent but they may change the

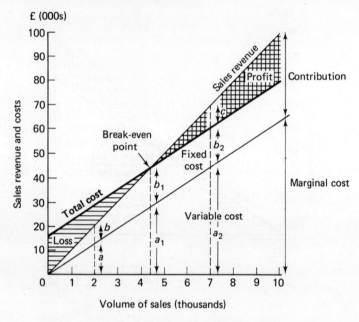

*Fig. 15.7 A contribution (break-even) chart*

*Notes:*
(i) At any volume of sales a vertical line from the sales axis to the sales revenue line shows:
  (*a*) the recovery of the marginal cost, and
  (*b*) the contribution.
(ii) Thus, for a sales volume of 2 000 units, the vertical line shows (*a*) the recovery of marginal cost and (*b*) part recovery of fixed costs.
(iii) At break-even point the vertical line shows ($a_1$) the recovery of the marginal cost and ($b_1$) contribution towards the whole of the fixed costs.
(iv) At a sales volume of 7 000 units the vertical line shows ($a_2$) the recovery of variable costs, ($b_2$) the recovery of fixed costs and (*c*) a contribution towards profit.

---

amount of profit depending on the proportion of low- and high-margin goods sold.

A graph can, therefore, be drawn from the available information and may be based on assumptions which are well-founded, but manufacturing and business conditions are continually changing and a reappraisal is necessary from time to time.

**High Fixed/Low Variable Cost compared with Low Fixed/High Variable Cost**
It has been shown in Fig. 15.5 and the calculations in Unit 15.6 that the margin of safety is approximately 56% of sales value in the case under discussion.

|  | £ |
|---|---|
| Sales | 100 000 |
| Sales at BEP | 44 444 |
| Safety margin | £ 55 556 = 55.556% |

This has been achieved in a situation where the fixed cost is relatively low and where the variable cost is fairly high. This is now compared with production where the fixed cost is much higher and there is a smaller segment of variable cost. The following costs are used in this example:

|  | £ | % |
|---|---|---|
| Sales | 100 000 | 100 |
| Direct materials | 20 000 | 20 |
| Direct wages | 10 000 | 10 |
| Variable overhead | 10 000 | 10 |
| Marginal cost | 40 000 | 40 |
| Contribution | 60 000 | 60 (C/S ratio) |
| Fixed cost | 40 000 | 40 |
| Profit | £20 000 | 20 |

$$\text{Sales at break-even point} = \frac{\text{Fixed cost}}{\text{C/S ratio}} = \frac{£40\,000}{60} \times 100$$
$$= £66\,667$$

The sales at break-even point are 66.667% of sales volume, which indicates that the margin of safety is approximately 33% compared with 56% in the previous example, and the C/S ratio is 60% compared with 36%. Profit is the same at £20 000. If it is assumed that production and sales increase by 10% the details are as follows:

| Cost statement | | | | | | |
|---|---|---|---|---|---|---|
|  | *Low fixed cost* | | | *High fixed cost* | | |
|  | £ | £ | % | £ | £ | % |
| Sales |  | 110 000 | 100.0 |  | 110 000 | 100.0 |
| Direct material | 33 000 |  | 30.0 | 22 000 |  | 20.0 |
| Direct wages | 22 000 |  | 20.0 | 11 000 |  | 10.0 |
| Variable overhead | 15 400 |  | 14.0 | 11 000 |  | 10.0 |
| Marginal cost |  | 70 400 | 64.0 |  | 44 000 | 40.0 |
| Contribution |  | 39 600 | 36.0 |  | 66 000 | 60.0 |
| *Less* Fixed cost |  | 16 000 | 14.5 |  | 40 000 | 36.4 |
| Profit |  | £23 600 | 21.5 |  | £26 000 | 23.6 |

Reduction in fixed cost as a percentage of sales

|  |  |  |
|---|---|---|
|  | 16% to 14.5% = 1.5% | 40% to 36.4% = 3.6% |
| Increase in profit | £3 600 | £6 000 |

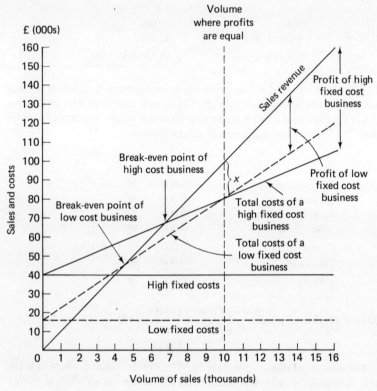

*Fig. 15.8 A break-even chart—effects of high and low fixed costs*

These figures show that for an increase of 10% in turnover, the profit in the business with high fixed costs is growing faster than in the business with low fixed costs. The effect on profit in high and low fixed cost situations is shown in Fig. 15.8.

Fig. 15.8 shows fixed and total costs of the low fixed cost business in a broken line and of the high fixed cost business in a continuous line. Normal sales are shown as a dotted line in the vertical position at 10 000 units. The chart shows that, at this volume, both undertakings have the same total cost and profit $(x)$. As turnover increases, the profits of the high fixed cost enterprise draw quickly away from the other business. It is vulnerable in a recession. In a boom, however, this enterprise can expand its profits at a greater rate. The low fixed cost business reaches the break-even point at a lower rate of activity and therefore has a greater margin of safety. This gives it more flexibility as it can stand a recession better than the high fixed cost business.

### The Sequential Profit Graph
Profit graphs tend to show the contribution as a straight line, and at one

particular angle. When several products are manufactured this type of graph obscures the fact that there is a product mix, with different sales levels and different amounts of contribution earned by each of the products. The sequential graph takes account of this situation and shows the contribution line as contribution accumulates for each of the products or product groups. It illustrates the amount of sales and contribution provided by each product, and as it extends from one product to the other it is a cumulative figure, but the individual sales and contribution can be read off the chart.

The slope of the product contribution line indicates the contribution/sales ratio and the graph is constructed by beginning with the highest ratio and finishing with any product which shows a negative contribution.

A profit graph is shown in Fig. 15.9 based on the following information:

| Product | Sales £ | C/S ratio % | Contribution £ | |
|---|---|---|---|---|
| A | 300 000 | 45 | 135 000 | |
| B | 240 000 | 60 | 144 000 | |
| C | 60 000 | (15) | (9 000) | [ ( ) indicates a |
| D | 150 000 | 20 | 30 000 | negative value.] |
| | 750 000 | 40 | 300 000 | |
| Less Fixed cost | | | 150 000 | |
| Profit | | | £150 000 | |

Contribution accumulates as follows:

| Product | Sales £ | C/S ratio % | Contribution £ | Sales £ | Cumulative contribution £ |
|---|---|---|---|---|---|
| B | 240 000 | 60 | 144 000 | 240 000 | 144 000 |
| A | 300 000 | 45 | 135 000 | 540 000 | 279 000 |
| D | 150 000 | 20 | 30 000 | 690 000 | 309 000 |
| C | 60 000 | (15) | (9 000) | 750 000 | 300 000 |
| | £750 000 | 40 | 300 000 | | |
| Less Fixed cost | | | 150 000 | | |
| Profit | | | £150 000 | | |

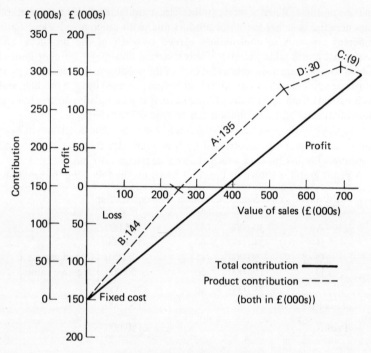

*Fig. 15.9 A sequential profit graph*

## 15.8    Differential Costing

Differential costing is a technique which uses marginal costs in the preparation of *ad hoc* information in which only the differences in cost and income between alternative courses of action are taken into consideration. There may be problems and constraints which limit the production of a particular product, and investigations may be carried out to consider alternative courses of making or buying. Whereas marginal costing refers to the routine system which ascertains marginal costs, where only variable costs are charged to cost units and fixed costs are written off in full against the contribution for that period, differential costing uses the information provided by marginal costs to consider alternative courses of action.

In profit planning, it may be necessary to consider the effect of price changes or to calculate the volume required to attain a certain increase in profits. It should be remembered that fixed costs and profits are interrelated as they represent contribution, and as sales and contribution are in direct proportion to each other, the C/S ratio can be used to estimate the sales required to attain a particular profit.

For example, with present sales of 10 000 units at £10 each, fixed costs of

£16 000, a C/S ratio of 36 per cent and profits of £20 000, what volume and sales value will be needed to increase profits by 45 per cent?

45% of £20 000 = £9 000 (Total profit £29 000)

$$\text{Sales required} = \frac{\text{Fixed cost} + \text{Profit}}{\text{C/S ratio}}$$

$$= \frac{£16\ 000 + £29\ 000}{36\%}$$

$$= \frac{£45\ 000}{36} \times 100 = £125\ 000 \ (12\ 500\ \text{units})$$

This is an increase of 2 500 units at £10 each which is equal to extra sales amounting to £25 000. As fixed costs have already been covered in the current turnover the extra could have been calculated as follows:

$$\frac{\text{Extra profit}}{\text{C/S ratio}} = \frac{£9\ 000}{36} \times 100 = £25\ 000$$

**Pricing Decisions**
In certain industries where there is a large amount of unused capacity, such as in undertakings carrying out jobbing work, it is often necessary to accept orders with a low contribution in order to provide work. In extreme circumstances any reasonable amount over marginal cost will provide contribution towards the fixed costs, enabling the firm to break-even and possibly show an acceptable profit. Unused capacity represents the loss of potential contribution and as long as future business will not be harmed by the acceptance of lower prices, it is often beneficial to reduce the normal price. Trade can expand by a variation of selling prices and the most profitable relationship between costs, prices and volume of business should be ascertained.

Proposals to reduce prices in order to increase sales should always be carefully investigated. This is because of the additional volume required to compensate for the decline in prices. A reduction in price reduces the C/S ratio, and shortens the margin of safety, because the break-even point is reached at a much greater volume of sales.

For example, if the unit price of £10 is reduced by 10 per cent to £9, the example given at the foot of p. 234 would appear as:

|  | £ |
|---|---|
| Sales 10 000 units @ £9 | 90 000 |
| *Less* Marginal cost | 64 000 |
| Contribution | 26 000 (C/S ratio 28.89%) |
| *Less* Fixed cost | 16 000 |
| Profit | £10 000 |

In order to maintain profits, extra volume is required.

$$\text{Sales required} = \frac{\text{Fixed cost} + \text{Profit}}{\text{C/S ratio}}$$

$$= \frac{£16\,000 + £20\,000}{28.89\%}$$

$$= £124\,611 \; (13\,846 \text{ units @ £9 each})$$

3 846 extra units will have to be sold just to hold the profit at £20 000. In connection with pricing, remember that a decrease in fixed or variable costs will improve the margin of safety as the break-even point will be reached at a smaller volume of sales.

## 15.9　Limiting Factor

Unless a plan or forecast is capable of fulfilment, it is a waste of time trying to calculate turnover and profits and to project them on a break-even chart. A *limiting factor* is the factor in the activities of an undertaking which, at a particular time, or over a period, limits the volume of output. The limiting factor is sometimes called the *key factor* or the *principal budget factor*. Marginal costing has been examined generally on the basis that only one product is manufactured, but a company may make a number of products with different rates of contribution and different production problems.

Sales are frequently a limiting factor because of lack of demand and other causes. Other limiting factors are a shortage of skilled labour or materials, a shortage of space or of suitable plant and equipment, or a lack of capital to provide the necessary facilities. In such circumstances, the area of constraint should be examined together with the contribution so that it can be seen which products are yielding the greatest individual contribution, and what steps can be taken to improve the situation. For example, floor space may be a limit to expansion and therefore it is advisable to examine departments or products and to compare the contribution provided, and to rank these products in order of profitability. Consider Example 15.2.

**Example 15.2**

| Product | Area (m²) | Contribution provided £ | Contribution per m² £ | Ranking |
|---|---|---|---|---|
| A | 5 000 | 22 000 | 4.40 | 1 |
| B | 4 800 | 10 800 | 2.25 | 3 |
| C | 10 200 | 26 520 | 2.60 | 2 |
| | 20 000 | £59 320 | | |

On the assumption that 2 000 square metres of floor space used for producing Product B could be adapted to make Product A without any changes in fixed costs or selling prices and if the turnover of A increases by 40 per cent the results would be as follows:

| Product | Area (m²) | Contribution provided £ |
|---|---|---|
| A | 7 000 | 30 800 |
| B | 2 800 | 6 300 |
| C | 10 200 | 26 520 |
| | 20 000 | 63 620 |
| Less Present contribution | | 59 320 |
| Increased contribution | | £ 4 300 |

This is a simplification of the practical problems because there may be other factors determining the turnover, such as sales of Product B having to be maintained in order to retain the customers who are purchasing our other products, and if B is not available may go elsewhere for A and C. Limiting conditions must be used in the best possible way, and when deciding what product or combination of products to manufacture, each item must be examined to determine the contribution per unit of limiting factor.

An analysis to show the contribution per unit of limiting factor should precede the forecast of a sales and production budget as it may be possible to change the normal sales mix in order to improve profitability. The analysis below indicates that Product X has the best contribution to sales at $38\frac{1}{2}$ per cent and the highest contribution per £ of materials, whereas Product Z has the best contribution per £ of wages. Decisions will be made after consideration of limiting factors and other conditions which may arise in a trading period.

| | Analysis of cost of production and sales | | | | | | Contribution per £ of | | |
| | | | Variable | Marginal | | | | | |
| Product | Materials | Wages | overhead | cost | Contribution | Sales | Sales | Material | Wages |
| | £(000s) | £(000s) | £(000s) | £(000s) | £(000s) | £(000s) | £ | £ | £ |
| X | 85 | 35 | 40 | 160 | 100 | 260 | 0.385 | 1.176 | 2.857 |
| Y | 160 | 90 | 90 | 340 | 180 | 520 | 0.346 | 1.125 | 2.000 |
| Z | 95 | 30 | 80 | 205 | 95 | 300 | 0.317 | 1.000 | 3.167 |
| | £340 | £155 | £210 | £705 | £375 | £1 080 | | | |

## 15.10  Make or Buy Decisions

If there is a shortage of capacity the remedy is to expand or to purchase certain items from an outside source. The amount of capital expenditure and the likely cost savings must be carefully considered. Purchasing may be advisable where suppliers have specialized equipment and can supply at reduced prices but the effect of fixed costs on internally made products must be taken into account.

The cost comparison should be between the supplier's price and the marginal cost of producing the goods on the premises. This is because it is assumed that the fixed costs have already been incurred and that the other costs are the variable costs. If there is a limiting factor, products which earn the highest rate of contribution per unit of limiting factor should be retained.

When facilities are available for production to be carried out at an economic price, it is advantageous to make the product oneself. Complete control is established over the quality of the materials used, the manufacturing process and delivery of the final product. If a product manufacturing process or design is unique, it may also be essential to make the item in order to maintain secrecy.

When a product is manufactured under licence, there may be a condition that all work is carried out by the licensee, and the item has to be made and not bought. The disadvantages of buying often mean that drawings, specifications, patterns, jigs, tools and dies have to be supplied, as well as advice on the manufacturing process. There is also the problem of late deliveries and the suspension of assembly when parts for the main product have not arrived. If items such as castings are supplied, and some are unsatisfactory and need to be replaced, there may be a considerable delay in completing products. A subcontractor may accept work and give satisfactory service when his business is slack, but may provide poor service when his own trade returns to normal.

If it is discovered that certain parts can be purchased at or near the making price, it is advantageous to buy them only when the production facilities made available can earn more than they did under the other process.

*Cost of bought-out items and cost of production*

| Article | A | B | C |
|---|---|---|---|
| | £ | £ | £ |
| Purchase price | 18.00 | 35.00 | 45.00 |
| Production: | | | |
| Man hours | 4 | 5 | 5 |
| Machine hours | 1 | 2 | 4 |
| Cost: | £ | £ | £ |
| Marginal cost | 20 | 25 | 30 |
| Fixed cost | 4 | 8 | 10 |
| Total cost | £24.00 | £33.00 | £40.00 |
| Excess of purchase price over marginal cost: | | | |
| Per article | (2.00) | 10.00 | 15.00 |
| Per man hour | (0.50) | 2.00 | 3.00 |
| Per machine hour | (2.00) | 5.00 | 3.75 |

With Article A, the purchase price is less than the marginal cost, so it is profitable to buy outside. Article A also shows the lowest rate of contribution per man hour, and if manpower is the limiting factor, again this article could be purchased outside. If manpower is so short that further outside purchases must be made, then Article B should be purchased outside. When machine power is the limiting factor, A is again the first choice for outside purchase, since it yields the lowest rate of contribution per machine, and C is the second choice at a contribution of £3.75.

## 15.11  Exercises

1. The managing director of MC Limited, a manufacturing company, has recently attended a short conference on 'Marginal costing for non-accounting executives', and has returned enthusiastic to learn more about marginal costing in operation. One particular idea which was discussed only briefly at the conference was a suggestion that management should be more interested in marginal costing than absorption costing, because profits are affected by relative volumes of production and sales in any one period.

You are required, as management accountant, to prepare a short paper discussing briefly the concepts of marginal costing and absorption costing and explaining what effect different volumes of production and sales have on profit reported under each system.                                              (*ICMA*)

2. (*a*) Explain what is meant in accountancy when reference is made to the break-even point.

(*b*) State the information which can be obtained from a break-even chart.

3. (*a*) What is the contribution/sales ratio?

(*b* What does it measure?

(*c*) On what does it depend with regard to a factory as a whole, and why could it alter from year to year?                                              (*ICMA*)

# Unit Sixteen
# Standard Costing

## 16.1 Introduction

A mass of cost data arises as a result of business transactions and manufacturing processes. This information is historical and either represents actual cost or records past performance. If this information is collected each year, the cost of performance in the current period can be compared with similar details recorded previously, but if there is no previous record, the cost accountant has to accept what is received without question. When comparisons are made and variations are disclosed, there is no real evidence of inefficient performance or of the payment of uneconomic prices because no standard of measurement is available to check the cost or the performance. For example, costs may be distorted by changes in the volume of production, and variations in buying or selling prices may hide the fact that productivity has improved or that inefficiency has occurred. No information is available to prove that the best use is being made of materials and labour or of plant and equipment, because no planning or investigation has been made to establish standards or to install procedures to measure the efficiency of the business. *Standard costing is a method of ascertaining costs and checking performance against standards, by comparing actual cost with standard cost and thereby revealing the extent of any variance which has taken place.*

An analysis is made of the causes of the variations so that, where necessary, corrective action can be taken to improve the situation. This is to maintain efficiency by executive action and is called *management by exceptions.* Management is not concerned with the mass of data which is equivalent to standard cost or standard performance, but only with the exceptional variations which occur during a production period.

A full system of standard costing involves a considerable amount of preparatory work because of the need to establish standards for all the elements of cost.

The Institute of Cost and Management Accountants defines standard cost as *a predetermined cost calculated in relation to a prescribed set of working conditions, correlating technical specifications and scientific measurements of materials and labour to the prices and wage rates expected to apply during the period to which the standard cost is intended to relate, with an addition of an appropriate share of budgeted overhead. Its main purposes are to provide bases for control through variance accounting, for the valuation of stocks and work-in-progress, and, in exceptional cases, for fixing selling prices.*

Standards are not set by guesswork but are determined by people with the necessary technical knowledge to assess scientifically what the cost or the performance should be under certain conditions.

## 16.2  Variance Accounting

**Standard Costing v. Budgetary Control**
The same basic idea applies to standard costing and to budgetary control for they are both predetermined and used as measuring sticks within a business. The term *variance accounting* is now used to describe the unified technique of budgetary control and standard costing, both of which compare planned performance with actual performance in the analysis of variances, but, for convenience, they are shown as separate Units in this book. The fundamental idea is predetermination of costs, followed during the operating period by a comparison of actual cost with the value of the allowance set, and the reporting of deviations from the set target. Whereas budgetary control fixes objectives for all aspects of income, expense and other functions of a business, standard costing is concerned with the detailed production operations and the products of a business. The setting of standards gives close attention to the study of work, the human factor, methods of production and the efficiency of operations, while budgetary control sets limits on spending, is generally less concerned with detailed analysis but more concerned with controlling the expenditure of cost centres.

## 16.3  Standard Conditions—Normal, Expected, Ideal

The introduction of standard costing requires a decision on the type of standards to set. Are they to be fixed on the basis of *normal conditions* or on *expected*, attainable conditions, or should the aim be to set standards based on best performance which can only be attained under *ideal conditions*? Production under normal conditions is not usually acceptable because output is based on normal capacity and average sales, probably with little attention being given to the efficiency of labour, machines or the economic use of materials.

Standards worked out on *expected* actual costs are based on the volume of production and efficiency which the manufacturer hopes to achieve, and on the prices which he expects to pay for materials and services. The standards allow for waste and a degree of inefficiency, which is unavoidable in most circumstances. A high level of efficiency is expected but the standards are realistic and are capable of attainment. *Ideal standards* are only attainable in perfect conditions, and as these seldom, if ever, occur, they are not a reasonable or realistic proposition. Such conditions would result in a continuous stream of unfavourable variances which would discourage effort, and have a disincentive effect on the employees. The best basis for standards is therefore expected, attainable conditions.

## 16.4  The Establishment of Standard Costs

Installing a system of standard costing may be a long and costly business, but once installed, the records are there for continuous use to check the efficiency of operations. The biggest problem probably concerns the revision of standards. When standards no longer apply because of changes in price, manufacturing methods or product specifications, they must be revised. The cost of revising standards may be excessive and requires a great deal of clerical effort. A period has to be chosen within which the *current standards* will apply and this is normally one year. If a system is to be operated for several years without revision, then *basic standards* can be established, using index numbers which change according to the movement in prices. This is not entirely satisfactory because over a period of years the index number is often not a true reflection of the current value.

### Studying the Product and the Processes

Before standards are set for materials, labour and expense, it is essential to carry out a careful examination of the products and manufacturing processes. Fixing standards in a large company requires the services of many people, particularly technical and accounting staff. In general, records have to be made of the type and quality of material to be stocked and used in the product, the sequence of operations in the manufacture, and the equipment and machinery to be used. In order to be effective, everything connected with the organization needs to be scientifically studied so that the standards set are fair, reasonable and correct and, when the operating results are measured, they should show how efficient or inefficient the departments and employees are within each period of control.

### Standard Unit of Work

*Standard hours* or *standard minutes* are the units used to measure the basic time for carrying out a piece of work, plus relaxation allowance and contingency allowance where applicable. The standard hour is a hypothetical hour which measures the amount of work which should be performed in that time by an experienced worker. In current practice, 60 or 1 standard units are produced in one hour when unrestricted work is carried out at standard performance. A standard unit of work is expressed in terms of standard minutes or standard hours.

### Standard Time

This is the total time in which a task should be completed at standard performance, that is, basic time, plus contingency allowance, plus relaxation allowance.

## 16.5   Material Standards (Direct Material)

Materials are controlled on the basis of *price and usage* after allowing for normal waste. The technical expert decides on the best and most economical material to use for each purpose, and, after allowing for wastage, specifies the exact size, quantity or weight required for each item included in the product to be manufactured. Such a review of materials is valuable as it often discloses a large range of different sizes and types of materials, many of which could probably be eliminated after a study of them all. A reduction in variety can lead to economies in purchasing, material handling and storage, and a reduction in the amount of capital invested in stocks.

**Standard Prices**

The buyer or purchasing officer prepares lists of materials and indicates the prices to be included in the standard cost for the period ahead. These prices will be based on current or forecast market prices, allowing for anticipated increases, or they may be based on the price paid in recent months together with any expected increases. In some cases it may be necessary to obtain quotations from possible suppliers. Standards will be set for purchased components as well as for raw materials.

## 16.6   Labour Standards (Direct Wages)

Wages are controlled according to the *rates paid* and the *efficiency* of the operator, measured by the time taken and the standard time allowed for each job. In order to control labour costs efficiently, the planning department or similar authority has to establish standards by:

(*a*) listing the operations necessary to make the product;

(*b*) specifying the department or production centre where the work is to be carried out;

(*c*) indicating the tools or equipment needed or the machine which is to be used;

(*d*) stating the grade of labour or grade of employees for each operation;

(*e*) setting the standard operation times in standard direct labour hours or expressing it in money where piece-work prices are in use.

**Standard Product Costs**

As costs have to be assembled for standard products, a standard cost form or card is prepared for each item to be produced. This shows the details mentioned above and, by using standard costing rates for wages and overheads, the operations can be priced and the complete cost can be shown. A standard wages rate has to be established for each grade of labour, and is the trade union rate for each grade, or the average rate paid where union rates do not apply. Account must be taken of any wage plans or special incentive schemes which are in use.

## 16.7   Overhead Standards (Fixed and Variable)

Overheads are controlled by the budgeted allowances for each cost centre and the actual expenditure, according to efficiency and the volume or capacity available. Management has to make decisions on the volume of production in each of the producing cost centres and the work to be carried out by the service cost centres. The decisions will probably be based on the normal capacity to manufacture. This figure is arrived at by taking maximum capacity and deducting from it an amount to cover the usual losses caused by, for example, holidays, material shortages, breakdowns and absenteeism.

The procedure for arriving at the overhead rate for each producing cost centre is similar but more precise than the method used in historical costing.

When fixing standards for materials, labour and overheads, advice is sought from experienced people, and work study techniques such as *time study* and *method study* will probably be used.

## 16.8   Variance Analysis

Variances are analysed into constituent parts as shown in Fig. 16.1 and the actual performance is compared with the planned performance. The main variances are:

### (*a*)  Operating Profit Variance

This is the difference between budgeted and actual operating profit. Operating profit arises from the normal activities of the business, such as the provision and sale of manufactured goods or services, before taking account of extraneous transactions such as those of a purely financial nature.

### (*b*)  Operating Profit Variance due to Sales

This consists of variances arising from selling prices and sales volume. It is the difference between the budgeted operating profit and the margin between the actual sales and the standard cost of those sales.

### (*c*)  General Administration Cost Variance

This is the difference between the total standard cost of general administration included in the total standard cost of the products sold, and the actual expenditure incurred on general administration.

### (*d*)  Marketing Cost Variance

This is the difference between the total standard cost of marketing included in the total standard cost of the products sold, and the actual expenditure incurred on marketing.

### (*e*)  Production Cost Variance

This is the difference between the standard cost of production achieved during the period, whether completed or not, and the actual cost incurred on such work.

The object of variance analysis is to detect the operating problems and to report them, so that corrective action may be taken where possible.

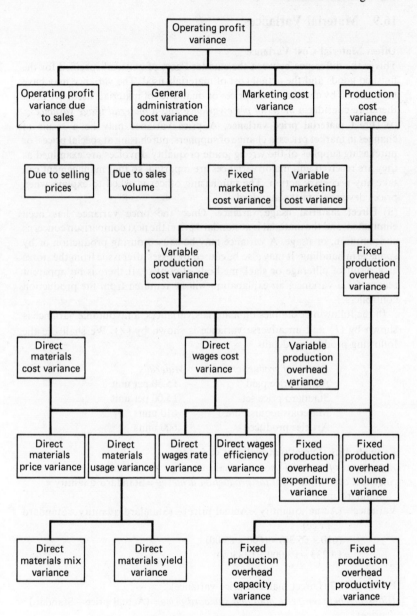

*Fig. 16.1 Variance analysis*

## 16.9    Material Variances

### Direct Material Cost Variance

This is the difference between the standard cost of material specified for the finished goods and the actual cost of materials used. The variance may have been caused by changes in the prices or quantities of materials used. We must therefore consider a *material price variance* and a *material usage variance*.

(i) **Direct material price variance.** A price variance may be a result of changes in market prices, a change of suppliers, purchasing at special prices, or purchasing supplies of the wrong grade or quality. Invoices are examined as they are received and major variances are reported, so that management can take any necessary action. The purchasing officer is asked to explain when prices deviate from the standard.

(ii) **Direct material usage variance.** Once the price variance has been eliminated, and the material is at standard price, the next comparison concerns consumption, or usage. A variance may be caused during production or by spoilage in handling. It may also be caused by losses after issue from the stores as a result of pilferage or slack methods of control. If there is no apparent reason for a variance, an explanation will be required from the production controllers.

In the following examples on materials variances, a favourable variance is shown by (*F*) and an adverse variance is shown by (*A*). We shall use the following production details.

| Details of production | Materials |
|---|---|
| Actual price paid | £5.30 per unit |
| Standard price set | £5.00 per unit |
| Materials requisitioned | 610 units |
| Articles produced | 600 units |

**Example 16.1** (Direct material cost variance)

*Actual cost of material used* = Actual quantity × Actual price
*Standard cost of material for production achieved* = Standard quantity × Standard price

Variance = (Actual quantity × Actual price) − (Standard quantity × Standard price)

$$= (610 \times £5.30) - (600 \times £5.00)$$
$$= £3\ 233 - £3\ 000 = \underline{\underline{£233(A)}}$$

**Example 16.2** (Direct material price variance)

*Difference between price paid and standard price* = (Actual price − Standard price)

*Materials used* = Actual quantity

Variance = (Actual price − Standard price) × Actual quantity

$$= (£5.30 - £5.00) \times 610$$
$$= £0.30 \times 610 = \underline{\underline{£183(A)}}$$

*Note:* The direct material price variance must be related to the material requisitioned or purchased, because the profit or loss caused by a variance in the price is in respect of the material actually supplied and used by the operator.

**Example 16.3** (Direct material usage variance)
*Actual quantity of material used* = Actual quantity
*Standard quantity for production achieved* = Standard quantity
Variance = (Actual quantity − Standard quantity) × Standard price
(*Note:* The material is at standard price)
$$= (610 - 600) \times £5.00 = £50(A)$$

*Note:* The material used by the operator exceeds the amount required to produce the goods as represented by the standard quantity. The usage variance indicates whether more or less material has been used than is needed to produce the standard quantity. Although the variance is expressed in money, it is related not to price but to the quantity of material actually used and the quantity which should have been used.

The direct material price variance and the direct material usage variance can now be reconciled with the direct material cost variance.

|  | £ |
|---|---|
| Direct material price variance | 183 (*A*) |
| Direct material usage variance | 50 (*A*) |
| Direct material cost variance | £233 (*A*) |

In this example, all the variances are *adverse*: too high a price has been paid and too much material has been used. When some variances are *favourable* and some are *adverse*, it is necessary to state them as *net* variances. This means that the smaller variance is set against the larger one to show the net effect. Thus, it would be possible to have an adverse material cost variance of £233 which was the result of an adverse usage variance (say, minus £300) but a favourable price variance (say, plus £67). The net effect is minus £233.

## 16.10 Labour Variances

### (a) Direct Wages Cost Variance
The direct wages cost variance is the difference between the standard and the actual cost of labour. This variance could have been caused by changes in the wages paid, or by changes due to over-achieving or under-achieving the standard output. We must therefore discover the *direct wages rate variance* and the *direct wages efficiency variance*.

(i) **Direct wages rate variance.** When dealing with variances it is sensible to ensure that they are not caused by clerical errors when the standard was set and calculated or when the comparison is made between standard and actual. Wage rate variance is similar to material price variance and may be the result of changes in wage rates because of awards, or a change in wage plans such as the introduction of piece-work, or because the wrong grade of labour has been used (such as an apprentice instead of a skilled worker, or a highly skilled worker performing low-grade work). When a different grade of worker is used, a note to this effect will probably be made on the job card, otherwise the foreman or supervisor will be contacted for an explanation.

(ii) **Direct wages efficiency variance.** This variance relates to the gain or loss made by achieving or failing to achieve the standard output per hour. It is as well to remember that the wages cost is now at standard cost because any rate variance has been removed. Therefore, these are time variances priced at the standard rate and are found by comparing the actual time with the standard time recorded on job cards. The excess time taken may be a result of incorrect instructions given to the employee, poor supervision, using materials of the wrong quality, or using tools, machinery or equipment which may be faulty or of the wrong type. Poor efficiency may also be caused by using workers who are insufficiently trained, or who are working in sub-standard conditions. Sometimes, organizational problems cause a hold-up in the supply of material, tools and so on. When employees are idle because of delays in material supplies and breakdowns of machinery, the idle time should be charged to an *Idle Time Account* so that management is aware of the problems that exist.

(b) **Examples of Labour Variances**
(*Note: When calculating labour variances, the standard cost is not actual hours at the standard rate but standard hours for the production achieved, at the standard rate.*)

| Details of production — labour | |
|---|---|
| Actual rate | £2.00 per hour |
| Standard rate | £1.90 per hour |
| Actual hours worked | 40 |
| Units produced | 15 at 3 standard hours each |

**Example 16.4** (Direct wages cost variance)
*Standard cost of labour* = Standard hours × Standard rate
*Actual cost of labour* = Actual hours × Actual rate
Direct wages variance = (Standard hours × Standard rate) − (Actual hours × Actual rate)
$$= (15 \times 3) \times £1.90 - (40 \times £2.00)$$
(*Note:* Standard hours for units produced)
$$= £85.50 - £80.00 = \underline{\underline{£5.50\ (F)}}$$

**Example 16.5** (Direct wages rate variance)
*Difference between wage rates* = Actual rate − Standard rate
*Hours worked* = Actual hours
Wage rate variance = (Actual rate − Standard rate) × Actual hours
$$= (£2.00 - £1.90) \times 40 = \underline{\underline{£4.00\ (A)}}$$

*Note:* This variance shows the rate of wages actually paid and the rate which should have been paid (standard rate) for the grade of worker selected to perform this work, as specified when the standards were set. The wage rate variance shows these rates and the wages paid above or below the standard cost. In this case, being adverse, the wage rate variance shows that £4 extra was paid because the operator was receiving 10 pence per hour above the standard rate.

**Example 16.6** (Direct labour efficiency variance)
*Difference in hours* = Actual hours − Standard hours for production achieved
Labour efficiency variance = (Actual hours − Standard hours for production achieved) × Standard rate
$$= [40 - (15 \text{ units} \times 3 \text{ hours})] \times £1.90$$
$$= -5 \times £1.90 = \underline{\underline{£9.50 \, (F)}}$$

*Notes:*
(i) Where the term (*F*) for favourable is used, the minus sign may be left out.
(ii) When there is a difference between the actual hours and the standard hours, for the production achieved (Units produced *times* Standard hours per unit), it indicates that the work has been carried out in a shorter or longer period of time than the standard hours allowed. The standard rate is used because the application of the price variance has reduced the actual rate paid to the standard rate. The profit or loss shown by the direct labour efficiency variance is the result of efficient or inefficient working, always provided that the rate is fairly set.

The direct wages cost variance is reconciled with the direct labour efficiency variance and direct wages rate variance.

|  | £ |
|---|---|
| Direct labour efficiency variance | 9.50 (*F*) |
| Direct wages rate variance | 4.00 (*A*) |
| Direct wages cost variance | £5.50 (*F*) |

This indicates payment of an excess wage rate and a favourable output which (when netted) equals the direct wages cost variance.

## (*c*) Production Ratios
The operating performance of labour can be measured in various ways to indicate the efficiency achieved, the level of activity, and the usage of capacity. One way is by calculating control ratios concerning production, when quantities of goods produced or services provided are expressed in either standard direct labour hours or standard machine hours.

The ICMA publication *Terminology of Management and Financial Accountancy* defines ratios concerning production as follows:
(i) **Production volume ratio.** The number of standard hours equivalent to the production achieved, whether completed or not, divided by (or expressed as a percentage of) the budgeted number of standard hours. This is often referred to as the activity ratio but the term is not recommended because *activity* is capable of different interpretations.

(ii) **Capacity ratio.** The actual number of direct working hours divided by (or expressed as a percentage of) the budgeted number of standard hours.

(iii) **Productivity (or efficiency) ratio.** The standard hours equivalent to the production achieved, whether completed or not, divided by (or expressed as a percentage of) the actual number of direct working hours.

**Example 16.7**

| | |
|---|---|
| Standard time | 4 hours per unit |
| Budget | 192 units (768 standard hours) |
| Actual production | 197 units (788 standard hours in 800 actual hours worked) |

*Production volume ratio*

$$=\frac{\text{Standard hours equivalent to the production achieved}}{\text{Budgeted standard hours}} \times 100$$

$$=\frac{788}{768} \times 100 = 102.6\%$$

*Capacity ratio*

$$=\frac{\text{Actual hours worked}}{\text{Budgeted standard hours}} \times 100$$

$$=\frac{800}{768} \times 100 = 104.2\%$$

*Productivity (or efficiency) ratio*

$$=\frac{\text{Standard hours equivalent to the production achieved}}{\text{Actual hours worked}} \times 100$$

$$=\frac{788}{800} \times 100 = 98.5\%$$

A comparison of budgeted and actual production shows that five extra units were produced and this accounts for the increase of 2.6 per cent in the volume of production. However, this volume was achieved in 800 hours, compared with 768 hours budgeted for the usage of capacity, and this accounts for the increase of 4.2 per cent shown by the capacity ratio. As the increase in the use of capacity was greater than the increase in the volume of production, this indicates that the efficiency was below 100 per cent.

These ratios are related to each other and the productivity or efficiency ratio can be calculated or proved by using the production volume ratio and the capacity ratio as follows.

$$\text{Efficiency ratio} = \frac{\text{Production volume ratio}}{\text{Capacity ratio}} \times 100$$

$$= \frac{102.6}{104.2} \times 100 = \underline{\underline{98.5\%}}$$

At the standard rate of production, 200 units should be produced in 800 hours.

$$\text{Efficiency ratio} = \frac{\text{Actual production}}{\text{Production at standard rate}} \times 100$$

$$= \frac{197}{200} \times 100 = \underline{\underline{98.5\%}}$$

The productivity or efficiency ratio is also referred to as the *rate of efficiency* or simply as the *efficiency*.

## 16.11 Overhead Variances

However carefully the overheads are estimated in order to arrive at a standard charge to be added to products for the expenses incurred, it is highly likely that variances will arise. If a standard overhead cost has been budgeted at £5 per unit and 2 000 units are produced, the overhead cost should be £10 000. If, in fact, the actual cost of overheads is £13 500, there is an unfavourable overhead variance of £3 500, while, if overheads only cost £9 800, there is a favourable overhead variance of £200. This variance should be analysed to find out the cause. Was it an expenditure variance (caused by wage increases to managerial staff, perhaps) or a capacity variance (caused by working at a higher or lower capacity than standard)? There are several types of variance which are described below and illustrated in charts (see Figs. 16.2 and 16.3).

### Fixed and Variable Overheads

Costs which vary in direct ratio to production are *variable overheads*. *Fixed overheads* represent the fixed costs of the organization and the fixed overhead cost per unit is set so that the total quantity represents the budget or the constant cost. If the budget quantity is not reached, a variance arises, because of the under-absorption or over-absorption that occurs.

The budget for the period will show separately the fixed and variable overheads and the budgeted or standard hours of production. The information will provide the details to calculate the *fixed overhead absorption rate* and the *variable overhead absorption rate* by dividing the cost in each case by the budgeted standard hours of production.

The use of *flexible budgets* is advisable as allowances should be set in accordance with the activity achieved. If there is a change in the number of working days a *calendar variance* can be calculated. It is part of the volume variance and is equivalent to the standard hours lost or gained.

### Controllable Variances

Variances are favourable or adverse and can be separated into those which are

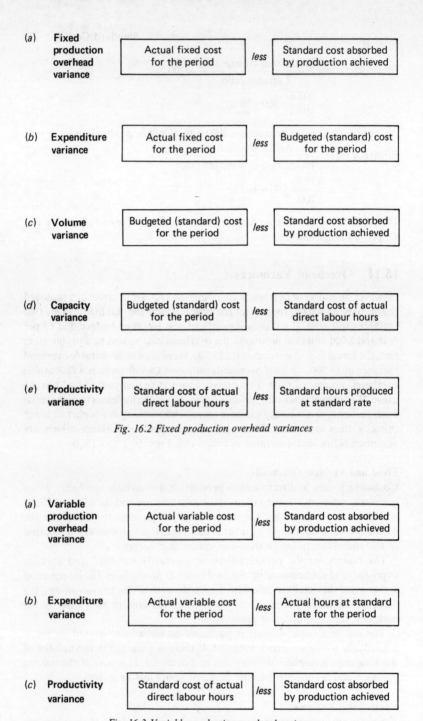

(a) **Fixed production overhead variance**

| Actual fixed cost for the period | *less* | Standard cost absorbed by production achieved |

(b) **Expenditure variance**

| Actual fixed cost for the period | *less* | Budgeted (standard) cost for the period |

(c) **Volume variance**

| Budgeted (standard) cost for the period | *less* | Standard cost absorbed by production achieved |

(d) **Capacity variance**

| Budgeted (standard) cost for the period | *less* | Standard cost of actual direct labour hours |

(e) **Productivity variance**

| Standard cost of actual direct labour hours | *less* | Standard hours produced at standard rate |

*Fig. 16.2 Fixed production overhead variances*

(a) **Variable production overhead variance**

| Actual variable cost for the period | *less* | Standard cost absorbed by production achieved |

(b) **Expenditure variance**

| Actual variable cost for the period | *less* | Actual hours at standard rate for the period |

(c) **Productivity variance**

| Standard cost of actual direct labour hours | *less* | Standard cost absorbed by production achieved |

*Fig. 16.3 Variable production overhead variances*

controllable and uncontrollable. A controllable variance is one which is the primary responsibility of a specified person, whereas an uncontrollable variance is one for which no individual can be held responsible, as, for example, a national wage award, or an increase in the cost of rent. An individual can, however, be answerable for the efficiency of a group of workers under his or her control or for material usage.

## 16.12 Analysing Overhead Variances

The terminology, methods of analysis and ledger entries about overhead variances vary considerably from business to business, and the published material on this subject tackles the problem in a variety of ways. It is essential to understand the basic terms before proceeding with the analysis:

**Budget**
This is a financial and quantitative forecasted statement, based on estimated cost and an anticipated volume of activity expressed in units, direct labour hours, machine hours, etc. A standard cost is established for hours and units.

**Volume**
The volume of production, whether budgeted or actual, is represented by the quantity of units produced or the number of standard hours of labour or machine time used in the production of those units. The cost of this volume is obtained by multiplying the volume by the predetermined (standard) cost. It should be noted that there is a budgeted (planned) volume and an actual volume. When expressed in hours, there are the standard hours planned and the standard hours produced.

**Production Actually Achieved**
This is the actual volume of production and represents the standard hours in the units produced. For example, the actual hours may be 20 500 and the number of standard hours per unit, 10. If 2 000 units are produced, the production actually achieved is equivalent to 20 000 hours and this produces an adverse variance of 500 hours at the standard rate per hour.

**Budget Cost Allowance**
Costs are ascertained during a costing period of, say, four weeks and this is the control period during which comparisons are made between budgeted and actual results. The *budget cost allowance* is the amount allowed to budget centres during this control period. A proportion of the annual budget is allowed for fixed cost, based on the benefits expected during the period and not on any actual payment made at that date. The allowance for variable cost is in direct proportion to the volume of production.

**Overhead Variance**
This is referred to as a cost variance or total variance and is the difference

between the actual cost of overheads and the standard cost absorbed in the production achieved. It is defined and analysed as fixed production overhead expenditure variance and variable production overhead expenditure variance, in the section on analysing overhead variances below.

Referring to the ICMA terminology, the variances consist of:

(a) **Fixed Production Overhead Variance**

This is the difference between the standard cost of fixed overhead absorbed in the production achieved, whether completed or not, and the fixed overhead attributed and charged in that period.

(b) **Variable Production Overhead Variance**

This is the difference between the standard variable production overhead absorbed in the production achieved, whether completed or not, and the actual variable production overhead.

Each of these variances may then be sub-divided:

(a) **Fixed Production Overhead Variance**

This is divided into *fixed production overhead expenditure variance* and *fixed production overhead volume variance*, with the latter sub-dividing yet again into a *capacity variance* and a *fixed cost productivity variance*. These are defined as follows:

(i) **Fixed production overhead expenditure variance.** This is the difference between the budget cost allowance for production for a specified control period and the amount of actual fixed expenditure attributed and charged to that period.

(ii) **Fixed production overhead volume variance.** This is that portion of the fixed production overhead variance which is the difference between the standard cost absorbed in the production achieved, whether completed or not, and the budget cost allowance for a specified control period. This may then be sub-divided into:

1. *Capacity variance.* This is that portion of the fixed production overhead volume variance which is caused by working at higher or lower capacity than standard. Capacity is often expressed in terms of average direct labour hours worked per day, and the variance is the difference between the budget cost allowance and the actual direct labour hours worked (valued at the standard hourly absorption rate).

2. *Fixed cost productivity variance.* This is that portion of the fixed production overhead volume variance which is the difference between the standard cost absorbed in the production achieved, whether completed or not, and the actual direct labour hours worked (valued at the standard hourly absorption rate).

(b) **Variable Production Overhead Variance**

This may be sub-divided into an *expenditure variance* and a *productivity variance* but sub-division is not recommended unless there are reasonable grounds for believing that the resultant sub-variances would be helpful. These are defined as follows:

(i) **Variable production overhead expenditure variance.** Variable overheads vary strictly with output (i.e. volume) but a variance may arise when there is a difference between the actual cost and the budget cost allowance as a result of a change in price after the budget was set.

(ii) **Variable production overhead productivity variance.** If the operations are inefficient so that the number of working hours is greater than the allowance in the budget, a variance will be caused by this low productivity. It may be found by taking the standard cost of the actual direct labour hours less the standard cost absorbed by the production achieved.

In order to analyse and report on the overhead variances, the following information is required for each control period:

budgeted standard hours and budgeted units of production;
actual standard hours of production and units produced;
budgeted cost of fixed and variable overheads;
actual cost of fixed and variable overheads;
fixed overhead absorption rate;
variable overhead absorption rate.

**Example 16.8** (Overhead analysis)

| *Budget* | | *Actual* | |
|---|---|---|---|
| Fixed overheads | £108 000 | Fixed overheads | £106 000 |
| Variable overheads | £90 000 | Variable overheads | £82 500 |
| Standard hours | 36 000 | Hours worked | 32 800 |
| Units of production | 6 000 | Units produced | 5 400 |

*Standard hours per unit*

$$= \frac{\text{Hours}}{\text{Units}} = \frac{36\,000}{6\,000} = 6$$

*Standard hours achieved by production*
= Units produced × Standard hours
per unit
= 5 400 × 6
= 32 400

(*continued overleaf*)

*Absorption rate per hour*
Fixed overhead

$$= \frac{\text{Budgeted fixed overhead}}{\text{Budgeted standard hours}}$$

$$= \frac{£108\ 000}{36\ 000}$$

$$= £3.00 \text{ per hour}$$

Variable overhead

$$= \frac{\text{Budgeted variable overhead}}{\text{Budgeted standard hours}}$$

$$= \frac{£90\ 000}{36\ 000}$$

$$= £2.50 \text{ per hour}$$

*Standard variable overhead absorbed in the production achieved*
= Standard hours achieved ×
　Variable overhead absorption rate

$$= 32\ 400 \times £2.50$$

$$= £81\ 000$$

*Variable overhead cost of actual hours, at variable overhead absorption rate*
= Hours worked × Variable
　overhead absorption rate

$$= 32\ 800 \times £2.50$$

$$= £82\ 000$$

*Notes:*
(i) It is necessary to calculate the budgeted standard hours per unit and the budgeted (standard) absorption rates for fixed and variable overheads which are 6 hours per unit and £3.00 and £2.50 per hour respectively.
(ii) For the actual results it is necessary to calculate the standard hours achieved by production and the variable overhead absorbed by this production which are 32 400 hours and £81 000 respectively.
(iii) The next calculation is to obtain the variable overhead cost for the actual hours worked which is £82 000.
This information shows that variable overheads cost £82 500 but for the hours worked they should have cost £82 000 and the value absorbed in the production achieved is only £81 000. There is also a variance between the budgeted fixed cost and the actual fixed cost.

*Overhead variance*
= Actual cost of overheads − (Standard hours produced × Overhead
　absorption rates)
= (Fixed overhead £106 000 + Variable overhead £82 500) − (Standard
　hours produced × Overhead absorption rates)
= £188 500 − [32 400 × (£3.00 + £2.50)]
= £188 500 − £178 200 = £10 300 (*A*)

This shows that the total overhead variance is an adverse or unfavourable one of £10 300, and this can now be shown as fixed and variable.

*Fixed production overhead variance*
= Actual cost − (Standard hours of production × Fixed overhead
　absorption rate)
= £106 000 − (32 400 × £3.00)
= £106 000 − £97 200 = £8 800 (*A*)

*Variable production overhead variance*
= Actual cost − (Standard hours of production × Variable overhead
    absorption rate)
= £82 500 − (32 400 × £2.50)
= £82 500 − £81 000 = £1 500 (*A*)

The fixed and variable overhead variances in this example are both adverse and the overhead variance of £10 300 is equal to the fixed £8 800 plus variable £1 500.

Analysing the fixed production overhead variance more fully, we have:
  (i) *Fixed production overhead expenditure variance*
      = Budgeted cost − Actual cost
      = £108 000 − £106 000 = £2 000 (*F*)

This is an expenditure variance and indicates that £106 000 has been charged for the period, and the budget cost allowance is £108 000, resulting in a favourable variance of £2 000.

  (ii) *Fixed production overhead volume variance*
      = (Budgeted (standard) hours − Standard hours of production) × Fixed
          overhead absorption rate
      = (36 000 − 32 400) × £3.00
      = 3 600 × £3.00 = £10 800 (*A*)

This is a volume variance which shows the extent of the difference between the production achieved and planned. It will be seen that the volume variance less the expenditure variance equals the fixed production overhead variance (£10 800 − £2 000 = £8 800).

Analysing the volume variance more closely we have:
  1. *Capacity variance*
      = (Budgeted (standard) hours − Hours worked) × Fixed overhead
          absorption rate
      = (36 000 − 32 800) × £3.00
      = 3 200 × £3.00 = £9 600 (*A*)

This is a part of the volume variance and shows that there is a deficiency of 3 200 hours. The factory has not used the facilities available and operated according to the plan, which has resulted in an under-absorption of £9 600 in fixed costs.

  2. *Fixed cost productivity variance*
      = (Hours worked − Standard hours of production) × Fixed overhead
          absorption rate
      = (32 800 − 32 400) × £3.00
      = 400 × £3.00 = £1 200 (*A*)

This loss in productivity is often referred to as an efficiency variance, and in this example there has been a loss in output, equivalent to 400 standard hours of production. For the quantity of units produced there are excess hours as a result of apparent inefficiency, and this has left an under-absorption of £1 200 of fixed costs. The capacity variance plus the productivity variance is equal to the volume variance (£9 600 + £1 200 = £10 800) and shows that there has been a loss in volume with operations not proceeding according to the plan. There has been inefficiency and a reduction in the level of activity allowed for in the budget.

Analysing the variable production overhead variance more fully, we have:
  (i) *Variable overhead expenditure variance*
      = Actual cost − Budget cost
      = £82 500 − £82 000 = £500 (*A*)

 (ii) *Variable overhead productivity variance*
      = (Hours worked − Standard hours of production) × Variable overhead absorption rate
      = (32 800 − 32 400) × £2.50
      = 400 × £2.50 = £1 000 (*A*)

The variable overhead expenditure variance plus the variable overhead productivity variance equals the variable production overhead variance (£500 + £1 000 = £1 500). The sub-division of the variable production overhead variance is not recommended unless there are reasonable grounds for believing that the information resulting from the sub-variances would be helpful. The information shown here indicates that the variable expenses cost £500 more than the allowance for the output achieved and there was an adverse variance of £1 000 caused by inefficient working when there was an excess of 400 working hours.

**Summary of overhead variances**

| (− means costs were less then expected) (+ means costs were more than expected) | Favourable (−) *F* | Adverse (+) *A* |
|---|---|---|
| *Fixed production overhead* | £ | £ |
| Expenditure variance | | −2 000 |
| Volume variance: | | |
| Capacity variance | +9 600 | |
| Productivity variance | +1 200 | |
| Total volume variance | | +10 800 |
| Total fixed production overhead variance | | +8 800 |
| *Variable production overhead* | | |
| Expenditure variance | +500 | |
| Volume variance | | |
| Productivity variance | +1 000 | |
| Total variable production overhead variance | | +1 500 |
| Total production overhead variance | | +£10 300 |

**Reports**

Variance analysis should be followed by the intelligent use of reports, so that investigations can be made to find out why the performance has failed to reach the level planned. The object of standard costing is to plan operations systematically in advance, in order to improve processes, methods and procedure, and to secure low costs as well as keeping spoilage, waste and loss to a minimum. It provides a check on the efficiency of supervision and of direct and indirect labour and shows to what extent plant capacity is being utilized. The reporting system should allow for a feedback of information so as to generate corrective action and to enable revisions to be made where necessary.

## 16.13   Sales Variances

Apart from cost variances which are so important to people concerned with manufacturing operations, there are other variances, some of which are concerned with sales revenue. These are somewhat complicated because they can be dealt with in different ways. In the early stages of costing they were dealt with on the basis of turnover or the level of sales, and the changes which occurred in sales revenue from period to period or between product groups. The present trend is towards margins because management is interested in the profit level which changes when sales revenue varies or the mix of sales is different. There are two methods in use which may be slightly confusing. It is outside the scope of this book to deal with this topic at an advanced level but they are covered briefly, using some imaginary figures.

(*a*) **Sales Turnover Method**

(i) **Sales value variance** = Budgeted sales − Actual sales
   $= £50\ 000 − £54\ 000 = £4\ 000\ (F)$

This is a favourable change in sales.

(ii) **Sales price variance** = Actual sales − Standard sales
   $= £54\ 000 − £48\ 000 = £6\ 000\ (F)$

This is a comparison between actual sales value and actual sales at standard values.

(iii) **Sales volume variance** = Budgeted sales − Actual sales at standard values
   $= £50\ 000 − £48\ 000 = £2\ 000\ (A)$

This indicates a change of actual quantities compared with the budget. The sales volume variance also consists of a quantity variance and a mix variance.

(*b*) **Sales Margin Method**

It is assumed that all costs will be at standard cost when calculating the variances.

(i) **Total sales margin variances**
   $= (\text{Actual sales} − \text{Standard cost of sales}) − \text{Budgeted profit}$
   $= (£54\ 000 − £43\ 200) − £10\ 000$
   $= £10\ 800 − £10\ 000 = £800\ (F)$

(ii) **Sales margin price variances**
= Actual profit − (Actual units sold × Standard margin)
= £10 800 − (480 × £20) = £1 200 (*F*)

(iii) **Sales volume variance** = Budgeted profit − Standard profit
= £10 000 − £9 600 = £400 (*A*)

The total sales margin equals the price variance plus the volume variance. The volume variance is also equal to a quantity variance plus a mixture variance.

## 16.14　Other Variances

There are many variances in use, some of which are peculiar to particular industries. We give a few examples:

### (*a*) Calendar Variance

This variance applies to overheads and is a result of the difference between the *number of working days* in the budget period and the number of working days in the period to which the budget applies. For example, fixed overhead costs would be under-recovered if, for some special reason, a working day was suddenly declared a public holiday.

### (*b*) Revisions Variance

This variance is the difference between a current standard cost and a revised standard cost, brought about by a change in costs or prices during a budget period. There may be a change in wage rates because of a national award, a permanent increase in certain expenses, or extra fixed payments to certain employees, for example. It is frequently of an uncontrolled type and the adjustment of standard costs should be held up until the next review of standards. The costs should be segregated by charging to a Revisions Variance Account.

### (*c*) Seasonal Variance

This relates to a volume variance, and is the difference between standards based on average output and output which is budgeted to allow for seasonal fluctuations.

### (*d*) Direct Materials Mixture Variance

A mixture variance is the difference between quantity of material used in the actual mixture and that used in the standard composition. A specification which indicates the standard materials to be used in the manufacture of a product will state the proportion of the different types of materials which are to be used. If there is a shortage of one or more of the specified materials, it is possible that the proportions can be changed or different materials may be used. These may be cheaper or more expensive and this will result in a mixture variance. A similar variance applies to direct labour, when different grades of labour are used.

### (e) Yield Variance

A yield variance arises when the expected yield (the standard yield) is not achieved for some reason. The standard yield or output may allow for a loss which occurs during the process, such as evaporation or some similar cause. There is therefore a planned loss, and if the actual loss is different there is a yield variance. This may be caused by, for instance, operating at an incorrect temperature. If there is no planned loss, then the actual output should be the same as the standard output and if the actual output is different then there is a yield variance. The standard yield specified less the actual yield gives a yield variance.

## 16.15 Book-keeping and Accounting for Actual and Standard Costs

There is a considerable variation not only in the methods of costing but also in the way costs are recorded. In this book it is not intended to deal exhaustively with the ledger accounts for costing but some aspects of the accounting procedure are given in this section.

If we are to record costs which, like other business transactions, are exchanges of value, then in the interests of accuracy and the information which can be provided, it is necessary to use double-entry accounting.

### (a) Separate Ledgers—the Financial Accounting Ledger and the Cost or Factory Ledger

Accounting, as we have seen, is divided into *financial* accounting and *cost* accounting and the external and internal transactions may be dealt with in two ledgers, the financial ledger and the cost ledger. It may be advantageous to operate the accounting system in this way as the costing system usually involves a vast amount of analysis and summarizing, with a continual transfer of values.

When separate ledgers are kept, the financial accountant keeps a *memorandum* Cost Ledger Control Account to record the items of cost to be included in the cost ledger. This is the account which connects the financial books with the accounts in the cost ledger. Another account in the cost ledger is referred to as either a Cost Ledger Contra Account or a General Ledger Adjustment Account. The entries are posted on the opposite side of the account to that normally made, and this procedure turns the cost ledger with its single entries into a self-balancing ledger. For example, Wages Account, which normally appears on the debit side, is shown in the General Ledger Adjustment Account on the credit side and the double-entry is made by a debit entry into a Wages Control Account.

### (b) Control Accounts

A Control Account shows the original amount extracted from the financial books and also the transfers to subsidiary (costing) ledgers or to other Control Accounts. For example, the Wages Control Account would show the debit for the wages for a particular period and credits to Work-in-progress Account, Production Overhead Account, and so on. In a large company, with many product groups, there would be a transfer to a separate Work-in-progress Account for each of the products.

### (c) Integrated Accounts—Only One Ledger

It is obvious that if separate ledgers are kept, there must be a duplication of entries as the information in both ledgers is similar in most respects. Therefore, unless there are sound reasons for keeping a separate set of accounts in a cost ledger, integral accounts are kept and all the accounting is dealt with in the financial ledger. The accounting system is formed in such a way that the cost control statements for management can be prepared from one set of accounts. With a proper coding system, the books of original entry can be analysed, summaries prepared and the information can be posted to Control Accounts such as the following:

Stores Ledger Control Account
Wages Control Account
Production Overhead Control
    Account

Sales Ledger Control Account
Debtors and Creditors Control
    Accounts
Work-in-progress Control Account

### (d) Cost Ledger

This is the principal book of account in the cost department when the staff operate their own set of accounts. This ledger includes all the accounts and Control Accounts in respect of the costing system, and there are usually subsidiary ledgers too. The detailed information shown in the subsidiary ledgers is recorded in total in the Control Accounts in the cost ledger which is self-balancing, therefore a trial balance can be extracted at suitable periods and a Costing Profit and Loss Account can be prepared. The main difficulty concerning the cost ledger is that although most of the costs are identical with those in the financial books, some items are different and it is therefore necessary to reconcile the profit in the cost ledger with that in the financial books.

Two points of possible disagreement may occur:

(i) **Depreciation.** The Cost Accounts may use a variable rate based on production, whereas the Financial Accounts will use the annual allowance where the cost is spread over a period of time. Sometimes, in order to maintain comparability of costs, the Cost Accounts will include depreciation although it is no longer charged in the financial books.

(ii) **Valuation of stocks and work-in-progress.** Stocks and work-in-progress will be included in the Financial Accounts at cost or at net realizable value but the Cost Accounts may record them at a valuation such as LIFO or at a value which includes excessive overheads.

(e) **Reconciliation of Cost and Financial Accounts**
The difference in costing and financial profit must be accounted for by preparing a Reconciliation Statement which lists the items responsible for the discrepancy between the two sets of accounts.

(f) **Costing Profit and Loss Statement in Standard Form**
The information in the cost ledger is used to prepare a Costing Profit and Loss Account which is shown in Figs. 16.4(a) and (b) in normal and standard form respectively (p. 264).

The Profit and Loss Account shown in (a) uses the historical costs recorded in the ledger and this is followed by a statement (b) using the same basic information but which enables management to see where the variances are.

(g) **Controlling and Reducing Costs**
The object of standard costing is to set objectives which can be attained and to stimulate employees and managers to reach the performance desired. The preparation of departmental operating statements reveals the efficiency achieved, and other types of statement provide information that can be used to introduce improvements and economies.

Profit and Loss Account
(for year ending December 31, 19..)

|  | £ | £ |
|---|---|---|
| Sales |  | 435 000 |
| Less Direct material | 290 000 |  |
| Direct wages | 33 000 |  |
| Production overhead | 87 000 |  |
| Cost of sales |  | 410 000 |
| Gross profit |  | 25 000 |
| Less Administration expenses | 3 000 |  |
| Selling expenses (fixed and variable) | 21 000 |  |
|  |  | 24 000 |
| Net profit to General Ledger Adjustment Account |  | £   1 000 |

*Fig. 16.4(a) Normal form of Profit and Loss Account*

Costing Profit and Loss Statement

|  | £ | £ | £ |
|---|---|---|---|
| Sales: 30 000 units @ £5 per unit |  |  | 450 000 |
| Direct material @ £9 per unit |  | 270 000 |  |
| Direct wages @ £1 per unit |  | 30 000 |  |
| Production overhead £2.50 per unit |  | 75 000 |  |
| Standard cost of sales |  |  | 375 000 |
| Standard gross profit |  |  | 75 000 |
| Administration (fixed) |  | 4 000 |  |
| Selling (fixed) |  | 6 000 |  |
| Selling 4% (variable) |  | 18 000 |  |
| Administration and selling expenses |  |  | 28 000 |
| Standard net profit |  |  | 47 000 |
| Less Variances |  |  |  |
| Adverse |  |  |  |
| Direct material |  | 20 000 |  |
| Direct wages |  | 3 000 |  |
| Production overhead |  | 12 000 |  |
| Sales price |  | 15 000 |  |
|  |  | 50 000 |  |
| Favourable |  |  |  |
| Administration | 1 000 |  |  |
| Selling expenses | 3 000 |  |  |
|  |  | 4 000 |  |
|  |  |  | 46 000 |
| Actual net profit |  |  | £   1 000 |

*Fig. 16.4(b) Standard form of Profit and Loss Account*

## 16.16   Exercises

1. What are the main differences between *historical costing* and *standard costing*?

2. Explain the meaning of the following terms used in a standard costing system:

   (a) efficiency variance;
   (b) capacity variance;
   (c) revisions variance;
   (d) calendar variance.

# Unit Seventeen

# Budgetary Control

## 17.1 Planning and Forecasting

The success of an enterprise is dependent on the objectives, policies and practices of those who direct it. The managers have to state their policy and determine the end results they want and, in so doing, must plan the activities necessary to achieve their objectives.

The old patterns of management, where intuition was used as a guide in directing an organization, have changed and been replaced by the establishment of control points which clarify responsibilities and accountability. Management is concerned with three factors of control:

(i) **The control of money.** The management of money is carried out by using ratio analyses (see Unit 18) for current assets and current liabilities, for inventory and sales, for fixed assets and net worth and similar items and the net return on invested capital.

(ii) **The direction of operations.** The management of operations is to do with day-to-day activities concerning sales, rate of stock turnover, operating expenses, gross margins, and so on, and the net profit on sales.

(iii) **The management of people.** This relates to customers and employees.

Budgetary control is a carefully worked out financial plan based on forecasts and best possible estimates that can be made at the date when the budgets are prepared. Those concerned with forecasting and planning future action must consult and communicate with many people in order to obtain vital information which is needed in the preparation of budgets. The purpose of the plan is to ensure that the business is operated as a unified whole rather than as a group of separate departments. Co-operation is essential if the plan is to be a success, and by assigning responsibilities to people in charge of a particular function of the business, a budget regulates spending.

There is a distinction between a forecast and a plan: the forecast is a prediction of what is likely to happen under certain conditions and is concerned with probabilities, whereas a plan is an objective which takes account of policy. The budget provides a means of control.

A budget has been defined as *a financial and/or quantitative statement, prepared prior to a defined period of time, of the policy to be pursued during that period for the purpose of attaining a given objective.*

*Budgetary control* is a technique for the establishment of budgets relating the responsibilities of executives to the requirements of a policy, and the continuous comparison of actual with budgeted results either to secure by individual action the objective of that policy or to provide a basis for its revision. These definitions are given in the Institute of Cost and Management Accountants' *Terminology of Cost Accountancy.*

## 17.2    Budget Committee

The volume of work and the problems associated with the preparation of budgets invariably requires the constitution of a *budget committee*. The chairman is usually the chief executive and the secretary, who carries out the routine work, is normally the *budget officer*. Much preliminary work has to be done and this is started at an early stage in order to prepare the final figures well before the new period begins. The budget committee consists of the senior executives of the business, whose function is to consider past performance by an analysis of income and expenditure, and to take account of present trends, and likely changes in the future. They will make their plans in accordance with the policy of the Board of Directors, and as interpreted by the managing director or general manager.

The budget officer confers with each person who is responsible for sectional budgets, and provisional figures will be agreed but notice has to be taken of the *principal budget factor* which is the factor which restricts the operations and progress of the business. It may be sales or a shortage of cash, materials, labour or other factors, and decisions will have to be made by the committee before the sectional budgets can be finalized, as this factor controls all the other budgets. The principal factor is the main restriction on operations but there may be other *limiting factors* similar to those mentioned above which also have to be taken into account.

## 17.3    The Budget Period

This is determined by the nature of the business and the type of budgets which are to be prepared. The natural period of time is one year but industries connected with fashion or seasonal trades may need a shorter period. Others may need a longer period, and capital expenditure budgets may be set for three to five years. However, frequent revision is usually essential, because of changes in prices and policies.

For purposes of control, budgets are broken down into shorter periods such as the cash budget, which is normally set on a monthly basis, and the budget for a supervisor which is probably on a weekly basis.

## 17.4    Functional Budgets

Budgetary control is a technique which is used in the management and direction of operations and is applied by the use of functional budgets for each activity in the business. Budgets differ slightly between one industry or organization and another, but the objective is the same. In order that control can be exercised when the period of operations begins, budgets are prepared which can be compared with the *operating statements* for each manufacturing or trading period. This comparison will disclose variances which, after examination and investigation, will generally reveal the cause of the difference between the actual cost and the allowance set. Before operations start, the budgets are summarized and the details provide information which is used to prepare the *master budget*. This budget is a forecasted Profit and Loss Account and all these budgets are completed by preparing a forecasted balance sheet.

Functional budgets include the following:

sales budget;
production budget;
manufacturing budget (direct materials, direct wages, factory overhead);
administration, selling and distribution cost budgets;
purchases budget;
cash budget;
plant utilization budget;
capital expenditure budget.

## 17.5   The Sales Budget

The preparation of this budget begins with a *sales forecast*, which is a difficult task because of fluctuations in sales which take place over the year. It is on this budget that many of the other budgets are based. The work of forecasting usually starts with an examination of the sales analysis for the current year as far as it is available. In the work of developing the forecast, the following details may be required:

(i)  unit sales by product lines;
(ii)  sales expected in each area or country;
(iii)  sales for each month;
(iv)  sales to customers or through agents at non-standard prices.

Policy conditions, such as a decision to increase production facilities by shift-working or to expand plant capacity, are taken into account. There may be changes in prices, and a forecast will have to be made of business conditions in general, including changes in population or in the income available to consumers. The initial forecast will be in quantities or units which will later be evaluated by using standard or budget prices or, where applicable, non-standard prices.

## 17.6   The Production Budget

The production budget is based on the sales budget and this relationship requires a co-ordination of sales and production policy so that sales targets can be aligned with the production capacity of the factory, after allowing for the available stocks and for supplies that can be obtained outside the factory. A production programme has to be drawn up which will indicate in terms of output the hours of work required to meet the requirements of the sales department. The budget is a statement of the units of product to be made and the hours of work expected from each department and cost centre. The objects are to manufacture the products so that they are available on the dates specified by the customer or the sales department and, at the same time, to maintain a reasonably low level of stocks in order to avoid excessive obsolescence.

## 17.7    The Manufacturing or Production Cost Budget

This budget sets out the allowed expenditure for the output indicated in the production budget. As this is a cost of production budget it is closely linked with the cash budget and the master budget. There are subsidiary budgets for direct materials, direct wages and overhead expenses, and the production budget referred to above could, if desired, be included under the heading of this section.

### (a) Direct Material Cost
Standard costing greatly facilitates the preparation of a materials budget, but when standard cost records are not available the details have to be obtained from previous costs or estimates which have to be adjusted so that they are relevant to the period when manufacture takes place.

### (b) Direct Labour Cost
A similar procedure applies to estimating the cost of wages. The hours shown in the production budget are used with the wage rates which are likely to apply during the period of production.

### (c) Overhead Expenses
This budget has to be assembled from a large amount of detailed information from past records, and updated to allow for changes in future costs and budgeted activity. It is compiled on the basis of departmental overhead expense budgets and cost centre budgets. These are laid out to conform with the expense classification records so that the budgeted costs are available for use in the manufacturing period when actual costs are compared with budgeted figures. Budgetary control is not only concerned with costs but should also, as a means of control, be concerned with quantities. As far as possible, the costs should be set alongside units of material and hours of labour. Controllable and uncontrollable costs are also important factors and costs can be analysed as fixed, variable and semi-variable. This is necessary when budgeted costs are fixed on the basis of allowances set out in a *flexible budget*, which is one where costs are separated into fixed, semi-fixed and variable, and where the budgeted costs are set for various levels of activity. In this way, the spending allowance for each item of overhead is adjusted to the volume of production and the allowance changes in relation to the level of activity attained. A flexible budget is shown in Table 17.1.

## 17.8    The Selling and Distribution Cost Budget

This deals with the costs of selling and distributing the goods or services of the

**Table 17.1 Flexible budget—works maintenance department**

| Activity | 0% | | | 95% | 100% | 105% | 110% |
|---|---|---|---|---|---|---|---|
| Expense | Fixed cost | Variable cost per hour | | 23 750 | Hours 25 000 | 26 250 | 27 500 |
| | £ | £ | | £ | £ | £ | £ |
| Materials | — | 1.00 | | 23 750 | 25 000 | 26 250 | 27 500 |
| Labour | 3 000 | 1.50 | | 38 625 | 40 500 | 42 375 | 44 250 |
| Salaries | 6 000 | — | | 6 000 | 6 000 | 6 000 | 6 000 |
| Tools and equipment | 800 | 0.50 | | 12 675 | 13 300 | 13 925 | 14 550 |
| Fuel | — | 0.30 | | 7 125 | 7 500 | 7 875 | 8 250 |
| Depreciation | 1 000 | — | | 1 000 | 1 000 | 1 000 | 1 000 |
| | £10 800 | | | £89 175 | £93 300 | £97 425 | £101 550 |
| Rate per hour | | | | £3.755 | £3.732 | £3.711 | £3.693 |

*Notes:*

(i) The budget is in steps of 5 per cent with a range between 95% and 110%. Certain items of expense are fixed, while others include a fixed charge and a variable charge. Where the cost includes both types of expense, the difference in cost between each column is a result of the change in activity or volume of output. For example, the change in hours for 5% activity is 1 250 hours, and in the case of labour, 1 250 hours at £1.50 is £1 875 which is the difference between each column and the next. At 100% activity the cost is £3 000 fixed cost plus 25 000 hours at £1.50 per hour, which gives £40 500. At 95% activity, the cost includes £3 000 fixed costs plus 23 750 hours at £1.50 per hour, which totals £38 625.

(ii) Normal capacity is represented by 100% and 25 000 hours. At this level the overhead rate per direct labour hour is £3.732 which includes:

$$\frac{\text{Fixed costs}}{\text{Hours worked}} = \frac{£10\ 800}{25\ 000} = £0.432$$

$$\frac{\text{Variable costs}}{\text{Hours worked}} = \frac{£93\ 300 - £10\ 800}{25\ 000} = £3.300$$

$$£3.732$$

business. It covers expenditure incurred in promoting sales, retaining custom, packing for transport, storage of finished goods, advertising and publicity and similar costs.

## 17.9 The Purchasing Budget

This budget includes all materials used in the business such as direct and indirect materials required for production, selling and administration, capital expenditure, and those used in research and development. Allowance is made for outstanding orders and closing stocks, and for any changes in the levels of stocks of raw materials, finished goods or bought out items.

The budget provides information to enable the purchasing department to arrange for goods to be supplied when prices are at the most economic level, or to take advantage of special prices. As this budget involves a large outwards flow of cash, it is related to the cash budget, and the plans made will give indications of the cash requirements, and, in some cases, may have to be adjusted to the availability of cash as shown in the cash budget.

## 17.10 The Cash Budget

A cash budget is a summary of the expected cash receipts and payments during the period of the budget. This budget is usually drawn up on a monthly basis and begins with the balance at the beginning of the year. After taking account of receipts and disbursements during the month, it shows the balance which is then carried forward.

*Cash receipts* include:
Payments by debtors, cash sales, dividends received, sales of assets (capital), loans received, and issues of shares and debentures.
*Payments* include:
Wages and salaries, payments to creditors, rent and rates, taxes, capital expenditure, dividends payable, commission payable and repayments of debentures.

The cash budget is an important one as it indicates whether cash is available to meet demands and whether additional finance will be required. It also shows any surplus cash which could be invested outside the business.

Note that the cash budget is drawn up on a receipts and payments basis, whereas the other budgets are concerned with income and expenditure and are related to activity. An example of a cash budget is given below.

**Example 17.1**
A company prepares budgets on a monthly basis for the quarter ending March 31, 19.1. In order to produce the necessary budgets, the following forecasts have been made for the five months from November 19.0 to March 19.1.

|  | Purchases | Sales | Overheads | Depreciation | Wages |
|---|---|---|---|---|---|
|  | £ | £ | £ | £ | £ |
| November | 77 000 | 157 500 | 14 000 | 1 050 | 42 000 |
| December | 50 400 | 87 500 | 11 200 | 1 050 | 28 700 |
| January | 42 000 | 100 100 | 10 500 | 1 050 | 29 400 |
| February | 52 500 | 105 000 | 11 500 | 1 050 | 37 800 |
| March | 58 100 | 126 000 | 12 600 | 1 050 | 38 500 |

Further information may be applicable to a cash budget:

(a) All purchases are on credit; suppliers will be paid two months after the date of the transaction.

(b) 20 per cent of sales are on credit. Debts are paid in the month after the transaction takes place. The balance of the forecast is in respect of cash sales.

(c) Overheads include charges for the following:

(i) Electricity—November £800; December £810; January £630; February £735; March £840. Quarterly accounts are received for this expense.

(ii) The electricity bill for the quarter ending December 31, 19.0 which is estimated to amount to £2 150, will be paid in January 19.1.

(iii) The rent is £8 400 per annum and is paid quarterly in advance on January 1, April 1, July 1 and October 1.

(iv) Annual rates are paid in advance on April 1 and October 1. The rates for 19.0/19.1 amount to £12 600; £6 300 has been paid in April and £6 300 in October.

(v) All other overheads are paid in cash as they occur.

(d) Wages are paid in cash as they become due for payment.

(e) Capital expenditure is in respect of office equipment to be received by the company in February 19.1. The cost is £7 000 and the account will be settled in March 19.1.

(f) The bank balance at January 1, 19.1 is expected to be £10 500. The cash budget is prepared and presented as shown in Fig. 17.1.

Cash budget for quarter ending March 31, 19.1

|  | January £ | February £ | March £ |
|---|---|---|---|
| Balance brought forward | 10 500 | (10 690) | (3 885) |
| *Receipts* | | | |
| Sales | 97 580 | 104 020 | 121 800 |
|  | £108 080 | £ 93 330 | £117 915 |
| *Payments* | | | |
| Purchases | 77 000 | 50 400 | 42 000 |
| Electricity | 2 150 | — | — |
| Rent | 2 100 | — | — |
| Rates | — | — | — |
| Other overheads | 8 120 | 9 015 | 10 010 |
| Wages | 29 400 | 37 800 | 38 500 |
| Capital expenditure | — | — | 7 000 |
|  | £118 770 | £ 97 215 | £ 97 510 |
| Balance carried forward: | (10 690) | (3 885) | £20 405 |

*Workings*

|  | Sales January | Sales February | Sales March | Purchases |
|---|---|---|---|---|
|  | £ | £ | £ |  |
|  | 100 100 | 105 000 | 126 000 | November £77 000 |
| *Less* 20% credit sales | 20 020 | 21 000 | 25 200 | (paid January) |
| Cash sales | 80 080 | 84 000 | 100 800 | December £50 400 |
| *Add* Credit sales from |  |  |  | (paid February) |
| previous month | 17 500 | 20 020 | 21 000 | January £42 000 |
|  | £ 97 580 | £104 020 | £121 800 | (paid March) |

Overheads

|  | £ | £ | £ |
|---|---|---|---|
| January | 10 500 February | 11 500 March | 12 600 |
| *Less* Electricity | 630 | 735 | 840 |
| Rent | 700 | 700 | 700 |
| Rates | 1 050 | 1 050 | 1 050 |
|  | 2 380 | 2 485 | 2 590 |
|  | £8 120 | £9 015 | £10 010 |

*Fig. 17.1 Example of a cash budget*

*Notes:*
(i) For the purpose of preparing budgets, the forecasts include *depreciation* which is a non-cash item and must not be included in a cash budget.
(ii) Overhead expenditure includes costs which are incurred on a credit basis and these must be deducted. The items must be included in the cash budget only when they are actually paid.

## 17.11   The Plant Utilization Budget

This budget is concerned with the facilities available to carry out the production programme. It shows the machine load of individual machines or groups of machines in different departments or cost centres.

This budget discloses which machines or departments are overloaded and steps can then be taken to:

> work overtime or increase the overtime hours;
> begin shiftworking or increase the number of shifts;
> place work with sub-contractors;
> transfer work to other departments;
> place work with other factories within the group;
> extend the plant.

If it is not possible to arrange for the desired volume of production, an amendment would have to be made to the sales and associated budgets. This could lead to spare capacity in other sections and efforts would then be needed to find ways of filling the gap.

## 17.12   The Capital Expenditure Budget

This refers to the purchase or manufacture of fixed assets for replacements, extensions as a result of expansion or overloading, and new techniques requiring modern machinery or equipment. The items included in this budget apply to the production, administration and selling functions of the business.

It is a long-term budget, usually set for three to five years and requires frequent revision because of changes in costs of land, buildings, machinery and equipment. With a long-term budget, there is often a change of outlook: new proposals are made, or a revision may be needed because of economic conditions.

This budget gives an indication of the cash requirements, and if financial resources are not available within the company, arrangements have to be made to borrow the cash so that the project can be carried out. It is always important to consider the effect of capital expenditure on the other budgets, in connection with the reduction or increase in costs or selling prices.

## 17.13   Other Budgets

There are many different types of budget which may be used in planning operations.

### (a) Research and Development Budget

This expenditure is concerned with the improvement of existing products, and the development of new ones or of new methods of production. It may involve the design of special machines or equipment, the testing of raw materials or pure research. Research and development expenditure may represent an essential part of a company's costs but it is an element which has to be carefully controlled. The usual procedure is for directors to sanction or appropriate an amount that they consider reasonable, which is either based on costs of a previous period or on the basis of requests made by the head of research. He will submit a programme of work to be carried out in the budget period, supported by estimated costs.

### (b) Personnel Budget

This budget provides details of the labour force required to carry out the work planned in the various budgets, and shows the direct and indirect workers in number, grades and wages. It is a manpower planning exercise which defines the labour force for the budget period and tends to stabilize the ratio of direct to indirect workers.

### (c) Administrative Expense Budget

Salaries are the most important item in this budget and most of the expenses can be estimated on the basis of previous costs with an adjustment for salary awards and likely increases in the budget period.

### (d) Forecast, Control and Appropriation Budgets

These terms apply to the way in which budgeted expense allowances are determined. The forecast budget provides a basis for planning and is sometimes called a *fixed budget* as opposed to a *flexible budget*, because the amounts are not adjusted for volume. The control budget is a flexible budget which determines the amount on a volume basis. The appropriation budget establishes a limit on spending, such as for advertising or research.

## 17.14 General Procedure

Budgetary control is a system which places responsibility where it belongs, and accounts for the term responsibility budgets. Co-operation among all those concerned with the operation of budgetary control is essential and details of the system should be explained to each of those involved.

Control is exercised by assigning responsibility and measuring results and then reporting the deviations from budget to those in charge of operations and expenditure. The budget officer analyses the variances and decides on the significance of the results. He should concentrate on those matters requiring attention in order to ascertain which variances are the result of internal operations and the actions of employees, and which variances are caused externally, and are probably uncontrollable. When preparing the reports, the budgeted figures and the actual costs should be set side by side and only the relevant facts should be reported, but adequate explanations should be given. Variations may be as a result of price changes (*price variances*) or gains or losses caused by volume (*volume variances*) or changed conditions (*revisions variances*). Other variations may be due to the use of methods different from those planned (*methods variances*) or to many other causes. *Controllable variances* are those for which a particular individual is responsible and which indicate success or failure in controlling the expenditure. This applies to items such as the usage of material and the employment and supervision of labour which results in different degrees of efficiency.

After allowing for comments from those receiving the reports, decisions should be made to take corrective action where this is possible and advisable, to make further investigations, to change the methods or to revise the budget.

## 17.15 An Exercise in Setting Budgets

This exercise and the budgets which follow have, of necessity, been simplified and abbreviated. The budgets are quarterly rather than monthly. A draft balance sheet has been prepared for the current year as certain details are required in the preparation of budgets and this balance sheet will be needed when the master budget is prepared (see Fig. 17.2, pp. 276–7).

## Balance sheet as at December 31, 19.0

| Assets employed | Cost £ | Less Depreciation £ | Value £ |
|---|---|---|---|
| *Fixed assets* | | | |
| Land and buildings | 392 500 | 3 000 | 389 500 |
| Machinery and plant | 100 000 | 17 800 | 82 200 |
| Motor vehicles | 25 000 | 11 000 | 14 000 |
| Office furniture | 5 000 | 2 000 | 3 000 |
| | £522 500 | £33 800 | 488 700 |

| | | |
|---|---|---|
| Quoted investments (market value £47 500) | | 47 475 |
| *Current assets* | | |
| Stock: General stores | 238 562 | |
| Finished goods (machines) | 27 400 | |
| | | 265 962 |
| Debtors | | 80 500 |
| Cash at bank and in hand | | 78 628 |
| | | 425 090 |
| *Less* Current liabilities | | |
| Creditors | 101 000 | |
| Wages due | 4 500 | |
| Preference dividend proposed | 17 500 | |
| Proposed ordinary dividend | 25 000 | |
| Corporation tax | 88 925 | |
| | | 236 925 |
| *Net current assets* | | 188 165 |
| | | £724 340 |

*(continued opposite, in vertical style)*

**Financed by**

|  |  | £ | £ |
|---|---|---|---|
| *Long-term liability* |  |  |  |
| 6% Debentures |  |  | 100 000 |

*Preference shareholders' interest in the company*       *Authorized*

250 000 7% Preference shares of £1 each fully paid      250 000     250 000

*Ordinary shareholders' interest in the company*        *Authorized*
£

250 000 Ordinary shares of £1 each,
fully paid       250 000     250 000

*Reserves*
Revenue reserves:

| | |
|---|---|
| Staff pension fund | 49 500 |
| General reserve | 73 000 |

| | | |
|---|---|---|
| Profit and Loss Account | 3 750 | |
| *Less* Preliminary expenses | 1 910 | |
| | | 1 840 |
| | | 124 340 |

Ordinary shareholders' equity      374 340

£724 340

*Note:* Stock of finished machines consists of

| | | |
|---|---|---|
| Product X 2 @ £2 600 = | £5 200 |
| Product Y 4 @ £2 400 = | £9 600 |
| Product Z 6 @ £2 100 = | £12 600 |
| | £27 400 |

*Fig. 17.2 Draft balance sheet*

**Preparing the Sales Forecast and Sales Budget**
The sales manager received reports from his area representatives of expected sales of machines in their regions, and from this he compiled Tables 17.2 and 17.3.

**Table 17.2    Estimated quarterly sales for year ending December 31, 19.1**

| Machine type | X | Y | Z | Totals |
|---|---|---|---|---|
| Quarter ending | | | | |
| March 31 | 35 | 56 | 42 | 133 |
| June 30 | 28 | 50 | 29 | 107 |
| September 30 | 19 | 39 | 24 | 82 |
| December 31 | 30 | 50 | 34 | 114 |
| Totals | 112 | 195 | 129 | 436 |
| Selling price | £3 600 | £3 200 | £2 880 | — |
| Total sales | £403 200 | £624 000 | £371 520 | £1 398 720 |

**Table 17.3    Estimated area sales for year ending December 31, 19.1**

| Machine type | X | | Y | | Z | | | Totals |
|---|---|---|---|---|---|---|---|---|
| Selling price | £3 600 | | £3 200 | | £2 880 | | | |
| | Units sold | £ | Units sold | £ | Units sold | £ | | £ |
| Area A | 35 | 126 000 | 125 | 400 000 | 70 | 201 600 | 230 | 727 600 |
| Area B | 17 | 61 200 | 27 | 86 400 | 20 | 57 600 | 64 | 205 200 |
| Area C | 27 | 97 200 | 18 | 57 600 | 15 | 43 200 | 60 | 198 000 |
| Area D | 33 | 118 800 | 25 | 80 000 | 24 | 69 120 | 82 | 267 920 |
| Totals | 112 | £403 200 | 195 | £624 000 | 129 | £371 520 | 436 | £1 398 720 |

From the detailed information received from the areas he prepared a sales forecast which was agreed with the chief executive and eventually this forecast was the basis of the sales budget. The forecast and budget are shown in Tables 17.4 and 17.5.

**Table 17.4   Sales forecast of machines for period ending December 31, 19.1**

|  | Current year 19.0 | Mar. 31 | June 30 | Sept. 30 | Dec. 31 | 19.1 Totals |
|---|---|---|---|---|---|---|
| Area A |  |  |  |  |  |  |
| Product X | 30 | 10 | 9 | 7 | 9 | 35 |
| Product Y | 120 | 35 | 32 | 28 | 30 | 125 |
| Product Z | 60 | 20 | 18 | 15 | 17 | 70 |
|  | 210 | 65 | 59 | 50 | 56 | 230 |
| Area B |  |  |  |  |  |  |
| Product X | 15 | 5 | 4 | 3 | 5 | 17 |
| Product Y | 30 | 8 | 7 | 5 | 7 | 27 |
| Product Z | 15 | 6 | 5 | 4 | 5 | 20 |
|  | 60 | 19 | 16 | 12 | 17 | 64 |
| Area C |  |  |  |  |  |  |
| Product X | 25 | 8 | 7 | 5 | 7 | 27 |
| Product Y | 16 | 5 | 5 | 4 | 4 | 18 |
| Product Z | 12 | 6 | 3 | 2 | 4 | 15 |
|  | 53 | 19 | 15 | 11 | 15 | 60 |
| Area D |  |  |  |  |  |  |
| Product X | 35 | 12 | 8 | 4 | 9 | 33 |
| Product Y | 28 | 8 | 6 | 2 | 9 | 25 |
| Product Z | 20 | 10 | 3 | 3 | 8 | 24 |
|  | 83 | 30 | 17 | 9 | 26 | 82 |
| *Totals* | 406 | 133 | 107 | 82 | 114 | 436 |

The column header row reads: Current year 19.0 | Quarter ending Mar. 31 June 30 Sept. 30 | 19.1 Totals Dec. 31

**Table 17.5   Sales budget for period ending December 31, 19.1**

| | Current year 19.0 | Standard price | Quarter ending Mar. 31 | June 30 | Sept. 30 | 19.1 Dec. 31 | Totals |
|---|---|---|---|---|---|---|---|
| | £ | £ | £ | £ | £ | £ | £ |
| **Area A** | | | | | | | |
| Product X | 120 000 | 3 600 | 36 000 | 32 400 | 25 200 | 32 400 | 126 000 |
| Product Y | 364 000 | 3 200 | 112 000 | 102 400 | 89 600 | 96 000 | 400 000 |
| Product Z | 182 800 | 2 880 | 57 600 | 51 840 | 43 200 | 48 960 | 201 600 |
| | 666 800 | — | 205 600 | 186 640 | 158 000 | 177 360 | 727 600 |
| **Area B** | | | | | | | |
| Product X | 58 000 | 3 600 | 18 000 | 14 400 | 10 800 | 18 000 | 61 200 |
| Product Y | 82 000 | 3 200 | 25 600 | 22 400 | 16 000 | 22 400 | 86 400 |
| Product Z | 53 000 | 2 880 | 17 280 | 14 400 | 11 520 | 14 400 | 57 600 |
| | 193 000 | — | 60 880 | 51 200 | 38 320 | 54 800 | 205 200 |
| **Area C** | | | | | | | |
| Product X | 92 000 | 3 600 | 28 800 | 25 200 | 18 000 | 25 200 | 97 200 |
| Product Y | 62 000 | 3 200 | 16 000 | 16 000 | 12 800 | 12 800 | 57 600 |
| Product Z | 41 000 | 2 880 | 17 280 | 8 640 | 5 760 | 11 520 | 43 200 |
| | 195 000 | — | 62 080 | 49 840 | 36 560 | 49 520 | 198 000 |
| **Area D** | | | | | | | |
| Product X | 115 000 | 3 600 | 43 200 | 28 800 | 14 400 | 32 400 | 118 800 |
| Product Y | 70 000 | 3 200 | 25 600 | 19 200 | 6 400 | 28 800 | 80 000 |
| Product Z | 62 000 | 2 880 | 28 800 | 8 640 | 8 640 | 23 040 | 69 120 |
| | 247 000 | — | 97 600 | 56 640 | 29 440 | 84 240 | 267 920 |
| *Totals* | £1 301 800 | — | £426 160 | £344 320 | £262 320 | £365 920 | £1 398 720 |

Using the sales forecast as a basis the budget committee considered the production forecast for the year, and it was decided to use the production facilities to manufacture a slightly larger quantity of machines than those shown in the sales budget. It was suggested that the surplus machines should be treated as stock at the year-end and shown as such in the master budget, but the sales department was to try to sell these machines as they became available. A statement of the stocks and planned production is as follows:

| Product | X | Y | Z |
|---|---|---|---|
| Budgeted sales | 112 | 195 | 129 |
| *Less* Estimated opening stock | 2 | 4 | 6 |
| Production required to meet the sales forecast | 110 | 191 | 123 |
| *Add* Closing stock | 7 | 11 | 16 |
| Planned production | 117 | 202 | 139 |

The works manager and production controller estimated the quarterly production as shown in Table 17.6.

**Table 17.6   Estimated quarterly production**

| Product | X | Y | Z | *Totals* |
|---|---|---|---|---|
| Quarter ending | | | | |
| March 31 | 37 | 59 | 45 | 141 |
| June 30 | 29 | 51 | 31 | 111 |
| September 30 | 20 | 40 | 26 | 86 |
| December 31 | 31 | 52 | 37 | 120 |
| Planned production | 117 | 202 | 139 | 458 |

Information is now available which indicates what is to be produced and the quantities, in terms of machines, to be produced in each quarter.

This information will enable the production budget to be produced in two ways:

(a) *Production volume* in terms of hours to be worked in each department;

(b) *Production cost* by using subsidiary budgets for the elements of cost.

The production records (Table 17.7) showed the direct labour hours required to manufacture the machines.

**Table 17.7   Direct labour hours per machine**

| Product | X | Y | Z |
|---|---|---|---|
| Department | | | |
| 1 | 226 | 180 | 170 |
| 2 | 216 | 200 | 176 |
| 3 | 130 | 120 | 103 |
| *Totals* | 572 | 500 | 449 |

On the basis of these hours of direct labour, the production budget (volume) for the year was prepared for each quarter, showing the number of machines to be produced and the hours of work for each type of machine in each of the departments (see Table 17.8).

**Table 17.8　Production budget for period ending December 31, 19.1**

| | Direct labour hours Quarter ending | | | | | | | | | |
| | Mar. 31 | | June 30 | | Sept. 30 | | Dec. 31 | | Totals | |
| | Units | Hours | Units | Hours | Units | Hours | Units | Hours | Units | Hours |
|---|---|---|---|---|---|---|---|---|---|---|
| **Department 1** | | | | | | | | | | |
| Product X | 37 | 8 362 | 29 | 6 554 | 20 | 4 520 | 31 | 7 006 | 117 | 26 442 |
| Product Y | 59 | 10 620 | 51 | 9 180 | 40 | 7 200 | 52 | 9 360 | 202 | 36 360 |
| Product Z | 45 | 7 650 | 31 | 5 270 | 26 | 4 420 | 37 | 6 290 | 139 | 23 630 |
| | 141 | 26 632 | 111 | 21 004 | 86 | 16 140 | 120 | 22 656 | 458 | 86 432 |
| **Department 2** | | | | | | | | | | |
| Product X | 37 | 7 992 | 29 | 6 264 | 20 | 4 320 | 31 | 6 696 | 117 | 25 272 |
| Product Y | 59 | 11 800 | 51 | 10 200 | 40 | 8 000 | 52 | 10 400 | 202 | 40 400 |
| Product Z | 45 | 7 920 | 31 | 5 456 | 26 | 4 576 | 37 | 6 512 | 139 | 24 464 |
| | 141 | 27 712 | 111 | 21 920 | 86 | 16 896 | 120 | 23 608 | 458 | 90 136 |
| **Department 3** | | | | | | | | | | |
| Product X | 37 | 4 810 | 29 | 3 770 | 20 | 2 600 | 31 | 4 030 | 117 | 15 210 |
| Product Y | 59 | 7 080 | 51 | 6 120 | 40 | 4 800 | 52 | 6 240 | 202 | 24 240 |
| Product Z | 45 | 4 635 | 31 | 3 193 | 26 | 2 678 | 37 | 3 811 | 139 | 14 317 |
| | 141 | 16 525 | 111 | 13 083 | 86 | 10 078 | 120 | 14 081 | 458 | 53 767 |
| *Totals* | 141 | 70 869 | 111 | 56 007 | 86 | 43 114 | 120 | 60 345 | 458 | 230 335 |

The purchasing officer made a general statement to the committee on the expected movement in prices during the budget period and he was requested to prepare and present to the budget officer a schedule of material prices for direct and indirect materials so that the budget for direct materials and the budget for factory overhead could be drawn up (Tables 17.9 and 17.10).

**Table 17.9    Production cost budget for period ending December 31, 19.1**

| Materials | Cost per machine | Mar. 31 | *Direct materials* Quarter ending June 30 | Sept. 30 | Dec. 31 | *Totals* |
|---|---|---|---|---|---|---|
| **Group A** | | | | | | |
| | £ | £ | £ | £ | £ | £ |
| Product X | 410 | 15 170 | 11 890 | 8 200 | 12 710 | 47 970 |
| Product Y | 380 | 22 420 | 19 380 | 15 200 | 19 760 | 76 760 |
| Product Z | 350 | 15 750 | 10 850 | 9 100 | 12 950 | 48 650 |
| | 1 140 | 53 340 | 42 120 | 32 500 | 45 420 | 173 380 |
| **Group B** | | | | | | |
| | £ | £ | £ | £ | £ | £ |
| Product X | 520 | 19 240 | 15 080 | 10 400 | 16 120 | 60 840 |
| Product Y | 460 | 27 140 | 23 460 | 18 400 | 23 920 | 92 920 |
| Product Z | 434 | 19 530 | 13 454 | 11 284 | 16 058 | 60 326 |
| | 1 414 | 65 910 | 51 994 | 40 084 | 56 098 | 214 086 |
| **Group C** | | | | | | |
| | £ | £ | £ | £ | £ | £ |
| Product X | 278 | 10 286 | 8 062 | 5 560 | 8 618 | 32 526 |
| Product Y | 219 | 12 921 | 11 169 | 8 760 | 11 388 | 44 238 |
| Product Z | 161 | 7 245 | 4 991 | 4 186 | 5 957 | 22 379 |
| | 658 | 30 452 | 24 222 | 18 506 | 25 963 | 99 143 |
| *Totals* | | £149 702 | £118 336 | £91 090 | £127 481 | £486 609 |

The personnel manager stated that the rates of wages payable during the period of the budget was estimated to be:

> Department 1    £1.00 per hour
> Department 2    £1.50 per hour
> Department 3    £2.00 per hour

The direct wages budget was drawn up by the budget officer by using the information shown in the production budget for the direct labour hours and the rates of wages already given. On the basis of the production forecast the committee considered the effect of this output and other matters on the cost of factory overheads. The works manager was asked to consult with departmental

**Table 17.10  Production cost budget for period ending December 31, 19.1**

| | Rate per hour | Direct wages Quarter ending | | | | | | | | | |
| | | March 31 | | June 30 | | September 30 | | December 31 | | Totals | |
| | £ | Hours | £ | Hours | £ | Hours | £ | Hours | £ | Hours | £ |
| **Department 1** | | | | | | | | | | | |
| Product X | 1.00 | 8 362 | 8 362 | 6 554 | 6 554 | 4 520 | 4 520 | 7 006 | 7 006 | 26 442 | 26 442 |
| Product Y | 1.00 | 10 620 | 10 620 | 9 180 | 9 180 | 7 200 | 7 200 | 9 360 | 9 360 | 36 360 | 36 360 |
| Product Z | 1.00 | 7 650 | 7 650 | 5 270 | 5 270 | 4 420 | 4 420 | 6 290 | 6 290 | 23 630 | 23 630 |
| | | 26 632 | 26 632 | 21 004 | 21 004 | 16 140 | 16 140 | 22 656 | 22 656 | 86 432 | 86 432 |
| **Department 2** | £ | | £ | | £ | | £ | | £ | | £ |
| Product X | 1.50 | 7 992 | 11 988 | 6 264 | 9 396 | 4 320 | 6 480 | 6 696 | 10 044 | 25 272 | 37 908 |
| Product Y | 1.50 | 11 800 | 17 700 | 10 200 | 15 300 | 8 000 | 12 000 | 10 400 | 15 600 | 40 400 | 60 600 |
| Product Z | 1.50 | 7 920 | 11 880 | 5 456 | 8 184 | 4 576 | 6 864 | 6 512 | 9 768 | 24 464 | 36 696 |
| | | 27 712 | 41 568 | 21 920 | 32 880 | 16 896 | 25 344 | 23 608 | 35 412 | 90 136 | 135 204 |
| **Department 3** | £ | | £ | | £ | | £ | | £ | | £ |
| Product X | 2.00 | 4 810 | 9 620 | 3 770 | 7 540 | 2 600 | 5 200 | 4 030 | 8 060 | 15 210 | 30 420 |
| Product Y | 2.00 | 7 080 | 14 160 | 6 120 | 12 240 | 4 800 | 9 600 | 6 240 | 12 480 | 24 240 | 48 480 |
| Product Z | 2.00 | 4 635 | 9 270 | 3 193 | 6 386 | 2 678 | 5 356 | 3 811 | 7 622 | 14 317 | 28 634 |
| | | 16 525 | 33 050 | 13 083 | 26 166 | 10 078 | 20 156 | 14 081 | 28 162 | 53 767 | 107 534 |
| *Totals* | | 70 869 | £101 250 | 56 007 | £80 050 | 43 114 | £61 640 | 60 345 | £86 230 | 230 335 | £329 170 |

heads in order to establish the extent of work to be carried out in respect of maintenance and services during the budget period.

This information was submitted to the budget officer to enable him to prepare a draft budget for presentation to the committee. After revision this appears as shown in Table 17.11.

**Table 17.11 Factory overhead budget for period ending December 31, 19.1**

| | Quarter ending Mar. 31 | June 30 | Sept. 30 | Dec. 31 | *Totals* |
|---|---|---|---|---|---|
| | £ | £ | £ | £ | £ |
| | Department 1 | | | | |
| Indirect material | 2 805 | 2 000 | 1 300 | 2 201 | 8 306 |
| Fuel and lighting | 2 214 | 1 100 | 1 000 | 1 500 | 5 814 |
| Repairs to machines | 1 510 | 1 400 | 1 370 | 1 425 | 5 705 |
| Indirect wages | 11 962 | 10 008 | 7 525 | 10 461 | 39 956 |
| Factory expenses | 7 029 | 5 998 | 4 786 | 6 032 | 23 845 |
| *Depreciation* | | | | | |
| Land and buildings | 250 | 250 | 250 | 250 | 1 000 |
| Machinery and plant | 451 | 451 | 452 | 452 | 1 806 |
| | 26 221 | 21 207 | 16 683 | 22 321 | 86 432 |
| | Department 2 | | | | |
| Indirect material | 3 073 | 2 300 | 1 900 | 2 350 | 9 623 |
| Fuel and lighting | 2 308 | 1 280 | 1 195 | 2 000 | 6 783 |
| Repairs to machines | 1 985 | 1 628 | 1 303 | 1 740 | 6 656 |
| Indirect wages | 14 784 | 11 055 | 8 104 | 13 021 | 46 964 |
| Factory expenses | 8 862 | 6 868 | 5 208 | 7 113 | 28 051 |
| *Depreciation* | | | | | |
| Land and buildings | 300 | 300 | 300 | 300 | 1 200 |
| Machinery and plant | 531 | 531 | 532 | 532 | 2 126 |
| | 31 843 | 23 962 | 18 542 | 27 056 | 101 403 |
| | Department 3 | | | | |
| Indirect material | 1 610 | 1 200 | 1 029 | 1 306 | 5 145 |
| Fuel and lighting | 1 200 | 670 | 623 | 1 060 | 3 553 |
| Repairs to machines | 1 049 | 825 | 763 | 850 | 3 487 |
| Indirect wages | 7 463 | 6 926 | 4 237 | 6 274 | 24 900 |
| Factory expenses | 4 500 | 3 510 | 2 902 | 3 982 | 14 894 |
| *Depreciation* | | | | | |
| Land and buildings | 200 | 200 | 200 | 200 | 800 |
| Machinery and plant | 247 | 247 | 247 | 247 | 988 |
| | 16 269 | 13 578 | 10 001 | 13 919 | 53 767 |
| *Totals* | £74 333 | £58 747 | £45 226 | £63 296 | £241 602 |

The costs recorded in the factory overhead budget and those in the direct wages budget provide the details which are required in order to calculate the absorption rates for preparation of the factory overhead (absorbed) section of the production cost budget (Table 17.12).

*Absorption rates: percentage on direct wages*

The formula is $\dfrac{\text{Budgeted overhead}}{\text{Budgeted direct wages}} \times 100$

*Department 1*

$$\frac{£86\ 432}{£86\ 432} \times 100 = \underline{100\%}$$

*Department 2*

$$\frac{£101\ 403}{£135\ 204} \times 100 = \underline{75\%}$$

*Department 3*

$$\frac{£53\ 767}{£107\ 534} \times 100 = \underline{50\%}$$

**Table 17.12    Production cost budget for period ending December 31, 19.1**

|  | % on Direct wages | Factory overhead (absorbed) Quarter ending | | | | |
|---|---|---|---|---|---|---|
|  |  | Mar. 31 | June 30 | Sept. 30 | Dec. 31 | Totals |
| Department 1 |  | £ | £ | £ | £ | £ |
| Product X | 100 | 8 362 | 6 554 | 4 520 | 7 006 | 26 442 |
| Product Y | 100 | 10 620 | 9 180 | 7 200 | 9 360 | 36 360 |
| Product Z | 100 | 7 650 | 5 270 | 4 420 | 6 290 | 23 630 |
|  |  | 26 632 | 21 004 | 16 140 | 22 656 | 86 432 |
| Department 2 |  |  |  |  |  |  |
| Product X | 75 | 8 991 | 7 047 | 4 860 | 7 533 | 28 431 |
| Product Y | 75 | 13 275 | 11 475 | 9 000 | 11 700 | 45 450 |
| Product Z | 75 | 8 910 | 6 138 | 5 148 | 7 326 | 27 522 |
|  |  | 31 176 | 24 660 | 19 008 | 26 559 | 101 403 |
| Department 3 |  |  |  |  |  |  |
| Product X | 50 | 4 810 | 3 770 | 2 600 | 4 030 | 15 210 |
| Product Y | 50 | 7 080 | 6 120 | 4 800 | 6 240 | 24 240 |
| Product Z | 50 | 4 635 | 3 193 | 2 678 | 3 811 | 14 317 |
|  |  | 16 525 | 13 083 | 10 078 | 14 081 | 53 767 |
| Totals |  | £74 333 | £58 747 | £45 226 | £63 296 | £241 602 |

The budget officer consulted the sales manager and other officials and prepared the administration overhead budget and the selling and distribution overhead budget. This was placed before the budget committee and approved.

The cost of administration (see Table 17.13), and the total direct wages from the production budget (see Table 17.10) provided the details for calculating the absorption rate for administration costs, and the total cost of selling and distribution (see Table 17.14) together with the total unit sales from the sales budget (see Table 17.4) provided the details for calculating the absorption rate for the selling and distribution expenses.

**Table 17.13    Administration overhead budget for period ending December 31, 19.1**

| | Mar. 31 | June 30 | Sept. 30 | Dec. 31 | Totals |
|---|---|---|---|---|---|
| | | Quarter ending | | | |
| | £ | £ | £ | £ | £ |
| Office expenses | 13 091 | 14 268 | 10 386 | 14 615 | 52 360 |
| Salaries | 8 160 | 8 160 | 8 598 | 8 598 | 33 516 |
| Directors' fees | — | 2 500 | — | 2 500 | 5 000 |
| Audit fees | 1 625 | — | — | — | 1 625 |
| Debenture interest | — | 3 000 | — | 3 000 | 6 000 |
| Depreciation (furniture) | 62 | 62 | 63 | 63 | 250 |
| Totals | £22 938 | £27 990 | £19 047 | £28 776 | £98 751 |

*Absorption rate: percentage on direct wages*

$$\text{The formula is } \frac{\text{Budgeted administration overhead}}{\text{Direct wages}} \times 100$$

$$= \frac{£98\ 751}{£329\ 170} \times 100 = \underline{\underline{30\%}}$$

**Table 17.14    Selling and distribution overhead budget for period ending December 31, 19.1**

| | Mar. 31 | June 30 | Sept. 30 | Dec. 31 | Totals |
|---|---|---|---|---|---|
| | | Quarter ending | | | |
| | £ | £ | £ | £ | £ |
| Travellers' salaries | 10 000 | 10 000 | 12 000 | 12 945 | 44 945 |
| Advertising | 2 000 | 2 500 | 2 500 | 3 125 | 10 125 |
| Motor expenses | 6 000 | 6 000 | 7 600 | 7 530 | 27 130 |
| Depreciation (motor vehicles) | 1 250 | 1 250 | 1 250 | 1 250 | 5 000 |
| Totals | £19 250 | £19 750 | £23 350 | £24 850 | £87 200 |

*Absorption rate: standard rate per machine*

The formula is $\dfrac{\text{Budgeted selling overhead}}{\text{Budgeted sales (units)}}$

$=\dfrac{£87\ 200}{436}=£200$

At this stage the information is available for preparation of budgeted machine costs (see Fig. 17.3) by using selling prices from the sales budget (Table 17.5), direct materials (Table 17.9) and direct wages (Tables 17.7 and 17.10) from the production cost budget, and the absorption rates from the overhead budgets. This will disclose the budgeted profit per machine and a calculation can be made to find the budgeted profit for the year.

---

*Notes to Fig. 17.3: Extra profits*

(i) The profit of £209 808 is the standard profit on the basis of standard cost in the current year.

(ii) As the standard costs have increased, an extra profit is made on the opening stock which is valued on a lower standard cost.

(iii) The opening stock of £27 400 includes direct materials, direct wages, factory overhead and administration overhead.

(iv) The corresponding costs in the current year are

$$
\begin{array}{lr}
 & £ \\
\text{X} \ \ 2 \times £2\ 860 = & 5\ 720 \\
\text{Y} \ \ 4 \times £2\ 520 = & 10\ 080 \\
\text{Z} \ \ 6 \times £2\ 248 = & 13\ 488 \\
\hline
 & £29\ 288 \\
\end{array}
$$

This gives an extra profit of (£29 288 − £27 400) = £1 888

As the calculation of £209 808 is based on machines which provided only the current standard profit, the standard profit must be increased because some machines made a higher profit. These were made more cheaply in a previous period.

|  | | | Product | | |
| --- | --- | --- | --- | --- | --- |
|  | | X | | Y | Z |
| *Materials* | | £ | | £ | £ |
| Group A | | 410 | | 380 | 350 |
| Group B | | 520 | | 460 | 434 |
| Group C | | 278 | | 219 | 161 |
|  | | 1 208 | | 1 059 | 945 |

*Direct labour*

|  | Hours | £ | Hours | £ | Hours | £ | |
| --- | --- | --- | --- | --- | --- | --- | --- |
| Department 1 | 226 | 226 | 180 | 180 | 170 | 170 | |
| Department 2 | 216 | 324 | 200 | 300 | 176 | 264 | |
| Department 3 | 130 | 260 | 120 | 240 | 103 | 206 | |
|  | 572 | 810 | 500 | 720 | 449 | | 640 |

*Factory overhead*

|  | % | | | | | |
| --- | --- | --- | --- | --- | --- | --- |
| Department 1 | 100 | 226 | | 180 | | 170 |
| Department 2 | 75 | 243 | | 225 | | 198 |
| Department 3 | 50 | 130 | | 120 | | 103 |
|  | | 599 | | 525 | | 471 |
| *Administration overhead (30%)* | | 243 | | 216 | | 192 |
|  | | 2 860 | | 2 520 | | 2 248 |
| *Selling expenses* | | 200 | | 200 | | 200 |
| Total cost | | 3 060 | | 2 720 | | 2 448 |
| Profit (15% on invoice value) | | 540 | | 480 | | 432 |
| Invoice value | | £3 600 | | £3 200 | | £2 880 |

*Note:* 15% on invoice value $=\dfrac{15}{85}$ of Total cost

|  | | £ |
| --- | --- | --- |
| Product X | 112 machines at a profit of £540 each = | 60 480 |
| Product Y | 195 machines at a profit of £480 each = | 93 600 |
| Product Z | 129 machines at a profit of £432 each = | 55 728 |
|  | | 209 808 |

*Add* Extra profit on previous year's stock (see *Notes opposite*)

X 2 at £260 = £520
Y 4 at £120 = £480
Z 6 at £148 = £888

|  | £ |
| --- | --- |
|  | 1 888 |
|  | £211 696 |

*Fig. 17.3 Budgeted machine costs*

**Budgeted Profit**

The purchasing officer together with the materials controller prepared the purchases budget for direct and indirect materials by taking the opening stocks and using information provided by the production budget (direct materials), and the factory overhead budget. These figures will be needed when the cash budget is drawn up, although the payment of accounts will depend on the terms of credit and the policy of the company in respect of when payment should be made. These budgets are shown in Fig. 17.4.

Purchases budget for period ending December 31, 19.1

| Materials | Stock Jan. 1 | Usage | *Direct materials* Balance | Purchases | Stock at end of quarter |
|---|---|---|---|---|---|
| Quarter ending March 31 | £ | £ | £ | £ | £ |
| Group A | 86 700 | 53 340 | 33 360 | 40 000 | 73 360 |
| Group B | 103 862 | 65 910 | 37 952 | 45 000 | 82 952 |
| Group C | 48 000 | 30 452 | 17 548 | 25 000 | 42 548 |
| | 238 562 | 149 702 | 88 860 | 110 000 | 198 860 |
| | Stock Apr. 1 | Usage | Balance | Purchases | Stock at end of quarter |
| Quarter ending June 30 | £ | £ | £ | £ | £ |
| Group A | 73 360 | 42 120 | 31 240 | 50 000 | 81 240 |
| Group B | 82 952 | 51 994 | 30 958 | 70 000 | 100 958 |
| Group C | 42 548 | 24 222 | 18 326 | 30 000 | 48 326 |
| | 198 860 | 118 336 | 80 524 | 150 000 | 230 524 |
| | Stock July 1 | Usage | Balance | Purchases | Stock at end of quarter |
| Quarter ending September 30 | £ | £ | £ | £ | £ |
| Group A | 81 240 | 32 500 | 48 740 | 32 000 | 80 740 |
| Group B | 100 958 | 40 084 | 60 874 | 40 000 | 100 874 |
| Group C | 48 326 | 18 506 | 29 820 | 18 000 | 47 820 |
| | 230 524 | 91 090 | 139 434 | 90 000 | 229 434 |
| | Stock Oct. 1 | Usage | Balance | Purchases | Stock at end of quarter |
| Quarter ending December 31 | £ | £ | £ | £ | £ |
| Group A | 80 740 | 45 420 | 35 320 | 53 180 | 88 500 |
| Group B | 100 874 | 56 098 | 44 776 | 77 299 | 122 075 |
| Group C | 47 820 | 25 963 | 21 857 | 29 204 | 51 061 |
| | 229 434 | 127 481 | 101 953 | 159 683 | 261 636 |
| *Totals* | | £486 609 | | £509 683 | |

Purchases budget for period ending December 31, 19.1

| | *Indirect materials* | | | | |
| | Mar. 31 | June 30 | Sept. 30 | Dec. 31 | *Totals* |
| | £ | £ | £ | £ | £ |
| Department 1 | 2 805 | 2 000 | 1 300 | 2 201 | 8 306 |
| Department 2 | 3 073 | 2 300 | 1 900 | 2 350 | 9 623 |
| Department 3 | 1 610 | 1 200 | 1 029 | 1 306 | 5 145 |
| | £7 488 | £5 500 | £4 229 | £5 857 | £23 074 |

Cash budget for period ending December 31, 19.1

| | | Quarter ending | | | |
| | Mar. 31 | June 30 | Sept. 30 | Dec. 31 | *Totals* |
| | £ | £ | £ | £ | £ |
| Balance brought forward | 78 628 | (65 664) | (50 684) | (31 586) | 78 628 (March) |
| *Receipts* | | | | | |
| Debtors | 364 462 | 372 000 | 289 000 | 390 077 | 1 415 539 |
| | 443 090 | 306 336 | 238 316 | 358 491 | 1 494 167 |
| *Payments* | | | | | |
| Creditors: Direct and indirect materials | 170 000 | 180 000 | 125 000 | 111 698 | 586 698 |
| Wages: Direct and indirect | 135 796 | 107 313 | 84 668 | 112 648 | 440 425 |
| Dividends: Preference | 17 500 | | | | 17 500 |
| Ordinary | 25 000 | | | | 25 000 |
| Taxation | 88 925 | | | | 88 925 |
| Fuel and light | 5 722 | 3 050 | 2 818 | 4 560 | 16 150 |
| Repairs to machines | 4 544 | 3 853 | 3 436 | 4 015 | 15 848 |
| Factory expenses | 20 391 | 16 376 | 12 896 | 17 127 | 66 790 |
| Office expenses | 13 091 | 14 268 | 10 386 | 14 615 | 52 360 |
| Directors' fees | | 2 500 | | 2 500 | 5 000 |
| Audit fees | 1 625 | | | | 1 625 |
| Debenture interest | | 3 000 | | 3 000 | 6 000 |
| Advertising | 2 000 | 2 500 | 2 500 | 3 125 | 10 125 |
| Motor expenses | 6 000 | 6 000 | 7 600 | 7 530 | 27 130 |
| Salaries | 18 160 | 18 160 | 20 598 | 21 543 | 78 461 |
| | £508 754 | £357 020 | £269 902 | £302 361 | £1 438 037 |
| Balance carried forward (=deficit) | (65 664) | (50 684) | (31 586) | 56 130 | 56 130 |

*Fig. 17.4 Purchases budgets and cash budget*

The cash budget has been prepared starting with the balance as shown in the balance sheet and using the figures shown in the operating budgets. The receipts from debtors will depend on the sales and the time-lag between the date of dispatch and the date of collection. The amount shown for each period is based on past experience, by taking into account the average collection period. For convenience, the forecast of cash payments for many items is based on the assumption that payment is made in the period when the expenditure is incurred.

At this stage, the operating budgets have been prepared and approved by the budget committee which must give the final approval. A product summary budget (see Fig. 17.5) is prepared followed by the master budget and the balance sheet.

### Product summary budget for period ending December 31, 19.1

| Product | X | Y | Z | Total |
|---|---|---|---|---|
| | £ | £ | £ | £ |
| Opening stock | | | | |
| (finished machines) | 5 200 | 9 600 | 12 600 | 27 400 |
| Direct materials | 141 336 | 213 918 | 131 355 | 486 609 |
| Direct wages | 94 770 | 145 440 | 88 960 | 329 170 |
| Factory overhead | 70 083 | 106 050 | 65 469 | 241 602 |
| Administration overhead | 28 431 | 43 632 | 26 688 | 98 751 |
| | 339 820 | 518 640 | 325 072 | 1 183 532 |
| Less Closing stock (machines) | 20 020 | 27 720 | 35 968 | 83 708 |
| | 319 800 | 490 920 | 289 104 | 1 099 824 |
| Selling expenses | 22 400 | 39 000 | 25 800 | 87 200 |
| | 342 200 | 529 920 | 314 904 | 1 187 024 |
| Profit | 61 000 | 94 080 | 56 616 | 211 696 |
| Sales revenue | £403 200 | £624 000 | £371 520 | £1 398 720 |

### Calculations
Opening stock (finished machines)

| | £ |
|---|---|
| Product X 2 @ £2 600 | 5 200 |
| Product Y 4 @ £2 400 | 9 600 |
| Product Z 6 @ £2 100 | 12 600 |
| | £27 400 |

Closing stock (finished machines)

| | £ |
|---|---|
| Product X 7 @ £2 860 | 20 020 |
| Product Y 11 @ £2 520 | 27 720 |
| Product Z 16 @ £2 248 | 35 968 |
| | £83 708 |

*Fig. 17.5 Product summary budget*

The master budget can now be prepared using figures shown in the budgets or summary budget and information extracted from the balance sheet for the year ending December 31, 19.0.

The master budget (Fig. 17.6, pp. 295–6) takes the form of a Budgeted Profit and Loss Account and a budgeted balance sheet. There are several sources of figures for their master budget; those for the Profit and Loss Account (column 1) are derived from the sources shown in column 2.

Profit and Loss Account

| Column 1 | Column 2 |
|---|---|
| Opening stock | Purchases budget or balance sheet 19.0 |
| Purchases | Purchases budget |
| Closing stock | Purchases budget |
| Direct material used | Derived from opening stock, purchases and closing stock; production cost budget or summary budget |
| Direct wages | Production cost budget or summary budget |
| Factory overhead | Factory overhead budget |
| Opening stock (finished machines) | Balance sheet 19.0 |
| Closing stock (finished machines) | Derived from opening stock, production budget and sales forecast. Valued by using budgeted machine costs |
| Administration overhead | Administration overhead budget |
| Selling expenses | Selling expenses budget |
| Corporation tax | Estimated at £100 000 |
| Appropriations | Proposed 20% ordinary dividend and other items as shown |

The balance sheet is prepared in the usual way by using the information in the previous balance sheet and adjusting the figures from the details shown in the budgets and the Profit and Loss Account.

**Workings**

*Debtors*

|  | £ |
|---|---|
| Balance 19.0 | 80 500 |
| Sales 19.1 | 1 398 720 |
|  | 1 479 220 |
| Cash receipts (from cash budget) | 1 415 539 |
| Balance 19.1 | £   63 681 |

*Creditors*

|  | £ | £ |
|---|---|---|
| Balance 19.0 |  | 101 000 |
| Purchases 19.1 |  |  |
| Direct materials | 509 683 |  |
| Indirect materials | 23 074 |  |
|  |  | 532 757 |
|  |  | 633 757 |
| Payments (cash budget) |  | 586 698 |
| Balance 19.1 |  | £ 47 059 |

*Wages*

|  | £ | £ |
|---|---|---|
| Balance 19.0 |  | 4 500 |
| Direct wages | 329 170 |  |
| Indirect wages |  |  |
| (Factory overhead budget) | 111 820 |  |
|  |  | 440 990 |
|  |  | 445 490 |
| Payments (cash budget) |  | 440 425 |
| Balance 19.1 |  | £   5 065 |

Budgeted Profit and Loss Account for year ending December 31, 19.1

| | £ | £ | % | % |
|---|---|---|---|---|
| Sales | | 1 398 720 | | 100 |
| *Production costs* | | | | |
| Direct materials | | 509 683 | | |
| Direct labour | | 329 170 | | |
| Factory overhead | | 241 602 | | |
| *Add* Opening stock | 238 562 | | | |
| *Less* Closing stock | 261 636 | | | |
| | | (23 074) | | |
| | | 1 057 381 | | |
| *Finished machines* | | | | |
| *Add* Opening stock | 27 400 | | | |
| *Less* Closing stock | 83 708 | | | |
| | | (56 308) | | |
| Cost of sales (deduct from sales above) | | £1 001 073 | | 71.6 |
| Gross profit | | 397 647 | | 28.4 |
| *Less* | | | | |
| Administration costs | 98 751 | | 7.1 | |
| Selling expenses | 87 200 | | 6.2 | |
| | | 185 951 | | 13.3 |
| Profit before taxation | | 211 696 | | 15.1 |
| *Less* Corporation tax | | 100 000 | | 7.1 |
| Profit after taxation | | 111 696 | | 8.0 |
| Balance brought forward | | 3 750 | | |
| Profit available for distribution | | 115 446 | | |
| *Appropriation of profits* | | | | |
| Preliminary expenses | 1 910 | | | |
| Transfer to general reserve | 25 000 | | | |
| Transfer to staff pension fund | 3 000 | | | |
| 7% Preference dividend | 17 500 | | | |
| Proposed ordinary dividend of 20% | 50 000 | | | |
| | | 97 410 | | |
| Balance (carried forward) | | £18 036 | | |

*Fig. 17.6 The master budget: (a) Budgeted Profit and Loss Account*

Budgeted Balance Sheet as at December 31, 19.1

| Assets employed | Cost | Depreciation | Value |
|---|---|---|---|
| *Fixed assets* | £ | £ | £ |
| Land and buildings | 392 500 | 6 000 | 386 500 |
| Machinery and plant | 100 000 | 22 720 | 77 280 |
| Motor vehicles | 25 000 | 16 000 | 9 000 |
| Office furniture | 5 000 | 2 250 | 2 750 |
| | £522 500 | £46 970 | 475 530 |

| | | |
|---|---|---|
| Quoted investments (market value £47 750) | | 47 475 |
| *Current assets* | | |
| Stock: General stores | 261 636 | |
| Finished machines | 83 708 | |
| | 345 344 | |
| Debtors | 63 681 | |
| Cash at bank and in hand | 56 130 | |
| | 465 155 | |
| *Less* Current liabilities | | |
| Creditors | 47 059 | |
| Wages due | 5 065 | |
| Proposed preference dividend | 17 500 | |
| Proposed ordinary dividend 20% | 50 000 | |
| Corporation tax | 100 000 | |
| | 219 624 | |
| Net current assets | | 245 531 |
| | | £768 536 |

| **Financed by:** | | |
|---|---|---|
| *Long-term liability* | | £ |
| 6% Debentures | | 100 000 |

| | | |
|---|---|---|
| *Preference shareholders' interest in the company* | *Authorized* | |
| 250 000 7% Preference shares of £1 fully paid | 250 000 | 250 000 |

| *Ordinary shareholders' interest in the company* | *Authorized* | |
|---|---|---|
| | £ | £ |
| 250 000 Ordinary shares of £1 fully paid | 250 000 | 250 000 |

| *Reserves* | | |
|---|---|---|
| Staff pension fund | 52 500 | |
| General reserve | 98 000 | |
| Profit and Loss Account | 18 036 | |
| | 168 536 | |
| Ordinary shareholders' equity | | 418 536 |
| | | £768 536 |

*Fig. 17.6 The master budget: (b) Budgeted Balance Sheet*

## 17.16    Variance Reporting

Variance reports are an essential part of a system of budgetary control. They are prepared for the period of activity, usually weekly or monthly, which is appropriate and suitable to the work performed or the expenditure which has to be incurred. There is a large number of these reports and they are sent to top management, foremen, supervisors and so on. Examples are shown in Tables 17.15 and 17.16.

**Table 17.15    Factory overhead cost report for quarter ending March 31, 19. .**

|  | Actual cost £ | Budgeted cost £ | Variance Favourable £ | Variance Adverse £ |
|---|---|---|---|---|
| Indirect material | 2 900 | 2 805 |  | 95 |
| Fuel and lighting | 2 250 | 2 214 |  | 36 |
| Repairs to machines | 1 398 | 1 510 | 112 |  |
| Indirect wages | 12 000 | 11 962 |  | 38 |
| Factory expenses | 6 999 | 7 029 | 30 |  |
| Depreciation | 701 | 701 |  |  |
|  | £26 248 | £26 221 | £142 | £169 |

Remarks: (if any).

## 17.17    Zero-based Budgets

This is a technique in budgeting which was introduced in 1960 by an American electronics company. It is a procedure for considering *relative values* and re-examining expenditure which, after review, has to be justified. This technique is claimed to improve cost control and to allocate resources more effectively. The usual procedure in budgeting is to start with the previous year's budgets and to adjust these on the basis of *comparative* costs by making allowance for changes in policy, costs and estimated future conditions. Zero-based budgeting, however, is carried out every three to five years. It splits budgets into activity levels and gives consideration to whether the required results can be obtained with a lower level of activity, or more cheaply. It is an exercise which questions every activity, establishes priorities and seeks alternative ways of providing services.

## 17.18    Continuous Budgeting

Rapidly changing price levels make annual budgeting difficult because when comparisons are made between actual costs and budgeted allowances, the results are unreliable indicators of true performance. Many companies now use a system which looks at current costs and conditions at the end of each

**Table 17.16    Area sales report for quarter ending March 31, 19. .**

| | Actual | | Budget | | Variance | |
|---|---|---|---|---|---|---|
| | Machines | Value | Machines | Value | Machines | Value |
| | | £ | | £ | | £ |
| **Area A** | | | | | | |
| Product X | 9 | 32 400 | 10 | 36 000 | 1 (A) | 3 600 (A) |
| Product Y | 33 | 106 000 | 35 | 112 000 | 2 (A) | 6 000 (A) |
| Product Z | 21 | 60 480 | 20 | 57 600 | 1 (F) | 2 880 (F) |
| | 63 | 198 880 | 65 | 205 600 | 2 (A) | 6 720 (A) |
| **Area B** | | | | | | |
| Product X | 5 | 18 000 | 5 | 18 000 | — | — |
| Product Y | 9 | 28 000 | 8 | 25 600 | 1 (F) | 2 400 (F) |
| Product Z | 6 | 17 000 | 6 | 17 280 | — | 280 (A) |
| | 20 | 63 000 | 19 | 60 880 | 1 (F) | 2 120 (F) |
| **Area C** | | | | | | |
| Product X | 8 | 28 800 | 8 | 28 800 | — | — |
| Product Y | 5 | 16 000 | 5 | 16 000 | — | — |
| Product Z | 8 | 23 040 | 6 | 17 280 | 2 (F) | 5 760 (F) |
| | 21 | 67 840 | 19 | 62 080 | 2 (F) | 5 760 (F) |
| **Area D** | | | | | | |
| Product X | 12 | 43 200 | 12 | 43 200 | — | — |
| Product Y | 5 | 16 000 | 8 | 25 600 | 3 (A) | 9 600 (A) |
| Product Z | 10 | 28 800 | 10 | 28 800 | — | — |
| | 27 | 88 000 | 30 | 97 600 | 3 (A) | 9 600 (A) |
| **Summary** | | | | | | |
| Product X | 34 | 122 400 | 35 | 126 000 | 1 (A) | 3 600 (A) |
| Product Y | 52 | 166 000 | 56 | 179 200 | 4 (A) | 13 200 (A) |
| Product Z | 45 | 129 320 | 42 | 120 960 | 3 (F) | 8 360 (F) |
| *Totals* | 131 | £417 720 | 133 | £426 160 | 2 (A) | £8 440 (A) |

quarter and adjusts the remaining budget values so that a more accurate assessment can be made. Every month or quarter new forecasts are made to give some indication of budget values over the next twelve months.

## 17.19    Advantages and Disadvantages of Budgetary Control

Budgetary control is a management function which is essential if control is to be established over the different sections of the business. It uses planning and forecasting in order to achieve the objects of the business and seeks to maintain effective performance by co-ordinating the various departments. In this respect budgeting uses consultative management and group participation, so that the activities of these departments can be synchronized. Its final objective is to secure control by measuring what has been accomplished, and by taking appropriate action where required.

The advantages of budgetary control are as follows:

(a) it compels management to make clear-cut statements concerning its policy and objectives;

(b) it plans and makes forecasts so that the costs of materials, wages and expenses are set at the most economical levels;

(c) it is a consultative procedure which demands co-operation in the preparation of budgets and the operations which follow, so that the results fixed by the budget can be attained;

(d) it establishes areas of responsibility and sets targets so that the people carrying the responsibility are aware of what must be achieved if the organization's objectives are to be realized;

(e) by controlling the spending of money which is regulated in accordance with a well-defined plan, it attempts to avoid a loss of resources;

(f) the organization is encouraged to examine its products, markets and methods in order that the maximum use can be made of the plant, equipment and assets of the business;

(g) management receives a warning when operations are not proceeding in accordance with the plan. This follows a comparison of budget with actual results when substantial deviations are investigated and reported.

The only disadvantage of budgetary control is that it is time-consuming and requires a high degree of accuracy in its forecasting. However, the great advance in micro-processor technology will allow much of this routine work in the future to be produced within minutes.

## 17.20 Exercises

1. Explain what you understand by a *budget* and a *forecast* and describe the procedure which is used when a business operates a system of budgetary control.

2. You have been appointed as the first management accountant to an old-established manufacturing business of medium size which has recently expanded rapidly beyond the capacity of its existing accounting system. It has been agreed by the board of directors that your priority task will be to prepare and introduce a system of budgetary control.

You are required to set out clearly:

(a) the problems you are likely to face in carrying out this task;

(b) the requirements which will have to be satisfied before the proposed budgeting system can operate successfully at the planning stage.

*(ICMA)*

# Unit Eighteen

# The Analysis of Accounting Information

## 18.1 Ratio Analysis

Elementary accounting records enable management to keep track of the many transactions taking place with debtors, creditors, shareholders, employees, bankers and others. When classified into the broad areas of purchases, sales, expenses, profits, assets and liabilities, the numerous accounts can be set against one another to show the results of the activities measured in profit or loss for the period, and net worth of the business. However satisfactory these results may be, they do not tell the full story of the business, such as how well or how badly it has fared compared with its competitors, compared with last year, or compared with the resources put into the business in terms of capital employed.

It follows that a set of final accounts is not the end of the accountant's work, but only the end of the beginning. We must now analyse the results achieved, and investigate various aspects of our organization's performance. Since many of these investigations involve comparisons, it is helpful if they are in simple mathematical terms. The percentage return achieved on capital invested is a more meaningful figure than the net profit actually achieved. Consider the following companies:

A Co Ltd   Profit £200 000
B Co Ltd   Profit £250 000

Company B appears to have achieved better results than company A. A little more information soon changes the picture:

A Co Ltd   Capital invested £200 000   Profit £200 000
B Co Ltd   Capital invested £5 000 000   Profit £250 000

We can now see that the results of Company A were much more satisfactory. On a capital outlay of £200 000 the profit was £200 000, a return of 100 per cent. Company B, by contrast, only achieved a return on capital invested of:

$$\frac{250\ 000}{5\ 000\ 000} \times 100 = \underline{\underline{5 \text{ per cent}}}$$

Clearly, the ratio of profit to capital employed is much more informative than the absolute profit figures. The latter are almost meaningless until compared with the resources put into the business in terms of capital employed.

**Ratio analysis** is a systematic way of comparing various aspects of a business, to bring out the relative success or failure of each facet of the organization's activities. We can compare department with department, branch with branch, salesman with salesman, product with product, accounting period with accounting period, our business with a comparable business, and so on. In general, each analysis results in a ratio: 2:1, 3:1, 4:1, etc., or a series of percentages such as 50 per cent on materials, 30 per cent on direct costs, 15 per cent on overheads and 5 per cent profit.

Although each ratio has its own formula and must be studied separately, they are all in fact interrelated and can be progressively explored to give a detailed analysis of every aspect of the business. They thus form a branching network of interrelated ratios, each successive group of branches analysing a more detailed area than the previous one. This is illustrated in Fig. 18.1. Each ratio is explained in more detail in the text in the sections indicated in the figure.

The analysis of a business revolves around two main areas, *profit performance* and *liquidity*. The profit performance is examined by considering the *return on capital employed* and the other ratios which can be developed from it, as shown in Fig. 18.1. The liquidity position is examined by considering the *working capital ratio*, and the *liquid, quick* or *acid-test ratio* (see Unit 18.9).

## 18.2    The Return on Capital Employed

The accountancy bodies examine this ratio, which is the most fundamental ratio of all, by looking at the capital employed from the point of view of the assets purchased with the capital, rather than the capital itself. It really makes no difference, for the two sides of a balance sheet are equal. Whether we look at the capital employed or at the assets purchased when we employ the capital does not make a lot of difference. It is, however, rather confusing for students, who would expect a ratio called *return on capital employed* to refer to the *capital employed* and not to the assets. Remember, then, that *the capital we employ and the assets we buy when we employ it have the same values.* First let us consider the relatively simple set of Final Accounts shown in Fig. 18.2 (pp. 304–5).

### Assets Base and Related Profit

Strictly speaking, the calculations of return on capital employed should be based on average capital employed throughout the year, but in practice the asset figures used are those on the final balance sheet for the year, and the profit figures are those of the final Trading and Profit and Loss Account.

The phrase *return on capital employed* is susceptible to different interpretations, and its formula gives different results according to the assets base chosen. To make this clear, consider the balance sheet in Fig. 18.2(*b*). The

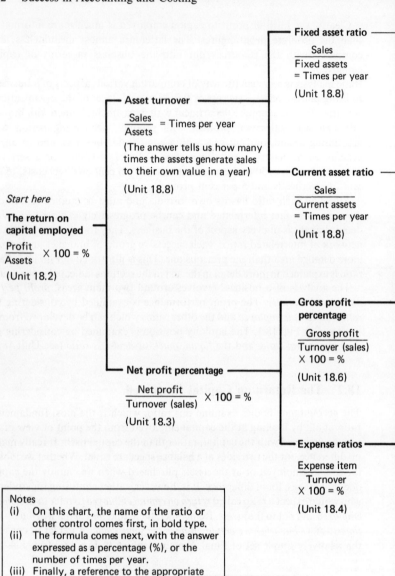

Fixed asset ratio

$$\frac{\text{Sales}}{\text{Fixed assets}}$$
= Times per year
(Unit 18.8)

Asset turnover

$$\frac{\text{Sales}}{\text{Assets}}$$ = Times per year
(The answer tells us how many times the assets generate sales to their own value in a year)
(Unit 18.8)

*Start here*

**The return on capital employed**
$$\frac{\text{Profit}}{\text{Assets}} \times 100 = \%$$
(Unit 18.2)

Current asset ratio

$$\frac{\text{Sales}}{\text{Current assets}}$$
= Times per year
(Unit 18.8)

Gross profit percentage

$$\frac{\text{Gross profit}}{\text{Turnover (sales)}} \times 100 = \%$$
(Unit 18.6)

**Net profit percentage**

$$\frac{\text{Net profit}}{\text{Turnover (sales)}} \times 100 = \%$$
(Unit 18.3)

Expense ratios

$$\frac{\text{Expense item}}{\text{Turnover}} \times 100 = \%$$
(Unit 18.4)

Notes
(i)   On this chart, the name of the ratio or other control comes first, in bold type.
(ii)  The formula comes next, with the answer expressed as a percentage (%), or the number of times per year.
(iii) Finally, a reference to the appropriate section of Unit 18 is given.

*Fig. 18.1 A branching-network diagram of control ratios*

e.g. $\dfrac{\text{Sales}}{\text{Plant and equipment}}$ = Times per year

(Unit 18.8)

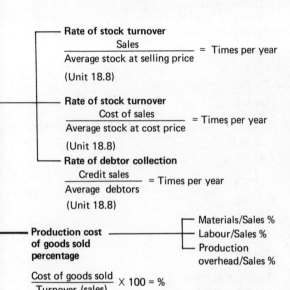

**Rate of stock turnover**

$\dfrac{\text{Sales}}{\text{Average stock at selling price}}$ = Times per year

(Unit 18.8)

**Rate of stock turnover**

$\dfrac{\text{Cost of sales}}{\text{Average stock at cost price}}$ = Times per year

(Unit 18.8)

**Rate of debtor collection**

$\dfrac{\text{Credit sales}}{\text{Average debtors}}$ = Times per year

(Unit 18.8)

**Production cost of goods sold percentage**
— Materials/Sales %
— Labour/Sales %
— Production overhead/Sales %

$\dfrac{\text{Cost of goods sold}}{\text{Turnover (sales)}} \times 100 = \%$

(Unit 18.7)

**Occupancy ratio**
— Rent/Sales %
— Rates/Sales %
— Lighting and heating/Sales %

**General administration ratio**
— Clerical wages/Sales %
— Salaries/Sales %
— Directors' fees/Sales %
— Management services/Sales %
— Research and development/Sales %

**Marketing and distribution ratio**
— Field force expenses/Sales %
— Advertising/Sales %
— Distribution costs/Sales %
— Market research/Sales %

Clearview Ltd

Trading and Profit and Loss Account for year ending December 31, 19. .

| | £ | | £ |
|---|---|---|---|
| Opening stock | 28 464 | Sales | 429 500 |
| Purchases | 210 788 | *Less* Returns | 3 500 |
| | 239 252 | | 426 000 |
| *Less* Closing stock | 73 100 | | |
| Cost of sales | 166 152 | | |
| Gross profit | c/d 259 848 | | |
| | £426 000 | | £426 000 |
| Bad debts | 3 040 | Gross profit | b/d 259 848 |
| Rent and rates | 3 800 | | |
| General expenses | 43 000 | | |
| Light and heat | 3 720 | | |
| Salaries | 45 212 | | |
| Debenture interest | 3 200 | | |
| | 101 972 | | |
| Net profit | c/d 157 876 | | |
| | £259 848 | | £259 848 |

Appropriation section

| | | | |
|---|---|---|---|
| Preliminary expenses | 1 880 | Balance (from previous year) | 3 740 |
| Reserve for future taxation | 40 000 | Net profit | b/d 157 876 |
| General reserve | 10 000 | | 161 616 |
| Preference dividend | 5 400 | | |
| Ordinary dividend | 20 000 | | |
| | 77 280 | | |
| Balance | c/d 84 336 | | |
| | £161 616 | | £161 616 |
| | | Balance | b/d 84 336 |

*Fig. 18.2(a) Final accounts for analysis*

Clearview Ltd balance sheet (abbreviated) (as at December 31, 19..)

| Fixed assets | £ | Ordinary shareholders' interest | £ |
|---|---|---|---|
| (Depreciation details omitted) | | Ordinary shares of £1 | 200 000 |
| Freehold buildings | 288 000 | Reserves | |
| Plant and machinery | 80 000 | Premium on shares    36 000 | |
| Furniture and equipment | 15 984 | General reserve    20 000 | |
| | 383 984 | Balance on | |
| | | Appropriation A/c  84 336 | |
| | | | 140 336 |
| Current assets | | | 340 336 |
| Closing stock   73 100 | | Less Preliminary expenses | 1 880 |
| Debtors   11 520 | | Ordinary shareholders' | |
| Balance at bank   58 536 | | interest | 338 456 |
| Cash in hand   956 | | Preference shareholders' interest | |
| Payments in | | 9% Preference shares | 60 000 |
| advance   250 | | 8% Debentures | 40 000 |
| | 144 362 | Reserve for future tax | 54 690 |
| | | Current liabilities | |
| | | Creditors   6 500 | |
| | | Salaries due   1 700 | |
| | | Debenture interest   1 600 | |
| | | Ordinary dividend   20 000 | |
| | | Preference dividend   5 400 | |
| | | | 35 200 |
| | £528 346 | | £528 346 |

Fig. 18.2(b) A balance sheet for analysis

Note: For convenience this balance sheet is displayed with both sides in the order of permanence, i.e. most enduring assets, and most enduring liabilities, first in each case.

total capital employed is £528 346, and it is employed to purchase assets which also total £528 346. One possible asset base is, therefore, £528 346, but what profits relate to this figure? Clearly, it must be the whole of the net profit, as well as the interest on debentures which has been deducted from the net profit in the Profit and Loss Account. The related profit is, therefore:

$$£157\,876 + £3\,200 = £161\,076$$

so the calculation is:

$$\text{Return on capital invested} = \frac{(\text{Net profit} + \text{Debenture interest})}{\text{Total assets}} \times 100$$

$$= \frac{161\,076}{528\,346} \times 100$$

$$= 30.49\%$$

The return on capital invested is seen to be 30.49 per cent—a very satisfactory rate of return compared with other alternative opportunities. Had we not invested in this company we might have invested in 9% debentures, or 7% preference shares or 4% National Savings at the Post Office. The opportunities are legion, and some investments clearly do better than others.

Not all investors in this company received the same reward, however. Even if the assets earned a return of 30.49 per cent overall, the preference shareholders only received 9 per cent and the debenture holders only received 8 per cent. So the extra 21.49 per cent from the preference shareholders actually went to swell the earnings of the ordinary shareholders, and so did the extra 22.49 per cent of the debenture holders' true earnings. These two groups sacrificed the higher dividend for the greater security they obtained by not investing in ordinary shares.

Looking at the liabilities side of the balance sheet again, we can see that ordinary shareholders' interest in the company is actually £338 456. This is the same as saying that the ordinary shareholders have purchased this value of assets for the business—the rest of the assets must have been purchased with the funds supplied by preference shareholders, debenture holders, tax moneys not yet paid, etc. What profits are related to this assets base of £338 456? From the accounts in Fig. 18.2(a) we can see that the correct profit figure to take is calculated as follows:

|  | £ | £ |
|---|---|---|
| Net profit |  | 157 876 |
| *Less* Preliminary expenses | 1 880 |  |
| Reserves for future taxation | 40 000 |  |
| Preference dividend | 5 400 |  |
|  |  | 47 280 |
| Profit attributable to ordinary shareholders |  | £110 596 |

The items deducted above are profits which have been used for other purposes—to reduce fictitious assets or to provide for taxation, or as a reward to the preference shareholders. The reward to the debenture holders was deducted before the net profit was arrived at. All the rest of the profit, including that placed to General Reserve Account, belongs to the ordinary shareholders. We can now calculate the return on capital invested by the ordinary shareholders. This is found by the formula:

$$\frac{\text{Related profit}}{\text{Asset base}} \times 100$$

$$= \frac{110\ 596}{338\ 456} \times 100 = \underline{\underline{32.68\%}}$$

We can see that the ordinary shareholders actually achieved a higher return than was earned overall by the assets, and a much higher one than that of the preference shareholders or debenture holders.

The range of assets bases, and related profits, is given in Table 18.1. Although the answers to the question 'What was the return on capital invested in this company?' vary according to the assets base and related profit (or loss) chosen, there cannot be any agreement on what is the best answer. It depends upon the particular aspect that interests the accountant conducting the investigation.

## 18.3   Net Profit Percentage

This ratio is fully described in *Success in Principles of Accounting* (p. 379). The formula is:

$$\frac{\text{Net profit}}{\text{Turnover}} \times 100$$

The main points are:

(*a*) Unless some dynamic situation has developed which is squeezing profit margins, the net profit percentage ratio should always be constant. Thus, if business done (i.e. sales or turnover) doubles, profits double but the *ratio* stays the same. Thus:

$$\text{Year 1} \quad \frac{10\ 000}{50\ 000} \times 100 = \underline{\underline{20\%}}$$

$$\text{Year 2} \quad \frac{20\ 000}{100\ 000} \times 100 = \underline{\underline{20\%}}$$

(*b*) If net profit percentage changes from one period to another there must be a cause — perhaps in the manufacturing section, the trading section or in the administrative side of the company's work. The cause can be found by examining the company's activities in minute detail by taking out *expense ratios* (see Unit 18.4).

(*c*) It is important to discover whether the fall in net profit percentage was a result of fluctuations in the items charged to the Profit and Loss Account, or of fluctuations in the gross profit taken forward into the Profit and Loss Account caused by changes in costs or receipts lower down in the organization.

Table 18.1  Assets bases and related profits (for calculating return on capital employed)

| Assets bases | Source | Related profit figure | Figures from Fig. 18.2 (a) and (b) |
|---|---|---|---|
| 1. Total assets | Total asset figure on balance sheet | Net profit *plus* any debenture interest deducted in Profit and Loss Account | $\dfrac{161\,076}{528\,346} \times 100$ |
| 2. Assets provided by long-term funds | Total assets *less* current liabilities | Earnings after tax, i.e. net profit *plus* debenture interest *less* tax appropriations | $\dfrac{121\,076}{493\,146} \times 100$ |
| 3. Assets provided by the owners | Total assets *less* current liabilities and long-term funds provided by debenture holders and other outsiders | Earnings after interest and tax, i.e. net profit *less* appropriation for future taxation (interest has already been deducted) | $\dfrac{117\,876}{398\,456} \times 100$ |
| 4. Assets provided by ordinary shareholders | Ordinary shareholders' interest in the company — same as 3 above but also deduct preference shareholding | Earnings after interest, tax and preference dividend, i.e. same as 3 above but also deduct the preference dividend | $\dfrac{112\,476}{338\,456} \times 100$ |

(*d*) It is not only increases in costs which affect the ratio, but also decreases in receipts. Thus, if administrative expenses rise they will eat into profit margins, but so will a failure to achieve income from sources which have been enjoyed in previous years. Thus, as far as the Profit and Loss Account is concerned, decreases in rent received, commission received, fees received, and so forth, reflect on the net profit percentage just as much as would increases in, say, bad debts, depreciation charges or interest payable.

Increases in costs and decreases in receipts require different types of remedial action. Costs must be lowered by aiming for greater efficiency. Decreased receipts must be recovered by a more aggressive pursuit of traditional incomes to re-establish the source of funds which for some reason has dried up.

**Example 18.1**
Using the figures from Fig. 18.2 what is the net profit percentage?

$$\text{Net profit percentage} = \frac{\text{Net profit}}{\text{Sales}} \times 100$$

$$= \frac{£157\ 876}{£426\ 000} \times 100 = \underline{\underline{37.06\%}}$$

When compared with the net profit percentage for the previous period, we would expect to find that this figure was a constant, and if it varies substantially we would want to know why.

The first thing to do is to check the gross profit percentage to see if this has also varied. If so, the change in net profit percentage may be a reflection of the change in gross profit percentage, which has simply been passed on into the Profit and Loss Account. If the gross profit percentage is constant over the two periods the fall in net profit percentage must be caused by the items listed in the Profit and Loss Account. We should therefore need to calculate *expense ratios* and also consider the amount of miscellaneous receipts, to discover where the changes have arisen. These are explained below.

## 18.4  Expense Ratios

Expense ratios are calculated as a percentage of turnover using the general formula:

$$\text{Expense ratio} = \frac{\text{Expense item}}{\text{Turnover}} \times 100$$

Thus from Fig. 18.2 (*a*) the following expense ratios could be calculated:

$$\text{Bad debts ratio} = \frac{£3\ 040}{£426\ 000} \times 100 = \underline{\underline{0.7\%}}$$

$$\text{Rent and rates ratio} = \frac{£3\ 800}{£426\ 000} \times 100 = \underline{\underline{0.89\%}}$$

$$\text{Salaries ratio} = \frac{£45\ 212}{£426\ 000} \times 100 = \underline{\underline{10.6\%}}$$

These ratios are not very informative by themselves, but compared with the same ratio for a previous period any one of them may reveal a significant alteration. For example, if the salaries for the previous year had been only 8.5 per cent of turnover, then clearly an unfavourable variance has arisen. The staff employed are not as effective this year as last. We can only tell what the difficulty is from our records. If staffing has not changed, then turnover must be down and we are losing customers. If staffing has increased, why is this? It may be that a certain amount of empire-building is going on. Perhaps extra staff have been taken on to meet extra work anticipated from a sales drive, but the sales resulting from that activity were not as great as expected. Possibly staff numbers have actually been reduced, but sales have fallen even more. It is no good working out ratios unless they are followed up in a practical way.

## 18.5    Miscellaneous Receipts

Just as it is helpful to know to what extent expenses have changed during the period under review, it is also helpful to know if receipts have changed. Thus, where income has been received from some regular source, such as sub-letting premises, or from commission on business, any decline in these receipts will cause a decline in net profit and therefore in net profit percentage.

There is no reason for such miscellaneous receipts to vary with turnover. Income received from sub-letting part of our premises does not mean extra rent will be received when our turnover increases. It might even be better, when calculating net profit percentage, to leave out that part of the profit provided by these miscellaneous profits, and only include profits directly related to turnover.

A fall in net profit percentage caused by this type of change is borne out by the fact that the gross profit percentage has not varied and the expense ratios are also relatively constant. The solution to the problem is to compare the receipts for the current period with those from the previous period, and discover what has caused any difference. As mentioned earlier, perhaps a tenant has been given notice to quit because we need the extra space for our own use, in which case little can be done about the loss of rent. Perhaps a source of income has been lost as a result of the collapse of a particular firm, or as a result of change in a customer's method of trading, or a loss of business has been caused by incompetence or bad customer relations.

## 18.6    Gross Profit Percentage

This is explained fully in *Success in Principles of Accounting* (p. 369). The formula is:

$$\text{Gross profit percentage} = \frac{\text{Gross profit}}{\text{Turnover}} \times 100$$

In Fig. 18.2 (a) the figures are

$$\text{Gross profit percentage} = \frac{£259\ 848}{£426\ 000} \times 100$$
$$= \underline{61.0\%}$$

Reasons for a fall in gross profit percentage include:

(a) theft of takings by staff;

(b) theft of stock by staff, or 'passing-out' of stock by staff to associates, or by shop-lifting;

(c) incorrect stocktaking;

(d) breakages and other forms of wastage;

(e) decreased rate of stockturn;

(f) poor buying, resulting in need to mark down stock to sell it;

(g) failure to pass on increases in purchase prices to the consumer, by slow action in raising selling prices:

(h) change in the mix of products.

## 18.7  Production Cost to Sales Ratio

In manufacturing enterprises where the goods manufactured are transferred to the Trading Account at production cost, the cost of goods sold can be calculated as a percentage of the sales figure. It will, of course, simply be the counterpart of the gross profit percentage (see Unit 18.6). Thus, in Fig. 18.2(a) above the gross profit percentage was found to be 61.0 per cent. The cost of goods sold (in Fig. 18.2(a) it is called the cost of sales) when expressed as a percentage of the sales is calculated as follows:

$$\text{Production cost to sales ratio} = \frac{\text{Cost of goods sold}}{\text{Turnover}} \times 100$$
$$= \frac{£166\ 152}{£426\ 000} \times 100$$
$$= \underline{39\%}$$

This is the counterpart of the gross profit percentage above (39% + 61% = 100%).

This production cost is made up of two parts, the *prime costs* and the *factory overhead*. Prime costs are further divisible into *material costs* and *labour costs* and each of these expenses can be expressed as an expense ratio, as described in Unit 18.4.

The formulae are:

$$\text{Materials to sales ratio} = \frac{\text{Material costs}}{\text{Turnover}} \times 100$$

$$\text{Labour to sales ratio} = \frac{\text{Labour costs}}{\text{Turnover}} \times 100$$

$$\text{Production overhead to sales ratio} = \frac{\text{Production overhead}}{\text{Sales}} \times 100$$

## 18.8   Asset Turnover (Capital Turnover)

In Fig. 18.1 the return on capital employed is shown as the primary ratio at the extreme left-hand end of the diagram, with the formula:

$$\text{Return on capital employed} = \frac{\text{Profit}}{\text{Assets}} \times 100$$

As in Table 18.1 (1), the assets base here is the *total assets* figure and the *related profit* figure is the *net profit plus debenture interest* figure which the *total assets* have generated. We can therefore calculate the return on capital employed as:

$$\frac{\text{Profit}}{\text{Assets}} \times 100$$

$$= \frac{£161\ 076}{£528\ 346} \times 100 = \underline{30.5\%}$$

Since we know the figure for sales (turnover), this primary ratio can now be divided into two in the following way, as shown by Fig. 18.1.

$$\frac{\text{Profit}}{\text{Assets}} = \frac{\text{Profit}}{\text{Sales}} \times \frac{\text{Sales}}{\text{Assets}}$$

$\dfrac{\text{Profit}}{\text{Sales}}$ is, of course, the net profit percentage, which may be calculated, using the profit figure related to the asset base under discussion, as follows:

$$\text{Net profit percentage} = \frac{\text{Profit}}{\text{Sales}} \times 100$$

$$= \frac{£161\ 076}{£426\ 000} \times 100 = \underline{37.81\%}$$

*Note:* This is slightly different from the net profit percentage calculated in Unit 18.3 because of the use of a different profit figure, related to a different assets base—as in Table 18.1.

$\dfrac{\text{Sales}}{\text{Assets}}$ is called the *asset turnover*. It indicates how many times the asset value is turned over during each period (generally one year) in sales of the product. We have already seen that the total assets are, in fact, of the same value as the total liabilities (i.e. the capital invested) so that the asset turnover could equally well be called the *capital turnover*.

In Fig. 18.2 we can calculate the asset turnover as

$$\frac{\text{Sales}}{\text{Assets}} = \frac{£426\ 000}{£528\ 346} = \underline{0.806\ \text{times}}$$

From the breakdown of the original ratio into two separate parts, it can be seen that these two ratios must be connected. We can show this by repeating the breakdown and then reuniting them.

$$\frac{\text{Profit}}{\text{Assets}} = \frac{\text{Profit}}{\text{Sales}} \times \frac{\text{Sales}}{\text{Assets}}$$

$$= 37.81\% \times 0.806\ \text{times} = \underline{30.5\%}$$

This shows that the return on capital employed is made up of a satisfactory rate of profit (37.81 per cent) but only turning over less than once in a year. This rate of turnover is therefore not very satisfactory, and the return on capital employed could be made more satisfactory if the asset turnover could be raised.

This type of analysis, based on a single set of figures, is not very helpful. It would be more satisfactory if similar calculations could be made over several years to show trends.

### Fixed Asset Turnover and Current Asset Turnover

The overall asset turnover can be further analysed into two parts. The formulae are:

(i) **Fixed asset turnover** $= \dfrac{\text{Sales}}{\text{Fixed assets}}$

The answer shows how many times the capital invested in fixed assets generated sales of the same value during the period. A decline in this turnover rate implies increasing excess capacity, inefficient use of fixed assets because of poor production planning, or, if plant has been expanded in expectation of increased trade, the expected sales have failed to materialize.

The investigation can be carried further by investigating each of the components of fixed assets in the same way—for example, a plant and equipment turnover ratio would be found by the formula: $\dfrac{\text{Sales}}{\text{Plant and equipment}}$

(ii) **Current asset turnover** $= \dfrac{\text{Sales}}{\text{Current assets}}$

This ratio tells us how many times the capital invested in current assets generated sales of the same value during the period. If this rate of turnover declines it means that there is a decline of efficiency somewhere in the system.

This is best investigated by extending the analysis to find the *rate of stock turnover* (see *Success in Principles of Accounting* p. 374) and the *sales/debtors ratio*.

The former can be calculated by either of the formulae given in Fig. 18.1, and shows how rapidly stock is turning over. The sales/debtors ratio, or *rate of debtor collection*, indicates how many times the debtors turn over in the year. Using imaginary figures we might have:

$$\frac{\text{Credit sales}}{\text{Average debtors}} = \frac{£336\,000}{£38\,000} = 8.8 \text{ times in the year.}$$

Dividing this figure into 12 months, 52 weeks or 365 days, we have:

$$12 \div 8.8 = 1.36 \text{ months}$$

$$52 \div 8.8 = 5.9 \text{ weeks}$$

$$365 \div 8.8 = 41.5 \text{ days}$$

The average debtor pays up in 1.36 months, i.e. 5.9 weeks or 41.5 days.

## 18.9    Solvency and Liquidity

Solvency is the ability to pay debts as they fall due. This means, in particular, the ability to pay external creditors, who have supplied goods or services. Other interested parties are the debenture holders, who want to receive their interest on the due date, and shareholders, who look forward to receiving whatever profits are appropriated as dividends by resolution of the company at the Annual General Meeting. It does not follow that because a company is making profits it has cash available to meet its pecuniary obligations. Cash generated by the firm's profit-making activities may have been spent by buying fixed assets, or may have been used to pay up short-term or long-term loans.

These types of expenditure affect the liquidity of the firm's assets. Liquid assets are either in cash form (balances of cash-in-hand or at the bank) or are readily convertible into cash, such as marketable investments. Stock is not liquid, for it is sometimes difficult to find a buyer, and fixed assets are not liquid, by definition. The problem of cash flows is discussed in Unit 19.

**Working Capital**

Working capital is that part of the capital which is required to run the business after the fixed assets have been obtained. It is, therefore, used to finance current assets, that is, to buy or manufacture stock, to finance debtors in the interval between the sale and the payment, and to provide cash as required. However, these activities can often be assisted by short-term credit as when creditors supply goods and payment is delayed. Therefore

Working capital = Current assets − Current liabilities.

Frequently the term *net working capital* is used to designate this figure. The ratio:

$$\frac{\text{Net working capital}}{\text{Sales}} \times 100$$

expresses net working capital as a percentage of sales and shows changes in working capital relative to the sales it is trying to finance. If the volume of business expands but the working capital to finance it is not increased, difficulties may arise in the future about meeting obligations. This is called *over-trading*. If the volume of business contracts, but the working capital to finance it is not reduced, the situation is called *under-trading*.

The ratios which are used for keeping track of liquidity problems are discussed in *Success in Principles of Accounting* (Unit 32.9). They are:

Current ratio = Current assets : Current liabilities

Liquid ratio = Current assets − Stock : Current liabilities

(This is sometimes also called the quick ratio or the acid-test ratio.)

The current ratio should preferably be somewhere near 2:1; twice as much current assets should be available as the possible claims from creditors and other current liabilities.

The liquid ratio should be at least 1:1, in other words, there should be sufficient funds available (cash, balances at the bank and immediately realizable investments) to meet all current obligations.

**Example 18.2**

Expanding Ltd have the following figures included in their final results for the two years shown:

|  | Year 1 £ | Year 2 £ |
|---|---|---|
| Sales | 560 000 | 834 000 |
| *Current assets* | | |
| Stock | 34 000 | 42 500 |
| Debtors | 11 600 | 23 500 |
| Bank balances | 26 000 | 28 500 |
| Cash-in-hand | 850 | 620 |
| Payments in advance | 180 | 250 |
| Current assets | £72 630 | £95 370 |
| *Current liabilities* | £23 500 | £38 000 |

| | | |
|---|---|---|
| Current assets | 72 630 | 95 370 |
| *Less* Current liabilities | 23 500 | 38 000 |
| Net working capital | £49 130 | £57 370 |

The ratios would be calculated as follows:

(i) **Net working capital to sales ratio** $= \dfrac{\text{Net working capital}}{\text{Sales}} \times 100$

Year 1 $\dfrac{£49\,130}{£560\,000} \times 100 = \underline{8.8\%}$

Year 2 $\dfrac{£57\,370}{£834\,000} \times 100 = \underline{6.9\%}$

The ratio shows that the net working capital available has fallen relative to the sales that it has to finance, and therefore needs watching in the future. Anything that can be done to keep cash balances healthy, to collect debts and reduce commitments to creditors should be considered.

(ii) **Current ratio** = Current assets : Current liabilities

Year 1 £72 630 : £23 500 = $\underline{3.1:1}$

Year 2 £95 370 : £38 000 = $\underline{2.5:1}$

The current ratio has fallen but is still more than adequate for the purposes of the business.

(iii) **Liquid ratio** = Current assets − Stock : Current liabilities

Year 1 £38 630 : £23 500 = $\underline{1.6:1}$

Year 2 £52 870 : £38 000 = $\underline{1.4:1}$

Again the ratio has fallen, but it is just about satisfactory at the moment. Management should keep a careful eye on the working capital position over the next few months.

**Table 18.2   Claimants' chart for accounting records**

| Type of claimant (i) | Nature of interest (ii) | Aspects of importance following from column (ii) (iii) | Helpful ratios etc. (iv) |
|---|---|---|---|
| 1. External creditors | Payment for goods or services supplied | (a) Are there enough current assets to pay current liabilities? <br> (b) Are these current assets liquid enough? <br> (c) Are there any prior claims on the assets if the company gets into financial difficulties? <br> (d) Are there any signs of difficulties ahead? | (a) Working capital ratio <br> (b) Liquid ratio <br> (c) Inspect Register of Charges (see Section 95, Companies Act 1948) <br> (d) Examine earnings record over recent years, and directors' report |
| 2. Debenture holders | Payment of interest for duration of the loan and refund of the capital according to the terms of issue | (a) Can the company pay the debenture interest? <br> (b) Is it honouring any arrangements about the eventual repayment (for example, to create a reserve fund)? <br> (c) Are there any signs of decreasing financial standing which might cast doubts on any ability to repay? <br> (d) Are further issues proposed which will have a prior claim over existing claims? | (a) Interest/times covered ratio (see Unit 18.14) <br> (b) Reference may be made to balance sheet and directors' report <br> (c) As above <br> (d) As above, but also inspect the Register of Charges from time to time |
| 3. Bankers | Repayment of any overdraft or loan granted. Security against the overdraft or loan | (a) What is the loan for, and for how long? <br> (b) How is it to be repaid? <br> (c) What security can be offered, and will its value change? <br> (d) Are there any prior rights already in existence? | (a) Keep a check on liquidity (see Unit 18.9) <br> (b) Review the firm's records at regular intervals <br> (c) Keep a check on the asset values and ensure that they do not diminish <br> (d) Check Register of Charges re prior rights |

| | Interest | Questions | Notes |
|---|---|---|---|
| 4. Small investors | Seek a good yield on the investment, and security of capital | (a) The trends in sales and in profits over recent years, and for the future (b) The yield on the investment (and alternative investments) (c) The liquidity position—can dividends be paid or are there cash flow problems? | (a) See Unit 18.15 (b) Earnings per share (see Unit 18.11) (c) Price/earnings ratio (see Unit 18.12) (d) Funds flow statements (see Unit 19) |
| 5. Large investors | Sound profit and growth prospects | (a) All aspects mentioned in this Unit (b) Major surveys for the future of industries and regions will be of interest to them | Sophisticated analysts available to study all aspects |
| 6. Ordinary shareholders | See groups 4 and 5 above | The inability of shareholders in large companies to bring any influence on the boards of directors is a cause of disinterest. It leaves the way open for take-over bids by those who can buy a controlling interest | See 4 and 5 above |
| 7. Employees | Adequacy of wages. Possible profit-sharing scheme for employees. Adequacy of and security of pensions | (a) What proportion of the total rewards went to labour during the period? Were wages adequate? (b) What proportions of the total rewards went to interest and profit? (c) Are pension arrangements satisfactory and are they safe in the event of, say, liquidation? | Distribution of value added concept (see Unit 18.15) |
| 8. Potential take-over bidder | Wishes to secure a controlling interest at a reasonable price | (a) What is the market price of the shares? (b) What is their true value? There may be hidden reserves of which the market is unaware. (These assets are valued below cost and can be sold off at their true value—hence asset stripping.) (c) How disgruntled are the shareholders? (Will they sell cheaply if disillusioned by investment in the company?) (d) Has there been under-trading, i.e. large cash balances not used, which can be put to work profitably elsewhere? | An evaluation of site values and other property. An evaluation relative to the present situation of the bidding company. It is possible that economies of large scale, shared working of facilities, storage space, distribution network, etc. can be achieved |

## 18.10    Claimants on the Organization

Every organization has claimants on it. These claimants have different interests and view the firm's financial situation from different points of view. An accountant may be approached by any one of these parties and requested to report on the affairs of a company, and naturally the client will expect the report to be relevant to his or her particular needs. In order to show the variety of interests, and measures and ratios which would help to throw light on the different aspects involved, a Claimants' Chart is shown in Table 18.2.

## 18.11    Earnings Per Share

When a company makes profits the shareholders expect to receive a dividend, but whether or not they receive one depends on the directors. They have the responsibility of running the company, and will recommend what dividend is to be paid. With preference shares, which are entitled to a fixed rate of dividend in preference to ordinary shareholders, it frequently happens that the directors will recommend the preference dividend to be paid in full. In prosperous times they will also recommend a reasonable dividend to be paid to the ordinary shareholders, but this is rarely the whole of the profit earned — if only because it is impossible to divide a sum of money exactly equally among a large number of shareholders. Thus, a profit of £29 735 to be divided among a shareholding of 100 000 £1 shares comes to 29.735 pence per share, and this cannot be paid out in legal tender which only goes down to pence and halfpence. Usually, a reasonable dividend is recommended and the rest is left in reserves of one sort or another.

There is, therefore, a difference between the dividend per share and the earnings per share and this difference gives an indication of the dividend policy of the directors. The following example illustrates two different dividend policies.

**Example 18.3**
The following figures relate to the results of two firms, Silver Ltd and Gold Ltd.

|  | Silver Ltd | Gold Ltd |
|---|---|---|
|  | £ | £ |
| Ordinary shareholding (shares of £1) | 100 000 | 250 000 |
| Profits | 38 000 | 95 000 |
| Recommended dividend | 8% | 25% |

    (a)  What are the earnings per share?
    (b)  What are the dividends per share?
    (c)  Comment on the dividend policy.

$$\text{Earnings per share} = \frac{\text{Profits}}{\text{Shareholding}}$$

| | Silver Ltd | Gold Ltd |
|---|---|---|
| | £ 38 000 | £ 95 000 |
| | 100 000 | 250 000 |
| Earnings: | 38 pence per share | 38 pence per share |

| | Silver Ltd | Gold Ltd |
|---|---|---|
| Dividends per share: | 8 pence per share (8%) | 25 pence per share (25%) |
| Retained earnings: | 30 pence per share | 13 pence per share |

While the earnings of the shares are the same, the distribution of earnings is very different, 8 per cent in one case and 25 per cent in the other. Clearly, the dividend policy of Silver Ltd is more restrained than that of the directors of Gold Ltd. The shareholders of Silver Ltd are forced to take a small dividend and see most of their profits ploughed back into the company. They may well be disgruntled as a result and open to offers by a take-over bidder who wishes to acquire their shares. The shareholders of Gold Ltd will be much more enthusiastic about the company, and less willing to see the directors replaced by another board.

Some shareholders, who have an adequate income already and are paying high rates of income tax, may actually prefer to have the earnings of their shares retained as reserves, and used to expand the business. They will prefer not to receive high dividends, but to take their profits in the form of an increased value of the shares when they eventually sell them—that is, as a capital gain. To prevent the avoidance of tax in very small companies controlled by less than five persons, there are special rules about the retention of profits, which make a proportion of them taxable at the higher rates whether they have been distributed or not.

## 18.12   Price/Earnings Ratio and Dividend Cover

When attempting to compare various classes of ordinary shares, the market price of the share has to be considered. While dividends are normally expressed as a percentage of the nominal value of the capital, the investor cannot buy shares at par except on the first day of issue (and often not even then). Thus, an investor who buys a £1 share in a popular company may pay much more—say £4—for the share. If the company then declares dividends of 20 per cent, the *dividend yield* is only 5 per cent to this particular shareholder. If the earnings retained are taken into account as well, it is possible to calculate an *earnings yield*. The link between dividend yield and earnings yield can be shown by calculating the *dividend cover*. Thus, if only 25 per cent of the earnings are actually distributed as dividend the dividend cover would be four times covered, since the actual profits are four times as great as the amount distributed to the shareholders.

Another method of showing this link is to calculate a price/earnings ratio. The calculation can be made using either the total value of the shares on the market, and the total earnings, or the value of a single share and the earnings per share. Thus, if a company which has earned £500 000 has two million shares on the market, with each £1 share valued at £2, the calculations would be as follows:

$$\text{Total market value of shares} = £4\text{m}$$
$$\text{Total earnings} = £500\ 000$$
$$\text{Earnings per share} = \frac{£500\ 000}{2\ 000\ 000} = 25 \text{ pence per share}$$

Price/Earnings (P/E) Ratio under the two methods would then be:

(a)  Total market value : Total earnings = £4m : £500 000 = 8:1

(b)  Price per share : Earnings per share = £2 : 25 pence = 8:1

P/E ratios have become the usual method of comparing the equities of companies; the lower the figure in the first part of the ratio, the better the return on the investment. Thus, a P/E ratio of 1:1 represents a 100 per cent return, while the P/E ratio of 8:1 above represents a $12\frac{1}{2}$ per cent return.

## 18.13   Capital Gearing

Companies finance their affairs in a variety of ways: by issuing ordinary or preference shares, by issuing debentures, by short-term loans, and so on. Since debentures offer great advantages at present over preference shares, they are more commonly used to raise fixed interest capital. (Strictly speaking, preference shares should be called fixed dividend capital.) The ratio of debentures to ordinary shares, i.e. of fixed interest funds to equity, is called *capital gearing* and has implications for investors. Thus, if the gearing is low (fixed interest funds small relative to equity), the effects on the amounts of profit becoming available for the investor in ordinary shares will be different from the effects when the gearing is high (fixed interest funds large relative to equity). In the first case, most of the funds needed to run the company are being obtained by the issue of ordinary shares. In the second case, most of the funds are coming from the issue of debentures.

Consider two companies with the capital structure shown below:

|  | A Ltd | B Ltd |
|---|---|---|
|  | £ | £ |
| 8% Debentures | 200 000 | 800 000 |
| Ordinary shares | 800 000 | 200 000 |
| Gearing (Fixed funds : Equity) | 1 : 4 | 4 : 1 |
|  | Low gear | High gear |

In a three-year period, profits vary as follows:

|  | A Ltd | | | B Ltd | | |
|---|---|---|---|---|---|---|
|  | Year 1 | Year 2 | Year 3 | Year 1 | Year 2 | Year 3 |
|  | £ | £ | £ | £ | £ | £ |
| Profits | 200 000 | 150 000 | 75 000 | 200 000 | 150 000 | 75 000 |
| Debenture interest (8%) | 16 000 | 16 000 | 16 000 | 64 000 | 64 000 | 64 000 |
| Net profit | 184 000 | 134 000 | 59 000 | 136 000 | 86 000 | 11 000 |
| Tax (say 50%) | 92 000 | 67 000 | 29 500 | 68 000 | 43 000 | 5 500 |
| Profit after tax | £92 000 | £67 000 | £29 500 | £68 000 | £43 000 | £5 500 |
| Rate of earnings on ordinary shares | 11.5% | 8.38% | 3.69% | 34% | 21.5% | 2.75% |

It can be seen that the percentage rate varies much more with the highly geared company (B Ltd) than with the low-geared company (A Ltd). Ordinary shareholders, therefore, avoid highly geared companies when the economy is depressed and prospects of profitability are poor, but favour them when the economy is booming, since there are very good prospects of a high dividend. For example, if in Year 4 profits rose to £300 000, the respective rates would be 17.75 per cent (A Ltd) and 59 per cent (B Ltd). The change in earnings rate over the previous year would be 4.8 times in the low-geared company, and 21.5 times in the high-geared company.

## 18.14   Interest (Times Covered)

Debenture holders are, naturally, concerned about whether a company is likely to have any difficulty in paying the debenture interest. The interest (times covered) ratio can be used to discover a company's capacity to pay its fixed interest charges. The formula is:

$$\text{Interest (times covered)} = \frac{\text{Profit (after tax)} + \text{Interest paid}}{\text{Interest paid}}$$

Thus A Ltd in the illustration used in Unit 18.13, had interest covers as follows:

$$\text{Year 1} \quad \frac{92\,000 + 16\,000}{16\,000} = \frac{108\,000}{16\,000} = 6.75 \text{ times}$$

$$\text{Year 3} \quad \frac{29\,500 + 16\,000}{16\,000} = \frac{45\,500}{16\,000} = 2.8 \text{ times}$$

While B Ltd had interest covers as follows:

$$\text{Year 1} \quad \frac{68\,000 + 64\,000}{64\,000} = \frac{132\,000}{64\,000} = 2.06 \text{ times}$$

$$\text{Year 3} \quad \frac{5\,500 + 64\,000}{64\,000} = \frac{69\,500}{64\,000} = 1.09 \text{ times}$$

## 18.15    Added Value Statements

The traditional method of showing the success or otherwise of a business is to prepare final accounts which include the Trading and Profit and Loss Account and an Appropriation Account. These accounts *show how the sales revenue has been applied* and are prepared mainly for the benefit of the management, the shareholders and the Inland Revenue. The final accounts are a conventional report on the company's activities, which were considered satisfactory in the past, but the final accounts disclose very little about the amounts paid out between the point where the income from sales was achieved and the point where the residue of that income was withdrawn as profits by the owners. The published accounts may be good accounting statements, but to those without accounting skills they may be difficult to understand.

In the interest of good industrial and public relations it is now considered essential not only to report to shareholders but also to other groups such as employees and consumers.

What is meant by *added value*? It is, of course, used in everyday language because of the system of value added tax — a method of taxing goods and services as they change hands from one person to another. As goods pass through the various stages of production, value is added to them, until they end up as finished goods ready for the consumer. Any business receives its raw materials, components, and so on at a certain price, and sells them at a higher price, the difference being the added value. This added value is the reward earned by the factors of production which have been employed in that particular firm. In economic terms, some of the added value will go as rent to the landlord, a great deal of it will go as wages to the workers, the factor 'labour'. The factor 'capital' will be paid interest for the services it has supplied, and the final part of the added value is the residue of profit which goes to those who took the risks of the enterprise — the ordinary shareholders. In this way an added value statement accounts to the whole community for the distribution throughout society of the added value created. Where did the wealth actually go?

Many companies now include value added statements with their annual reports, as it is recognized that these show how the sales revenue has been applied in a way which is easily understood by all those interested in the company's activities.

The information supplied, in addition to the cost of materials and services, is given under four headings:

(i) amounts paid to employees and in providing amenities for them;
(ii) amounts reinvested for the replacement of assets and the expansion of the business;
(iii) amounts paid to central and local government;
(iv) amounts paid to those who provide the capital.

A value added statement should show clearly the following elements:

(*a*) The amount paid for raw materials, goods and services, which forms a large percentage of the income from sales.

(b) The proportion of added value received by employees in the form of wages, salaries and other rewards is evidence of the amounts received by those who give their time and effort to the business.

(c) The amount paid to government (which may appear in the form of notes) in respect of corporation tax, rates, National Insurance contributions, import duty, value added tax, income tax deducted from employees' wages and salaries, and the amount deducted from interest on debenture stocks.

(d) The amount paid to shareholders and the holders of debentures.

(e) The amount reinvested in the company, including retained profits, depreciation and deferred tax.

The distribution of added value can be shown as in Fig. 18.3.

|  | £(000s) | Pence per £ of sales |
|---|---|---|
| Sales | 2 325 | 100 |
| Less Cost of materials and services | 1 651 | 71 |
| Added value | 674 | 29 |

Added value was distributed in the following ways:

|  | % of Added value | Pence |
|---|---|---|
| Rewards to employees | 28 | 8.0 |
| Amounts payable to central and local government | 48 | 14.0 |
| To providers of capital | 10 | 2.9 |
| For replacement of assets and expansion of the business | 14 | 4.1 |
| Total per £ of sales | 100 | 29.0 |

*Fig. 18.3 Example of display of distribution of added value*

Using the same sales value and added value a more detailed statement is shown in Fig. 18.4.

Sales value was applied in the following ways:

| | Year 19.1 | | | Year 19.0 | | |
|---|---|---|---|---|---|---|
| | £(000s) | £(000s) | % | £(000s) | £(000s) | % |
| (a) To pay the suppliers of materials and services | | 1 651 | 71.0 | | 1 423 | 72.2 |
| (b) As added value | | | | | | |
| *For the benefit of employees* | | | | | | |
| Wages and salaries | 186 | | | 167 | | |
| *Less* Income tax and National Insurance | 40 | | | 42 | | |
| | 146 | | | 125 | | |
| Pension scheme (non-contributory) | 28 | | | 22 | | |
| Profit-sharing | 4 | | | 3 | | |
| Welfare and provision of amenities | 8 | | | 7 | | |
| | | 186 | 8.0 | | 157 | 8.0 |
| *To central and local government* | | 326 | 14.0 | | 269 | 13.6 |
| *To providers of capital* | | | | | | |
| Interest on loan capital | 16 | | | 13 | | |
| *Less* Income tax | 2 | | | 2 | | |
| | 14 | | | 11 | | |
| Dividends to shareholders | 53 | | | 42 | | |
| | | 67 | 2.9 | | 53 | 2.7 |
| *For replacement of assets and expansion of the business* | | | | | | |
| Depreciation | 21 | | | 18 | | |
| Retained profits | 74 | | | 51 | | |
| | | 95 | 4.1 | | 69 | 3.5 |
| *Sales revenue* | | £2 325 | 100% | | £1 971 | 100% |

*Fig. 18.4 Distribution of added value*

When there is a source of income from investments and associated companies, or profits and losses on foreign exchange, the value added by manufacturing and trading is adjusted before dealing with the distribution of added value, under the headings of (a) employees (b) government (c) providers of capital and (d) reinvestment in the business.

The added value statement is an effective form of communication which focuses attention on the major areas of finance and keeps everybody adequately informed. An actual presentation from the accounts of Bass Ltd is reproduced by courtesy of the directors in Fig. 18.5.

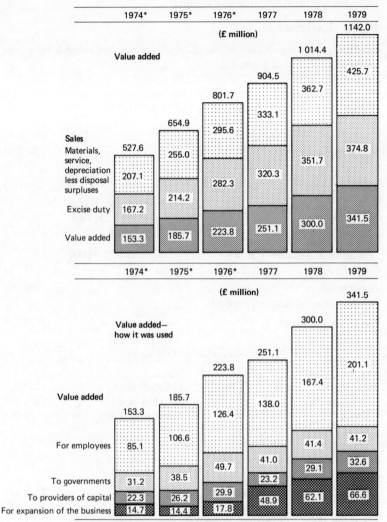

| | 1974* | 1975* | 1976* | 1977 | 1978 | 1979 |
|---|---|---|---|---|---|---|
| | | | (£ million) | | | 1142.0 |

**Value added** 1014.4, 904.5, 801.7, 654.9, 527.6

425.7, 362.7, 333.1, 295.6, 255.0

**Sales**
Materials, service, depreciation less disposal surpluses: 207.1, 214.2, 282.3, 320.3, 351.7, 374.8

Excise duty: 167.2

Value added: 153.3, 185.7, 223.8, 251.1, 300.0, 341.5

| | 1974* | 1975* | 1976* | 1977 | 1978 | 1979 |
|---|---|---|---|---|---|---|
| | | | (£ million) | | | 341.5 |

**Value added—how it was used**
300.0, 251.1, 223.8, 201.1, 185.7, 167.4, 153.3, 138.0, 126.4

**Value added**

For employees: 85.1, 106.6, 41.0, 41.4, 41.2

To governments: 31.2, 38.5, 49.7, 23.2, 29.1, 32.6

To providers of capital: 22.3, 26.2, 29.9, 48.9, 62.1, 66.6

For expansion of the business: 14.7, 14.4, 17.8

*Before change in accounting policy for deferred taxation

*Fig. 18.5 A value added statement* (reproduced by courtesy of Bass Ltd)

*Notes:*

(i) **Value added.** Sales exclude VAT, which is collected on behalf of governments. In 1979, sales totalled £1 142 million. However, £374.8 million had to be paid out in Excise Duty directly to governments, and a further £425.7 million was needed to pay the group's suppliers of the raw materials, goods and services needed to make, sell and distribute its products. This figure includes the wear and tear on assets and is reduced by surpluses on disposals of assets. After charging these amounts there was £341.5 million left. This is the value added.

(ii) **How was the value added used?** The biggest proportion went to pay the wages and other costs of employing people. It also provided the money for dividends and taxation and was a vital source of funds for investment in the business.

## 18.16   Exercises

1. Discuss the significance of actual profit figures and relative figures in assessing company performance.

2. The following is a summary or the final accounts of Trevor Nash (Cambridge) Ltd for the year ending December 31, 19...

|  | £ | £ |
|---|---|---|
| Net sales: Cash |  | 300 000 |
| Credit |  | 128 000 |
|  |  | 428 000 |
| Stock at January 1, 19.. | 26 240 |  |
| Purchases | 237 500 |  |
|  | 263 740 |  |
| *Less* Stock at December 31, 19.. | 35 000 |  |
| Cost of sales |  | 228 740 |
| Gross profit |  | 199 260 |
| Selling and administration expenses |  | 88 722 |
| Net profit before tax |  | £110 538 |

Balance sheet as at December 31, 19..

|  | £ |  | £ |
|---|---|---|---|
| *Fixed assets* | 288 175 | Ordinary shares | 250 000 |
| *Current assets* |  | Revenue reserves | 155 339 |
| Stock | 35 000 | Current liabilities | 37 054 |
| Debtors | 11 500 |  |  |
| Investments | 40 000 |  |  |
| Cash | 67 718 |  |  |
|  | 154 218 |  |  |
|  | £442 393 |  | £442 393 |

From the above information, calculate:

(*a*) the rate of stock turnover;
(*b*) working capital ratio;
(*c*) liquid capital ratio;
(*d*) debtors' turnover and average credit period taken, given that the average debtors are £11 000;
(*e*) return on total assets employed;
(*f*) the ordinary shareholders' interest in the company;
(*g*) the return on the ordinary shareholders' interest (disregarding tax).

# Sources and Applications of Funds

## 19.1 Final Accounts and Funds Flow

The Trading, Profit and Loss Account and the balance sheet are conventional statements which may satisfy the needs of many interested persons but they fail to disclose certain facts connected with cash flow and the movement of funds. The information provided is insufficient to enable us to decide whether the profits and funds have been used wisely. Further information is required in order to show how effective management has been in the control of income and expenditure, and the traditional final accounts must be supplemented by a statement to indicate the funds available during the operating period and how they have been utilized.

## 19.2 Statement of Standard Accounting Practice No. 10

SSAP 10 was issued in 1975 and applies to all enterprises other than small businesses with a turnover or gross income less than £25 000 per annum. Its object is to establish the practice of providing Source and Application of Funds Statements as part of audited accounts. These statements reveal the movements in capital, assets and liabilities during the year, and their effect on the net liquid funds. A minimum standard of disclosure is laid down.

The information to be disclosed consists of:

(a) profit or loss for the period;

(b) adjustments for items not using (or providing) funds;

(c) dividends paid;

(d) acquisitions and disposals of fixed and non-current assets;

(e) funds raised by increasing the issued capital, or funds expended in its redemption;

(f) funds raised by increasing, or expended in repaying or redeeming medium- or long-term loans;

(g) an analysis of the changes in working capital;

(h) movements in net liquid funds.

Among the items listed above, two require explanation.

(i) **Net liquid funds.** These consist of cash at the bank and in hand, and cash equivalents (e.g. investments held as current assets) less bank overdrafts and other borrowings repayable within one year of the accounting date.

(ii) **Adjustments for items not using or providing funds.** This refers to non-cash items where the item is an internal transaction, such as depreciation which does not involve a use of funds. When depreciation is charged to the Profit and Loss Accounts, it reduces the profits available for distribution but there is no outflow of cash as with other expenses charged to Profit and Loss Account.

The funds are still available within the system, and increase liquidity. It is therefore important to remember that the total depreciation charged for the year has to be added to the net profit before tax in order to obtain the total funds generated from operations.

## 19.3  Preparation of a Statement of Source and Application of Funds

The details for this statement are extracted from the Profit and Loss Account, the balance sheet and the balance sheet for the previous year.

### Definition of Funds

Every business has a cash flow, but it is incorrect to assume that at the point of sale the balance of cash is increased by the amount of the profit, as this only applies when all transactions are on a cash basis. As soon as credit trading with debtors and creditors is introduced the situation changes, and is further complicated when cash provided by profits is used to increase stocks or to purchase fixed assets. All these are flows of funds or movements of financial resources which affect the working capital. In preparing the statement we analyse the flow of funds by dealing with the changes which have taken place between the beginning and end of the year.

Imagine that on January 1, 19.1 £100 000 is invested in a trading company.

### Bank Account

| 19.1 | £ |
|---|---|
| Jan. 1 Capital | 100 000 |

### Capital Account

|  |  | 19.1 | £ |
|---|---|---|---|
|  |  | Jan. 1 Bank | 100 000 |

The *source of funds* is represented by the credit balance in the Capital Account and the *application of funds* (use of funds) is shown as a debit in the Bank Account. If, at the end of the year, no trading or transactions have taken place and on January 1, 19.2, a further £50 000 is invested, the capital becomes £150 000 and the balance at bank is £150 000. An increase in a credit balance is a source of funds (£50 000) and an increase in a debit balance is an application of funds (£50 000). However, this is only half the story. A comparison can be made between the two years to provide the details for the statement.

| | | Year 19.1 | Year 19.2 | Difference |
|---|---|---|---|---|
| | | £ | £ | £ |
| *Liabilities* | Capital | 100 000 | 150 000 | +50 000 (Source) |
| *Assets* | Bank | 100 000 | 150 000 | +50 000 (Application) |

Statement of Source and Application of Funds
(for year ended December 31, 19.2)

| Source of funds: | £ |
|---|---|
| Capital | 50 000 |
| Application of funds: | |
| Bank | 50 000 |

If the contribution of extra capital is a source of funds, the repayment of capital must be the reverse, an application of funds, while the source of funds for the repayment must be the Bank Account, which consequently has a decreased balance. A full record of sources and applications of funds therefore takes account of movements in both directions and the difference between two balance sheets can be shown as:

| *Assets* | *Liabilities* |
|---|---|
| Increase = Application of funds | Increase = Source of funds |
| Decrease = Source of funds | Decrease = Application of funds |

Arranging a bank loan to purchase machinery is a source of funds which leads to an increase in liabilities. The purchase of the machinery is an application of funds which leads to an increase in assets. The repayment of the loan decreases the liabilities. The loan disappears (an application of funds) and the cash at bank is reduced. Cash, an asset, is the source of funds, and is used to extinguish the loan.

*Book-keeping entries and their effect on the flow of funds*
 (*a*) Debits which reduce liabilities are applications.
 (*b*) Debits which increase assets are applications.
 (*c*) Credits which increase liabilities are sources.
 (*d*) Credits which reduce assets are sources.
The rule is: debits are applications, credits are sources.

**Example 19.1**
January 1: Wages due £1 000, paid January 5
January 5: Stock £1 000, purchased on credit

Wages Account (see (*a*) above)

| 19.. | | £ | 19.. | | £ |
|---|---|---|---|---|---|
| Jan. 5 | Bank | 1 000 | Jan. 1 | Amount due | 1 000 |

Bank Account (see (*d*) above)

| 19.. | | £ | 19.. | | £ |
|---|---|---|---|---|---|
| Jan. 1 | Balance | 30 000 | Jan. 5 | Wages | 1 000 |

Stock Account (see (*b*) above)

| 19.. | | £ | 19.. |
|---|---|---|---|
| Jan. 1 | Balance | 10 000 | |
| Jan. 5 | Creditor | 1 000 | |

### Creditor's Account (see (c) above)

| | 19.. | £ |
|---|---|---|
| | Jan. 1 Balance | 15 000 |
| | Jan. 5 Stock | 1 000 |

*Liabilities*

| | Jan. 1 | Jan. 5 | Changes | |
|---|---|---|---|---|
| | £ | £ | £ | |
| Capital | 24 000 | 24 000 | — | |
| Wages due | 1 000 | — | −1 000 | (Application) |
| Creditors | 15 000 | 16 000 | +1 000 | (Source) |
| | £40 000 | £40 000 | — | |

*Assets*

| | £ | £ | £ | |
|---|---|---|---|---|
| Bank | 30 000 | 29 000 | −1 000 | (Source) |
| Stock | 10 000 | 11 000 | +1 000 | (Application) |
| | £40 000 | £40 000 | — | |

It can be seen that funds have been applied to pay the accrued wages and to increase the amount of stock, and the *source* of these funds is cash at bank and the creditors who are providing the business with funds. A similar situation exists when there are debtors, but in this case funds are *applied* (used) to accommodate the debtors until they pay for goods or services.

Sometimes there is a transfer between different liabilities or different assets by an increase in one item and a decrease in another. For example, when fixed assets are sold for cash, there is a reduction in total value of fixed assets and the net liquid funds, and working capital is increased.

Before considering an actual example of the preparation of a statement of source and application of funds, it is helpful to list the activities which provide a source of funds, and those which show an application of funds.

| Activities which produce a source of funds | Transactions and changes shown as: |
|---|---|
| Capital introduced | The original capital provided by owners, partners, and shareholders |
| Additional capital received | Increased capital representing further investment by the owners |
| Profit from operations | Net profit as shown in the Profit and Loss Account, adjusted for items which are not a movement of funds, such as a profit or loss on the sale of fixed assets, or depreciation on fixed assets |

| | |
|---|---|
| Long-term borrowing | New loans or debentures or increases in these items |
| Short-term borrowing | New funds or an increase in borrowing |
| Sale of assets other than current assets | Decrease in value of fixed assets, investments and loans to others |
| Movement in current assets | Decrease in current assets |
| Movement in current liabilities | Increase in current liabilities |
| **Activities which show an application of funds** | **Transactions and changes shown as:** |
| Loss from operations | Loss as shown in Profit and Loss Account adjusted for items which are not a movement of funds |
| Repayment of long-term loans and debentures | Decrease in long-term liabilities |
| Purchase of fixed assets and investments and loans made to others | An increase in fixed assets, investments and loans to others |
| Repayment of short-term borrowing | Reduction or elimination of short-term borrowing, shown by a reduction in current liabilities |
| Introduction of or addition to a current asset | Increase in current assets |
| Withdrawal of profits and cash by owners and partners; dividends and repayment of capital to shareholders | Payments in form of drawings or dividends. Reduction in share capital |

When preparing a funds statement, the information which is required is readily available. In examination work, however, you may have to adjust the figures provided in order to obtain the correct amounts of profit on operations, profit on sale of fixed assets, depreciation charged, and so on.

The procedure for selecting the items and amounts for the Statement is as follows:

(*a*) Compare the two balance sheets and indicate by plus or minus signs the changes which have occurred. Ensure that the amounts are correct by adding the value of the changes in each section of the balance sheet in order to reconcile the total change in liabilities with the total change in the value of the assets.

(*b*) Begin the statement with the *Net profit before taxation* arising from trading, then add or deduct from this figure profit or losses on *Extraordinary items* such as exchange differences, goodwill written off, fire losses, etc.

(*c*) The next section is headed *Adjustments for items not involving a movement of funds*. Depreciation has to be added back as no movement of funds take place when the depreciation entries are made. Profits and losses on sale of fixed assets or sale of investments have to be dealt with in a similar way. The profit or loss does not involve a movement of funds; it is the value of the actual sale which has to be recorded and this is shown later under the heading *Funds from other sources*. A loss on the sale of assets (which has reduced the profit, but not the funds available) must be added back, while a profit on the sale of assets (which has increased the profit, but not the funds available) must be deducted. The total of this section is shown as *Total funds generated from operations*.

(*d*) Now deal with the *Funds from other sources* such as the proceeds of share issues or new loans. Also, show the amount realized on the sale of investments or fixed assets, and any miscellaneous items providing funds. This completes the section on *Sources of funds*.

(*e*) The applications of funds are as follows:

(i) Include the change in the cost of fixed assets to arrive at the purchase price of fixed assets. If there have been disposals, ignore the change in balance sheet values and refer to the information provided on the movement of fixed assets.

(ii) Include the value of any investments purchased, loans repaid and any redemption of shares or debentures.

(iii) With dividends, show the actual amount paid which is probably the previous year's proposed dividend.

(iv) With taxation, show the actual amount paid. This may be the taxation in the previous year's accounts, but when the amount is not obvious, proceed as follows: pick up the current and deferred tax from the previous year and the tax debit (including amounts of over- or under-provision for previous years) from this year's Profit and Loss Account. The tax paid can now be found by deducting the total amount of tax shown in the balance sheet for the current year.

These entries will complete the applications and the total can be deducted from the *Source of funds*. The difference is the *Change in working capital* representing the surplus (or deficit) of funds. This amount can be verified by finding the difference between the working capital in the two balance sheets after deducting taxation and dividends.

(*f*) We must now provide an analysis of the increase or decrease in working capital including the movement in net liquid funds. To obtain this, refer to the changes in current assets and current liabilities, but ignore taxation and dividends.

## 19.4   An Example Illustrating the Procedure in the Preparation of a Statement of Source and Application of Funds

A company makes a profit of £82 000 for the year ending December 31, 19.8. This amount was arrived at after allowing for depreciation, but before allowing for taxation and appropriations. It represents the profit on trading and an amount which was due to the disposal of fixed assets.

The following information relates to the purchase and disposal of machinery and plant during the year ended December 31, 19.8: (*a*) purchases £45 000; (*b*) sales £15 000; (*c*) book value of sales £14 000. An extension to buildings and premises was completed at the end of the year. We can now compare the two balance sheets in order to establish the changes which have taken place since the beginning of the year.

Balance sheets

| December 31, 19.7 | | | | December 31, 19.8 | | | |
| Cost £(000s) | Deprec-iation £(000s) | Value £(000s) | Assets employed: *Fixed assets* | Cost £(000s) | Deprec-iation £(000s) | Value £(000s) | Net changes £(000s) |
|---|---|---|---|---|---|---|---|
| 40 | – | 40 | Goodwill | 40 | 4 | 36 | – 4 |
| 250 | 5 | 245 | Land and buildings | 270 | 10 | 260 | + 15 |
| 300 | 58 | 242 | Machinery and plant | 325 | 88 | 237 | – 5 |
| 69 | 15 | 54 | Fixtures and fittings | 69 | 17 | 52 | – 2 |
| £659 | £78 | 581 | | £704 | £119 | 585 | + 4 |
| | | 68 | Investments | | | 105 | + 37 |
| | | | *Current assets* | | | | |
| | | 47 | Stock | | | 63 | + 16 |
| | | 50 | Debtors | | | 65 | + 15 |
| | | 1 | Rates in advance | | | – | – 1 |
| | | 10 | Cash at bank | | | – | – 10 |
| | | 108 | | | | 128 | — |
| | | £757 | | | | £818 | +£61 |

| | | | Financed by | | | |
| | | £(000s) | *Share capital* | | £(000s) | £(000s) |
|---|---|---|---|---|---|---|
| | | 250 | Ordinary shares | | 250 | – |
| | | 50 | Capital reserves | 100 | | + 50 |
| | | 62 | Revenue reserves | 18 | | – 44 |
| | | 112 | | | 118 | — |
| | | 362 | | | 368 | + 6 |
| | | 200 | 7% Preference shares | | 150 | – 50 |
| | | 562 | | | 518 | – 44 |
| | | | *Long-term liability* | | | |
| | | 50 | 9% Debentures | | 70 | + 20 |
| | | | *Current liabilities* | | | |
| | | 80 | Creditors | 89 | | + 9 |
| | | 35 | Taxation | 40 | | + 5 |
| | | 30 | Dividends proposed | 36 | | + 6 |
| | | Nil | Bank overdraft | 65 | | + 65 |
| | | 145 | | | 230 | — |
| | | £757 | | | £818 | +£61 |

Additional information – Movement of assets

| *Machinery* | December 31, 19.7 £ | 19.8 Purchases £ | 19.8 Sales £ | 19.8 Depreciation £ | December 31, 19.8 £ |
|---|---|---|---|---|---|
| Cost | 300 000 | + 45 000 | – 20 000 | – | = 325 000 |
| *Less* Depreciation | 58 000 | | – 6 000 | + 36 000 | = 88 000 |
| Net | £242 000 | +£45 000 | – 14 000 | 36 000 | =£237 000 |
| Selling price | | | 15 000 | | |
| Profit on sale | | | £1 000 | | |

(*continued overleaf*)

*Depreciation*

| | |
|---|---:|
| Goodwill | 4 000 |
| Buildings | 5 000 |
| Fixtures and fittings | 2 000 |
| | 47 000 |
| *Add* Profit available for distribution | 82 000 |
| | 129 000 |
| *Less* Profit on sale of machinery | 1 000 |
| Profit from operations *plus* Depreciation | £128 000 |

Comparison of the balance sheets discloses the following changes:

| | *Changes*<br>£ | | *Source*<br>£ | *Application*<br>£ |
|---|---|---|---:|---:|
| Goodwill | − 4 000 | No movement of funds for the £4 000 written off. It must be included with the depreciation and added to profit to find the total generated from operations. | | |
| Land and buildings | + 15 000 | Extension to buildings £20 000 (£270 000—£250 000) is an application. Depreciation of £5 000 is not a movement of funds, and, as described above, must be added back to profit. £20 000 applied *less* £5 000 depreciation =£15 000. | | 20 000 |
| Machinery and plant | − 5 000 | See Movement of assets for details of changes. Expenditure of £45 000 is an application and £15 000 from sales is a source. Depreciation £36 000 is not a movement of funds, but must be added back to profit as above. | 15 000 | 45 000 |
| Fixtures and fittings | − 2 000 | No movement of funds for depreciation which must be added back to profit. | | |
| Investments | + 37 000 | An increase indicates a purchase of investments and is an application. | | 37 000 |
| | | | *c/fwd*  £15 000 | £102 000 |

| | Changes | | Source | Application |
|---|---|---|---|---|
| | £ | b/fwd | £15 000 | £102 000 |
| Stock | +16 000 | An increase in stock is an application but is shown in the Statement of Source and Application of Funds as an increase with the increases and decreases in working capital. | | 16 000 |
| Debtors | +15 000 | Another increase which is an application and is shown with the working capital. | | 15 000 |
| Rates in advance | − 1 000 | This was a movement of funds in the previous year as an application. In the current year the profit figure is reduced but there is no movement of funds and this amount is now a source, shown as a decrease in working capital. | 1 000 | |
| Cash at bank | −10 000 | A reduction in cash is a source and a movement in net liquid funds which decreases the working capital. | 10 000 | |
| | | The previous items are assets employed. This next section deals with the financing of those assets. In this section a decrease in liabilities is an application. | | |
| Preference shares | −50 000 | This indicates a repayment or outflow of funds and is an application. | | 50 000 |
| Capital reserves | +50 000 | This is the creation of a capital redemption reserve fund to offset the reduction of capital caused by the redemption of preference shares (Section 58 of the Companies Act 1948). There is no movement of funds. | | |
| | | c/fwd | £26 000 | £183 000 |

|  | Changes | | Source | Appli-cation |
|---|---|---|---|---|
|  | £ | b/fwd | £26 000 | £183 000 |
| Revenue reserves | −44 000 | The decrease represents the capitalization of revenue reserves (£50 000) offset by an appropriation of profits (£6 000). The former does not involve a flow of funds. The latter can be ignored since it is included in the profit figure. | | |
| Debentures | + 20 000 | An increase is a source of funds | 20 000 | |
| Creditors | + 9 000 | The creditors are financing the business by a further £9 000. They are a source of funds when there is an increase, but the amount is not shown as a source but as a decrease in working capital. | 9 000 | |
| Taxation | + 5 000 | The provision for taxation is not a movement in the current year and £40 000 is included in the profit before tax. The movement or application is £35 000 paid in respect of the previous year. Ignore the change of £5 000. | | 35 000 |
| Proposed dividend | + 6 000 | The proposed £36 000 is not a movement and is included with profit. The movement is £30 000 as an application for the amount proposed in the previous year. Ignore the change of £6 000. | | 30 000 |
| Bank overdraft | + 65 000 | Like creditors above, this is a source of funds which is included as a movement in net liquid funds and decreases the working capital. | 65 000 | |
|  | | c/fwd | £120 000 | £248 000 |

|  | Changes |  | Source | Appli-cation |
|---|---|---|---|---|
|  | £ | b/fwd | £120 000 | £248 000 |
| Profit | +82 000 | Profit before taxation is a source of funds. The £82 000 is adjusted by deducting £1 000 for the profit on sale of machinery as this is not a funds flow. This is then increased by the non-cash item, depreciation at £47 000. | 128 000 | |
|  |  |  | £248 000 | £248 000 |

We are now in a position to summarize these points in a Statement of Source and Application of Funds.

### Statement of Source and Application of Funds
### (for year ended December 31, 19.8)

| | £ | £ |
|---|---|---|
| Sources of funds | | |
| Net profit before taxation | | 82 000 |
| *Adjustment for items not involving a movement of funds* | | |
| Depreciation | 47 000 | |
| Profit on sale of machinery | (1 000) | |
| | | 46 000 |
| *Total funds generated from operations* | | 128 000 |
| *Funds from other sources* | | |
| Issue of debentures | 20 000 | |
| Sale of machinery | 15 000 | |
| | | 35 000 |
| *Total extra funds made available* | | 163 000 |
| *Application of these funds* | | |
| Extension to buildings | 20 000 | |
| Purchase of machinery | 45 000 | |
| Purchase of investments | 37 000 | |
| Repayment of preference shares | 50 000 | |
| Dividends paid | 30 000 | |
| Payment of taxation | 35 000 | |
| | | 217 000 |
| *Excess of application of funds* | | £(54 000) |

(The excess has to be financed by change in
   working capital)
Increase (decrease) in working capital

| | |
|---|---:|
| Increase in stock | 16 000 |
| Increase in debtors | 15 000 |
| Increase in creditors excluding taxation and proposed dividends | (9 000) |
| Rates in advance | (1 000) |

*Increase in net current assets (apart from liquid items)*  21 000
Financed by movements in net liquid funds

| | | |
|---|---:|---:|
| Decrease of cash at bank | £10 000 | |
| Bank overdraft | £65 000 | (75 000) |

*Increased indebtedness to finance excess expenditure on fixed*
                                                    *assets*   £(54 000)

It should be noted that the amounts paid in respect of dividends and
taxation are included among the applications but the provisions for dividends
and taxation are excluded as individual amounts from the working capital
section at the bottom of the statement.

The increase (decrease) in working capital can be proved as follows:

Working capital<br>(year ended December 31, 19.7)

| | £ | £ | £ |
|---|---:|---:|---:|
| Current assets | | | 108 000 |
| Current liabilities | | 145 000 | |
| *Less* Provision for taxation | 35 000 | | |
| Proposed dividends | 30 000 | | |
| | | 65 000 | 80 000 |
| | | | £28 000 |

Working capital<br>(year ended December 31, 19.8)

| | £ | £ | £ |
|---|---:|---:|---:|
| Current assets | | | 128 000 |
| Current liabilities | | 230 000 | |
| *Less* Provision for taxation | 40 000 | | |
| Proposed dividends | 36 000 | | |
| | | 76 000 | |
| | | | 154 000 |
| | | | (£26 000) |

Decrease in working capital = £28 000 − (£26 000) = (£54 000)

The taxation and dividends must also be excluded from the working capital when reconciling the change in working capital with the amount shown in the statement. The accounts in this exercise show a reduction in working capital of £54 000. It should also be noted that, in practice, there is a requirement to produce a statement of source and application of funds for both the period under review and for the corresponding previous period.

When listing the amounts as sources and applications, it is important to remember to exclude working capital items from this section of the statement as they have to be shown as increases or decreases of working capital at the bottom of the statement.

**Conclusions about SSAP 10**

The statement of source and application of funds (SSAP 10) has to be provided as a supplementary statement to the accounts. It has been shown that the details in the statement represent the funds received by the business during the year from operational profits, depreciation, issues of shares and debentures, sale of fixed assets and sale of investments, etc. The statement also shows how these funds have been used to purchase fixed assets and investments, to repay loans and to pay dividends, taxation, etc. The net amount represents the change in working capital and this is analysed to show the items included in this change such as debtors, creditors, stock and the movement in net liquid funds of cash and bank overdraft. Although in the early stages of producing these statements it may help if comparative balance sheets show the changes, it is essential to understand the basic principles of accounts and the effect which transactions have on the business, so that the source and application of funds are clearly understood.

## 19.5 Cash Flow Statements

Statements are sometimes requested to show the increase or decrease in cash during the year, or to show the cash flows, and to reconcile the net amount with the cash in the balance sheet. This is the cash flow statement which contains virtually the same details laid out differently, as the funds statement. The *funds flow statement* shows the sources and applications and the changes in working capital, whereas the *cash flow statement* shows the sources of cash and its use, and indicates whether or not there has been an increase or decrease in cash. Alternatively, if the statement reconciles the cash flow with the closing balance of cash in the balance sheet, we begin with the closing balance in the previous balance sheet and end the statement with the cash figure in the current balance sheet. The cash flow statement includes the working capital items with the sources or applications and not as a separate list as in the funds statement. The following examples use the same details as used in the source and application of funds statement shown previously. The first shows the cash flows during the year; the second shows the same cash flows but picks up the opening balance, and concludes with the closing balance.

(a) Cash Flow Statement (for year ended December 31, 19.8)

| Source of cash | £ | £ |
|---|---:|---:|
| Profit from operations including an adjustment for depreciation | | 128 000 |
| Issue of debentures | 20 000 | |
| Sale of machinery | 15 000 | |
| Increase in creditors | 9 000 | |
| Rates in advance | 1 000 | |
| | | 45 000 |
| | | 173 000 |
| *Less* Application of cash | | |
| Extension to buildings | 20 000 | |
| Purchase of machinery | 45 000 | |
| Increase in investments | 37 000 | |
| Repayment of preference shares | 50 000 | |
| Dividends paid | 30 000 | |
| Payment of taxation | 35 000 | |
| Increase in stock | 16 000 | |
| Increase in debtors | 15 000 | |
| | | 248 000 |
| | | £(75 000) |

| Deficit of cash flow financed as follows: | £ |
|---|---:|
| Use of cash balance at bank January 1, 19.8 | 10 000 |
| Bank overdraft obtained December 31, 19.8 | 65 000 |
| | £(75 000) |

(b) Cash Flow Statement (for year ended December 31, 19.8)

|  | £ | £ |
|---|---|---|
| Balance as at December 31, 19.7 |  | 10 000 |
| Source of cash | £ |  |
| Profit from operations including an adjustment for depreciation | 128 000 |  |
| Issue of debentures | 20 000 |  |
| Sale of machinery | 15 000 |  |
| Increase in creditors | 9 000 |  |
| Rates in advance | 1 000 |  |
|  |  | 173 000 |
|  |  | 183 000 |
| Application of cash | £ |  |
| Extension to buildings | 20 000 |  |
| Purchase of machinery | 45 000 |  |
| Increase in investments | 37 000 |  |
| Repayment of preference shares | 50 000 |  |
| Dividends paid | 30 000 |  |
| Payment of taxation | 35 000 |  |
| Increase in stock | 16 000 |  |
| Increase in debtors | 15 000 |  |
|  |  | 248 000 |
| Balance at December 31, 19.8 (Bank overdraft) |  | £(65 000) |

## 19.6 Exercises

1. The summarized balance sheets at the end of the last two completed financial years of Kotidy Ltd are as follows:

### Balance sheets as at December 31

|  | 19.3 £ | 19.4 £ |  | 19.3 £ | 19.4 £ |
|---|---|---|---|---|---|
| Land and buildings | 332 000 | 320 600 | Issued capital | 700 000 | 700 000 |
| Machinery and plant | 345 000 | 436 000 | General reserve | 112 000 | 112 000 |
| Stock in hand | 79 800 | 101 260 | Profit and Loss A/c |  |  |
|  |  |  | balance | 18 500 | 18 500 |
| Work-in-progress | 130 000 | 120 400 | Net profit for year | — | 91 500 |
|  |  |  | Proposed dividend | 70 000 | — |
| Debtors | 167 200 | 231 540 | Debentures | 100 000 | 75 000 |
| Cash at bank | 85 000 | — | Creditors | 138 500 | 205 000 |
|  |  |  | Bank overdraft | — | 7 800 |
|  | £1 139 000 | £1 209 800 |  | £1 139 000 | £1 209 800 |

The cost price of the fixed assets at the balance sheet dates was as follows:

Land and buildings: 19.3, £340 000; 19.4, £340 000.
Machinery and plant: 19.3, £383 000; 19.4, £523 000.

A dividend of $12\frac{1}{2}$ per cent is proposed for the year ended December 31, 19.4. Taxation is to be ignored.

Compile a Sources and Applications of Funds Statement for the year ended December 31, 19.4, which should show the movement in working capital and net liquid funds.

# Unit Twenty
# Inflation or Current Cost Accounting

## 20.1 The Problem of Changing Prices in Inflationary Times

Inflation accounting is an important topic and will probably remain so for some time to come. Historical cost accounts fail to show the impact of changing prices, and in inflationary times more realistic information is required to enable management to take steps to maintain real capital and provide for the replacement of materials and assets. Discussions have taken place over many years, both here and abroad, on how best to record the effects of inflation. The debate concerns the kind of accounting system which should replace or supplement the historical system which has serious defects under prolonged and acute inflation.

Every business has its own capital structure, which in normal circumstances enables it to provide the fixed and current assets which are required to operate the business without difficulty. If there is a reasonable degree of price stability, the working capital is sufficient to cope with the normal level of operations, but under inflationary conditions extra funds are required to pay for the increased expenses and the replacement of fixed assets and stock. Unless there is an awareness of the problem, under-costing takes place and the future of the business can be put in jeopardy, with insufficient funds available to continue production. The following examples illustrate the problem.

### (a) Replacement of Stock
A company stocks a particular component which it issues on a FIFO basis. The items are purchased for £30 each and sold for £45 each but the company has been notified that future supplies will cost £36. Under historic cost accounting, the gross profit is £15 but as the present stock is sold it will have to be replaced by new purchases which require an extra £6 for each unit. The effect of inflation is to turn the gross profit of £15 into an operating profit of £9 and a holding gain of £6. The surplus available has been reduced from £15 to £9.

### (b) Increases in Working Capital
In inflationary times, extra working capital is required. Where a business has to finance a larger quantity of debtors each year because of price increases, this extra finance has to be provided by the shareholders. Of course the reverse is true if there are creditors; the more creditors, the more easily the business can be financed with their funds. Hence the depressing tendency in inflationary times for firms to postpone payment for as long as possible, so that their affairs are financed by their suppliers. This means that the business has to allow for the extra funds needed to finance the business in the interval between making sales and receiving payment. Equally, a business supplying services, not goods,

requires working capital until its customers actually pay the invoices for services rendered. This adjustment will be reduced, however, to the extent to which suppliers are prepared to give credit.

### (c) Replacement of Fixed Assets

A company has a machine which cost £10 000, and which has an estimated life of ten years with no residual value. The current price of a similar machine is £15 000. It is depreciated on the straight-line basis, so at the end of Year 5 the provision for depreciation is £5 000 (5 × £1 000) and the book value is £5 000. The current situation is that in order to replace the machine, annual depreciation should be £1 500 per annum, and there is a *backlog* of depreciation of £2 500 (5 years at £500). Although the book value is shown as £5 000, the value to the business is £7 500; but evidently under-costing is taking place, as £500 per annum is being treated as profit instead of cost. Replacement of the asset will eventually involve a reduction in working capital.

### (d) The Rewards to Factors of Production

Turning from accountancy to the general economic background to business (which has grave implications for the accountant), historical cost accounting overstates the profit earned and can lead to serious errors in the distribution of wealth in society. We can only distribute wealth if we have created it. The rewards paid to the factors of production—land, labour and capital—together make up the total value of the wealth created in a society, but the way in which this distribution is arranged reflects the relative strengths of the respective bargaining powers of the factors. The rewards to land and to capital are essentially long-term arrangements, made in the form of leases on the one hand and stocks, shares and other securities on the other. These arrangements are not easy to revise, but because of the marketing arrangements which Stock Exchanges have developed we can usually escape from a bad bargain if we are desperate enough, at some capital cost. Labour (which includes most of management) by contrast not only has a short-term engagement but is highly organized. If historical cost accounting overstates the profit earned by ignoring the erosion that is occurring as a result of inflation, the strong forces of labour demand higher wages from this fictitious profit, and reduce the rewards to the other factors—but particularly the rewards to capital.

Historical cost accounting no longer gives a true and fair view of the state of a business, but a biased and totally incorrect view. If this bias is disregarded historical accounting alone can easily cause the collapse of an enterprise employing thousands of people. Wild fluctuations in costs and prices erode the capital base of a business, cause cash flow problems and make marketing and production much more difficult. When there is a persistent increase in prices, by obtaining and accounting for current replacement costs, it is possible to show the effect of changing price levels on profit margins, cash flow and working capital.

The problem has been to decide on the most satisfactory way of adjusting historical cost accounts, and thus produce a set of current cost accounts which do give a true and fair view of a company's affairs. After several abortive attempts, the Accounting Standards Committee finally produced the Statement of Standard Accounting Practice No. 16, on March 31, 1980.

## 20.2  SSAP 16: Current Cost Accounting

The solution to the problem of inflation accounting proposed by SSAP 16 is as follows:

(a) The trading profit, calculated on the historical cost basis, shall be adjusted to give instead a *current cost operating profit*. There will be three adjustments, as follows:

(i) **A cost-of-sales adjustment (COSA).** This adjusts for the higher replacement prices to be paid to buy more stock once the present stock has been sold. This problem has been outlined in Unit 20.1(a).

(ii) **A monetary working capital adjustment (MWCA).** This allows for the need for extra working capital, as outlined in Unit 20.1(b).

(iii) **A depreciation adjustment.** This increases the depreciation normally charged, to cover *the rise in prices of the fixed assets consumed in the period*. This problem has been explained in Unit 20.1(c).

The result of these adjustments will therefore mean that the historical cost profit has been turned into a *current cost operating profit*.

(b) This current cost operating profit may, however, have been over-adjusted, and give an unfair view of the company's true profits. This is because some of the net operating assets of the business will have been obtained by borrowing. Since borrowing is always expressed in monetary terms, the repayments are not affected by inflation. Thus a loan of £1m borrowed in Year 1 and repayable in Year 2 will still be only £1m even if the price of goods has risen by 20 per cent because of inflation. In inflationary times, borrowers benefit because they repay in devalued currency. For this reason we need to reduce the allowances made in (a) above by a figure which reflects the proportion of borrowed money in our financial arrangements.

This is the so-called *gearing adjustment*. The total of the adjustments given in (a) above is reduced by the proportion that *net operating assets financed by borrowing* bears to *total net operating assets*. The gearing adjustment is necessary in order to show the profit attributable to the shareholders, and is calculated after interest, taxation and extraordinary items have been taken into account. The result of adjusting the current cost operating profit found in (a) above by the gearing adjustment is called the *current cost profit attributable to the shareholders*.

Unit 20.1(d), above, considered the rewards to factors and the way in which all employees expect to share in the success of their firms. We can see that if employees use the high profits being made as an argument for an increase in wages, this is a fair argument if it is based on the current cost profit attributable to shareholders. In the past, the argument was based upon the historical cost profits, which were not really being made. The increased standard of living enjoyed today is really at the expense of the capital used to re-tool companies, while the low profits being earned encourage investors to invest in foreign countries, and is causing the decline of many United Kingdom firms. This economic argument shows how important inflation accounting is in the wider context of the economic situation.

## 20.3    The Presentation of Current Cost Accounts

The Standard calls for annual financial statements, in the form of a Current Cost Profit and Loss Account and a current cost balance sheet. Firms are to publish both Current Cost Accounts and Historical Cost Accounts, with appropriate notes. It is for the firm to decide whether to make the Current Cost Accounts the main accounts, and the Historical Cost Accounts subsidiary, or vice versa.

**Current Cost Reserve**
The current cost balance sheet includes an additional reserve, referred to as the current cost reserve, which includes, where appropriate:

(a) unrealized revaluation surpluses on fixed assets, stock and investments;

(b) realized amounts equal to the cumulative net total of the current cost adjustments, that is:

    (i) the depreciation adjustment (and any adjustments on the disposal of fixed assets);

    (ii) the two working capital adjustments;

    (iii) the gearing adjustment.

Before proceeding to prepare typical accounting statements, it is necessary to consider the definitions given in SSAP 16 for some of the terms in use in the Standard, and these are given in Unit 20.4.

## 20.4    Explanatory Notes on Various Aspects of Current Cost Accounting

(i) **Holding gains.** A holding gain is one that accrues to a company by virtue of holding assets (for example, stock), at a time when prices are rising. Such gains may be realized or unrealized and represent *the difference between the value to a company of an asset at any point, and the original cost incurred in purchasing that asset.*

(ii) **Operating gains.** These are profits earned as a result of the company's activities, and are represented by *the difference between the amounts realized for a company's output and the value to the business of the inputs* (see (iv) below).

(iii) **Extraordinary gains.** These consist of *the difference between the amounts realized for items which do not form part of a company's normal output, and their value to the company at the time of disposal.*

(iv) **Value to the business.** This is the *net current replacement cost* or the *recoverable amount*, if it is recognized that there has been a permanent diminution in the value of an asset. The recoverable amount is *the greater of the* *net realizable value and, where applicable, the amount recoverable from its further use.*

(v) **Net operating assets.** These comprise the fixed assets (including trade investments), stock and monetary working capital dealt with in an *historical cost* balance sheet.

(vi) **The operating capability of the business.** This is the amount of goods and services which the business is able to supply with its existing resources in the relevant period, that is, with the resources represented in accounting terms by *the net operating assets at current cost* (as defined above).

(vii) **Current cost operating profit.** This is the surplus from ordinary activities, after allowing for the impact of price changes on the funds needed to continue the existing business and maintain its operating capability. It is calculated before interest on net borrowing and taxation.

(viii) **Monetary working capital.** This is the aggregate of trade debtors, pre-payments, and trade bills receivable, plus stocks not subject to a cost of sales adjustment, less trade creditors, accruals and trade bills payable (in so far as they arise from day-to-day operating activities of the business as distinct from transactions of a capital nature). In cases where exclusion would be misleading, monetary working capital can include cash floats and that part of bank balances or overdrafts arising from fluctuations in the volume of stock, trade debtors and trade creditors. With banks and other financial businesses, this definition is extended to cover other assets and other liabilities from day-to-day operations as distinct from transactions of a capital nature.

(ix) **Net borrowing.** This is the excess of the aggregate of all liabilities and provisions (including convertible debentures and deferred tax, but excluding proposed dividends) other than those included within monetary working capital and other than those which are, in substance, equity capital *over* the aggregate of all current assets other than those subject to a cost of sales adjustment and those included within monetary working capital.

## 20.5 Standard Accounting Practice

The Standard applies to listed firms quoted on a Stock Exchange, and to all unlisted firms with a turnover of more than £5 million, or with balance sheet totals at the start of any year *exceeding* £2½ million of assets, or with 250 or more employees, for all annual financial statements relating to accounting periods starting on or after January 1, 1980. The Standard does not apply to insurers, to most property investment and property-dealing entities, nor to non-profit-making organizations.

It is expected that even those firms which are not required to follow its rules will wish to use those parts of the Standard which are relevant. Such firms should certainly consider their situation with regard to changing prices in inflationary times.

### Current Cost Profit and Loss Account

This should show:

(a) the current cost operating profit or loss, derived from the historical cost trading profit (before interest on net borrowing as defined above) by adjustments for cost of sales, monetary working capital and depreciation;

(b) interest or income relating to the net borrowing on which the gearing adjustment has been based;

(c) gearing adjustment;

(d) taxation;

(e) extraordinary items;

(f) current cost profit or loss (after tax) attributable to shareholders.

A reconciliation should be provided between the profit or loss before charging interest and taxation calculated on the historical cost basis and the current cost operating profit, and this should show:

(a) depreciation adjustment;

(b) cost of sales adjustment (COSA);

(c) monetary working capital adjustment (MWCA) and, where appropriate, interest relating to monetary working capital;

(d) other material adjustments made to profits calculated on the historical cost basis when determining current cost operating profit.

The adjustments for cost of sales and monetary working capital may be combined.

### Current Cost Balance Sheet

Assets and liabilities are to be included as far as practicable on the following bases:

(a) Land and buildings, plant and machinery, and stocks subject to a cost of sales adjustment—at their value to the business.

(b) Investments in associated companies, either at the applicable proportion of the associated companies' net assets stated under this Standard or, where such information is not readily available, at directors' best estimate. Allowance for premium or discount on acquisition should be made as stated under (e) below.

(c) Other investments (excluding those treated as current assets) at directors' valuation. Where the investment is listed and the directors' valuation is materially different from mid-market value, the basis of valuation and the reasons for the difference should be stated.

(d) Intangible assets (excluding goodwill) at the best estimate of their value to the business.

(e) Goodwill (premium or discount) arising on consolidation on the basis set out in SSAP 14 (Group Accounts). Where goodwill is carried at an amount established before the introduction of SSAP 14, it should be reduced to the extent that it represents revaluation surpluses relating to assets held at the date of the acquisition.

(f) Current assets, other than those subject to a cost of sales adjustment, on the historical cost basis.

(g) All liabilities on the historical cost basis.

Reserves in the current cost balance sheet should include revaluation surpluses or deficits and adjustments made to allow for the impact of price changes, to arrive at current cost profit attributable to shareholders. Amounts to reduce assets from net current replacement cost to recoverable amount should be charged to the Profit and Loss Account.

When a full historical balance sheet is disclosed, the current cost balance sheet may be in summarized form. Notes should disclose the totals of net operating assets and net borrowing and their main elements. The balance sheet should be supported by summaries of the fixed asset accounts and the movement on reserves.

Notes attached to the current cost accounts should describe the bases and methods adopted in preparing the accounts particularly in relation to:

(a) the value to the business of fixed assets and the depreciation thereon;

(b) the value to the business of stock and work-in-progress and the cost of sales adjustment;

(c) the monetary working capital adjustment;

(d) the gearing adjustment;

(e) the basis of translating foreign currencies and dealing with translation differences arising;

(f) other material adjustments to the historical cost information;

(g) the corresponding amounts for the previous year.

### Earnings per Share

Listed companies should show the current cost earnings per share based on the *current cost profit attributable to equity (ordinary) shareholders before extraordinary items.*

This section covers the main aspects of current cost accounting but for a complete guide to current cost accounting you should refer to the Statement of Standard Accounting Practice No. 16 (available from the Institute of Chartered Accountants in England and Wales) and to the Guidance Notes on SSAP 16 (issued by the Accounting Standards Committee of the main accounting bodies).

## 20.6   Calculation of Current Replacement Cost

When it is necessary to determine current values, you can refer to relevant indices or, where appropriate, to suppliers' price lists. Indices may be general or specific, when they apply to particular types of assets, or they may be drawn up internally to meet the needs of a particular business. The Central Statistical Office publishes a booklet, each April, August and December, entitled *Price Index Numbers for Current Cost Accounting*, available from HMSO. Other useful publications include *Current Cost Accounting — A Guide to Price Indices for Overseas Countries*, and a monthly supplement in *Business Monitor*, both available from HMSO. Care should be taken when fixing values because changes in design and technological progress may make it possible to replace an asset at a price well below that calculated by some form of indexation. Indices are averages, and so can be used for blocks of similar assets. They measure the average changes between points in time, and are ratios expressed as percentages. Prices at the base date have an index number of 100 and the price which is being indexed is given a number which is a percentage of the base date price.

### Example 20.1

(a)  Base date price £20                    Index number $= 100$

(b)  Price at next date £25

$$\text{Index number} = \frac{\text{Price}}{\text{Base date price}} \times 100 = \frac{£25}{£20} \times 100 = 125$$

(c)  Price at following date £30

$$\text{Index number} = \frac{£30}{£20} \times 100 = 150$$

There is a 25 per cent increase in value between (a) and (b), a 50 per cent increase between (a) and (c), and the increase between (b) and (c) is 20 per cent $\left( \dfrac{£30}{£25} \times 100 \right)$. Table 20.1 shows this information more concisely.

**Table 20.1 Increase in value of index**

| Year | Index with base year L | Increase over previous year % | Factor for Year N |
|------|------------------------|-------------------------------|-------------------|
| L    | 100                    | —                             | 1.5               |
| M    | 125                    | 25                            | 1.2               |
| N    | 150                    | 20                            | —                 |

Index numbers prior to the base date year can be calculated as required. The factor is useful when a large number of calculations have to be made. It is the ratio of the index in Year N to the index in the year of interest. To find the current cost of any item at Year N we multiply the cost of the item in any previous year by the appropriate factor. Thus if a firm has two machines, one purchased in Year L for £800, and the other in Year M for £20 000, the current costs in Year N would be:

First machine: £800 × 1.5 = £1 200

Second machine: £20 000 × 1.2 = £24 000

We have been dealing with a simple index or *price relative* (see *Success in Statistics* Unit 10) but it may be advisable and more convenient in certain cases to group items or classes of materials together in order to simplify the work of pricing. This is carried out using a procedure which takes account of the relative importance of each item in the group, and which produces a weighted index number. It is not the purpose of this section to deal with statistics as an exercise, but to emphasize the use and importance of index numbers in the process of arriving at current costs

## 20.7 Revaluation of Fixed Assets and the Depreciation Adjustments

To arrive at the value of fixed assets, the replacement cost has to be found and the assets restated at their current value to the business. Another way of arriving at a value is through the application of relevant indices to existing gross book values. When there has been a permanent diminution in value it is necessary to calculate the *recoverable amount*. This is either

(*a*) *the current realizable amount net of realization expenses* or

(*b*) when the asset continues in use for a period, *the amount which can be recovered by its use and the value of the net amount realized at the date of eventual disposal.*

Having arrived at a value the next step is to calculate the depreciation charge and compare it with the charge included in the historical cost accounts; this may involve *backlog depreciation*.

**Backlog depreciation.** The restatement of the value of fixed assets requires an adjustment to accumulated depreciation, and the extra depreciation for earlier periods is called backlog depreciation. This is not charged to revenue but to the current cost reserve (reducing the revaluation surpluses resulting from price changes). Backlog depreciation represents the effect of current price changes on past consumption, and so is not charged in arriving at the operating result.

The basis of the depreciation charge in the Current Cost Profit and Loss Account is the difference between the *current cost in the accounting period* and the *amount shown in the historical accounts.* Current cost accounting measures the amount required to maintain the present operating capability of a business, and the transfer to or from current cost reserve is the net amount of the restatement of the gross current replacement cost and the restatement of the accumulated depreciation.

**Revaluation of plant and machinery**

**Example 20.2**

|  |  | £ |
|---|---|---|
| Year 1 | Purchase price | 1 500 |
| Year 1 | Index number at date of purchase | 104 |
| Year 5 | Index number at end of current period | 182 |
| Year 5 | Estimated gross replacement cost: | £ |

$$=\frac{182}{104}\times £1\ 500 = \qquad\qquad 2\ 625$$

Year 5    Revaluation surplus transferred to current cost reserve:

$$£$$
$$=£2\ 625 - £1\ 500 = \qquad\qquad 1\ 125$$

The fixed asset will be index-linked and the amount adjusted from year to year.

Index number at beginning of Year 6 = 182
Index number at end of Year 6 = 195

$$\text{Effect of price change during year} = \left(\frac{195-182}{182}\right)\times £2\ 625$$

$$= £187.5 \text{ (Transfer to current}$$
$$\text{cost reserve)}$$

Gross replacement cost at end of Year 6 = £2 625 + £187.5 = £2 812.5

*Note*: The same result is obtained from the calculation based on the date of purchase i.e.

$$\frac{£1\ 500}{104}\times 195$$

$$= £2\ 812.5$$

The amounts shown above as transfers to the current cost reserve will be reduced by the depreciation adjustment.

**Depreciation adjustment**
**Example 20.3**
Life of asset estimated at 10 years, with no scrap value.
Depreciation method: straight line.

Depreciation on historical cost basis = 10% of cost (£1 500)
= £150 (annually)

Depreciation on current cost basis = 10% of current cost (£2 625)
= £262.5 (Year 5)

*Depreciation adjustment* required = £262.5 − £150
= £112.5 (Year 5)

*Backlog depreciation* = 4 years at £112.5
= £450

Transfer to *Current cost reserve* = £450 Backlog + Current year adjustment of £112.5
= £562.5

The net amount transferred as a *credit* to the current cost reserve is the revaluation surplus of £1 125 *less* the increase in depreciation of £562.5 = £562.5.

| Year 5 | Cost or valuation | Depreciation | Net |
|---|---|---|---|
| *Plant and machinery at* | £ | £ | £ |
| Historical cost | 1 500 | 750.0 | 750.0 |
| Current cost | 2 625 | 1 312.5 | 1 312.5 |
| Difference as current cost reserve | £1 125 | £562.5 | £562.5 |

Year 6

*Depreciation adjustment* = (10% of £2 812.5) − £150 = £131.25 charged to Current Cost Profit and Loss Account.

*Backlog depreciation* = 10% of current cost (Year 6) − 10% of current cost (Year 5) × 5 = (£281.25 − £262.5) × 5 = £18.75 × 5
= £93.75

Amount transferred to current cost reserve = £131.25 + £93.75
= £225

Net amount transferred as a *Debit* to the current cost reserve = Depreciation £225 − Revaluation surplus £187.5 = £37.5

(*continued overleaf*)

| Year 6 | Cost or valuation | Depreciation | Net |
|---|---|---|---|
| *Plant and machinery at* | £ | £ | £ |
| Historical cost | 1 500.0 | 900.0 | 600 |
| Current cost | 2 812.5 | 1 687.5 | 1 125 |
| Difference as current cost reserve | £1 312.5 | £787.5 | £525 |

The amount now shown in the current cost reserve (Year 6) is £525. This is a reduction of £37.5 on the previous year (£562.5—£525) because of the *debit* of £37.5 in Year 6.

## 20.8   Calculations and Examples in the Production of Current Cost Accounts

Items from the Historical Accounts shown below are used as examples in this Unit, and calculations are units of thousands of pounds.

Historical Cost Profit and Loss Account
(for the year ended December 31, 19.6)

|  | 19.6 |
|---|---|
|  | £(000s) |
| Turnover | 7 000 |
| Trading profit | 700 |
| *Less* Net interest payable | 125 |
|  | 575 |
| Corporation tax | 80 |
| Profit attributable to shareholders | 495 |
| Proposed dividends | 40 |
| Retained profit of the year | £455 |
| Retained profits/revenue reserves: |  |
| Retained profit of the year | 455 |
| Revenue reserves at the beginning of the year | 835 |
| Revenue reserves at the end of the year | £1 290 |

Historical cost balance sheet as at December 31, 19.6

| 19.5 £(000s) | 19.5 £(000s) | | 19.6 £(000s) | 19.6 £(000s) |
|---|---|---|---|---|
| | 2 000 | Fixed assets | | 2 000 |
| | 500 | *Less* Depreciation | | 600 |
| | 1 500 | | | 1 400 |
| | | Current assets | | |
| 750 | | Stock | 1 050 | |
| 1 050 | | Trade debtors | 1 300 | |
| 200 | | Cash | 200 | |
| 2 000 | | | 2 550 | |
| | | *Less* Current liabilities: | | |
| 600 | | Trade creditors | 700 | |
| 100 | | HP creditors | 70 | |
| 265 | | Overdraft | 200 | |
| 100 | | Taxation | 80 | |
| 30 | | Proposed dividend | 40 | |
| 1 095 | | | 1 090 | |
| | 905 | Net current assets | | 1 460 |
| | £2 405 | | | £2 860 |
| | | *Financed by* | | |
| | £(000s) | | | £(000s) |
| | 700 | Share capital | | 700 |
| | | Reserves: | | |
| | 835 | Revenue | | 1 290 |
| | 1 535 | Shareholders' capital and reserve | | 1 990 |
| | 750 | Convertible debentures | | 750 |
| | 120 | Deferred tax | | 120 |
| | £2 405 | | | £2 860 |

It is assumed that the change in stock levels will occur fairly evenly during he period and costs are calculated on a FIFO basis.

For simplicity, calculations in all the workings shown below are taken from the following list of index numbers.

Each index number corresponds to the middle of the month concerned. The base date is January 19.2 in the previous decade.

| Year 19.5 | October | 188 | Year 19.6 (continued) | July | 200 |
|---|---|---|---|---|---|
| | November | 190 | | August | 200 |
| | December | 192 | | September | 200 |
| | | | | October | 220 |
| Year 19.6 | January | 192 | | November | 227 |
| | February | 192 | | December | 250 |
| | March | 196 | | | |
| | April | 197 | Year 19.7 | January | 250 |
| | May | 198 | | February | 250 |
| | June | 200 | | March | 252 |

The simple monthly average based on twelve months to the end of year 19.6 is

$$\frac{2\ 472}{12} = \underline{\underline{206}}$$

The following index numbers are taken or derived from the above list.
(a) Mid-November 19.5                                              190.0
(b) November 30, 19.5 (average of Nov. and Dec.)                   191.0
(c) December 31, 19.5 (average of Dec. and Jan.)                   192.0
(d) Mid-October 19.6                                               220.0
(e) November 30, 19.6 (average of Nov. and Dec.)                   238.5
(f) December 31, 19.6 (average of Dec. and Jan.)                   250.0
(g) Simple monthly average based on 12 months to December 31,
19.6                                                               206.0

### Fixed Asset Revaluation Surplus, Backlog Depreciation and Depreciation Adjustment

In this exercise there are no additions or disposals during the financial year. It is assumed that the assets were purchased on the same date and have a life of 20 years, and there will be no scrap value at the end of that period. In practice, it is necessary to relate disposals and accumulated depreciation to the year of acquisition. It is also necessary to use an appropriate index number, applicable to the year of purchase, for each of the assets. This will probably be taken from the publication, *Price Index Numbers for Current Cost Accounting* and will enable the gross current cost to be calculated for each of the assets. The current cost accumulated depreciation can be established by using the gross current cost, calculating the annual amount and the total depreciation related to the life of the asset. This information provides the details to work out the cost of the depreciation adjustment for the year and the backlog depreciation. In the examples which follow, the depreciation is calculated on the straight-line basis.

*Historical cost*

| Fixed assets | *Historical* | *Depreciation* | *Net* |
|---|---|---|---|
| (purchased Jan. 1, 19.1) | *cost* | | |
| | £(000s) | £(000s) | £(000s) |
| at December 31, 19.5 | 2 000 | (500) | 1 500 |
| at December 31, 19.6 | 2 000 | (600) | 1 400 |

*Current cost*

The index number at date of acquisition is 150.

Gross current cost at December 31, 19.5

$$=\frac{\text{Historical cost}}{\text{Index number at date of acquisition}} \times \text{Index number at December 31, 19.5}$$

$$=\frac{£2\ 000}{150} \times 192 = £2\ 560$$

Revaluation surplus included in current cost reserve = Current cost − Historical cost

$$=£2\ 560 - £2\ 000 = £560$$

Annual depreciation at current cost $=\dfrac{£2\ 560}{20}=£128$

Backlog depreciation

= Accumulated depreciation at current cost − Accumulated depreciation at historical cost to Year 19.5

$$=£128 \times 5 - (£100 \times 5)$$

$$=£640 - £500$$

$$=£140 \text{ (debited to current cost reserve)}$$

Net amount charged to current cost reserve (Year 19.5)

= Revaluation surplus − Backlog depreciation

$$=£560 - £140$$
$$=£420$$

Gross current cost (Year 19.6)

$$=\frac{£2\ 000}{150} \times 250 = £3\ 333$$

Revaluation surplus as at December 31, 19.6

$$=£3\ 333 - £2\ 000 = £1\ 333$$

Revaluation surplus credited to current cost reserve (Year 19.6)

$$= £1\,333 - £560\ (\text{Year } 19.5) = £773$$

Depreciation adjustment (Year 19.6)

= Annual charge at current cost − Annual charge at historical cost

$$= \frac{£3\,333}{20} - £100$$

$$= £166.65 - £100$$

$$= £66.65\ (\text{say } £67)\ (\text{debited to Profit and Loss A/c})$$

Accumulated depreciation at current cost as at December 31, 19.6

$$= 6 \text{ years} \times £166.65 = £999.90\ (\text{say } £1\,000)$$

Backlog depreciation for Year 19.6

= [Annual charge at current cost (Year 19.6) − Annual charge at current cost (Year 19.5)] × 5 years

$$= (£166.65 - £128) \times 5$$

$$= £38.65 \times 5 = £193.25\ (\text{say } £193\,)\ (\text{debited to current cost reserve})$$

Net amount charged to current cost reserve for Year 19.6

= Revaluation surplus − Backlog for year

$$= £773 - £193 = £580$$

The double entries for this are shown in Unit 20.11 and this particular entry of £580 appears as a credit of £773 offset by a debit of £193 in the Current Cost Reserve Account.

The workings have provided the details for the Current Cost Final Accounts as follows:

| Current cost balance sheet | Valuation | Less Depreciation | Net |
|---|---|---|---|
| Fixed assets | £(000s) | £(000s) | £(000s) |
| at December 31, 19.5 | 2 560 | 640 | 1 920 |
| at December 31, 19.6 | 3 333 | 1 000 | 2 333 |
| Increase in value | 773 | 360 | 413 |
| Adjustment for historical cost | | −100 | +100 |
| Depreciation adjustment 19.6 Current Cost Profit and Loss Account | | − 67 | + 67 |
| Transfer to current cost reserve | 773 | 193 | 580 |

*Notes:* (The figures referred to are in thousands of pounds.)

(i) The asset has been increased on the balance sheet by £773, and depreciation has been increased by £360 to give a net increase in value of £413.

(ii) However, some of this depreciation has been provided out of this year's profits — £100 for the ordinary historical cost depreciation, and £67 for the cost of sales adjustment. This means that the assets available have increased by £580 (£413 increased fixed assets and £167 of cash flows now available in the system because they will not be designated as available for distribution as profits).

(iii) This increased asset value must be balanced by reserves, which are recorded in the Current Cost Reserve Account. It is in the form of £773 (revaluation credited to the reserve) offset by £193 of backlog depreciation (debited to the reserve).

## Working Capital Adjustments

Working capital includes finished stock, work-in-progress (stock) and monetary working capital. Current cost operating profit is derived by making three main adjustments to the historical cost trading profit before charging interest on net borrowing. These adjustments consist of

(*a*) depreciation;

(*b*) cost of sales;

(*c*) monetary working capital adjustments.

### (*a*) Depreciation

In the example above the depreciation adjustment was £67 for the year and it should be noted that backlog depreciation is not deducted in the Current Cost Profit and Loss Account but is included in the balance sheet in the current cost reserve as well as in the amount deducted as depreciation.

### (*b*) Cost of Sales Adjustment

This is the difference between the value to the business and the historical cost of the stock consumed in the period. In inflationary conditions, it is necessary to secure extra funds which are needed to replace, at current prices, the stock consumed. Materials are often held in stores for long periods and there is a time-lag between the receipt of goods and the date when they are issued. When stock is issued and priced on a FIFO basis, the historic cost is usually well below the replacement cost and the profit recorded is misleading, as extra money is needed to purchase and replace the materials consumed. For example, petrol is usually held for a short time, whereas spare parts may be held for a much longer time, and the replacement cost and profit of different items varies considerably. An estimate has to be made of different types of materials to establish the period for which they are held.

It is necessary to know the length of time so that appropriate indices can be selected when calculating the value of the opening and closing stock. The cost of sales adjustment is reached by taking the purchases at their recorded value, but the value of the opening and closing stock is restated by a method known as *averaging*.

**Averaging method.** The use of this method enables the cost of sales in the historical cost accounts to be adjusted to the current cost of sales at the date of consumption. The purchases and other costs incurred remain unaltered, but the opening and closing stock is converted to the average current cost during the period. The index, or indices, may be selected in a similar way to those for depreciation, by reference to the CSO booklet *Price Index Numbers for Current Cost Accounting*.

As the historical value of opening stock is probably recorded from low prices and historical closing stock from high ones, the effect of revaluation is to increase the opening stock and decrease the closing stock. This is because of the time-lag in the issue of stock and the use of the FIFO method. The high prices at the end of the year do not affect the costs of the current year. It is normally necessary to ascertain the average age of the opening and closing stocks so that the price index numbers appropriate to those dates may be applied. An adjustment is necessary for the balance sheet valuation but where ageing does not give a significantly different answer, the index numbers at the balance sheet date may be used and no adjustment is needed for balance sheet valuation.

**Example 20.4**

Purchases for the year amount to £7 500 thousands.

*(All units in this example are thousands of pounds)*

*Historical costs*

Opening stock is recorded in the balance sheet as £750 and consists of stock purchased over the last three months of 19.5. Closing stock is recorded in the balance sheet at £1 050 and consists of stock purchased over the last five months of the current year 19.6.

Using the averaging method, the COSA is calculated in the following steps:

|     |     |
| --- | --- |
| (i) Index for opening stock (mid-November 19.5) | 190 |
| Index for closing stock (mid-October 19.6) | 220 |
| Average index for year to December 31, 19.6 | 206 |

(Reference has been made to the table of index numbers given earlier.)

(ii)  From the historical cost of the closing stock, deduct the historical cost of the opening stock to get the total increase:

$$£1\ 050 - £750 = £300$$

(iii)  Isolate the effect of the volume change from the average current cost of closing stock.

$$\left( \frac{\text{Historical cost closing stock}}{\text{Closing index number}} \times \text{Average index number} \right) \; less$$

$$\left( \frac{\text{Historical cost opening stock}}{\text{Opening index number}} \times \text{Average index number} \right)$$

$$= \left( \frac{£1\,050}{220} \times 206 \right) - \left( \frac{£750}{190} \times 206 \right)$$

$$= £983 - £813$$

$$= \underline{\underline{£170}}$$

(iv) From the total increase (ii), deduct the volume increase (iii), to give the *Cost of sales adjustment* (the price increase):

$$= £300 - £170 = \underline{\underline{£130}}$$

The above method is represented by the following formula:

$$COSA = (C - O) - I_a \left( \frac{C}{I_c} - \frac{O}{I_o} \right)$$

$O$ = Historical cost of opening stock
$C$ = Historical cost of closing stock
$I_a$ = Average index number for the period
$I_o$ = Index number appropriate to opening stock
$I_c$ = Index number appropriate to closing stock.

The additional costs in the trading period caused by price changes may also be calculated in the following way:

(i) Imagine a situation where there is no opening or closing stock, and all purchases are sold during the year. The cost of sales is equivalent to the total purchases, and at current cost.

(ii) Where there is a time-lag between purchases and sales, so that particular items of stock appear in opening and closing stocks, and goods are issued on a FIFO basis, the cost of sales does not represent current cost. The figure for opening stock is set too low, and has to be increased to bring it up to replacement cost, by using the average index. In the case discussed above, this means:

$$\frac{£750}{190} \times 206 = \underline{\underline{£813}}$$

(iii) Similarly the closing stock figure is too high, for it includes goods at current prices which have to be reduced to the average for the year. When this *reduced* closing stock figure is deducted to give us the cost of sales, it will make the cost of sales *greater*. In this case, the closing stock figure is:

$$\frac{£1\,050}{220} \times 206 = \underline{\underline{£983}}$$

(iv)  When the Trading Account is re-stated using these adjusted figures we have:

|  | Historical cost £(000s) | Current cost £(000s) | Additional cost £(000s) |
|---|---|---|---|
| Opening stock | 750 | 813 | + 63 |
| Purchases | 7 500 | 7 500 | — |
|  | 8 250 | 8 313 | + 63 |
| *Less* Closing stock | −1 050 | − 983 | − 67 |
| Cost of sales | 7 200 | 7 330 | +130 |

*Balance sheet value of stock at current cost*

A separate calculation is required to ascertain the value of stock to the business as at the date of the balance sheet:

(i)  Relevant index numbers at December 31, 19.5 and December 31, 19.6. These are found by calculating the average of the mid-December and mid-January index numbers.

December 31, 19.5   $\dfrac{192+192}{2}=192$    December 31, 19.6   $\dfrac{250+250}{2}=250$

(ii)  Calculate the current cost:

$$\text{Current cost}=\frac{\text{Historical cost}\times\text{Average index for December and January}}{\text{Average index number during purchasing period}}$$

Opening stock 19.6   $£750\times\dfrac{192}{190}=£758$

Unrealized revaluation surplus $=£758-£750=£8$

Closing stock 19.6   $£1\,050\times\dfrac{250}{220}=£1\,193$

Unrealized revaluation surplus $=£1\,193-£1\,050=£143$

Increase in unrealized revaluation surpluses   $+£135$

The unrealized revaluation surplus of £135 is credited to the Current Cost Reserve Account together with the COSA £130 (total £265). The current cost of stock in the balance sheet is £1 193.

### (c)  Monetary Working Capital Adjustment (MWCA)

A business has to finance sales on credit, and when prices are increasing, extra finance has to be found until the accounts are settled. A converse effect occurs when purchases are made on credit, as the supplier finances the credit and has to find the extra funds required. The MWCA represents that part of the change in the amount of monetary working capital resulting from changes in price, and excludes changes arising from volume. This adjustment allows for the maintenance of net working capital other than stocks, and is calculated on a similar basis to the COSA. Although it is usually concerned with 'Debtors less Creditors', in a business where liquid assets are important, MWCA may include liquid assets in the total. When there is a growth in trade debtors, the historical profit is reduced by the amount which is required to finance the increase in debtors, but this amount is reduced if there is also a growth in trade creditors. The appropriate index is applied to the net balance of monetary assets. Examples may be taken from firms in different situations.

**Example 20.5**
A manufacturing company has large stocks and deals with both suppliers and customers on credit terms.
Items (inter alia) on the balance sheet are:

|  |  | £m |
|---|---|---|
| Stock |  | 78 |
| Debtors less Creditors |  | 17 |
| The adjustments to historical cost profit might be |  |  |
| *Profit and Loss Account* |  | £m |
| Historical cost profit (say) |  | 71 |
| *Current cost adjustments* | £m |  |
| Depreciation | 2.5 |  |
| Cost of sales | 19.0 |  |
| Monetary working capital | 3.5 |  |
|  |  | 25 |
| Current cost operating profit |  | £46m |

The monetary working capital adjustment takes account of the firm's need to finance a considerably larger volume of debtors because of inflation.

**Example 20.6**
A supermarket deals in cash only with its customers, but holds large stocks and exacts long credit periods from its suppliers.

| Balance sheet items |  | £m |
|---|---|---|
| Stocks |  | 52 |
| Creditors |  | 38 |
| The adjustment to historical cost profit might be |  |  |
| *Profit and Loss Account* |  | £m |
| Historical cost profit (say) |  | 88.0 |
| *Current cost adjustments* | £m |  |
| Depreciation | 3.0 |  |
| Cost of sales | 16.0 |  |
|  | 19.0 |  |
| *Less* Monetary working capital | 7.8 |  |
|  |  | 11.2 |
| Current cost operating profit |  | £76.8m |

This time there are no debtors but creditors are kept waiting and hence help the firm to finance its affairs. The adjustment is *deducted*.

**Example 20.7**
A bank has no trading activities requiring a cost of sales adjustment, but in inflationary times is obliged to hold larger liquid assets, which it is therefore entitled to include in its monetary working capital calculations.

| Balance sheet items | | £m |
|---|---|---|
| Fixed assets | | 40 |
| Advances and other liquid assets less | | |
| deposits | | 800 |

The adjustments to historical cost profit might be

| *Profit and Loss Account* | | £m |
|---|---|---|
| Historical cost profit (say) | | 137 |
| *Current cost adjustments* | £m | |
| Depreciation | 2 | |
| Monetary working capital | 27 | |
| | | 29 |
| Current cost operating profit | | £108m |

**Example 20.8** (see historical cost balance sheet—Unit 20.8 above).
Monetary working capital consists of trade debtors and trade creditors only. At each date, debtors exceed creditors and it is assumed that the average age of the opening and closing monetary working capital (MWC) is one month.

The opening MWC is (£1 050—£600)=£450
The closing MWC is (£1 300—£700)=£600

(i) Ascertain the relevant index numbers

$$\text{Index for opening MWC November 30, 19.5} = \frac{190+192}{2} = 191.0$$

$$\text{Index for closing MWC November 30, 19.6} = \frac{227+250}{2} = 238.5$$

Average index for year to December 31, 19.6=206.0

(ii) From the balance sheet value of the closing MWC, deduct the balance sheet value of the opening MWC:

$$£600-£450=£150$$

So extra monetary working capital of £150 is needed to run the business, but some of this may be because of changes in volume, and not to changes in prices (inflation).

(iii) Isolate the effect of the volume change: from the value of the closing MWC, deduct the value of the opening MWC (adjusting both values to the average price for the period).

$$\left( \frac{\text{Balance sheet value of closing MWC}}{\text{Closing index number}} \times \text{Average index number} \right) \ less$$

$$\left( \frac{\text{Balance sheet value of opening MWC}}{\text{Opening index number}} \times \text{Average index number} \right)$$

$$= \left( \frac{£600}{238.5} \times 206 \right) - \left( \frac{£450}{191} \times 206 \right)$$

$$= £518 - £485 = £33$$

(iv) From the result in (ii), the total increase, deduct the result in (iii), the volume increase, to give the MWCA, the price increase:

$$£150 - £33 = £117$$

The debtors exceed the creditors and the adjustment is a charge against profits. When the creditors exceed the debtors, and prices are rising, the adjustment is a *credit* to profit.

Where the MWC is a net liability greater than the value of stock, the excess is not funding working capital and so should be excluded when calculating the MWCA. The excess will, in consequence, be included in net borrowing for the purpose of calculating the gearing adjustment.

The above method is identical to that used for COSA and is represented by the following formula:

$$\text{MWCA} = (C - O) - I_a \left( \frac{C}{I_c} - \frac{O}{I_o} \right)$$

$O$ = Opening MWC
$C$ = Closing MWC
$I_a$ = Average index number for the period
$I_o$ = Index number appropriate to opening MWC
$I_c$ = Index number appropriate to closing MWC

## 20.9   Gearing Adjustment

Gearing applies to the way a business is financed. It generally refers to the composition of issued capital between fixed interest securities and ordinary shares. SSAP 16 requires preference shares to be included within the shareholders' interest. The profit is therefore attributable to all shareholders, ordinary and preference. The total adjustment for depreciation, cost of sales and monetary working capital has to be reduced in the proportion that net operating assets, financed by borrowing, bear to the total net operating assets.

### Net Operating Assets

These consist of fixed assets, stock and *monetary working capital* included in the historical cost balance sheet. The Current Cost Profit and Loss Account shows the current cost operating profit made up of the historical profit less the *total* of the current cost adjustments. This profit is then increased by the value of the adjustments financed by the net borrowing, less the interest paid on the sums borrowed. The reason why the profit is increased in this way is that the portion of inflationary costs, being financed out of borrowing, does not represent a loss to *this* business, except for the interest payable. Since the loans received will be paid back in devalued currency, the loss will be borne by the *lender* and not the *borrower*. It would therefore be wrong to deduct *all* the inflationary effects from the profits.

### Calculation of the Gearing Adjustment

The gearing proportion is the ratio of net borrowing to the average net operating assets over the year, taken at their current cost values. The amount of the net operating assets is the sum of

(*a*) fixed assets, including trade investments, i.e. investments that are not classified as current, and

(*b*) stock and monetary working capital.

The total of (*a*) and (*b*) is, of course, the same as the sum of

(*c*) net borrowing, and

(*d*) shareholders' interest (defined to include proposed dividends) taken from the current cost balance sheet. However, this is not much help to us, since we cannot calculate the total shareholders' interest until we have calculated the gearing ratio. This is because the gearing adjustment will affect the current cost reserve which is part of the shareholders' interest. We must, therefore, use the net borrowing figures and the net operating assets figures.

The gearing proportion can thus be calculated as follows:

(i) Ascertain the *average net borrowing* during the period. If it is negative because monetary assets included exceed monetary liabilities, no adjustment is needed as the excess is not part of the net operating assets. The average may be taken to be the simple average of the opening and closing balances, unless there have been substantial changes in borrowings during the period, or other events so that a weighted average would give a more appropriate indication. Let the average net borrowing be $L$.

(ii) Ascertain the *net operating assets* figure, which is the same as the average net borrowing ($L$) plus the shareholders' interest ($S$). (This must be so because they are the two sides of the same balance sheet.)

(iii) The *gearing proportion* is the ratio of the average net borrowing to the net operating assets:

$$\frac{L}{L+S}$$

(iv) If the sum of the current cost adjustments is taken as $A$ the gearing adjustment is:

$$\frac{L}{L+S} \times A$$

**Example 20.9** (continuing to use the figures given in Unit 20.8)

| | Opening £(000s) | Closing £(000s) |
|---|---|---|
| Net borrowing (as defined on p. 347) | | |
| Convertible debentures and deferred taxation | 870 | 870 |
| HP creditors | 100 | 70 |
| Bank overdraft | 265 | 200 |
| Taxation | 100 | 80 |
| Cash | (200) | (200) |
| Total net borrowings | £1 135 | £1 020 |

(Cash is deducted, under the definition. It is the only current asset not included in the cost of sales adjustment and the monetary working capital adjustment.)

$$\text{The average net borrowing } L = \frac{£1\,135 + £1\,020}{2} = \frac{£2\,155}{2} = \underline{£1\,077.5}$$

| *Net operating assets* | Opening £(000s) | Closing £(000s) |
|---|---|---|
| Fixed assets (net) | 1 920 | 2 333 |
| Stock | 758 | 1 193 |
| Monetary working capital | 450 | 600 |
| Total (the average of which equals $L + S$) | £3 128 | £4 126 |

$$L + S = \frac{£3\,128 + £4\,126}{2} = \frac{£7\,254}{2} = \underline{£3\,627}$$

So the gearing proportion $\dfrac{L}{L+S}$ is:

$$\frac{1\,077.5}{3\,627} \times 100 = \underline{29.7\%}$$

The gearing adjustment is calculated by applying this percentage to the total current cost adjustments.

| | £ |
|---|---|
| Depreciation adjustment | 67 |
| Cost of sales adjustment | 130 |
| Monetary working capital adjustment | 117 |
| Total adjustments | £314 |

| *Gearing adjustment* | = 29.7% of £314 |
|---|---|
| | = £93 |

## 20.10    Earnings Per Share

SSAP 16 requires listed companies to show the current cost earnings per ordinary (equity) share based on the current cost profit attributable to the ordinary shareholders before extraordinary items.

The formula is:

$$\frac{\text{Current cost profit attributable to equity shareholders (not counting extraordinary items)}}{\text{Ordinary share capital}}$$

The answer (usually given in pence per share) tells the shareholder the true earnings on his investment in the prevailing conditions.

In this example (see Unit 20.11 for the full display) the amounts are given in thousands of pounds and the earnings per share is:

$$\frac{£274}{£700} = \underline{\underline{39 \text{ pence per share}}}$$

*Note:* The earnings per share applies only to the ordinary shares (the equity), yet the current cost profit attributable to shareholders applies to all shareholders, so a company having both ordinary and preference shares would need to eliminate the element for the preference shareholders from both parts of the calculation.

*Operating profit return*
Another useful ratio is the operating profit return, found by the formula:

$$\frac{\text{Current cost operating profit}}{\text{Average net operating assets}} \times 100$$

In this example, the ratio is:

$$\frac{£386}{£3\,627} \times 100 = \underline{\underline{10.6\%}}$$

## 20.11    Display of Current Cost Accounts

The following Current Cost Profit and Loss Account is an example of a layout of this account.

## Current Cost Profit and Loss Account
### for year to December 31, 19. .

|  |  |  | £(000s) |
|---|---|---|---|
| Turnover |  |  | 7 000 |
| Historical cost trading profit before interest |  |  | 700 |
| *Less* Current cost operating adjustments |  |  | 314 |
| Current cost operating profit |  |  | 386 |
| *Add* Gearing adjustment |  | 93 |  |
| *Less* Interest on net borrowing |  | 125 |  |
|  |  |  | −32 |
| Current cost profit before taxation |  |  | 354 |
| Taxation |  |  | 80 |
| Current cost profit attributable to shareholders |  |  | 274 |
| Dividends |  |  | 40 |
| Retained current cost profit for the year |  |  | £234 |

The current cost balance sheet is therefore as shown on p. 370. To help you follow the derivation of the current cost figures, the various double entries in the Current Cost Accounts are given on pp. 371–2. The Current Cost Profit and Loss Account has also been repeated in non-vertical style so that the double entries can be followed (p. 373).

### Summarized Current Cost Balance Sheet
### at December 31, 19.6

| 19.5 £(000s) | £(000s) | | 19.6 £(000s) | £(000s) |
|---|---|---|---|---|
| | | *Assets employed* | | |
| | 2 560 | Fixed assets | | 3 333 |
| | 640 | *Less* Depreciation | | 1 000 |
| | 1 920 | | | 2 333 |
| | | *Net current assets* | | |
| 758 | | Stock | 1 193 | |
| 450 | | Monetary working capital (net) | 600 | |
| 1 208 | | Total working capital | 1 793 | |
| (30) | | Proposed dividend | (40) | |
| (265) | | Other current liabilities (net) | (150) | |
| | | (70 + 200 + 80 — 200 cash) | | |
| | 913 | | | 1 603 |
| | £2 833 | | | £3 936 |
| | | *Financed by:* | | |
| | | *Share capital and reserves* | | |
| | 700 | Share capital | | 700 |
| 428 | | Current cost reserve | 1 297 | |
| 835 | | Other reserves and retained profit | 1 069 | |
| | 1 263 | | | 2 366 |
| | 1 963 | | | 3 066 |
| | 750 | Convertible debentures | | 750 |
| | 120 | Deferred tax | | 120 |
| | £2 833 | | | £3 936 |

The Current Cost Accounts are as follows:

### Fixed Assets Account

| 19.5 | | | £(000s) | 19.5 | | | £(000s) |
|---|---|---|---|---|---|---|---|
| Jan. 1 | Balance | b/d | 2 000 | Dec. 31 | Balance | c/d | 2 560 |
| Dec. 31 | Current cost reserve (revaluation) | | 560 | | | | |
| | | | £2 560 | | | | £2 560 |
| 19.6 | | | £(000s) | 19.6 | | | £(000s) |
| Jan. 1 | Balance | b/d | 2 560 | Dec. 31 | Balance | c/d | 3 333 |
| Dec. 31 | Current cost reserve (revaluation) | | 773 | | | | |
| | | | £3 333 | | | | £3 333 |
| 19.7 | | | | | | | |
| Jan. 1 | Balance | b/d | 3 333 | | | | |

### Provision for Depreciation Account

| | | | £(000s) | 19.5 | | | £(000s) |
|---|---|---|---|---|---|---|---|
| Dec. 31 | Balance | c/d | 640 | Dec. 31 | Balance (Historical) b/d | | 500 |
| | | | | Dec. 31 | Current cost reserve (5 years @ £28) | | 140 |
| | | | £640 | | | | £640 |
| 19.6 | | | £(000s) | 19.6 | | | £(000s) |
| Dec. 31 | Balance | c/d | 1 000 | Jan. 1 | Balance | b/d | 640 |
| | | | | Dec. 31 | Profit and Loss A/c: | | |
| | | | | | Historical cost | | 100 |
| | | | | | Adjustment | | 67 |
| | | | | | Current cost reserve (Backlog 5 @ £38.65) | | 193 |
| | | | £1 000 | | | | £1 000 |
| | | | | 19.7 | | | £(000s) |
| | | | | Jan. 1 | Balance | b/d | 1 000 |

### Current Cost Reserve Account

| 19.5 | | | £(000s) | 19.5 | | | £(000s) |
|---|---|---|---|---|---|---|---|
| Dec. 31 | Depreciation | | 140 | Dec. 31 | Fixed assets (revaluation) | | 560 |
| Dec. 31 | Balance | c/d | 428 | Dec. 31 | Stock (revaluation) | | 8 |
| | | | £568 | | | | £568 |
| 19.6 | | | £(000s) | 19.6 | | | £(000s) |
| Dec. 31 | Depreciation (backlog) | | 193 | Jan. 1 | Balance | b/d | 428 |
| Dec. 31 | Gearing adjustment | | 93 | Dec. 31 | Fixed assets (revaluation) | | 773 |
| Dec. 31 | Balance | c/d | 1 297 | Dec. 31 | Profit and Loss A/c: | | |
| | | | | | Cost of sales adjustment | | 130 |
| | | | | | Monetary working capital adjustment | | 117 |
| | | | | Dec. 31 | Stock (revaluation) | | 135 |
| | | | £1 583 | | | | £1 583 |
| | | | | 19.7 | | | £(000s) |
| | | | | Jan. 1 | Balance | b/d | 1 297 |

### Stock Adjustment Account

| 19.5 | | | £(000s) | 19.5 | | | £(000s) |
|---|---|---|---|---|---|---|---|
| Dec. 31 | Current cost reserve | | £ 8 | Dec. 31 | Balance | c/d | £ 8 |
| 19.6 | | | £(000s) | 19.6 | | | £(000s) |
| Jan. 1 | Balance | b/d | 8 | Dec. 31 | Balance | c/d | 143 |
| Dec. 31 | Current cost reserve | | 135 | | | | |
| | | | £143 | | | | £143 |
| 19.7 | | | | | | | |
| Jan. 1 | Balance | b/d | 143 | | | | |

Current Cost Profit and Loss Account for year to December 31, 19..

| 19.6 | | £(000s) | 19.6 | | £(000s) |
|---|---|---|---|---|---|
| Dec. 31 | Depreciation (adjustment) | 67 | Dec. 31 | Historical net profit | 700 |
| | | | Dec. 31 | Current cost reserve (gearing adjustment) | 93 |
| | | | | | 793 |
| Dec. 31 | Current cost reserve (cost of sales adjustment) | 130 | | | |
| Dec. 31 | Current cost reserve (monetary working capital adjustment) | 117 | | | |
| Dec. 31 | Interest on net borrowing | 125 | | | |
| | | 439 | | | |
| Dec. 31 | Current cost profit before taxation c/d | 354 | | | |
| | | £793 | | | £793 |
| Dec. 31 | Taxation | 80 | Dec. 31 | Profit before taxation | 354 |
| Dec. 31 | Current cost profit after taxation c/d | 274 | | | |
| | | £354 | | | £354 |
| Dec. 31 | Proposed dividend | 40 | Dec. 31 | Profit after taxation | 274 |
| Dec. 31 | Balance being retained current cost profit for year c/d | 234 | | | |
| | | £274 | | | £274 |
| | | | 19.7 | | £(000s) |
| | | | Jan. 1 | Balance       b/d | 234 |

## 20.12   Exercises

1. Why is some type of price level accounting essential in inflationary times?

2. Explain how the changing volumes of stock and the granting of trade credit affect profits in inflationary times. How does SSAP 16 adjust for these two aspects of inflation?

3. What is a gearing adjustment? Why is it necessary? How is it calculated?

# Index